ORIENTAL VEGETABLES

ORIENTAL VEGETABLES

The Complete Guide for Garden and Kitchen

Joy Larkcom

Illustrations by Elizabeth Douglass

Kodansha International
Tokyo • New York • London

Copyright © 1991 by Joy Larkcom.
All rights reserved.

Distributed in the United States by Kodansha
America, Inc., 114 Fifth Avenue, New York,
New York, 10011. Published by Kodansha
International Ltd., 17–14, Otowa 1-chome,
Bunkyo-ku, Tokyo 112 and Kodansha America, Inc.

Printed in Great Britain.

ISBN 4-7700-1619-0

First edition, 1991. Published simultaneously in
Great Britain by John Murray Ltd.

**Library of Congress Cataloging-in-
Publication Data**

Larkcom, Joy.
   Oriental vegetables : the complete guide for
   garden and kitchen/
Joy Larkcom : illustrations by Elizabeth
Douglass. — 1st ed.
     p.   cm.
   Includes index.
   ISBN 4-7700-1619-0
   1. Vegetables, Chinese.   2. Vegetables. Japanese.
   3. Cookery
(Vegetables)   I. Title
SB351.C54L37   1991
635—dc20   91–11185
                    CIP

Contents

Illustrations

The author and publishers would like to thank the following for permission to reproduce photographs: Jacqui Hurst: 1, 10, 15; Pamla Toler: 4, 9, 13, 20, 21; American Takii Inc.: 18; Photos Horticultural: 19.

*To my husband Don
who made it all possible and in
loving memory of my parents
'Larky' and Dorothy*

Introduction

For many years my long-standing love affair with Chinese vegetables was largely unrequited. It was hard to get seed and it was hard to get information. When China began to open its doors more freely to Westerners in the 1970s, it was tantalizing to hear first-hand accounts of communes growing literally hundreds of different vegetables: I longed to find out more about them.

It has always seemed curious to me that, while Western gardens have been enriched beyond measure by the trees, shrubs and flowers that plant hunters brought back from China, there has never been a parallel introduction of oriental vegetables. Yet the diversity and productivity of Chinese vegetables, especially the many types of 'greens', must have been there to see. Some, it is true, slipped through the bamboo curtain. Browsing through my 1885 vegetable 'Bible', *The Vegetable Garden* by M M Vilmorin-Andrieux to give it its full title, I was astonished to see how many oriental vegetables *were* mentioned over a hundred years ago—burdock, Chinese yam, the climbing spinach basella, Chinese cabbage, pak choi, hardy mustards, gourds. . . . But they were presented as recently introduced curiosities rather than vegetables genuinely worthy of cultivation to enhance the cuisine.

Once I began growing Chinese vegetables in earnest, I realized I had stumbled on a treasure trove of tasty, vigorous, highly adaptable vegetables. They were crying out for their secrets to be revealed to the West. Again, this was most true of the brassicas (crucifers), so many of which proved ideally suited to the cooler months of autumn to spring, when the choice of vegetables in temperate climates is limited.

Two other qualities of these vegetables immediately impressed me. First, they can be grown fast and intensively, especially when cultivated as 'cut-and-come-again' crops (more on this later). This makes them ideal for the small gardens, tiny plots, and containers in which so many people have to grow their vegetables today. Second, many are highly nutritious, lending themselves to quick, healthy stir-frying or steaming, and, when harvested young, to use in salads. They seemed tailor-made for our overcrowded, health-conscious times and for the growing numbers of people turning to ethnic cooking of one kind or another.

Why has it taken so long for the West to 'discover' these lovely vegetables? I think one reason is the utter confusion surrounding their names. The strange Chinese names are unpronounceable for a start, but in addition many vegetables have several names, and the same names are applied to several vegetables.

When I started investigating Chinese vegetables I felt I was embarking on a giant jigsaw puzzle. The immediate task was to sort out what was what . . . to find the pieces with edges. Then the 'centre' had to be filled in by teasing out the secrets of cultivation, by finding which varieties performed best in the West, by collecting hints on cooking and so on. I've been working on the jigsaw for over ten years and am now much wiser—but needless to say, there are still a few missing pieces.

The first stage was to grow as many oriental vegetables as I could in our East Anglian garden. I tried to get Chinese seed, but it was almost impossible to get consistent seed supplies from mainland China. Traditionally, Chinese farmers save their own seed, a function taken over today by the communes. It is an eminently sensible practice, as over the years strains are selected which are adapted to the locality. But it means there is little need for seed companies as we know them, and therefore few avenues for exporting seed. There are, however, several Taiwanese companies exporting seed, and some of their varieties are suitable for the West. There are also Chinese seed companies in Hong Kong, but on the whole the varieties suitable for Hong Kong's tropical climate are not suited to our temperate climate. As I later discovered in the USA, many Chinese and other Asiatic groups growing oriental vegetables in the West still rely on their families back home to supply them with vegetable seed.

The immediate answer lay in Japan. The Japanese, deprived of native vegetables in their mountainous islands, long ago appreciated the potential of their giant neighbour's diversity of vegetables. Using Chinese material, they started selecting and breeding oriental vegetables, producing some outstanding new varieties. Through their international, export-oriented seed companies they are now making them available to the West. They are also popularizing them in Japan: oriental vegetables have become quite 'chic' with the sophisticated Japanese consumer.

In the past few years it has been fun growing these new vegetables and getting to know them, slowly attaching 'personalities' to the names. An early favourite was the fern-like 'Mizuna' greens. One soon got to appreciate not just its hardiness, prettiness and versatility, but its tolerance. Drop a tray of 'Mizuna' seedlings upside down, pick them up, replant them and they'll be fine. Neglect them for weeks in a seed tray: they'll grin and bear it and recover. But neglect a seed tray of Chinese cabbage, and in no time you'll find they have bolted, or become a slug's breakfast. They're the fastidious aristocrats among the oriental vegetables, demanding nothing but the best from the start.

I would love to be able to say I have grown all the vegetables covered in this book, but there are still some I haven't grown myself. In these cases I've had to rely on other people's experience, or what can be gleaned from the information on seed packets or in seed catalogues (which in some cases had to be translated from Japanese). It is never *quite* the same as your own, first-hand experience.

But, despite all the knowledge I gained, there was a missing element, and the more research I did at home, the more I dreamed of seeing these vegetables growing where they came from—in China. No-one interested in vegetable growing, or indeed in any branch of agriculture, can fail to be inspired by the Chinese people. Against enormous odds they have achieved remarkable levels of sustainable productivity, using systems of composting, irrigation, and intercropping evolved over centuries of agriculture. Two thousand years ago they were cultivating the aquatic plant *Azolla*, in association with a blue-green alga, to fix nitrogen in water to fertilize the rice crop. Today they lead the world in using biological control rather than

chemical sprays to control insect pests. With the new-found realization of the frailty of our planet, Chinese methods, rooted as they are in conservation and recycling, command new respect. Moreover, vegetables are enormously important in China: the average vegetable consumption per head is said to be higher than in any western European country or the USA. They are the warp and woof of Chinese cookery, found in some form in most dishes. As a vegetable fanatic, I *had* to go to China.

Arranging a vegetable study tour was fraught with difficulties. It took several frustrating years of letter writing and submissions before permission was granted for an official visit, organized through the Royal Society in this country and the China Association of Science and Technology. In the meantime I became a very part-time student in Cambridge, trying to learn a little horticultural Chinese. This would probably have been impossible had it not been for two years spent in China with my parents when I was eleven years old. Long forgotten sounds were brought out of hiding at the back of my now middle-aged brain and, before I left, I was able to communicate a little in Chinese.

In September 1985 a party of four of us, including photographer Pamla Toler, left for a three-and-a-half-weeks study tour. We visited Beijing in the north, Nanjing and Shanghai 'half-way down' on the east, then Chengdu, a thousand miles inland in the west, and finally Guangzhou (Canton), in the south. My most important piece of equipment was the beautifully written list of common and alternative Chinese vegetable names which my Chinese teacher, Charles Aylmer, had painstakingly prepared for me.

Wherever we travelled, we were touched by the warmth of the Chinese people, and their willingness to show us their crops and tell us about their cultivation. Professors in the research stations and universities, peasants we interrupted at work in the fields, our guides (whom I plagued mercilessly for recipes), market officials, street

sellers, even passers by, all responded enthusiastically to our many questions. More and more pieces of the jigsaw were being filled in.

Perhaps as important as the facts and figures was the harvest of images I brought back with me . . . the old couple straining at the barrel-shaped night soil cart on a noisy Chengdu road; the headscarfed, giggling girls planting celery with the ubiquitous 'vegetable planting knife', which could have doubled as a kitchen meat cleaver; the Biblical quality of the sun-drenched courtyard in a Beijing commune where Chinese chives were being winnowed for seed; and Chinese chives again in Guangzhou, in the beautiful narrow, raised island beds surrounded by water, where row upon row of plants was being blanched under an army of neatly lidded terracotta pots, each lid held down with a blob of gleaming fresh mud.

And then there were the culinary memories. Some of the richest came in our first week in Beijing, which included a superb meal in a famous vegetarian restaurant where every dish could have been a painting. Another was the meal prepared by the cook at the Beijing Vegetable Research Station guest house. He wanted to give us a glimpse of the many ways Chinese vegetables are prepared. There were already a dozen dishes on the table when we arrived, late as usual, and I made a sketch of them and brief notes. Shall I make your mouth water?

'Beauty Heart' radish Julienne strips, each pink with a tiny lime-green tip (the green outer skin of the radish). Sugar sprinkled on top. *Garlic flower stem* Short, bright green pieces of stem cooked with very finely sliced pork. Delicious. *Chinese cabbage* Very crisp. Cooked by putting Chinese pepper in very hot peanut oil for a few minutes then pouring it over the cabbage. *Green radish* Simply cut finely and served plain. Looked lovely; tasted very sweet. *Winter melon* One-inch chunks

cooked, with constant flicking, in the wok.

Cucumber Rolled up in little coils like a swiss roll, to give alternating layers of dark green skin and lighter coloured flesh. Very pretty.

Aubergine Peeled, softened in hot oil, removed from wok. Subsequently reheated with garlic, onion, soy sauce and sugar. Delicious too.

Stem lettuce Very pale green. Cooked with Sichuan pepper.

Luffah Very thin green slices, mixed with pork pieces.

Oyster mushroom Added to fine slices of fried beef, plus a little salt, cornstarch and a couple of tablespoons of water.

Lotus stem Strips 2 in (5 cm) wide, stuffed with minced pork, fried in batter.

Climbing spinach (Basella) Done in hot oil, with a little salt and fresh garlic. *Very* good.

Carrots with two kinds of radish, green and white All cut in rectangular pieces, cooked in oil in wok for a few minutes before adding a flour paste, plus a little sugar.

Pak choi rape Very dark green. Cut in 8-in (20-cm) strips; cooked with tiny shrimps.

Another excitement in Beijing was finding someone to demonstrate the carving of 'Beauty Heart' radish. This unique, rose-fleshed north-Chinese radish can be as large as a pint beer mug. It was magic to see it deftly carved into delicate flowers and butterflies by an expert lady cook.

From China I travelled on alone for brief visits to Hong Kong, Taiwan and Japan. Again I was overwhelmed by the helpfulness of everyone I met, and was fascinated to see slightly different techniques, new varieties, and some new crops. Yet more pieces in the jigsaw fell into place. The main reason for going to Japan was to make contact with the Japanese seed companies, but it proved an exceptionally fruitful week in many ways. A visit to the immaculate trial grounds of Takii Seeds (on their 150th anniversary) gave me a unique opportunity to see the latest brassica

varieties. A dawn visit to the Kanda wholesale market in Tokyo (equally immaculate), opened my eyes to a completely new range of vegetables—and just when I was beginning to think I knew something about oriental vegetables. The green stems of sweet coltsfoot, the crinkled green and red leaves of perilla, the various types of mountain yam and the tiny red seedlings of *Polygonum hydropiper* were among many I had never seen before.

Two years later I went to North America, on the last leg of my research trail. I wanted to see what Oriental communities in the West were growing. What fun it was, enlisting the help of enthusiastic American and Canadian friends, to track down Korean and Chinese growers in New Jersey, to admire the 'more Chinese than China' vegetable farms along the banks of the Fraser in Vancouver, and to visit the Indochinese community gardens in the heart of Seattle. These were restricted to Asian refugees over sixty-two years old . . . and I think I saw more variety on that small terraced, urban hillside than in the rest of the American continent. On a fascinating farm south of Los Angeles, run by a Taiwanese couple, the Hsiaos, I was to catch up again with Chinese chives, this time being blanched under low black plastic film tunnels instead of terracotta pots.

It was only after my return that I learnt of the exciting developments at Willow Run Farms in Michigan, a greenhouse operation on a reclaimed landfill site. Here baby pak choi, purple mustards and amaranthus are among the exotic vegetables being grown hydroponically in greenhouses heated with the recovered methane gas. A nice coupling of ancient oriental vegetables and modern Western technology.

In this book I have tried to pull together as much information as possible on the cultivation of oriental vegetables. Pride of place has gone to the brassicas (crucifers)—members of the cabbage family.

More than any other group, they comprise an exciting new range of plants, easily grown in temperate climates. Moreover, many of the hardier forms will flourish in unheated greenhouses or frames in winter and early spring, promising a 'Green Revolution' as far as our winter vegetable eating habits are concerned.

The other vegetables covered fall into three categories. First, are those which can be grown easily in temperate climates—for example Chinese chives and chrysanthemum greens or 'shungiku'. Second are vegetables requiring higher temperatures or a longer growing season; these could be considered 'sub tropical'. In cool climates they require greenhouses or some kind of protection to perform well, though will thrive outdoors in warmer climates. Water spinach (*Ipomea aquatica*) and amaranthus are two examples from this group. These have been treated less fully.

The third group consists of minor vegetables, herbs, wild plants and curiosities such as the water vegetables and some of the tubers. These are only covered briefly.

For reasons of space I have had to omit some well known vegetables which are widely grown in China and Japan. Those left out tend to be American rather than Asiatic in origin and association, or are already familiar and described in popular gardening books, or differ little from Western forms. Aubergine, melon, okra, peppers, spinach, sweet potato, tomatoes, and water melon are among those omitted, along with vegetables which are essentially tropical in nature.

The second part of the book is devoted to gardening techniques, emphasizing methods particularly appropriate for oriental vegetables. I should mention here that, like generations of Oriental gardeners, I grow organically without the use of chemical fertilizers, pesticides, fungicides, or weedkillers. So, by and large, the methods suggested are 'organic' and any products mentioned are currently approved by organic authorities in the British Isles.

A note about names

As mentioned earlier, the naming of Chinese vegetables is highly confusing. China is an enormous country, and inevitably vegetables are called by different names in different parts of the country, the same name sometimes being used for several vegetables. (The same situation occurs in Europe. Several vegetables are known as 'broccoli'; there are countless ambiguities in wild plant names.) The problem is compounded by the two principal Chinese languages, Mandarin and Cantonese, which when 'anglicized' have given rise to a host of ingenious spellings in attempts to capture the Chinese pronunciation.

Another source of confusion lies in the fact that many of the oriental vegetables were first introduced to the West by immigrant communities in the USA and Canada, using dialect names. And now there's a sort of American-Chinese, largely derived from these names. In addition there are Japanese names and, in some cases, Japanese approximations of the Chinese names.

To make it easier for Westerners, misleading European names have quite often been attached to various oriental vegetables, generally by the seedsmen introducing them. Take, for example, the lettuce generally listed in seed catalogues as 'celtuce' or 'asparagus lettuce' and not infrequently described as a cross between celery and lettuce. It is neither celery nor asparagus nor a cross between celery and lettuce: it is an Asiatic lettuce grown not for its leaves, but for its stem. Calling it 'stem lettuce' seems far more sensible. Similarly the so-called 'Chinese okra' is not okra at all: it is a luffa. The name 'celery mustard' is used for several vegetables, none of which is celery or mustard. And so it goes on.

In scientific circles there is still argument about the correct *botanical* name for some of the oriental vegetables, notably the brassicas.

The point to remember is that these vegetables did not evolve over the centuries in neat little categories . . . they are a continuum of types. So there *are* genuine borderline cases and, in the absence of scientific agreement, who is to say what is correct? So treat all names with a little suspicion. When buying seed or identifying oriental vegetables, use all available clues, such as catalogue descriptions, illustrations, the appearance of the vegetables, to make sure you are getting what you want.

My use of names in this book is based on the following criteria:
1. The correct botanical name (as far as it can be ascertained).
2. The most widely used Chinese or Japanese name.
3. The most *sensible* European name, which comes closest to conjuring up the plant in the mind's eye, and distinguishing it from any others.

At the beginning of each section I have listed some of the alternative names I have found in use today. As far as possible, Chinese names are written in the Latinized phonetic alphabet 'pinyin'.

A note on climate

I hope this book will be useful to many gardeners in the Western world, growing in a range of climatic conditions.

As all my own experiments and trials have been done in the British Isles, I have taken the mild, temperate British climate as the norm. The variabilities of our climate have been brought home to me forcibly over the two years I have been working on the book. The first summer, 1988, was among the coldest and wettest this century, followed by an extraordinarily mild winter with very little frost. The second, 1989, was among the hottest and driest this century! 1990 proved even hotter and drier. But, allowing for these vagaries, this is a climate where the average annual *minimum* temperatures are about 20°F (−7°C)—and such temperatures are rarely maintained for more than a few days at a time. Spring cabbages, spinach, hardy

greens, are typical of vegetables which survive outdoors most winters. The average mean temperature in the *hottest* month of the year (generally July) is roughly 60°F (15.6°C). This means that a question mark always hangs over the success of warm-season crops grown outdoors in summer, such as French beans, aubergines, sweet corn, peppers. In the northern parts of the country at least, they need to be grown under cover to guarantee success.

Throughout the book I have used the following terms as a rough guide to climate, hoping this will enable gardeners elsewhere to adapt the information to their own conditions.

Temperate climate Conditions prevailing in the British Isles as outlined above.

Warm climate Areas with longer, hotter summers than the British Isles, where warm-season vegetables listed above can be grown outdoors in summer. This would eventually merge into a subtropical climate.

(For information on daylength, see Glossary, page 201.)

A note on seeds

The choice of oriental vegetable seeds is still limited in Western seed catalogues, though the situation is improving steadily. Seedsmen tend to be conservative, preferring to play safe with old favourites. It is up to us gardeners to urge them to list new vegetables and the improved varieties which are being developed. Today's novelties could well be tomorrow's best sellers. There's a Chinese proverb (how could I leave the introduction without a Chinese proverb?) which roughly translated means 'Plant beans, get beans; plant gourds, get gourds'—the Eastern equivalent of 'you reap as you sow'. Please, seedsmen of the West, give us the beans and the gourds.

A note on varieties

The vegetables in this book can be divided into those which are already well known in the West, and those still relatively unknown.

In the first category headed Chinese cabbage is the obvious example; many varieties are available and, as a result of breeding programmes, new improved varieties are constantly being launched. So any recommendations run the risk of rapidly becoming obsolete. In these cases I will confine myself to indicating the factors to look for in choosing varieties. Otherwise be guided by information in current seed catalogues and up-to-date sources such as gardening magazines and radio and television programmes.

With the lesser known vegetables, for example the loose-headed Chinese cabbage, there is at present little choice in the West. I list any good available varieties, and as a source of future reference, briefly describe oriental varieties which deserve to be introduced, or are typical of *types* which have been covered in the text.

A note on measurements
Throughout the book measurements are given in imperial, with metric approximations in brackets. Conversions are not always exact, but are accurate enough for all practical purposes.

An experimental approach
Anyone growing oriental vegetables needs a little of the pioneer spirit. Compared with the vegetables which have been the mainstay of Western gardens for centuries, relatively little is known about them . . . though I hope this book will close some of the gaps. So keep good records, noting which varieties, what sowing times, and what growing methods did best in your conditions. If you feel bewildered about where to start in this vast new field of vegetables, turn to 'Starting Points' on page 200 for a few signposts.

Be experimental too about cooking. Traditional Chinese cooking methods such as steaming and stir-frying are now widely adopted in the West and are ideal for many oriental vegetables. But these vegetables can equally be adapted to Western recipes. For example, the young leaves of mustards and pak choi are wonderful in salads. And don't be tied to conventional ideas. Supermarkets reject the heads of Chinese cabbage once the embryonic flower shoots have started to develop. But those shoots are delicious. Try them.

Within the main text I have given some indication of how each vegetable is normally used and cooked. The separate recipe section at the end describes the basic recipes for a number of the vegetables covered. Several have been gleaned from enterprising cooks. I am most grateful to Ken Toyé, the 'Singing Chef' of Ipswich, for his help in compiling this section.

Finally, I would always be interested in hearing from anyone who wishes to share their experiences in growing or cooking oriental vegetables.

1991   Montrose Farm,
Hepworth, Diss,
Norfolk IP22 2PY
England

Part 1

Vegetables, edible wild plants and herbs

Brassicas

General introduction

I mentioned in my introduction to the book that of all the oriental vegetables the brassicas (crucifers), a group roughly defined as members of the cabbage family, should prove the most rewarding for Westerners to get to know and grow. An amazingly diverse group, it includes the sturdy, bud-like heads of Chinese cabbage (already well known in the West), the crisp white-stemmed pak chois, choy sum and Chinese broccoli with their delicious flowering shoots, the pretty fern-leaved 'Mizuna greens'; and the many types of mustard. Within the mustards there are exceptionally hardy varieties with beautiful purple-hued leaves, compact-headed mustards, and forms with weirdly swollen but highly prized stems and roots.

An endearing feature of the brassicas is their natural vigour. Seed normally germinates very fast, and seedlings and plants develop so rapidly you can almost see them grow. (Within 5½ weeks of transplanting a Chinese cabbage can attain a weight of 2 lb (1 kg): a lettuce would only reach 8 oz (225 g) in the same period.) Most of the oriental brassicas mature in less than four months, much faster than cabbages, cauliflowers and brussels sprouts, which take anything from 5–12 months from sowing to harvest.

To me these oriental brassicas epitomize everything that is 'healthy' about vegetables. In the dull grey days of mid-winter I am constantly struck by the shiny deep green of the 'Komatsuna' spinach mustards. They *radiate* good health. The same message comes from thick-sown patches of pak choi, and the fresh, emerald greens of the loose-headed Chinese cabbages. They have the glow of young vegetation in the first days of spring—except where caterpillars and slugs have gained the upper hand. They *are* healthy of course. Leafy vegetables are excellent sources of vitamins, minerals and fibre, with dark green leafy vegetables being a notable source of protein.

Mizuna intercropped with sweet corn

Many oriental brassicas are beautiful plants as well. I love the crinkly, crêpe-like texture of the rosette pak choi leaves; some mustards have the same quality. 'Mizuna' and the strap-leaved 'Mibuna' are decorative plants by any criterion. Nor is 'handsome' too strong a word for the striking appearance of some of the pak chois and cabbages—notably the creamy centred 'fluffy' types. All these plants find their way into my decorative vegetable garden.

I should digress here to say that I have always felt a vegetable garden should be pretty—and that even a tiny city or suburban garden can grow vegetables *and* look attractive. To demonstrate this I have created two small areas within my kitchen garden where the beds are laid out in formal and semi-formal patterns. They are called *potagers* after the traditional French vegetable garden, or *potager*, where vegetables and flowers were integrated. Here, using varieties chosen for their decorative as well as culinary qualities, vegetables are grouped together and interplanted with herbs and edible flowers to create colourful patterns and textured effects.

Climatic factors

The natural season for many oriental brassicas—for example Chinese cabbage, many pak chois, choy sum and Chinese broccoli—is summer and autumn. They are ideally suited to areas with cool summers and mild winters but, given protective cover in winter, will often crop happily through into spring. They can also be grown in spring and early summer, but if temperatures drop there is a strong tendency to bolt prematurely. Something can usually be salvaged by cutting young leaves just before the plants bolt, or indeed, by utilizing the bolted shoots. (For more on bolting see The bolting problem below.)

Quite a large group of oriental brassicas, including many of the mustards and the milder flavoured 'spinach mustards', are very hardy. Although some varieties can be grown for much of the year, they are most useful as winter crops. In temperate climates they can be grown in the open in winter, but if given protection, they will crop even more lushly, giving useful pickings from autumn through to spring or even early summer.

Stages of use

A characteristic of the oriental brassicas is that, besides harvesting as mature plants, many can be used at various stages during their life cycle.

Cut-and-come-again seedlings

1 AS CUT-AND-COME-AGAIN SEEDLINGS Seed can be sown fairly thickly, and the young seedlings cut when 2–4 in (5–10 cm) high, always cutting *above* the cotyledons or seed leaves. They will usually regrow within a few days, giving a second, then sometimes even a third, cut a few days later—hence the term 'cut-and-come-again'. These young seedlings are exceptionally tasty and nutritious. Because returns are so high, it is an ideal method for people limited to very small gardens or container growing. (See also Plant Raising, cut-and-come-again, page 155.)
2 CUT-AND-COME-AGAIN, MATURE AND SEMI-MATURE CROPS In this case mature and maturing leaves are cut an inch or so (3 cm) above ground

Cut-and-come-again: re-sprouting shoot on a semi-mature plant

level. With 'heading' brassicas, this can be done after the mature head has formed, leaving the stump to re-sprout. It can also be done at any intermediate stage of growth, or where a head seems unlikely to develop due to seasonal factors. It is a particularly useful practice in the winter months, encouraging a plant to continue producing fresh leaf. It also, in my experience, enables plants to survive temperatures several degrees lower than one would normally expect: a relatively bare stump has far more resistance to frost than a full-headed, leafy plant. The stump may look desolate in mid-winter, but it will survive, and burst into life again as soon as temperatures rise in spring.

Another approach is to harvest outer leaves of the plants as soon as they are an edible size. The Rodale Research Center in the United States, who have trialled oriental greens extensively in frames and solar greenhouses in winter, use this method to get earlier pickings. They point out, however, that total yields are higher if you wait for a plant to develop to its full size.
3 FLOWERING SHOOTS While several oriental brassicas are grown specifically for the young flowering shoots—choy sum and Chinese broccoli are the best known examples—we have discovered that the flowering shoots of almost *all* the oriental brassicas are deli-

cious, especially when grown under cover in the winter months. They are so tender and sweet we use them raw in salads. Moreover, the plants, no doubt bent on flowering to ensure the continuation of their kind, produce what seems to be an endless supply of flowering shoots, quite on the scale of a robust purple-sprouting broccoli plant. On the whole flowering shoots get tough faster, and are less prolific, when grown outdoors in summer.
4 SPROUTED SEEDS The seeds of any brassicas can be sprouted, provided they have not been treated or dressed in any way. (See Seed Sprouting, page 132.)

Flowering shoots

Fitting oriental brassicas into Western gardens

The strikingly fast growth of the oriental brassicas makes it easy to slot them into established gardening patterns. There are several options:
Spring As cut-and-come-again seedling catch crops.
Summer As 'follow-on' crops sown or planted in mid-summer after the first crops of, for example, early potatoes, peas or broad beans, have been lifted.
Autumn Follow-on crops after the main summer crops have been har-

vested, using either quick-maturing varieties or seedling cut-and-come-again crops. In many gardens ground is left empty at this time of year.

Winter The hardy types can be grown outdoors, and the less hardy types in cold frames, polytunnels or unheated greenhouses, again, utilizing ground that is often idle during the winter months.

Cultivation

All the rules of good gardening apply to oriental brassicas, but because they grow so fast, they are in some ways more demanding than other vegetables. The following are a few points of special relevance to their cultivation. (For basic cultivation see Part 2, pages 150 ff.)

Plant raising

Like any vegetables, oriental brassicas can either be sown *in situ* and thinned to the correct distance apart, or raised in seed beds or under cover and transplanted.

In perfect soil and climatic conditions excellent results can be obtained by sowing *in situ*. However, most oriental brassicas respond so well to being raised in some kind of module that it is recommended as standard practice for any plants being grown to a substantial size. This applies even at times when there is little bolting risk (see below). Plants raised in modules are much stronger than those sown *in situ* or in crowded seed trays, there is less risk of pest attack in the vulnerable early stages, and the ground where they will eventually grow can be used for another crop until they are ready. (See also Plant Raising, use of modules, page 153.)

The bolting problem

Under certain conditions a number of the oriental brassicas have a tendency to bolt, i.e. to produce flowers and run to seed rather than form a good leafy head. The causes of bolting are complex and interrelated. To a greater or lesser extent the following factors all play a part:
Low temperatures in the early stages of growth This is thought to be the single most important factor. Low temperatures, both when seeds are germinating and in the early stages of growth, lead to the initiation of flowers instead of leaves. Put very simply, young plants need to 'clock up' a certain number of heat units to prevent bolting: once this has been done they can be subjected to lower temperatures without damage.

Daylength With many species there is a greater tendency to bolt in long days (more than 12–14 hours of daylight) than in shorter days. In the northern hemisphere the bolting risk is therefore highest in spring and early summer.

Genetic factors Some types of brassicas are inherently less prone to bolting than others. This makes it possible to select and develop varieties with improved bolting resistance.

Stress Various kinds of 'stress' such as the 'shock' of transplanting, lack of water, over-watering, or sudden temperature changes can exacerbate the tendency to bolt.

MINIMIZING THE RISK OF BOLTING IN EARLY SOWINGS Several steps can be taken to minimize the risk of bolting when sowing bolt-prone brassicas at risky times of year, e.g. in spring.

• Raise plants in a protected environment, such as a heated propagator or heated greenhouse.

• Sow seeds in some form of module. These enable good root systems to be developed, and minimize the shock when the plants are eventually transplanted into their permanent positions. (See also Plant Raising, use of modules, page 153.)

• Germinate seed at high temperatures, at least 64–68°F (18–20°C), and ideally about 72°F (22°C). Once seeds have germinated and the plants have developed three or four leaves they should be grown on at a temperature of around 60°F (16°C) for 4–6 weeks. Make sure, however, that the seedlings have plenty of light and do not become drawn.

• If unexpectedly low temperatures are forecast, try and give plants extra protection, for exam-ple with a low plastic film tunnel or a sheet of bubble film.

It is impossible to be precise about how long any particular variety needs to be kept above a specific temperature to avoid bolting: the information simply isn't available. As a rough guide, however, the Rodale Research Center found that spring-sown oriental greens were liable to bolt if average temperatures remained below 50°F (10°C) for 2–3 weeks.

• Choose varieties recommended for their bolting resistance. New, improved varieties are constantly being developed suitable for earlier sowing: look out for them in seed catalogues.

If you encounter problems in growing headed brassicas early in the year, confine yourself to cut-and-come-again seedling crops, where a cut can be taken before the plants bolt. Even so, it is worth selecting varieties with bolting resistance. This may enable you to have two or three cuts instead of one. How welcome those early, fresh pickings can be after a long winter.

Soil fertility and manuring

Oriental brassicas grow successfully on any type of soil, from sands to clays, *provided they are fertile*. You cannot expect good, or even passable, crops unless the soil is in a high state of fertility. It is a waste of time trying to grow them on poor dry soils. Like all leafy crops, they need high levels of nitrogen to sustain their growth.

Plenty of organic manure or compost must be worked into the soil, and any techniques which help to build up soil fertility—good drainage, the use of raised beds, green manuring, mulching with organic materials—are to be encouraged. Peter Chan, the well-known Chinese gardener in California, works a band of compost into the soil a couple of inches deep when planting Chinese cabbage.

If growth seems less vigorous than expected, plants can be given a boost with a liquid feed once or twice during growth. For most brassicas, key times for supplementary feeding are within a month of planting and in the early stages of head development. (See also Part 2, Soil Fertility, pages 141 ff.)

Watering

Oriental brassicas also need a great deal of water. (It is estimated that a Chinese cabbage requires 5 gallons (22.7 litres) of water during its growing period.) Working plenty of organic matter into the soil helps to ensure a reservoir of moisture, but in dry conditions plants will need watering. Chinese cabbage and the pak chois have rather shallow root systems, so unlike Western brassicas, where the rule is to water occasionally but very heavily, these brassicas respond to being watered a little and often.

Mulching

Keeping the soil surface covered, i.e. mulched, is an excellent horticultural practice—one of the immediate benefits being that it slows moisture evaporation from the soil. Thumbing through a Taiwanese seed catalogue the other day I couldn't help noticing that all the crops photographed in the fields were mulched, either with rice straw or with black plastic film. Many Westerners who have grown oriental brassicas have commented on how they respond to being mulched, and this has been my experience.

The ideal mulch is a layer of organic material a couple of inches deep—but it is not always easy to obtain. Alternatively use the cheap plastic mulches now available. (See also Weeds, mulching, watering, page 157.)

Mulches may have a role to play in reducing pests and disease. Mulches with aluminium film, and to a lesser extent mulches with black film, have been shown to reduce aphid attacks. It also struck me recently that oriental brassicas grown in winter in my polytunnel were freer from disease where mulched, in this case with white plastic film. It is certainly worth trying. (See also Pests and Disease, reflecting mulches, page 174.)

Pests and disease

'We have joined the Pe Tsai diner's club, where we come across all sorts of interesting people on the same wavelength. These are mostly slugs, woodlice, caterpillars and mice. . . .' That was a postcard from my father on his attempts to grow Chinese cabbage in his (slug and snail infested) Cornish garden. I may have reservations about the woodlice and mice, but it is true that the soft, tender leaves of the oriental vegetables attract slugs, caterpillars, flea beetle and sometimes aphids to a greater extent than ordinary brassicas. The more tender the leaves, the more vulnerable they are to attack.

Conventional methods of control—chemical or organic—are effective. It is just that extra vigilance is called for to catch the villains before they have done serious damage. Growing brassicas under very fine mesh nets and fibrous films has also proved an effective means of protecting them from pests such as flea beetle, aphids, cabbage root fly and egg-laying caterpillars and moths. (See Pests and Disease, Barriers, page 174.)

Clubroot is the most potentially serious disease with oriental brassicas, making cultivation difficult in areas with clubroot-infected soil. With fast-maturing brassicas the problem can be contained to some extent by raising plants in pots or modules for transplanting. (See also Pests and Disease, page 178.)

Remedies for disease are few and the answer lies in prevention: good growing practices and hygiene. Here we have much to learn from the assiduous way the Chinese and Japanese remove all crop residues, dead leaves, debris and so on from the fields—eventually recycling them as compost. (See Pests and Disease, Hygiene, page 173.)

In practice I have had few diseases problems with oriental brassicas, other than bacterial rots on Chinese cabbage.

Protected cropping

The term 'protected cropping' embraces a range of devices and structures from cheap low plastic film tunnels supported by wire hoops, to glass and plastic film cloches, to traditional cold frames and modern solar frames, to 'walk in' polytunnels, unheated greenhouses, and the ultimate luxury, heated greenhouses. Mulching films, made of plastic film or woven nylon, are also very useful forms of protected cropping.

Through the higher temperatures obtained under cover, protected cropping extends the growing season by a couple of months. In temperate climates this enables more tender crops to be grown in summer and winter. Moreover, by sheltering plants from wind, protected cropping leads to significantly higher yields and better quality crops. Research has shown that sheltering plants from even *light* winds increases yields dramatically.

PROTECTED BRASSICAS IN WINTER Hitherto in Europe protected cropping has been mainly used, in the winter months, for traditional crops like spinach and winter lettuce, and more recently endive and chicory, which perform better in low winter light than lettuce. What hasn't been appreciated is how well many of the oriental brassicas grow in winter, given a little protection. Here at Montrose Farm in East Anglia we often have as many as twenty different varieties of oriental greens in our unheated polytunnel in mid-winter, their healthiness contrasting vividly with the miserable growth of vegetables remaining in the open.

Winter night temperatures can be very low, even in protected structures. Conversely they can be surprisingly high during the day when the sun shines. But, as the Rodale Research Center have pointed out, oriental vegetables have the ability both to 'bounce back' after low temperatures, and to tolerate the high day temperatures which may follow. Rodale also found them to be much more productive than spinach or lettuce. Top of their productivity league were headed and loose-headed types of Chinese cabbage (the

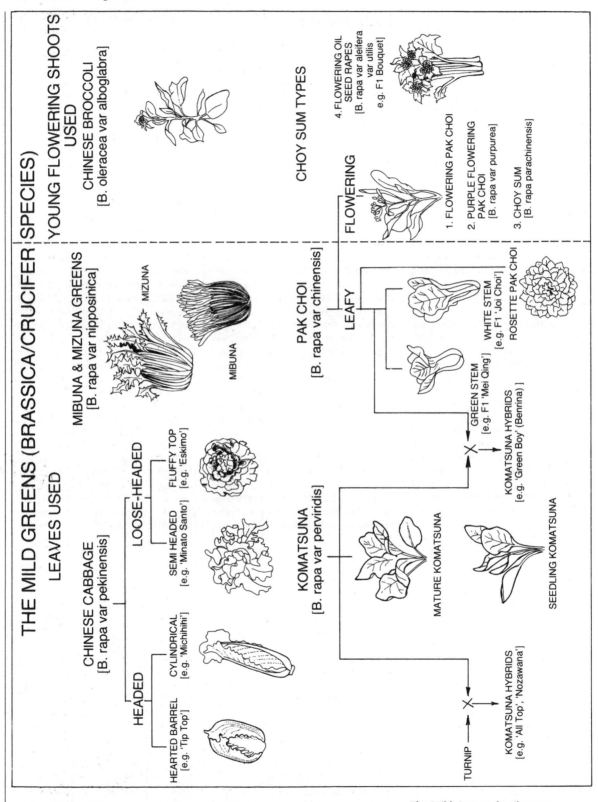

THE MILD GREENS (BRASSICA/CRUCIFER SPECIES)

LEAVES USED

YOUNG FLOWERING SHOOTS USED

CHINESE BROCCOLI
[B. oleracea var alboglabra]

CHOY SUM TYPES

FLOWERING

1. FLOWERING PAK CHOI
2. PURPLE FLOWERING PAK CHOI
   [B. rapa var purpurea]
3. CHOY SUM
   [B. rapa parachinensis]
4. FLOWERING OIL SEED RAPES
   [B. rapa var aleifera var utilis
   e.g. F1 Bouquet]

CHINESE CABBAGE
[B. rapa var pekinensis]

HEADED

HEARTED BARREL
[e.g. 'Tip Top']

CYLINDRICAL
[e.g. 'Michihiri']

LOOSE-HEADED

SEMI HEADED
[e.g. 'Minato Santo']

FLUFFY TOP
[e.g. 'Eskimo']

MIBUNA & MIZUNA GREENS
[B. rapa var nipposinica]

MIZUNA

MIBUNA

PAK CHOI
[B. rapa var chinensis]

LEAFY

GREEN STEM
[e.g. F1 'Mei Qing']

WHITE STEM
[e.g. F1 'Joi Choi']

ROSETTE PAK CHOI

KOMATSUNA HYBRIDS
[e.g. 'Green Boy' (Benrina)]

KOMATSUNA
[B. rapa var perviridis]

MATURE KOMATSUNA

SEEDLING KOMATSUNA

TURNIP ⟶ ✕ ⟶

KOMATSUNA HYBRIDS
[e.g. 'All Top', 'Nozawana']

The Mild Greens: family tree

headed varieties were usually cut at a rosette stage, as they rarely make full heads in the winter), followed by pak choi, oriental mustards, spinach and lettuce.

I am convinced we should exploit these oriental brassicas to the full in the autumn-to-spring period, harnessing their vitality in low cost forms of protected cover. The winter vegetable scene could be transformed. They can be used cooked or raw in salads, for in the lower light of winter conditions, leaves are thinner, less fibrous and more tender than when grown outdoors in summer. Another bonus: there are few pest problems in the winter months—and less need to use any kind of pesticides. (See also Part 2, Protected cropping, page 161.)

Grouping the oriental brassicas

For most gardeners the scientific classification of the oriental brassicas is of little help in finding one's way through these unfamiliar vegetables. So for practical purposes I've divided them into two main groups based on flavour: the *mild greens*, and the *mustard greens*:

The *mild greens* include types cultivated for their leaves and types cultivated for their flowering shoots and stems: all are relatively mild-flavoured. (See the illustrated table on page 12.)

The *mustard greens* are hotter in flavour, the flavour varying from a gentle hint of 'something interesting' to an extremely pungent flavour.

Confusion over the correct names for the brassicas is labyrinthine. (See 'A note about names' in the previous chapter.) For example, should the bulk of the mild greens (Chinese broccoli excepted) be called *Brassica rapa* or *B. campestris?* I hope I am swimming with the tide in opting for the former. Forgive me, eminent botanists, if I am wrong.

Inter specific hybrid brassicas

With modern technology different species can be crossed, sometimes by the actual fusion of cells, to create 'new' vegetables. The original impetus for such programmes was not so much to create new vegetables as to transfer good genetic qualities from one species to another—for example to work the natural resistance to bacterial soft rot found in the common European cabbage into Chinese cabbage, which is highly susceptible to such rots. Some promising new vegetables are emerging in the process.

So far few of these hybrids have been grown on any scale, but they could be introduced in the not too distant future. A hybrid between ordinary cabbage and komatsuna, 'Senposai' ('one thousand treasure vegetable'), is already being marketed in Japanese seed sprouting kits for children. The flavour is much like ordinary cabbage.

Headed Chinese cabbage

Family *Cruciferae*
Latin name *Brassica rapa* var *pekinensis*
Other names in use* Celery cabbage, Chinese leaves; napa and wong bok (barrel type); Michihili (tall cylindrical type)
Mandarin Da bai cai ('big white vegetable'); huang ya cai ('yellow tooth vegetable'); jie qiu bai cai ('headed cabbage')
Cantonese Bok choy; wong nga pak; wong bok; siew choy
Japanese Hakusai

* NB There are many other names in use for Chinese cabbage, sometimes variety names being used as a general term for Chinese cabbage. Chinese cabbage is also frequently called 'pak choi', but it is best to reserve 'pak choi' for the type described on page 121.

Background

Chinese cabbage did indeed originate in China, the earliest record in Chinese literature being in the fifth century AD. No wild Chinese cabbage has ever been found. It was probably a cross, which occurred naturally in cultivation, between the southern 'pak choi' and the northern turnip. A romantic theory is that this cross first occurred at the city of Yangzhou, the junction of the northern and southern sections of the Grand Canal, which linked north and south China.

The original Chinese cabbages were untidy, loose-headed things,

Use

Although Chinese cabbage is almost invariably sold as a mature head, gardeners can grow it as a seedling crop, or cut the semi-mature heads for intermediate-sized leaf, or use the sweet flowering shoots. (See Brassicas, General introduction, Stages of use, page 9.)

There need be little waste with Chinese cabbage. The outer wrapper leaves of a mature head may have to be discarded if they are tattered and weatherbeaten, but of the rest, the leaf blade, the midrib and the white leaf bases are all very tender and edible. Seedling leaves tend to be rather rough and hairy; where this is the case they are best cooked rather than eaten raw. Plant

Chinese cabbage: barrel headed
hearted type

but gradually different types evolved, probably in response to different climatic conditions. The firm-headed types, for example, developed in northern areas with a long cool summer; looser-headed types evolved in the hotter south (Chinese cabbage *doesn't* like it hot). Over the course of time different regions developed their own early, mid-season and late varieties, giving rise to literally hundreds of varieties with subtly varying characteristics.

Only relatively recently has Chinese cabbage become the ubiquitous vegetable it is in modern China. During the winter consumption of stored cabbage in north China is said to be over 120 lb (50 kg) per head—reputedly 80 per cent of all vegetables consumed.

Chinese cabbage didn't reach Japan until the 1860s. It was introduced to America late in that century, probably by immigrants or missionaries returning from China. It has only become established in Europe in the last fifteen or twenty years, but it has become popular so rapidly that it is now the one oriental vegetable everyone recognizes.

The first Japanese varieties were bred in the 1920s, and most of the varieties grown in the West today are Japanese F1 hybrids.

Characteristics

Chinese cabbage is annual or biennial, but grown as an annual. It looks rather like a well-fed cos lettuce, and not at all like the typical flat or rounded Western cabbage. It

forms an upright head, sometimes of very tight, overlapping leaves, sometimes a looser head. Heads vary enormously in shape and size, (see Types below), and when well grown can weigh anything from about 3 lb (1.4 kg) up to 10 lb (4.5 kg).

Depending on the variety, the colour of the outer leaves ranges from dark green to a very delicate pale green, with some traditional Chinese varieties being almost yellow-leaved. The inner leaves are always paler, sometimes blanched to a creamy whiteness in the centre of a tight head. Leaves vary from smooth and almost rounded in shape to frilled and wavy, sometimes with a rougher, hairier texture. In some varieties the leaves display a characteristic network of prominent white veins radiating from a thick, succulent midrib. The wrinkled appearance is so like the skin of a walnut the Chinese call this the 'walnut' type.

Another characteristic of Chinese cabbage is the broad, swollen base of the leaf midrib, midrib bases often overlapping to form a very solid, white 'butt' to the head. The leaves are generally very crisp, and the nearer they are to the centre of the heart the crispier and crunchier they are. Seedling leaves are often hairy, a characteristic generally lost with age.

Types

There are three main types: the tall cylindrical, hearted and loose-headed.

Chinese cabbage: cross section of
barrel type

breeders are trying to produce less hairy varieties.

The Chinese cabbage flavour is very delicate. Some varieties tend to sweetness, others are starchier, some are more watery than others. In China different varieties are considered suited for different purposes.

In the kitchen

With its fresh appearance and the crispy texture of shredded leaves it is now being widely adopted as a salad vegetable, even usurping iceberg lettuce in the hamburger and sandwich trade.

Chinese cabbage needs only light cooking or the flavour is destroyed. For this reason it should never be subjected to the traditional English treatment for cabbage—boiling in water. The Chinese are said to have a hundred methods of cooking it: in soups; as a steamed or stir-fried vegetable on its own; combined with other vegetables or with fish, meat and poultry; in fillings and stuffings.

In the West it is being used increasingly as a substitute for 'ordinary' cabbage in recipes such as stuffed cabbage, as well as being cooked 'Chinese-style'. In China, Japan and Korea enormous quantities of Chinese cabbage are used to make salted and fermented pickles such as the famous Korean *kimche*, a valuable source of vitamins during long winter months. Leaves are sometimes dried and used in soup. Dried, very finely chopped cabbage is mixed with garlic, '5 spices' and salt (70 per cent cabbage, 20 per cent garlic, 10 per cent spices and salt in one commercial brand) to make the Chinese *dongcai*. This is used to flavour fish dishes as well as soup.

(See also Recipes, page 188.)

Chinese cabbage: cylindrical type

Cylindrical type

This has long erect leaves, forming a compact but tapering head without wrapping leaves over the top. This type is sometimes tied when nearing maturity to make the inner leaves whiter.

The plants are generally 15–18 in (38–46 cm) tall and 4–6 in (10–15 cm) wide; the leaves are usually dark green. They are relatively slow growing, generally over 70 days from sowing to harvest. Most are more susceptible to bolting than the hearted types. In China they are used for the autumn fresh crop and for storage, being considered the sweetest and the best quality of the stored cabbages. Typical varieties are 'Michihili' and F1 'Jade Pagoda'.

Hearted type

These have large compact heads, with the leaves closely wrapped, usually over the top, to make a dense heart of paler leaves. The heads have several characteristic shapes, including 'stocky barrel', 'long barrel', and 'flat-topped'.

Hitherto most of the varieties available in the West have been Japanese or European-bred 'stocky barrel' types, with the weight tending to be in the lower half of the head. They have compact, broad to oblong heads, on average 8–10 in (20–25 cm) high and 6–9 in (15–23 cm) wide, often with 'walnut' veining on the leaves. Leaf colour ranges from light to dark green. They are quick-maturing (55–70 days), and relatively slow bolting. They are used for early and summer crops, both outdoors and under cover. They are generally used fresh, but can also be stored. Typical varieties are the F1 hybrids 'Tip Top' and 'Nagaoka'.

Indigenous Chinese varieties of hearted cabbages tend to be taller, many do not have closely overlapped leaves, and are more likely to bolt. So seed acquired from China may not do well in the West.

The 'flat-topped' types are rather squat and top-heavy. These varieties are generally adapted to tropical conditions, and few are at present grown in the West.

Loose-headed type

See next chapter.

Note Many crosses have now been made between the different types of Chinese cabbage, so modern varieties do not necessarily fit neatly into one of the above categories, and may display the characteristics of several groups.

Climate

Chinese cabbage likes coolish weather during its main growing period: temperatures about 55°–68°F (13°–20°C) are ideal. Where summer daytime temperatures rise above 95°F (35°C) ordinary varieties are unlikely to form hearts and are prone to disease. Under these conditions the tropical varieties should be grown.

At the cold end of the spectrum mature heads will stand light frost, i.e. 3–5 degrees of frost, depending on the variety and how much shelter they have (it is the combination of wind and low temperatures which is the killer.) Woven films can be used to give Chinese cabbage extra protection against frost in spring and autumn. (See also Film protection, below.)

In my experience, *semi-mature* heads treated as a cut-and-come-again crop in a polytunnel will survive temperatures as low as 14°F (−10°C). Varieties with greater resistance to cold are continually being developed. Look out for them in seed catalogues and use them for early and late sowings.

Rainfall Unless irrigation is available, Chinese cabbage should not be grown in areas with low rainfall during the growing period. The roots of most varieties are very shallow and have little resistance to drought.

Site/soil

Summer crops are best in an open situation, though they will tolerate light shade. Outdoor spring and autumn crops benefit from shelter from cold winds. Frost pockets should be avoided.

Chinese cabbage needs deep, rich, well-drained soil, with a high level of organic matter so that it retains moisture and plant roots run freely. Very light, very heavy and very poor soils should be avoided. (See also Brassicas, General introduction, Soil fertility and manuring, page 10.)

The soil pH should be between 6.5 and 7. Where there is a risk of clubroot infection, the pH should be raised to 7 or above by liming.

Rotation Chinese cabbage is a member of the brassica group of vegetables, and is very susceptible to clubroot and bacterial soft root, both soil-borne diseases. To avoid the build up of disease it should be rotated with unrelated crops, ideally over six or seven years.

Soil preparation Thorough preparation of the soil is essential for Chinese cabbage. If possible grow it on a bed system to minimize soil compaction. In China and Japan it is sometimes grown on ridges, both to overcome poor drainage and, by improving the air flow around the base of the plant, to help prevent bacterial disease. (See also Part 2, The bed system, page 147.)

Cultivation
Bolting

Chinese cabbage varieties vary considerably in their susceptibility to bolting if exposed to cold in the early stages. It is important to choose appropriate varieties for each sowing and, in cold periods, to germinate the seed and grow on seedlings at high temperatures. Remember, though, that something can usually be salvaged from semi-mature bolting plants with the cut-and-come-again treatment, and by harvesting bolted shoots. (See also Brassicas, General introduction, Stages of use, page 9, and The bolting problem, page 10.)

Intercropping

There is some evidence from the Asian Vegetable Research and Development Center in Taiwan that interplanting Chinese cabbage with dill and garlic lessens attacks by caterpillars.

When to grow what
Mature headed crop
(1) Late spring and early summer outside
    a) if started indoors *or*
    b) if planted out under protection
(2) Summer and autumn outside
(3) Autumn and early winter under cover

Seedling crop
(1) Spring under cover
(2) Late spring, early summer, autumn in the open
(3) Autumn, early winter under cover

Semi-mature cut-and-come-again heads and flowering shoots
(1) Spring to autumn outside
(2) Autumn to early winter under cover
For cultivation of these different crops, see below.

The mature headed crop
(1) LATE SPRING/EARLY SUMMER OUTDOOR CROP This is a chancy business, and is only worth trying in mild areas, where there is a sheltered spot to plant out.
    Delay sowing until about 2 weeks before the last frost in your area. Use a bolt-resistant variety,

and sow in modules in a heated greenhouse or propagator. If possible maintain temperatures of between 68 and 77°F (20–25°C) for the first 3 weeks. If this is difficult, aim for 64°F (18°C). Harden off carefully (see Part 2, Plant raising, Hardening off, page 153) before planting out at the 4–5 leaf stage. This early crop can be covered with a woven film after planting (see below).
    In the British Isles sowings can be made in the ground in late May and early June, *provided* floating mulches are used.
(2) SUMMER AND AUTUMN SOWING OUTDOORS In the temperate British Isles climate headed Chinese cabbage grows best outdoors, with the least risk of bolting, if sown roughly between mid-June and mid-August. On average plants will mature 8½–10 weeks after sowing, being ready for use from mid-August until about the end of October. Mid-July sowings will mature fastest. Make the last sowing at least 8 weeks before the first frost is expected in your area.
    Either sow *in situ* or in modules and transplant, the latter being preferable. Bare root transplants are not recommended. (See also Brassicas, General introduction, Plant raising, page 10.)
In situ sowings In the British Isles sowings can be made outside from late May or early June until July or August, depending on the district and the variety used. Use bolt-resistant varieties for the early sowings in May and early June; even so, there is still some risk of bolting if there are sudden snaps of cold weather.
    Sow thinly in drills ½–¾ in (15–20 mm) deep, keeping the rows at least 12 in (30 cm) apart. Water the drills thoroughly before sowing if conditions are at all dry. (See also Part 2, Plant raising, Sowing in adverse conditions, page 151.)
    Seed will normally germinate within 3–4 days. Start thinning when the plants have 4–5 true leaves, generally about 3 weeks after sowing. Thin in stages to 12–15 in (30–37 cm) apart. The wider the spacing, the larger the plants

will grow: 12 in (30 cm) apart each way is adequate for average-size barrel types; the cylindrical types can be a little closer. Plantings that will mature in late autumn can be a little further apart, allowing air to circulate more freely and making them less prone to rots.
    In the early stages of growth keep a sharp look out for damage by slugs and flea beetles and take appropriate measures. Crops can be sown under woven film to protect them from insects such as flea beetle, cabbage root fly and caterpillars. (See Pests and disease, Barriers, page 174.)
Transplanting Sow direct in modules, or in seed trays and transplant into modules. Transplant into the permanent positions after 4–6 weeks, at the 4–5 true leaf stage, at the spacings suggested for the direct sown crop.
(3) AUTUMN/EARLY WINTER CROP UNDER COVER I have found this a very useful crop, coming in at a time when fresh vegetables are scarce. The plants are grown in cold frames, unheated greenhouses or polytunnels during the winter months, making excellent use of ground that is often idle in winter. Some seasons this autumn-planted Chinese cabbage has supplied me with fresh pickings from late October, right through to May the following year. Use the most cold-resistant cylindrical varieties available. Failing that, reasonable results can be obtained with barrel types.
    Sow in the late summer or early autumn. Either sow *in situ* or in modules for transplanting. The latter gives more flexibility: one is often waiting for a summer greenhouse crop to be cleared to make for autumn plantings. Plant at normal spacing if you intend to have a headed crop initially. With a little luck, solid heads will be formed by early winter, and these can be cut, leaving the stumps in the soil to resprout. Closer spacing, 5–6 in (12.5–15 cm) apart, is sufficient for a cut-and-come-again crop of semi-mature heads.
    At this time of year plants sometimes produce only a rosette of

loose leaves instead of a full head. Treat them as a semi-mature cut-and-come-again crop. The leaves, being grown under cover, are exceptionally tender and can be used in salads or cooked. The plants will continue to grow in warm spells throughout winter. If temperatures never rise much above freezing they will remain dormant, but will start growing when temperatures rise in sunny spells in early spring. In late spring they will produce flowering shoots in copious quantities. Flower buds, stems and small leaves on the flowering shoots are all tender enough to use raw or cooked.

FILM PROTECTION FOR THE OUTDOOR CROP In the British Isles fibrous films (also known as floating mulches or film covers) are proving useful on the Chinese cabbage crop. The films are laid over the crop and anchored at the edges. (See Part 2, Protected cropping, Film covers, page 167.) Trials are still being completed, but from results so far the following uses are recommended. (Note that perforated plastic films are quite unsuitable for protecting Chinese cabbage.)

● Early sowings and planting can be covered with film, both to raise temperatures, and give protection against flea beetle, cabbage root fly, aphids and caterpillars. Crops planted in early May can be left covered until nearing maturity; if planted in late May, remove the covering after 2–3 weeks before temperatures become too high. Crops mature about a week earlier than they would otherwise.

● Late sowings can be covered to give a couple of degrees protection against autumn frost and protection against pests. Cover when sowing or planting. In this case planting can probably be delayed until about the third week in August.

EXTRA PROTECTION WITH LOW PLASTIC FILM TUNNELS AND CLOCHES Early and late in the season extra protection can be given with low polytunnels or cloches, provided the crop is well ventilated. (See also Part 2, Protected cropping, Low tunnels, page 166.)

Seedling crops

Chinese cabbage gives very quick and high returns grown as a cut-and-come-again seedling crop. (See Plant raising, Cut-and-come-again seedling crops, page 155.) Where slugs are taking a toll of headed cabbage, consider growing seedling crops instead. Slug damage is probably no less severe—but it is less noticeable than on a headed crop!

Use quick-maturing varieties. If required for use in salads, use the smoothest-leaved varieties available.

Germination and growth are very rapid. Make the first cut when two true leaves have formed, which is sometimes within 15 days of sowing. Two or three more cuts can usually be made, depending on the season, cutting seedlings until they are 4–5 in (10–12.5 cm) high.

Seedling crops require far more seed than headed crops. As most of the Chinese cabbage varieties available are relatively expensive F1 hybrids, this would make it a costly business. If you are unable to obtain cheaper, open pollinated varieties, consider saving your own seed for this purpose. (See also Plant raising, Saving seed, page 154.)

(1) SPRING SOWINGS UNDER COVER Sow indoors, in frames, unheated greenhouses or polytunnels, from very early spring onwards, provided soil temperatures are above 40°F (5°C). Sowing can continue for several weeks, but once indoor temperatures start to soar during the day, the plants, being so close together, will start to run to seed.

(2) LATE SPRING TO AUTUMN SOWINGS OUTDOORS Sow outside in a sheltered spot once the soil has warmed up. Make the first sowings under cloches or protected with fibrous film. Further sowings can be made until early summer. In midsummer seedling sowings tend to run to seed too rapidly to be worthwhile. Sow again outdoors in late summer and early autumn for an autumn crop.

(3) LATE AUTUMN/EARLY WINTER SOWINGS UNDER COVER Final sowings can be made in a frame, green-house or polytunnel in late autumn and early winter. Probably only one cut can be made before growth ceases because of low winter temperatures. However, if the plants survive the winter, a further very useful cut may be made in early spring.

Semi-mature cut-and-come-again heads and flowering shoots

Wherever Chinese cabbage is grown for mature heads, it can be cut before the head is formed and treated as a semi-mature cut-and-come-again crop. The leaf harvested will be less white and crispy than from a mature head. After several cuts the plants will run to seed and the young flowering shoots can be eaten. During the summer months flowering shoots must be picked very young, at the bud rather than flower stage, as they toughen rapidly.

Where Chinese cabbage is grown primarily as a semi-mature cut-and-come-again crop, grow plants 5–6 in (12.5–15 cm) apart.

(1) Spring to autumn sowings outside See The mature headed crop (1) and (2) above.

(2) Autumn to early winter sowings under cover See The mature headed crop (3) above.

Further care

Chinese cabbage is a greedy, leafy crop, with much the same nutritional requirements as lettuce. (See also Brassicas, General introduction, Soil fertility and manuring, page 10.)

Chinese cabbage is always thirsty, and ensuring that plants are never short of water is the best guarantee of a healthy crop. Heavy downpours on dry soils can cause cracking and lesions on the developing head, which encourage rots. The remedy is never to allow the soil to dry out. As mentioned earlier, the roots are shallow, so water a little and often.

Mulching after planting, with either organic material or a plastic mulch, both helps to retain soil moisture and to prevent bacterial rots, to which Chinese cabbage is prone. (See also Part 2, Weeds, mulching and watering, page 157.)

Head tying

The heads of the cylindrical types are sometimes tied as the plants are nearing maturity to make the inner leaves whiter and more tender. It may also give them a little protection against frost. Tie healthy plants, when the foliage is dry, tying them towards the top of the plant, either with string or by slipping a broad rubber band over the head. They are ready within a couple of weeks.

Containers

Headed Chinese cabbage is not a good subject for containers, as the risk of drying out is too high. Seedling Chinese cabbage could be grown in containers. (See also Part 2, Containers, page 169.)

Pests and disease

Chinese cabbage is susceptible to a wider range of pests and diseases than most of the oriental brassicas. The most serious pests are flea beetle, slugs, various caterpillars, cabbage root fly and aphids. The most serious diseases are clubroot, bacterial soft rot, powdery mildew and alternaria leaf spot.

(See also Brassicas, General introduction, Pests and disease, page 11, and Part 2, Pests and disease.)

Harvesting

Time from sowing to harvest, varies from about 55 days, for the early maturing barrel types, to 100 days, for the late maturing, cylindrical types. Seed catalogues often quote a 'days to maturity figure' for each variety, but these should be treated as no more than a rough guide, as so much depends on local conditions. Harvest heads when they feel solid, and show no sign of caving in beneath the fingers when pressed firmly with both hands.

Cut just above the soil surface. If they are being marketed, leave a couple of wrapper leaves around the head to protect them in transit. Otherwise strip them down to the firm central head.

During the summer mature Chinese cabbages will not stand long before young flower stems start to form within the heads. Although heads at this stage are frowned upon commercially, gardeners will find they are still very palatable. The flowering shoots eventually burst out of the head.

In the autumn cold-tolerant varieties will stand outside for several weeks, provided it is cold and dry. They will deteriorate fairly rapidly in wet conditions, unless protected with cloches. Aim to harvest them before frost, though they will withstand a few degrees of frost without damage. Warm spells following frost, however, will lead to increased rotting.

Storage

In a domestic refrigerator Chinese cabbage will keep in a fridge for several weeks, even months. To minimize the risk of listeria, remove any soil, and store them in paper bags or loose, out of contact with other food. Never store them in plastic bags.

In cellars and sheds Chinese cabbage can be stored for two to three months in a frost-free cellar or shed. The temperature should not rise much above 39°F (4°C), or they will start to rot. The ideal temperature is 34°F (1°C), with about 85 per cent humidity.

In cold frames Uproot the plants on a dry day, and either replant them in the soil of a cold frame, or lay them on wooden slats in the bottom of the frame. Where winter temperatures go below freezing, cover them with an 8–12 in (20–30 cm) thick layer of straw, or other insulating material. Close the frame in cold weather, but open it on warm days. They should keep sound for several months.

Although traditionally roots were cut off and plants trimmed before storage, the modern tend-

ency is to store them with the roots and outer leaves intact—provided the foliage is dry when lifted. Whatever storage method is used, examine the plants every 3–4 weeks, removing any diseased or decaying leaves.

Oriental methods of storage In China and Japan Chinese cabbage is stored for periods of 4–5 months by the methods given below, which are suitable only for areas with very cold, very dry winters. Under these conditions the outer leaves wilt and form a dry husk which protects the heart. Barrel-shaped cabbages are the main storage types, though cylindrical heads are also stored.

● In open sheds, in piles about 3–5 ft (1–1.5 m) high, butts facing outwards, covered with straw mats.

● In the field, roots intact, stacked closely in piles about five rows deep, covered with straw matting.

● In the field, piled in layers of two to three heads, separated by layers of sand and soil. The heap is built on a layer of sand covered by straw, and covered with a final layer of soil and sand, which is added to as temperatures get lower.

● In shallow pits, packed upside down with the roots intact and protruding above soil level, where they are covered with soil.

● In specially constructed deep pits and underground chambers. Cylindrical types are often stored this way, stacked with roots intact. The heads continue to develop and blanch, to give high-quality cabbage.

Varieties

There are now a great many varieties of headed Chinese cabbage listed in Western catalogues. In selecting them note the following points:

● The quality and reliability of the F1 hybrids is far superior to any open pollinated varieties, though the latter can be used for seedling cut-and-come-again crops.

● For the *earliest* sowings, choose bolt-resistant barrel-headed types.

● For the *latest* sowings, choose cold-resistant cylindrical types.

Loose-headed Chinese cabbage

The Chinese call this group 'no head cabbage': they are considered varieties of Chinese cabbage. Western catalogues usually list them as 'loose' or 'semi-headed' Chinese cabbage. In evolutionary terms they predate the headed Chinese cabbages, the theory being that very loose-headed cabbages evolved first, then semi-headed types, then the 'fluffy headed' types, and finally the headed cabbages. I find them a very attractive, versatile and easily grown group. They deserve to be much more widely grown in the West. Fortunately, enterprising seedsmen are starting to introduce them and to breed new varieties.

Chinese cabbage: loose headed type

Characteristics

The group embraces a range of types, from very loose, rather sprawly, open-headed varieties to the much denser, aptly named 'fluffy top' type. There is a lot of variation within the group, but a typical loose-headed variety has a funnel-shaped, rosetted head, and the leaves are frequently a very pretty light green colour, sometimes almost yellow, tending to be paler in the centre. There are also varieties with darker green leaves.

In some varieties the leaf surface is crêpe-like or 'savoyed'; others are lightly crinkled. But again there are smooth and glossy-leaved varieties. Leaf texture ranges from soft to very crisp, as found in the central leaves of mature 'fluffy tops'.

The leaf midribs are sometimes swollen at the base like headed Chinese cabbage, with the leaves seeming to spring from the ground. In others the midribs are small and the leaves are borne on narrow leaf stalks.

The 'fluffy top' varieties, sometimes described as 'self blanching', have frilled leaves. The outer leaves are light green, but when nearing maturity the tips of the central leaves turn a contrasting pure white or buttery yellow, giving the characteristic 'fluffy' appearance—and explaining the old Chinese variety names of 'flower cabbage' or 'golden cabbage'. The colour change is a useful indication that they are ready for harvesting.

Mature loose-headed varieties can reach weights of 4–5 lb (1.8–2.2 kg); but the 'fluffy tops' tend to be more substantial, mature heads sometimes weighing up to 8–9 lb (3.6–4 kg).

Climate, site/soil

See Headed Chinese cabbage, page 15.

Decorative value

These are pretty cabbages to grow. A group of mature creamy centred 'fluffy tops' makes a striking patch in the vegetable garden; the lighter coloured varieties look wonderful intercropped with dark vegetables such as red cabbages; the darker leaved varieties have a healthy handsomeness. I use them all in my decorative *potager*.

Chinese cabbage: 'fluffy top' type

Use

Like headed Chinese cabbage, the loose-headed types can be harvested at any stage from seedling leaves to mature heads. Some varieties lend themselves to being harvested when the heads are small, making very attractive greens. (See also Brassicas, General introduction, Stages of use, page 9.)

The flavour depends on the variety, but is generally a very pleasant, mild flavour, sometimes slightly 'nutty', sometimes sweet. Some varieties become sweeter after a touch of frost. The darker leaved varieties tend to be closer to European cabbage in flavour.

In the kitchen

Loose-headed cabbage can be cooked in any method suitable for Chinese cabbage, and in any recipe calling for 'greens'. It is also excellent raw in salads. The light coloured varieties, and especially the crispy 'fluffy tops', look most appetizing in salads.

In China and Japan the loose-headed cabbages are very popular for pickling. They are, however, unsuitable for storage.

Cultivation

(See also Brassicas, general introduction, Cultivation, page 10.) In my experience loose-headed cabbages are easier to grow than headed Chinese cabbage, for several reasons:

- They mature more rapidly, heads often being ready within 55–70 days of sowing in spring and summer (2–3 weeks faster than many varieties of Chinese cabbage).
- They tend to have more resistance to bolting.
- They tend to have more resistance to cold.
- They are more disease-resistant.

The bad news is that flea beetles, slugs and caterpillars appreciate their tender flavour and must be controlled. (See also Headed Chinese cabbage, Pests and disease, page 18.)

Growing methods

Loose-headed Chinese cabbage can be:
—direct-sown as a seedling crop
—direct-sown or transplanted, for cutting as a semi-mature plant.
—direct-sown or transplanted, for cutting as a small or mature head.

Where mature plants are wanted, the best quality plants are obtained by raising them in modules and transplanting. (See Part 2, Plant raising, Use of modules, page 153.) However, as loose-headed cabbages are less prone to bolting than headed Chinese cabbage, planting 'bare root transplants' is less risky than it is with Chinese cabbage.

When to sow

Generally speaking, the loose-headed Chinese cabbages can be grown outdoors for most of the growing season in temperate climates. They can be grown under cover in the winter months, provided temperatures do not fall much below freezing point. Varieties differ in their requirements, so should be checked before sowing.

Standard loose-headed varieties

SPRING

(1) Under cover Sowings can be made very early in the year, provided soil temperatures are above 41°F (5°C). For the fastest returns, make the first sowings cut-and-come-again seedling crops: it may be possible to make the first cuts within 4–5 weeks of sowing.

Where grown for harvesting young, or as a semi-mature cut-and-sow-again crop, space plants 8–10 in (20–25 cm) apart.

For a mature headed crop space plants from 12–20 in (30–50 cm) apart, depending on variety. Delay these sowings until late spring.

(2) Outdoors The Rodale Research

Center concluded that for the earliest outdoor harvest of Chinese cabbage, spring-sown, loose-headed varieties should be used, the seedlings being least likely to bolt if exposed to cold. Spring-sown crops grow very rapidly, producing very tender leaves.

Sow outdoors from early spring onwards, once the soil has warmed up, at spacings recommended for indoor sowings above.

SUMMER Growth is very fast in the summer months, but plants are more liable to become fibrous and coarse if left standing. Loose-headed cabbages are at their best in cool weather.

In temperate climates outdoor sowings can be made throughout the summer months, though it is best to avoid very hot periods.

AUTUMN Though growth is slower and yields lower in autumn and winter these are extremely useful crops.

(1) Outdoors In temperate climates seedling crops can be sown until early autumn; plants sown earlier can be planted out in early autumn. Where bad weather is likely it is advisable to cover these crops with cloches or low tunnels in late autumn to improve their quality. (See Brassicas, General introduction, Protected cropping, page 11.)

(2) Under cover (unheated) Provided the soil is still warm sowings of seedling crops can be made in late autumn and early winter. Plants can also be transplanted under cover in late summer and well into autumn, to mature during late autumn and early winter. Unless severe frosts are experienced under cover—in which case the plants may rot and die—they should continue to provide greens in early spring.

(3) Under cover (slightly heated) The Rodale Research Center grew a wide range of loose-headed greens in a double-layered polythene covered greenhouse, with the temperature kept between 40–42°F (4–6°C). They were sown in August and planted the third week in November. The first cuttings of immature plants were generally made within 50 days after planting, and

of mature plants 80–100 days after planting. They provided greens from October to March or April. They were fed with a liquid organic fertilizer twice a month from planting until the first cutting, and from then on once a month.

Fluffy top varieties

There is little data about the performance of 'fluffy top' varieties in the West. They are generally more susceptible to cold than the standard loose-headed varieties, and most are likely to bolt from early sowings. In common with other brassicas, they appear to withstand lower temperatures when grown as seedlings, or semi-mature cut-and-come-again crops.

Seedlings and semi-mature cut-and-come-again crops
—Sow spring through to summer in the open.
—Sow early spring and early autumn under cover.

Mature heads
—In temperate climates sow in mid-summer.
—In warm climates sow from late summer to early autumn.

Varieties

Few varieties of loose-headed Chinese cabbages are widely grown in the West at present. The following list includes some which have had limited trials, and others available from Japanese sources. New varieties are likely to be introduced in the future. Be guided by up to date literature for appropriate sowing dates.

SANTO (SHANTO/SHANDONG) GROUP
These were the original loose-headed Chinese cabbages introduced to the West. They are rather spreading in habit and characterized by fresh, light green leaves with white midribs. In mature heads the central leaves can become blanched, heads weighing up to 5 lb (2.3 kg). They fall into two distinct types:
—Round-leaved, with smooth leaves with smooth margins.
—Serrated-leaved, with frillier leaves and serrated margins.
The varieties below are among sev-

eral improved varieties being marketed by Japanese seedsmen:

'Maruba Santo' Fairly tall, round-leaved, bunches neatly. Fast-growing; more heat-tolerant than most varieties.

'Minato Santo' ('Minato Bekana') Vigorous, fast-growing, brilliant green wavy leaves. Slow-bolting, cold tolerant. Survived winter temperatures of 10°F (−12°C) in my unheated polytunnel.

'Ogato Santo' ('Large leaved Santo') Tall cylindrical head, 28 in (70 cm) when mature. Frilled leaves with slightly swollen white leaf bases; inner leaves yellowy white. Said to be easily grown, recommended for spring sowing.

SHIRONA GROUP May be a cross between Chinese cabbage and pak choi. Large leaves varying from light to dark in colour; leaf stalks flat, white, very tender and crisp. Fast growing, good resistance to cold and heat, suitable for sowing throughout the growing season. I

found plants overwintering under cover formed small crunchy hearts within the heads in spring. Use the most bolt-resistant varieties if growing a headed crop in early spring.

SAVOY-LEAVED GROUP

'Chirimen' ('Crêpe') Beautiful old variety with unique, lightish green, crêpe-textured leaves. Plants grow about 12 in (30 cm high). In temperate climates only suitable for summer sowing.

'Hikoshima Haruna' (Hikojima Haruma') Beautiful variety with large lightly savoyed leaves with white, slightly swollen leaf bases. Cold-resistant, slow-bolting, easily grown, reasonably productive in Rodale winter greenhouse trials.

'Vitamin Green' Distinct variety, dark green, thick, lightly savoyed leaves curling outwards. Vigorous, slow-bolting, exceptionally hardy; flavour close to European cabbage. Grown mainly as autumn to spring crop. In temperate climates sow in late summer; in warm climates in

autumn. In my experience it flourished all winter in unheated polytunnel.

'Hiroshimana' Unique, vigorous, strong; smooth, almost glossy, medium to dark green rather pointed leaves. Swollen leaf bases and midribs pale green. Large plants, up to 22 in (56 cm) diameter, 14 in (35 cm) high. Appears reasonably hardy; can be sown most of the year, except for hot weather, mid-summer sowings. In *very* cold areas sow in summer only. For harvesting as small heads, ready 40–45 days after sowing, space plants 4 in (10 cm) apart. For large heads, normally ready 60–70 days after sowing, space plants 17–19 in (42–48 cm) apart.

'FLUFFY TOP' VARIETIES

'Eskimo', 'Kashin' (Flower heart), **'Kogana', 'Winter Queen'** Only 'Eskimo' has reasonable bolting resistance and is suitable for late spring and early summer sowings for a mature crop.

Pak choi

Latin name *Brassica rapa* var *chinensis*

Other names in use   Chinese celery cabbage, Chinese white cabbage, mustard cabbage*

Mandarin   Bai cai ('White vegetable'); qing cai ('green vegetable'); xiao bai cai ('little white cabbage')

Cantonese   Pak choi; bok choy

Japanese   Chingensai (green-stemmed types); shakushina (white-stemmed types); taisin

* It is also sometimes called non-heading and loose-headed Chinese cabbage, but in my view it is best to keep these terms for the types of Chinese headed cabbage described in the previous chapter.

Background

Pak choi is older than Chinese cabbage, and is known to have been cultivated in China since the fifth century AD. Originally a south Chinese vegetable, it has now spread throughout China and the rest of Asia, Europe and America and, with recently developed varieties, to tropical countries such as Nigeria and Brazil. So the white butts of neatly stacked pak choi have become a familiar sight in markets the world over.

Characteristics

Pak choi is biennial, though if checked or grown in adverse conditions it will run to seed in its first year.

Use

Stages of use

One of the beauties of pak choi is its versatility. The whole plant is edible—leaves, crunchy leaf stalks and young flowering shoots—and it can be used at virtually any stage. I have an energetic lady supervisor in a Shanghai market to thank for a graphic demonstration of what amounts to the 'ages of man' in pak choi, which she illustrated with samples of market produce seized from nearby stalls.

Large seedling stage

This is known in China as the 'chicken feather' stage. The small, separate leaves are no more than 3–4 in (7.5–10 cm) long, with the leaf stalks undeveloped. This stage can be reached within 2 weeks of

The word 'bonny' springs to mind in describing pak choi, perhaps because of its pert, upright stance and general air of well-being. The classical pak choi is a loose head of up to a dozen, glossy green leaves with smooth margins. The leaves contrast dramatically with the very white leaf stalks, which often broaden at the base into a characteristic spoon-like shape. The leaf stalks vary in length from several inches to about a foot. Some varieties of pak choi have a close resemblance to Swiss chard.

There are many forms, some with very light green leaves, some with very cupped, 'ladle'-shaped leaves. The leaf stalks also vary enormously. They tend to be thick, broad and stiff in the newer varieties popular with Westerners, but in the 'soup spoon' *Tai Sai* varieties the Chinese prefer, they have a willowy, swan's neck gracefulness. They can be flat or rounded. In several varieties characteristic of the Shanghai area the leaf stalks are a pretty light green.

Varieties range in size from large, very robust plants 24 in (60 cm) or more high, to the perfectly formed miniature or squat pak chois, only 3–4 in (8–10 cm) high. Large plants can weigh over 4 lb (2 kg), with very little wastage.

The pak chois are shallow-rooted and very fast growing. On the whole the younger the plants the more tender they are. They may become stringy if grown slowly or in very hot weather. The green-stemmed types generally stand up to adverse conditions better than most of the white-stemmed.

Pak choi: white stemmed type

sowing in good growing conditions.

'Little cabbage' stage
Here the plant has developed into a tiny head with about six, more substantial leaves with pronounced, slightly swollen leaf stalks. They are about 4 in (10 cm) tall. This stage is reached about a month after sowing. In the USA they are known as 'baby' pak choi.

Mature pak choi
These would be fully developed plants, standard varieties varying in height from 8–9 in (20–23 cm) to 2 ft (60 cm). This stage is reached anything from 5–8 weeks after sowing in summer, though it will take longer in the winter months.

Note: the precise sizes and the time taken to reach the above stages will depend on variety, season, and growing conditions.

Flowering shoots
The young flowering shoots form in the centre of the plant, either as a result of premature bolting in the first season, or in the natural course of events when a plant has overwintered and is in its second season. In Chinese communities pak choi is often grown as a substitute for flowering 'choy sum'. (See Flowering brassicas, page 27.)

Dried pak choi
There is a long tradition of drying pak choi leaves for use in the winter months. When I visited the hillside gardens for retired Asians in the heart of Seattle, I was mystified by the large, browning leaves draped over a line like washing. Later I learnt they were pak choi leaves, being dried in the sun for use in soup and other dishes. (See also Storage, page 25.)

In the kitchen

The flavour of pak choi leaves is quite different from that of Chinese cabbage—more 'interesting', with a hint of very mild mustard to it. (Pak choi leaves are also more nutritious than Chinese cabbage leaves.) The Chinese say the 'soup spoon' *Tai Sai* varieties and the green-stemmed varieties are the best flavoured, and my tasting notes tend to support this. The dwarf *Canton* varieties are also considered sweet and good flavoured.

The leaf stalks are notable for their refreshingly crisp and juicy texture rather than their flavour, which can be bland. In some varieties they tend to be watery. The white-stemmed varieties are generally juicier than the green. The flowering shoots are sweet flavoured.

For salads I prefer pak choi 'chicken feather' seedlings to any other oriental brassicas: they are crisp, succulent, and have such a fresh, healthy-looking colour. But leaves from mature plants can be cut into small pieces, and the leaf stalks can be sliced, for use in salads.

Like Chinese cabbage, pak choi can be cooked in countless ways: simple stir-frying; added to soup for the final minutes of cooking; as an ingredient in meat, fish, chicken and noodle dishes. In Taiwan the little pak chois are served with their leaves splayed out in a star-like shape. The leaf stalks require slightly longer cooking than the leaves, but neither requires more than a couple of minutes at the most.

In the Orient coarser-leaved varieties of pak choi are very popular for making salt pickles, for which there are many traditional recipes.

(See Recipes, page 194.)

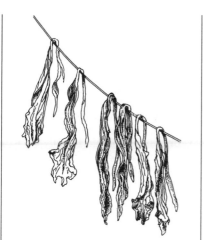

Pak choi leaves drying

Pak choi: soup spoon type

Pak choi: green stem type

Types

There are no cut and dried divisions within the pak choi group, with the exception of the unique 'rosette pak choi', which is a true subdivision of the pak chois (see Rosette pak choi, page 26). However, it is easier to understand the pak chois if they are divided into arbitrary groups on the basis of their appearance. (Note that new varieties being developed may erode the present distinctions between these types.)

Chinese white pak type

A sturdy-looking type, with light to dark green, fairly thick leaves, often curling outwards. The leaf stalks are very white, wide, shortish and generally flat, sometimes overlapping at the base of the plant. Plants tend to be of medium size, around 12 in (30 cm) high. They are vigorous, but vary in their cold-tolerance and tendency to bolt. Highly productive F1 hybrids, such as 'Joi Choi', have been introduced.

Soup spoon type

These are less sturdy, elegantly 'waisted' plants. The leaves and leaf stalks are thinner than in the previous type, which may account for the superior flavour. The leaves are lightly cupped and ladle-like—another term used to describe them. The leaf stalks are white, semicircular, and tend to overlap each other at the base where they broaden out into what is always described as the 'soup spoon' shape. (In fact the bases of most pak choi varieties bear *some* resemblance to Chinese soup spoons!)

They are vigorous, versatile varieties, with good tolerance to cold and heat. Most are tall varieties, about 18 in (45 cm) when mature, though some shorter forms of the soup spoon type are grown in Asia. Good varieties include 'Japanese White Celery Mustard', 'Nikanme', 'Seppaku ('Snow White') Tai Sai', Tai Sai.

Green leaf stalk type

This type is unique in that the leaf stalks are a beautiful, light green; they are broad, flattish, and widen out at the base in the approved pak choi manner. The leaves are rounded, smooth and emerald green. The plants are compact and sturdy and are usually harvested when small, about 6 in (15 cm) tall, though they can be left to grow much larger. The outer leaves are generally smaller than the inner leaves, so can be trimmed off for marketing.

These pak chois grow rapidly and can be sown throughout the growing season. They are probably the hardiest of all types (see Climate below). They are considered excellent quality, tender and well flavoured. Originating in the Shanghai area, 'Shanghai' was the first variety introduced to the West. The F1 'Mei Qing' (pronounced 'may ching' and meaning 'beautiful green') is the first F1 hybrid of this type and an excellent variety, with good bolting resistance when sown in spring. In the USA this is being grown all year round for 'baby' pak choi, maintaining the temperature at 65–70°F (18–21°C).

Squat or Canton type

The smallest and most compact pak chois come in this group. They have short, dark green slightly savoyed leaves, and short, thick, white leaf stalks. They can be harvested as baby pak chois from a very small size—just a few inches high. The tender leaves are considered among the best flavoured, in much the same class as the 'soup spoon' type.

They are better adapted to warm weather than most of the pak chois, but are very apt to bolt in a cool climate. In temperate climates the secret is to sow them in midsummer and harvest them as early as possible (the leaves tend to get thicker in cold weather). Varieties include 'Canton' and 'Canton Dwarf', the latter probably being the best for European conditions.

Several varieties classified as 'tropical' probably come into this category. Their use is not restricted to the tropics as the name might imply.

Climate

Most of the pak chois are naturally relatively cool-season crops, the ideal temperature during growth being in the 60s (°F) (15–20°C). However there are varieties adapted to hotter weather.

In temperate regions pak choi can be grown for most of the growing season, but it undoubtedly grows best in late summer and autumn. Crops sown in spring are apt to bolt before maturing, though there is plenty of scope for growing seedling crops or cutting plants young. (See The bolting problem, below). Most varieties tolerate light frosts, some, notably the green leaf stalk varieties, tolerate more severe frosts for short periods. In our unheated polytunnels the varieties 'Joi Choi', 'Mei Qing' and 'Shanghai' have all survived 14°F (−10°C) when kept small by cut-and-come-again cropping.

In North China pak choi is overwintered in cold frames, in which temperatures are maintained several degrees above freezing. (See also Protected cropping, Chinese solar frames, page 165.)

Site/soil

Like Chinese cabbage, pak choi has a relatively shallow, finely branched root system, so must be grown in fertile, moisture-retentive soil. Lack of moisture at any stage during growth leads to premature bolting and poor quality plants. (See also Headed Chinese cabbage, page 13.)

Decorative value

With the pert crispness of the small varieties, the lush, contrasting green and whites of the white-stemmed forms and the generally pleasing appearance of the green-stemmed forms, pak choi always looks attractive growing—except where caterpillars and slugs have been allowed to work overtime. Densely grown patches of 'chicken feather' pak choi can be most effective in a decorative garden, creating a wonderfully even carpet of green.

Both the fast-maturing seedling patches and mature plants, which resprout over a long period after cutting, are highly productive and recommended in small gardens.

Cultivation

Although similar to Chinese cabbage in its requirements and grown in much the same way, pak choi is generally easier to grow. This is partly because it matures faster: mature heads can be ready 35–55 days after sowing, depending on the variety and the season. It is also less susceptible to disease. (For cultivation see also Brassicas, general introduction, page 8.)

The bolting problem

Like Chinese cabbage, pak choi has a tendency to bolt prematurely from spring sowings, and in high summer temperatures mature heads may not stand long without bolting. The problem can be avoided in spring by growing seedling crops, and in summer by harvesting as early as possible. The following steps can be taken to minimize bolting when growing a mature crop. (See also Brassicas, General introduction, The bolting problem, page 10.)

IN SPRING

● Delay sowing if the weather is cold.

● Choose cold-tolerant varieties where known. (Unfortunately seedsmen rarely state clearly which varieties *are* cold tolerant.) In my experience 'Chinese White Pak', 'Joi Choi', 'Mei Qing' and the 'Tai Sai' varieties are the best in cold spring conditions.

● For the first outdoor planting, raise plants in a propagator, initially at a temperature of at least 64°F (18°C). Note, however, that raising pak choi at high temperatures does not seem to offer quite the same guarantee against subsequent bolting as it does with Chinese cabbage. Harden off well before planting outside.

● Protect the earliest outdoor sowings with cloches, low polytunnels or film covers. These have proved very effective in growing good

early crops of pak choi. (See Protected cropping, Film covers, page 167.)

IN SUMMER

● Choose heat-tolerant varieties. The green-stemmed pak chois and Canton varieties seem the best adapted to high temperatures.

● Water very frequently to prevent the soil from drying out and to encourage steady growth.

● Shade crops with shading net.

When to grow what

By and large, follow the sowing times and methods suggested for Headed Chinese cabbage (see page 16). There is, however, a little more flexibility if using the best modern pak choi varieties.

In my experience the following are the most useful sowings of pak choi:

● Seedling crops under cover in early spring.

● Mid-summer to autumn sowings for the outdoor headed crop. In temperate regions it may be possible to grow good crops from early summer to autumn. The last outdoor sowings can be made 6 weeks before the first frost is expected.

● Late summer, early autumn sowings transplanted under cover in autumn for use in winter and spring. For these use green-stalked varieties, 'Tai Sai' types and cold-resistant varieties like 'Chinese White' and F1 'Joi Choi'.

● Autumn seedling crop under cover.

ALL YEAR ROUND PRODUCTION IN GREENHOUSES Pak choi is now grown commercially all year round in greenhouses, with successive sowings in soil blocks. Seed is germinated at high temperatures, around 68°F (20°C), but temperatures are dropped after germination to 50°F (10°C) or less. It may be raised again to about 68°F (20°C) for a week or so after planting. Good ventilation is very important in summer, or the plants are likely to suffer from bacterial rot.

Sowing methods

Seedling crops are either broadcast or sown in wide drills. Headed crops are either sown *in situ* and thinned to the appropriate spacing, or raised in seed boxes or some kind of module and transplanted. (See also Plant raising, Sowing methods, page 151; Use of modules, page 153.)

Thinning can start when seedlings are about 4 in (7.5 cm) high. Thinnings can be eaten or, in cool weather and moist conditions, transplanted. Transplanting can normally be done 3–4 weeks after sowing.

Spacing

Spacing varies according to the variety and the size of plant required. 'Chinese White', for example, can be spaced about 6 in (15 cm) apart if small plants are wanted, or up to 18 in (45 cm) if large plants are required. Average spacing for medium-sized varieties would be 7–10 in (18–23 cm) apart. Small varieties can be 4 in (10 cm) apart, or 1–2 in (2.5–5 cm) apart, in rows 7 in (18 cm) apart.

INTERCROPPING As pak choi grows so fast and can be harvested young, it is very useful for intercropping. Seedling patches make useful catch crops at almost any time of year: I frequently sow strips between large brassicas such as cauliflowers and brussels sprouts.

In summer plant it between tall crops such as peas or beans, or beneath sweet corn. It will benefit from the light shade. It is frequently intercropped in China, for example, grown beneath climbing beans and climbing gourds, or alongside Chinese chives, on ground that will later be used to earth up the chives for blanching.

Another Chinese trick is to sow pak choi and carrot seed mixed together. For these sowings I mix two teaspoons of carrot with one of pak choi. In the early stages of growth the carrots look as if they will be overwhelmed by the pak choi, but the pak choi is pulled young, leaving the carrots to mature very satisfactorily. Also, the pak choi seems to bestow some protection against carrot fly, perhaps simply by confusing the flies when they are on the wing.

Further care

See Headed Chinese Cabbage, page 17.

Containers

Seedling pak choi and small young plants can be grown satisfactorily in containers. They do best in spring, late summer and autumn; the risk of the soil drying out is usually too high in mid-summer. (See also Part 2, Containers, page 169.)

Pests and disease

The most serious pests are flea beetle, cabbage caterpillars, cutworm, cabbage root fly and slugs. The most serious diseases are clubroot and bacterial rots. (See also Brassicas, general introduction, page 18, and Part 2, Pests and Disease, page 172.)

Harvesting

Pak choi should always be picked when the leaves and leaf stalks look fresh and crisp. It can either be harvested a few leaves at a time, picking the outer leaves when they reach a useful size, or by cutting a whole head ½–¾ in (1.5–2 cm) above ground level. For home use cut the heads rather than pull them up, as they always resprout vigorously, giving pickings over a long period.

Some pak choi varieties, for example 'Joi Choi', are very brittle, the outer leaves snapping off. If they are being marketed, leave them to wilt slightly for an hour or so before packing to avoid 'breakages'.

Storage

Pak choi is best used fresh as it doesn't store well under domestic conditions, though it can be kept for a day or two in the cool compartment of a fridge. (See Headed Chinese cabbage, Storage, page 18.) White-stemmed varieties can be kept in a cool store just above freezing point for a week, green-stemmed varieties for a little

longer, trimming the leaves afterwards.

In the north of China mature plants are dug up at the onset of winter and transplanted into frames as 'false plants'. Soil is drawn up around the leaves, so they may continue to grow.

DRYING PAK CHOI The Chinese separate the leaves of white-stemmed pak choi, and blanch them in boiling water for a few minutes until the colour changes. They are hung out in the sun to dry for a few days, and brought into the cool at night. Sometimes the leaves and stems are 'kneaded' when damp to break the fibres. Dried leaves can be kept for many months. They are sometimes found on sale in Chinese stores.

I found leaves dried well simply by hanging them in the kitchen until they were crisp. When cooked in soup they reconstituted very rapidly, giving it a good flavour.

Varieties

Compared with Chinese cabbage, relatively few pak choi varieties are available in the West. Knowing how a particular variety listed in seed catalogues will perform is something of a gamble. When trying a variety for the first time I would suggest making small sowings at different times—spring, summer and autumn—to see how it performs under your conditions. Given the versatility of pak choi, there will always be something to harvest. It is just a question of when it grows best, and how well it stands up to cold conditions in spring and winter, or very hot weather in summer. Most varieties will fit into one of the types described on page 23.

Rosette pak choi

Latin name *Brassica rapa* var *rosularis**

Other names in use Flat cabbage/pak choi; flat black cabbage/pak choi

Mandarin Wu ta cai ('black lying flat vegetable'); ta ge cai ('lying flat vegetable'); tai gu cai ('very ancient vegetable'); hei cai ('black vegetable'); piao er cai ('gourd ladle vegetable')—the semi-prostrate form.

Cantonese Tai koo choi

Japanese Tatsoi; tasai

* Sometimes also var *narinosa* or var *atrovirens*

Characteristics

This distinctive pak choi is believed to be of ancient origin. Its very thick, lustrous leaves are such a dark green they appear to be black. They are arranged in a dramatic rosette of very regular, concentric circles, which sometimes lies flat on the ground. In some varieties the leaves are erect in summer, but lie flat in cold weather.

Types

There are a number of types, ranging from the classic prostrate form at one end of the spectrum to the semi-prostrate at the other. Inevitably, the characteristics of the different varieties merge into one another as new varieties are developed.

Prostrate type

The thick leaves are more or less round, though the leaf width can vary from less than an inch to several inches. Some varieties have flat, smooth leaves, but in others the leaves are very puckered, giving the centre of the plant the crimped look of an old-fashioned rose. The leaf stalks are short, light green or ivory in colour, varying in length from 1–4 in (2.5–10 cm) high. These are the hardiest forms. They are much slower growing than the standard pak choi.

Semi-prostrate type

These are larger and more irregular in form. A typical variety grows 6–10 in (15–25 cm) high, though

Rosette pak choi: erect form (*above*) and prostrate form (*below*)

some are larger; they can be up to 20 in (50 cm) in diameter. They tend to have larger, less rounded leaves with longer leaf stalks, the leaves often being very crinkled. They are less hardy but faster growing than the prostrate types. The Chinese variety 'Hei Bai Cai' ('black-and-white vegetable') falls into this group.

New forms

More productive hybrids and varieties of rosette cabbage are being developed, mainly in Japan. Some have wider and whiter leaf stalks and much larger leaves, making them more like a typical pak choi in appearance. The striking-looking variety 'Sankeiyukina', with large,

Use

Like ordinary pak choi, rosette pak choi can be used at any stage: seedling leaves, small rosettes, large plants, and the young flowering shoots. The leaves are tougher and stronger flavoured than standard pak choi, but many consider it a superior flavour. Traditional Chinese wisdom is that the smaller-leaved forms are the best flavoured, and that the flavour is enhanced after a touch of frost. It is reputed to be very nutritious, with twice the mineral content of pak choi. Young leaves and small rosettes can be used raw in salads.

In the kitchen

This is such a ground-hugging plant that grit is apt to collect in the leaf stalks, which should be cleaned carefully. Leaves can be cooked individually, or in little clusters of four or five leaves broken off together.

This vegetable is cooked in much the same way as pak choi. It is often used in soups, to which it imparts a delicate flavour; it can also be stir-fried and seasoned with nutmeg; wilted slightly, sautéed with olive oil and garlic, and added to pasta along with grilled peppers (a suggestion from Alice Waters). It can also be made into a sauce to accompany meats.

crêpe-like leaves, seems to be a new form of rosette pak choi in spite of being labelled a mustard.

Climate

Rosette pak choi is a cool-weather crop, notable for its resistance to cold. The prostrate varieties withstand winter temperatures of 23–15°F (−5 to−10°C), and stand up to snow well. In my experience they are less likely to survive prolonged *wet* winter weather. The less hardy semi-prostrate varieties are tolerant of light frosts.

There have been limited trials with rosette pak choi in the West, but it seems to be slower-bolting in spring than most pak chois. Some varieties are tolerant of hot summer weather, others less so.

Soil/site

See Pak choi, page 24.

Decorative value

With its unique shape and very dark colour, rosette pak choi ranks high as a decorative vegetable. A patch of mature plants makes a striking bit of ground cover. I've used both mature and young plants to edge vegetable beds in my decorative *potager* and they could equally be used to edge flower beds. The young rosettes, when about 3 in (7.5 cm) in diameter, have a particularly appealing, cheeky look about them.

Cultivation

Rosette pak choi is grown like ordinary pak choi but, being less lush and slower growing, it is a little less demanding where soil fertility is concerned. Which is not to say it won't respond to good growing conditions. (See also Pak choi, page 24.)

When to sow what

Mature headed crop

LATE SUMMER/EARLY AUTUMN This is the traditional time to sow rosette pak choi in China, and I have found it the most satisfactory and useful sowing. In temperate climates sow:
(1) Mid-summer for an outdoor crop.
(2) In late summer for a winter crop in unheated greenhouses.
The protected crop has very tender leaves, which regenerate more rapidly after cutting in winter and early spring than the outdoor crop.
SPRING/EARLY SUMMER SOWINGS These sowings are more likely to bolt, and quality may not be good in high summer temperatures. However, some successful early sowings have been reported. New varieties may be better adapted to early sowings than traditional varieties.

Seedling crop

(1) Sow under cover in early spring and late autumn.
(2) Sow outdoors from late spring to late autumn.
Seedlings are ready for cutting 3–4 weeks after sowing, depending on the season. Growth is fastest in late summer.

Spacing

The more space rosette pak choi is given, the larger the plants will grow. For harvesting as smallish rosettes, thin or plant about 6 in (15 cm) apart. For larger plants space them 12–16 in (30–40 cm) apart, depending on the variety.

Containers

Headed rosette pak choi is relatively slow growing and low yielding, so would not be recommended for containers on productivity grounds, though it might well be on decorative grounds. It could be grown as a seedling crop—though again, would be less productive than other pak chois.

Harvesting

Plants take up to 8 weeks to mature, growth being fastest in the late summer months. Either
• Pick individual leaves as required.
• Cut the centre rosette of small leaves.
• Cut the head an inch or so above the base of the plant. It will regrow, though not as rapidly as ordinary pak choi.

Pests and disease

In my experience the most serious pests are slugs, cutworm and flea beetle. (See also Part 2, Pests and disease, page 172.)

Flowering brassicas: choy sum and co.

The flowering shoots of almost any brassica can be eaten when they are still young and tender. However, there are several oriental vegetables which are grown *primarily* for their flowering shoots—the oriental equivalent of sprouting broccoli and calabrese. Like their European counterparts, they tend to throw out a succession of shoots after the first, main shoot, has been harvested.

To say there are 'several' is an over-simplification: this is one of the jungles of Chinese vegetables—with different vegetables often called the same name, the same vegetable called by several names, and botanists still arguing about which is the correct name. For practical purposes it is best to look on them as an extended family, with the family likeness still apparent in some fairly distant relatives. The key member of the family is what is known in Cantonese as 'choy sum'—'choy' meaning vegetable, 'sum' meaning heart or flowering stem. It is one of the most popular vegetables in China. The

Choy sum: typical shoot

name 'choy sum' is so widely used in the West, it seems the most appropriate to give to the group as a whole.

The following are the principal members of this 'extended family':

Choy sum (*Brassica rapa* var *parachinensis*) (sometimes *B. chinensis* var *parachinensis*)

Purple-flowered choy sum (*Brassica rapa* var *purpurea*)

Flowering pak choi (*Brassica rapa* var *chinensis*)

Edible oil seed rapes (*Brassica rapa* var *oleifera* and var *utilis*) (Various hybrid flowering rapes have been developed primarily from this group.)

'Broccoletto' types (*Brassica rapa* 'Ruvo' group)

(For Chinese broccoli (*Brassica alboglabra*), a quite distinct vegetable also grown for its flowering shoots, see the next chapter.)

Let me introduce these vegetables separately, before covering their use and cultivation.

Choy sum

English names   Flowering white cabbage; mock pak choi

Mandarin   Cai xin ('flower stem/heart vegetable'); cai tai (for varieties with many flowering shoots from one leaf axil)

Cantonese   Choy sum; pak tsoi sum

Background and characteristics

Choy sum is a native of mainland China and is widely grown there, especially in the south. On our autumnal visit to Guanzhou the bright green leaves and contrasting yellow flowers of pak choi made striking belts of colour in long, raised beds—each bed an island surrounded by a flooded ditch. Clouds of cabbage white butterflies hovered optimistically overhead! (See also Part 2, The bed system, page 147.)

An annual plant, it is rather like bolted pak choi in appearance, though individual plants vary enormously. Some are spreading in habit, some upright, with height varying from 8–22 in (20–56 cm). In less than optimum conditions they are quite spindly, though under good conditions they grow vigorously and can spread to about 18 in (45 cm).

They are characterized by the yellow flowers, borne on slightly fleshy stalks ¼–½ in (0.5–1 cm) in diameter, and 6–8 in (15–20 cm) long. The flower stalks are lightly grooved, and are usually light green in colour but sometimes white. The flower stalks, when the flowers are in bud, are the main edible part. Leaves are light or dark green, generally rather oval or egg-shaped, with slightly serrated margins. They differ in size depending on the variety, but are generally smaller and less substantial than pak choi leaves.

Varieties

In China a number of distinct varieties have been selected, often on the basis of the number of days they require to mature: e.g. '40', '50', '60', '80', '90 days'.

At present named varieties are rarely available in the West, and work needs to be done to select the best yielding varieties for different seasons in temperate climates. Japanese seed companies are beginning to do so, and to develop more vigorous F1 hybrids.

Use of flowering brassicas

The flowering shoots are the main parts used. Sometimes the leaves are used, or whole plants are harvested young, or with developing flower shoots. The flowering shoots are tender and sweet. The main stem, as the flowers just start to appear, is said to be the best flavoured part.

In the kitchen

The flower shoots can be used in salads, provided they are harvested when young and tender. The open flowers can be used as decoration. I particularly like to use the purple-flowered choy sum and F1 'Bouquet' in winter salads, when colour is at a premium. Plants grown under cover are the most tender and best for this purpose.

The Chinese normally cook the flowering brassicas. They are steamed, lightly boiled or stir-fried, cooked for no more than a couple of minutes so the flavour is preserved. They are often mixed in meat, chicken and prawn dishes, or simply seasoned with oyster sauce. They have a pleasant, bright colour when cooked, the purple-flowered choy sum turning green.

The choy sum group can be used to make pickles, the rapes probably being most popular for this purpose. The Japanese recommend their hybrid flowering rapes for pickling. F H King, in his classic on Chinese and Japanese agriculture *Farmers of Forty Centuries* (1911), describes barrowloads of rape, tied in bundles a foot long, destined to be salted for winter use . . . (20 lb (9 kg) salt to every 100 lb (45 kg) of rape). This is a lactic acid fermentation, analogous to the manufacture of sauerkraut. (See also Recipes, page 187.)

Purple-flowered choy sum

Mandarin   Hong cai tai ('red shoots'); zi cai tai ('purple shoots')
Cantonese   Hong tsoi sum; hon tsai tai
Japanese   Beninabana; kosaitai

Characteristics

The purple colouring differentiates this vegetable from pak choi. The flower stalks, leaf stalks and leaf veins are often deep purple, while the leaves are dark green or purple. The leaves vary a great deal in size, but are usually serrated, rather like turnip leaves.

The colours intensify in cold weather, making it a colourful plant in the winter months—the pale yellow flowers contrasting with the foliage.

It grows vigorously in fertile soil, producing up to forty pencil-thick, flowering shoots. Like choy sum, it can be fairly skimpy in poor conditions.

Varieties

There are a number of varieties in China with varying characteristics —some hardier than others. We saw a brilliantly coloured local variety in Chengdu. At present there is little choice in the West, and there is scope for the introduction of suitable improved varieties.

Flowering pak choi

Background and characteristics

This is the pak choi described in the previous chapter (for names, see page 21). Chinese communities in the West often select varieties of pak choi to grow as choy sum, even though they consider the shoots inferior in flavour. Their merit lies in being easier to grow than choy sum.

Pak choi grown as choy sum (known as 'bok choy sum') is one of the main autumn crops in Vancouver's Chinese market gardens. A new strip is sown every week: it has started to germinate before the sower's footprints have faded from the sandy soil.

Varieties

Medium-sized varieties of pak choi are generally used for the purpose, harvesting the flowering shoot emerging from the centre of the plant.

Edible oil seed rapes

Mandarin name   You cai ('oil vegetable'); cai hua ('vegetable flower'); pu tung bai cai ('common cabbage')
Cantonese   Yau tsoi/yu choy ('oil vegetable')
Japanese   Aburana, natane

Characteristics

This group of Chinese rapes have well-developed seeds, which for centuries have been used in China as a source of oil for lamps and cooking. They also have a long history of being cultivated for their leaves and flowering shoots. Incidentally, this is not the oil seed rape now widely grown in the West.

The rapes look very similar to choy sum when growing, though the leaves tend to be glossier. When I grew edible rapes and choy sum side by side in my garden the rape seemed to be marginally more vigorous and more upright in stance.

Varieties

A traditional variety is sometimes listed in Western catalogues.

Hybrid flowering rapes

Characteristics

The hybrid flowering rapes are an exciting plant breeding development from Japan. From a gardener's point of view they are the best value of the choy sum tribe. The flowering shoots are much thicker than those of the traditional rapes, and have a beautiful flavour.

The hybrid flowering rapes retain their freshness better than other types of choy sum and travel well. The stocky 4-in (10-cm) long bundles of yellow-budded shoots I saw in the Kanda wholesale market in Tokyo looked exceptionally appetizing. The Japanese even use them as cut flowers!

Their colour and texture make them pretty garden plants. I grow them in my decorative *potager*, from which the more straggly choy sum and ordinary edible rape would be excluded.

Varieties

F1 'Bouquet' is the first of these varieties to reach the West. It is much higher yielding than the tra-ditional rapes, normally about 18 in (45 cm) high, growing up to 30 in (75 cm) when bolting. It has very attractive, savoyed leaves of a fresh light green—thicker in tex-ture than choy sum or rape leaves. One of its parents is the crêpe-leaved, loose-headed Chinese cab-bage 'Chirimen'. (See Loose-headed Chinese cabbage, Varieties, page 20.)

Flowering rape 'Bouquet'

Broccoletto types

This group includes various fast-growing greens such as 'broccoli raab', 'cima di rapa' and 'broc-coletti'. These traditional European peasant crops are grown for the flowering shoots, and may be an-cient offshoots of choy sum. They are mentioned here as they could be grown as substitutes for the Chinese forms.

They are generally sown in late summer, autumn or spring, often simply broadcast thinly, but some-times transplanted about 12 in (30 cm) apart to get a more pro-ductive plant. The shoots should be picked before they run clear of the leaves. The serrated, rather coarse-looking leaves are also edible. Leaves and shoots have a slightly mustardy taste raw, which be-comes a flavour of character when cooked.

Climate

Most of the choy sum group are temperate weather crops. (See also Sowing times, below.)

Soil/site

The flowering brassicas need to be grown fast in fertile, moisture re-tentive, but well drained soil or they will be miserable, tough and stringy instead of tender and suc-culent.

Cultivation

Sowing method

The flowering brassicas are fast growing and are usually closely spaced. They are often sown *in situ*, either broadcast or in rows. They should be sown shallowly; the more shallow they are sown, the faster they germinate. They can also be transplanted, though this is normally reserved for the earliest outdoor crop if started off indoors, or for a late crop planted under cover.

(For sowing times and spacing, see each group below.)

Further care

Where flowering brassicas are being cut continually, a liquid feed after each cut can be beneficial. (See also Part 2, Soil fertility, Liquid feeding, page 144.)

The choy sum group tend to have small shallow roots, so need to be watered frequently but lightly. (See also Brassicas, General introduction, Watering, page 11.)

Containers

On the whole the choy sum group are not very suitable, or high enough yielding, for containers. The purple-flowering pak choi and hybrid rape F1 'Bouquet' would be the best bets.

Pests and disease

Although any of the common bras-sica pests and diseases can affect the flowering brassicas, they seem to have more resistance than the larger, slower-growing oriental brassicas. They tend to be in the ground for a relatively short period, which may partly account for this.

In my experience flea beetle is the most likely pest in the early stages. In some years we have had a serious problem in early summer with brassica pollen or blossom beetles, which attack the buds on the flowering shoots. (See also Part 2, Pests and disease, page 172.)

Harvesting

The flowering brassicas are on average ready for cutting 40–60 days after sowing. It is important to choose the right moment to start harvesting. In summer growth can be very rapid, and a couple of days' delay can make the difference be-tween delicious tenderness and a fibrous, unpalatable, flowering stem. With the exception of the hybrid flowering rapes, they wilt very fast after picking, and are best used immediately.

Pick flowering shoots when a couple of flowers have opened. A commercial grower told me that, on a field scale, he starts cutting when 10 per cent of the plants have yellow flowers. With some varieties of choy sum an additional indicator is a dark green ring, seen in a cross section of a cut stem, which develops when the stem is becoming fibrous.

Harvest the main stem first. Cut or break off the shoots 5–6 in (13–15 cm) long or, in the case of purple-flowering choy sum, 8–12 in (20–30 cm) long, leaving three or four leaves on the stem. Side shoots will develop from the leaf axils over several weeks: anything from a couple to a prolific crop, depending on the variety and the conditions.

In some cases the whole plant is harvested young when the first flowering shoot develops. This is often the practice where flowering pak choi is used.

Sowing times and spacing

Choy sum

Sowing times Choy sum is the most tender of the group and is not frost-hardy. With the present varieties reasonably high summer temperatures are required for sturdy plants to develop.

Growing choy sum *well* is a tricky business: it seems to be a question of finding the right climatic conditions and the right variety. In temperate climates the most successful sowings are in mid- and late summer, making the last sowing 6 weeks before the first frost is expected. Earlier and later sowings

can be made under cover, though spring sowings have a tendency to bolt prematurely, with plants making spindly growth, unless they are germinated at high temperatures. In common with other flowering brassicas, choy sum is a good follow-on crop after early potatoes, peas and onions.

Spacing Plants can be grown at anything from 3–8 in (8–20 cm) between plants, allowing wider spacing for more vigorous varieties. In one commercial greenhouse plants are direct sown in rows 7 in (18 cm) apart, spacing seeds 1–2 in 2.5–5 cm) apart. The wider spacing is used for the more vigorous strains.

Choy sum is a good subject for intercropping. In the Guangzhou island beds it was being grown between rows of peas, the fast-growing choy sum being cleared before the peas required the 'middle ground' for expansion.

Purple-flowering choy sum

Purple-flowering choy sum grows best in cool weather, and is a fairly hardy plant, surviving temperatures down to about 23°F (−5°C).

In temperate climates it grows best from late summer to autumn sowings, for harvesting in early winter. Harvesting can continue into spring in a mild winter. It can also be sown in autumn and transplanted under cover for a winter to spring crop. Most varieties seem to bolt prematurely from spring and early summer sowings.

In warm areas it can be sown outdoors in autumn for winter to spring harvesting. In areas with cool summers it can be sown in summer for an autumn harvest.

Spacing Purple-flowering choy sum can be direct sown or transplanted. Plants can grow fairly large, and on average are spaced about 15 in (38 cm) apart.

Edible rapes

Edible rapes need lower summer temperatures than choy sum and are hardier, surviving light frosts. In temperate climates the most successful sowings are in spring and autumn. Mid-summer sowings are liable to bolt prematurely. For spacing see Choy sum above.

F1 'Bouquet' In temperate climates, late summer and early autumn outdoor sowings are recommended for this variety and are very successful; but I have had good results from early summer sowings. In frost-free areas it is a good winter crop outdoors, while in temperate climates it is an excellent winter and spring crop in unheated polytunnels and solar frames. In my experience F1 'Bouquet' will survive several degrees of frost when grown under cover in winter, but outdoors may fall victim to a combination of damp and low temperatures.

It can be sown *in situ* or transplanted. It is spaced 6–8 in (15–20 cm) apart.

Chinese broccoli

Latin name *Brassica oleracea* var *alboglabra*
Other names in use Chinese kale; white flowering broccoli
Mandarin Gai lan; jie lan
Cantonese Kaai laan tsoi; kailan

Background

Chinese broccoli is much closer to the European cabbage than to any of the Chinese cabbages. It probably originated in the Mediterranean, possibly sharing a common

ancestor with European calabrese. Botanically, it is very close to the famous Portuguese 'Tronchuda' cabbage. It was introduced to China in ancient times.

It is a most attractive vegetable— deliciously flavoured and an en-

Use

It is mainly the young flowering stems, with the flower buds and the small leaves on the flowering stems, which are eaten. The stems may need to be peeled if the outer skin has become tough. Whole plants are sometimes harvested young. Larger leaves can be eaten, but they don't have the delicate flavour of the flower stems. Like choy sum, the

dearingly willing, easy grower. It made one of our favourite vegetable dishes during our visit to China.

Characteristics

Normally an annual, Chinese broccoli is very different in appearance from the other oriental brassicas. It is a rather stout plant, most varieties growing to about 18 in (45 cm) when mature, though some are much shorter. The leaves are thick, and although essentially green or a distinct blue-green, most varieties have a characteristic grey, waxy look. Depending on the variety, they can be dull or glossy, smooth or wrinkled, round or narrow and pointed.

The flower stems, for which it is cultivated, are chunky, succulent and very smooth, on average ½–¾ in (1–2 cm) in diameter. The whole flowering shoot is much 'meatier' than the choy sum shoots, though less compact and substantial than the European calabrese shoots. The flowers are larger than most brassica flowers and usually white. There are also yellow-flowered varieties, and possibly, in China, a red-flowered variety.

It is a vigorous, fast-growing plant, producing secondary shoots over a long period after the main flowering shoot has been cut.

Climate

Chinese broccoli is easygoing in its climatic requirements. On the one hand it will grow in weather which would be uncomfortably hot for European cabbages, cauliflowers and calabrese; on the other it will tolerate several degrees of frost once it is past the seedling stage.

Soil/site

See Choy sum, page 30.

Cultivation

Provided it is being grown in fertile, moisture-retentive soil, Chinese broccoli seems to be one of the easiest of the flowering brassicas to cultivate.

Chinese broccoli

When to sow

MAIN CROP In temperate climates Chinese broccoli can be sown throughout the growing season, from late spring to early autumn. However, the heaviest yields are obtained from mid- to late summer sowings, maturing in late summer and autumn. In cool areas delay sowing until mid-summer, as earlier sowings may bolt prematurely.

EARLY CROP In temperate areas an early crop, maturing in early summer, can be obtained by starting plants off indoors in early spring, and planting out after hardening them off well, around the time when the last frosts are expected. Peter Chan, the well-known Chinese gardener living in Oregon, describes how, in the case of an unexpected late frost, he waters the plants before the early morning sun hits them, so protecting them from frost damage. His plants start cropping in early May, and he finds they continue cropping until November.

LATE CROP Late summer and early autumn sowings can be transplanted under cover in autumn to give a crop during the winter months. The plants may survive until spring unless temperatures drop very low. Growth will be slow in winter, but will pick up again in spring.

Sowing method

The method depends on whether plants are being harvested young, or allowed to grow into large plants for picking over a long period. Re-

young flower shoots, flower buds and flowers can all be used in salads.

In the kitchen

Chinese broccoli is generally cooked in much the same way as choy sum, usually stir-fried, either on its own or with meat, chicken or prawns.

I will always associate it with my first insight into the drama of a working Chinese kitchen—in a Guangzhou guest house. Can I digress to put you in the picture? Gas burners were roaring with typhoon ferocity under a row of 2-ft-wide woks, which seemed to be engulfed by leaping flames. Reassuring bowls of water stood between each wok. Two cooks were working with the split-second timing of jugglers, controlling the gas taps on the floor with their toes so their hands were free to manipulate the woks. The broccoli stems had been cut into pieces 3–4 in (7.5–10 cm) long. First they were cooked in the wok for about 90 seconds in fast boiling water with a little oil in it. The cook held the edge of the wok with a wet cloth, tossing the stems with a ladle. After testing a stem with his finger nail to see if it was tender, out they came, cold water was slung over them to cool them, and they were put on one side. The wok was then cleaned by ladling water into it (causing a mighty sizzle), boiling it vigorously, and equally vigorously sweeping it with several strokes of a straw wok brush. The dirty water was swooshed into a channel at the front of the bench.

Battered prawns were cooked next, and about 10 minutes later the broccoli was back in the wok with the prawns for a final warming and seasoning with sugar, vinegar, ginger and oyster sauce. (See also Recipes, page 187.)

commendations for spacing vary considerably, indicating that Chinese kale, rather like calabrese, is not very sensitive to spacing. Later-maturing, more vigorous varieties would benefit from generous spacing.

Young plant harvesting Sow broadcast or in rows about 4 in (10 cm) apart, thinning plants to 4–6 in (10–15 cm) apart. These are harvested whole as the flowering shoots start to appear.

Larger plants Sow *in situ* or transplant when about 3 in (7.5 cm) tall. Space plants from 10–15 in (25–38 cm) apart. Closer spacing can be used if you are short of space.

Further care
See Choy sum, page 30.

Containers
Chinese broccoli is rather unwieldy for containers unless harvested as young plants. (See also Part 2, Growing in containers, page 169.)

Pests and disease
Although Chinese broccoli can be affected by any of the common brassica pests and diseases, on the whole it is a healthy plant. Its rather waxy leaves appear to give some protection from flea beetle, slugs and caterpillars, but it can be affected by pollen beetle.

Peter Chan comments that the plants, being large, sometimes work themselves loose in strong winds, making an attractive egg-laying spot at soil level for cabbage root fly. Where this is a risk, earth up the stems to give the plants extra support.

Chinese broccoli is susceptible to downy mildew. (See also Part 2, Pests and disease, page 172.)

Harvesting
Chinese broccoli is slower growing than choy sum, but can be cropped over a longer period.

Large plants take on average 60–70 days to mature. Plants can often be harvested three times, taking the main flowering shoot first, then two further cuts of the side shoots which develop subsequently. After that growth tends to become too thin to be worth harvesting. Pick or cut the main flowering shoot just before the first flowers open, but no later. At this stage the shoots are generally no higher than the surrounding leaves and are about 6 in (15 cm) long.

In hot weather growth is very fast, and plants must be harvested continually or they will bolt prematurely, with shoots becoming tough.

The whole plant can also be harvested young, rather than waiting for the mature plant to develop. It may be ready within about 6 weeks of sowing.

Varieties
In China there are numerous varieties, divided into 'early', 'mid' and 'late' groups according to their natural flowering season and their resistance to heat and cold. To date only a handful are listed in the West, though more may become available in future.

'White-flowered' Standard tall variety; bluey-green leaves and white flowers.

F1 'Green Lance' White-flowered hybrid, more vigorous and even than the standard variety.

'Yellow-flowered' (Chinese Yellow Broccoli) Much smaller plant, 5–8 in (13–20 cm) tall. Generally recommended as a summer crop, but the Rodale Research Center in Pennsylvania found a spring crop yielded better than white-flowered kale.

The komatsuna group

Latin name *Brassica rapa* var *perviridis* or var *komatsuna*
Other names in use Mustard spinach, spinach mustard*
Japanese Komatsuna ('small pine edible leaf')

* Both are misleading, as it is neither spinach nor mustard.

Background
I am tempted to give the komatsuna group the 'most under-rated vegetable' award. They are among the hardiest and most productive winter vegetables I have come across, their flavour a happy compromise between the blandness of cabbage and the sharpness of most oriental mustards. They are also very easy to grow. Yet until now they have rarely earned a mention in Western books on vegetable growing.

'Komatsuna' is a kind of leafy turnip. Modern taxonomic research indicates that it probably evolved in the Far East from pak choi. The Japanese consider it one of the few pure Japanese vegetables, and probably cultivated it from ancient times. Today it is mainly grown in Japan, Korea and

Use
Stages of use
The komatsunas can be eaten at any stage. They are often grown as seedling crops, but are also spaced well apart and allowed to develop into large plants, when the leaves are used more like cabbage. They can also be harvested at intermediate stages: for example the whole plant may be harvested when it has about five leaves. The leaf stems are usually quite juicy and tender, and the flower shoots are sweet and succulent, though they can become quite hot-

Taiwan: it seems almost unknown in China. Nor have I seen it on sale in Europe, though it is being grown for fresh use and processing in the United States. The variety 'Komatsuna', which has given its name to the group, was originally found growing near Tokyo.

Like the flowering pak choi group, the komatsunas should probably be regarded as an extended family. Plant breeders, mainly in Japan, are crossing various closely related vegetables in the *Brassica rapa* group—pak choi, Chinese cabbage, leaf turnip and 'Komatsuna' itself, to produce an interesting range of new forms and varieties. Like the flowering brassicas, these have their individual characteristics but a strong family likeness.

The family includes:

Komatsuna/pak choi crosses
E.g. 'Benri-na' ('Green Boy').

Komatsuna/turnip green crosses
E.g. F1 'All Top', 'Nozawana'.

Foliage and fodder turnips
E.g. 'Shogoin', 'Typhon'.

Characteristics

Annual or biennial, depending on when sown. Members of the komatsuna group are generally large plants, anything up to 18 in (45 cm) tall, 20 in (50 cm) wide, and much taller when flowering. Some hybrids can reach a height of 8–14 in (20–35 cm) 20–30 days after sowing.

Leaves tend to be large, on average up to about 7 in (18 cm) wide and up to 12 in (30 cm) long in mature plants. They are usually dark green, smooth and often very glossy—giving them a look of healthy wellbeing. Some varieties have a 'matt' surface. The varieties with turnip parentage tend to be rougher looking and coarser textured, with more serrated leaf edges. The leaf stalks are usually a lightish green and thin, quite unlike the swollen leaf stalks of pak choi and Chinese cabbage. In some

Komatsuna: mature plant

Komatsuna: seedlings and young plants

varieties they are several inches long and bare; in others they are 'leafy' to near the base.

Some varieties develop semi-swollen tap roots, rather like turnips in appearance.

When they run to seed a vigorous crop of fairly substantial, yellow-flowered flowering shoots is produced.

Climate

The most notable characteristic of the komatsunas is their cold-tolerance. Several varieties have survived winter temperatures here of −12°C (10°F) under cover. Outside they were severely knocked back, but not killed, by −14°C (6.8°F). In temperate climates they can be cropped for most of the year. They are much less likely to bolt prematurely in cold spring and early summer than most of the oriental brassicas. They also have con-

flavoured as the plants mature.

At any stage, the leaves will regrow rapidly after cutting to give a further crop. (See Brassicas, General introduction, Stages of use, page 9.)

In the kitchen

The flavour of komatsuna could be described as midway between cabbage and mustard, with a pleasant hint of spinach. It tends to be blander and closer to cabbage in younger leaves—developing a little 'kick' in the older leaves. While writing this (in November), I went out to our polytunnel to fetch a leaf of 'Green Boy' to examine. By the time I had got back to the house I found I had absentmindedly eaten it. Proof of the pudding? The komatsunas are reputedly very nutritious, being particularly rich in calcium. Whole young leaves, parts of larger leaves, young stems and flowering shoots can be used in salads.

Leaves can be cooked by any methods used for oriental greens: boiled lightly or steamed, stir-fried, combined with other greens, used in soups. I have successfully substituted 'Savanna' for cabbage in a cabbage/yoghurt recipe. In Holland komatsuna is substituted for kale in the traditional 'stamppot' where potatoes, kale and sausage are boiled together.

In Japan komatsuna is pickled, varieties such as 'Nozawana' being especially recommended for the purpose. (See also Recipes, page 191.)

Fodder crops

Some varieties, especially those with turnip parentage, can also be used as fodder crops. Don't be put off by this: many forage crops are very palatable, especially when used young.

siderable resistance to heat. The variety 'Savanna' can be grown all year round in the tropics, provided there is adequate moisture.

Site/soil

The outdoor crops need an open site. Being large, fast-growing brassicas they require fertile, moisture-rententive soil. (See Brassicas, General introduction, page 10.)

Cultivation

When to sow

OUTDOORS The komatsunas can be sown outdoors from early spring to autumn, as long as the ground is workable.

UNDER COVER IN SPRING The earliest sowings can be made in unheated polytunnels, greenhouses and cold frames, as soon as the soil has warmed up. In some areas this could be as early as January or February. These sowings can be followed by the first outdoor sowings, which can be under cloches or low polytunnels, or protected by woven film. (See Part 2, Protected cropping, page 161.)

UNDER COVER IN AUTUMN Similarly, the last outdoor sowings in late summer or early autumn can be covered by cloches, low tunnels etc. to encourage faster growth.

The main winter sowings for large plants can be made in late summer, transplanting under cover in autumn.

The last *in situ* sowings of a seedling crop can be made in late autumn under cover. In frost-free conditions, or in a heated greenhouse, sowing could continue into November and December.

In my experience the following are the most useful sowings:
Seedling crop
(1) Early spring under cover
(2) Spring and early summer outside
(3) Late autumn under cover
Mature crop
(1) Mid-summer, for the autumn and outdoor winter
(2) Late summer to transplant under cover in autumn

These mature crops provide greens during winter and early spring. The indoor crop will be of better quality during the winter months, but will run to seed faster in early spring, providing continuous pickings of flowering shoots.

The productivity of the outdoor crop will be more dependent on the severity of the winter, but I have known varieties of komatsuna to survive in winters where virtually all other greens perished. Flowering shoots produced in spring tend to be tougher than those from the indoor crop.

Sowing methods

Seedling crop
Sow *in situ*, either in wide drills or broadcast, spacing seeds 1 in (2.5 cm) apart. (See also Part 2, Plant raising, Sowing methods, page 151.)

Mature crop
You can raise plants in some kind of module and transplant. This is much more satisfactory than the use of bare rooted transplants. (See also Plant raising, Use of modules, page 153.) Otherwise, sow *in situ*, thinning in stages to the required distance apart. As the leaves can be used at any stage, all thinnings can be eaten.

Spacing for the mature crop will depend on the variety, and the size of plant required. As a rough guide, for small plants space 2 in (5 cm) apart; for large plants 10–12 in (25–30 cm) up to 18 in (45 cm) apart.

Protected cropping

In spite of being very cold-tolerant, the quality of the komatsunas will be improved in the winter months if they are protected. They grow exceptionally well in unheated greenhouses and tunnels from autumn to spring, apparently unaffected by the low light levels. The healthy glossiness of their leaves is quite striking in a dreary winter.

Under commercial conditions seedling crops of komatsuna are grown under cover all year round. These are harvested when about 8 in (20 cm) high.

Further care

The komatsunas are a little less demanding than Chinese cabbage, but do require a fertile soil. (See also Brassicas, General introduction, Soil fertility, page 10.)

The komatsunas tend to have a better and deeper root system than many oriental brassicas, giving them reasonable resistance to drought. They are less likely to bolt prematurely in dry conditions. However, like any leafy greens, they perform best if never short of water.

Containers

Best use of containers would be made by growing komatsunas for harvesting at the seedling or young plant stage. (See also Part 3, Containers, page 169.)

Pests and disease

The komatsuna group is characterized by its robustness: they are a healthy group of plants. In my experience the most common pests are flea beetle, slugs, and cutworm. Aphids may cause damage in very hot weather; the outdoor winter crop may be attacked by pigeons. Turnip mosaic virus is a problem in some areas. (See also Part 2, Pests and disease, page 172.)

Harvesting

Depending on the variety and the time of year average days to harvest would be:
—*Seedling crops* 20–35 days
—*Small plants* 35 days (summer)–60 days (winter)
—*Large plants* 55 days (summer)–80 days (winter)
Cut seedlings at any stage from about 3 in (10 cm) high. Cut these and young plants about ¾ in (2 cm) above ground level, so the plants will resprout. Normally at least two cuttings can be made; sometimes more.

Mature plants can be cut whole, or individual leaves harvested as required. Most of the komatsunas can be harvested fairly continuously over several months.

In spring constant picking or cutting of the flowering shoots will encourage more to grow.

Varieties

As the komatsuna group becomes more appreciated in the West, it is likely that an increasing number of new varieties will become available. The following brief notes are on varieties I have grown or seen growing to date.

F1 'All Top' ('Big Top') Developed from Japanese turnip greens; dark green leaves, less glossy and somewhat coarser than 'Komatsuna'. Extremely fast growing and vigorous; it can develop into very large plants, 2 ft (60 cm) high. Adapted to a wide range of climatic conditions, from cold to tropical; also recommended for areas with high rainfall and high humidity. Can be grown all year round; very useful for winter greenhouse crop, and early seedlings under low polytunnels. Can be cut or grazed as a forage crop. Produces turnip-like roots. (The US variety 'Topper' is quite similar.)

'Benri-na' ('Green Boy') Japanese cross between 'Komatsuna' and pak choi. 'Benri-na' means 'convenient leaf'. Upright plant, slender, dark green leaves, long leaf stalks, so easily bunched. Fast-growing and very adaptable.

'Komatsuna' The 'original' spinach mustard. (See Background, above.) Large glossy leaves, versatile, hardy, fast growing. 'Late Komatsuna' is larger, very slow bolting, recommended for late sowing.

'Nozawana' Developed from turnip greens originated in a snowy, mountainous region in Japan. Recommended for cold and mountainous areas, though also heat-tolerant. Large serrated edged, slightly coarse leaves. Can grow into a huge plant over 3 ft (90 cm) high. In frost and snow leaves become purplish, and reputedly more tender and sweeter. Leaves and leaf stalks very popular in Japan for pickling. Eventually produces turnip-like roots.

'Osome Komatsuna' Improved, fast-growing, heavy-yielding variety. Can grow densely about an inch (2.5 cm) apart, cutting when 12 in (30 cm) tall. Easily bunched long leaf stalks. Excellent winter crop here in unheated polytunnel. Flowering shoots became hot just before bolting in spring, but excellent cooked.

F1 'Savanna' Cross between several komatsuna varieties. Lush leaves, fast-growing, early-maturing, very vigorous. Adapted to hot and cold conditions; slow-bolting. In commercial production regrows rapidly after mechanical harvesting. Can be used for forage.

'Shogoin' Strictly speaking a Japanese turnip; included here because grown mainly for its broad, serrated leaves, resembling many in the komatsuna group. Leaves used in salads or cooked. Cool weather crop, best sown in spring for a late spring crop, or from mid-summer on for autumn and early winter crop. Not as resistant to dry conditions as other komatsuna varieties. Greens can be harvested within 25–30 days; turnip roots after about 75 days. Roots can grow up to 6 in (15 cm) diameter; best eaten much smaller. Can be used for forage.

'Tendergreen' Very similar to 'Komatsuna'. Large glossy leaves, slow-bolting, good resistance to heat, drought and low temperatures.

'Typhon' ('Typhon Holland Greens') Cross between stubble turnip and Chinese cabbage, bred primarily as fodder crop. Young leaves mild flavoured, excellent cut-and-come-again crop, usable in salads or cooked. Larger leaves rather coarse. Very hardy; may wilt in very hot weather.

'Uzuki' Glossy leaves, slow bolting, suitable for all year production.

'Yayoi' Similar to Uzuki, larger leaves.

Mizuna greens

Latin name *Brassica rapa* var *nipposinica* or var *japonica*
Other names in use Kyona, Mizuna mustard, pot herb mustard
Mandarin Shui cai ('water vegetable')
Japanese Mizuna ('water/juicy vegetable'); Kyona ('Kyoto greens'); Kyomizuna

Background

Botanically, mizuna (pronounced *mee*zuna) is closely related to the leafy turnips. Although almost certainly Chinese in origin, it has been grown and cultivated since ancient times in Japan, and is generally considered a Japanese vegetable.

Characteristics

Mizuna is an exceptionally pretty plant. It forms a bushy clump—almost a giant rosette—of finely dissected, feathery leaves, which are a dark, glossy green. The relatively short leaf stalks are slender, white and juicy—hence the 'juici-

Use

Mizuna can be used at any stage, from small seedlings to a large plant. The flowering shoots are also edible. It is mild flavoured; the younger and smaller the leaves, the more tender they are. Older leaves can become fibrous.

In the kitchen

In the West mizuna has become prized as an off-season salad vegetable. Its glossy, dark green leaves are both pretty and healthy looking. They also make an excellent garnish.

It can be cooked by any method used for oriental greens, for example: in soups; steamed; stir-fried alone, with other vegetables, or with meat, poultry or fish. In the Napa Valley in the United States resourceful chefs are using mizuna in stuffed chicken breasts, in seafood ravioli, mixed with root vegetables and so on. The leaf stalks require slightly longer cooking so should be trimmed off and cooked separately. In the Far East mizuna is primarily a pickling vegetable.

(See also Recipes, page 192.)

ness' in the Chinese and Japanese names. The clumps tend to be about 9 in (23 cm) high and can spread to about 18 in (45 cm) in diameter. In the F1 hybrid varieties the leaves are broader and less serrated, giving a higher-yielding but equally striking plant.

Mizuna is naturally a very vigorous, healthy plant, regrowing rapidly after cutting. Mature heads of old varieties probably weighed little more than a couple of pounds (1 kg); some new varieties can weigh up to 13 lb (6 kg).

Climate

Mizuna is both heat and cold tolerant. In the USA it has continued growing without bolting at temperatures over 90°F (32°C). As for extreme cold, small plants struggled through our most severe winter in an unheated polytunnel, when indoor temperatures went down to 3°F (−16°C). Larger plants growing outdoors died—but probably as much from the melting snow lingering on the leaves as from sheer cold.

Mizuna normally stands up to wet conditions well. However, in dry conditions growth may be stunted and plants will appear to bolt prematurely, or produce very tough foliage.

Site/soil

Mizuna grows best on an open site, though summer crops can be grown in light shade. It tolerates a wide range of soil types, provided the soil is reasonably fertile and moisture-retentive. In these conditions I have never found supplementary feeding necessary.

Decorative value

With its glossy, deep green, fernlike foliage, mizuna is a very ornamental plant. Patches of mizuna in a flower bed are a wonderful foil to brightly coloured annuals. It makes a stunning edge to a vegetable or flower bed, and can be interplanted and used for underplanting with great effect. It retains its rosette shape and goes on looking good even when the leaves are being cut regularly for use. Both mature plants or seedlings can be used in any of these cases: parallel drills of seedlings quickly grow to form a dense carpet over the ground.

Cultivation

Mizuna can be grown as seedlings, as semi-mature and as mature plants. It responds well to cut-and-come-again treatment at any stage. (See also Brassicas, General introduction, Stages of use, page 9.)

Sowing methods

Mizuna is one of the most bolt-resistant of the oriental brassicas, even when sown in spring, so it is not necessary to sow in modules.

Either sow *in situ*, thinning to the correct distance apart, or sow in a seed tray or seed bed and transplant. Plants are normally ready for transplanting 2–3 weeks after sowing. (See also Part 2, Plant raising, page 150.)

When to sow

SPRING For the earliest pickings sow a seedling crop under cover, *in situ*, as soon as the soil has warmed up. For the earliest outdoor crop, sow indoors in seed trays, transplanting outdoors as soon as soil conditions permit.

LATE SPRING UNTIL EARLY AUTUMN Outdoor sowings can continue from late spring until autumn, but the cropping period will be shorter and the quality poorer in very hot weather.

LATE AUTUMN In temperate climates make the final sowing *in situ* under cover in late autumn, for a cut-and-come-again seedling crop. At the same time sowings made in early autumn can be transplanted under cover for a headed crop. These will crop throughout winter and well into the following spring.

Spacing

This can be varied according to the size of plant required.

—Small plants: 4 in (10 cm) apart
—Medium-sized plants, and plants that will be cut fairly frequently in winter: 8–9 in (20–22.5 cm) apart
—Large plants: 12–18 in (30–45 cm) apart

Intercropping

Mizuna is very useful for intercropping and undercropping. For example, narrow bands of seedling mizuna can be sown between widely spaced brassicas when the latter are first planted. I often grow mizuna under sweet corn, either planting it, or sowing wide drills, when the corn is planted in early summer. It will continue growing long after the corn has been harvested, sometimes into the following year (see illustration on page 8).

Protected cropping

Mizuna's resistance to cold makes it an excellent crop for unheated greenhouses and other forms of

Mizuna greens: broad-leaved type

protection during the winter months. It continues growing longer than most vegetables, seemingly unaffected by low light levels.

Containers

Being decorative and productive, Mizuna is a suitable subject for containers, either grown as a seedling crop or as large plants.

Pests and disease

Mizuna is normally a very trouble-free plant, flea beetle and slugs being the most likely pests. (See also Part 2, Pests and disease.) An unusual problem was encountered at Pragtree Farm in Washington State, USA, where the giant garden mushroom (*Strophularia rugosa annulata*) was being grown in the garden. It actually killed the mizuna!

Harvesting

Mizuna is very fast growing. The first cuts of seedling crops can sometimes be made within 2–3 weeks of sowing. (See also Part 2, Plant raising, Cut-and-come-again, page 155.) Heads can also be harvested whole.

The secret with mizuna is to cut plants regularly so that a fresh crop of tender leaves is continually being produced. Depending on the time of year, as many as five cuts can be made from one plant, the same plants sometimes cropping for up to ten months before they run to seed.

Varieties

Until recently there was only one open pollinated variety of Mizuna available. A number of hybrid varieties have now been developed in Japan. They are more uniform and productive, have better leaf quality, and sometimes lighter coloured leaves than the old varieties. They are generally classified as early, medium and late, indicating their suitability for different seasons.

'Tokyo Beau' Broad leaves, good cold resistance, excellent variety for winter.

'Chicken mustard' ('Thousand headed mustard')
Although usually classified as a *'Juncea'* mustard (see next chapter), this long-established Chinese vegetable may be closely related to mizuna. It has similar, deep green, deeply cut leaves. It must be sown in late summer, or it will bolt prematurely. It is probably not very hardy. It is traditionally used for pickles, but can be cooked or used in salads when young.

Mibuna greens ('Mibu greens')

Background

Mibuna is one of the most recent vegetables to break through the bamboo curtain. It appears to be closely related to mizuna—though no-one is sure. Like mizuna, it is regarded as a Japanese vegetable, with a long history of cultivation in Mibu, in the Kyoto prefecture. I made its acquaintance when a friend sent me a packet of seed from Japan. With its unusual appearance it has attracted a lot of favourable attention since I started growing it here.

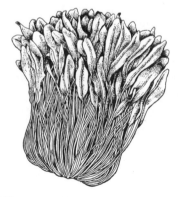
Mibuna greens

Characteristics

Mibuna is characterized by its long narrow leaves, which grow into a very elegant and striking spray-like clump. The leaves are ½–1½ in (1–4 cm) wide and 12–18 in (30–45 cm) long, depending on variety, often with rounded tips. The clumps can be 22 in (56 cm) in diameter. Leaves are dark or light green and tend to become lighter coloured when grown under cover, especially in winter. The leaf stems are slender and greenish in colour. The largest hybrids can produce plants up to 6.5 lb (3 kg) in weight.

Climate

It is essentially a cool weather plant, less adapted to extremes of heat and cold than mizuna, though in my garden it has survived 21°F (−6°C) outside. Mature plants are

Use

Mibuna is mild flavoured, though more distinct and slightly stronger flavoured than mizuna. Most people seem to like the taste very much. The flavour tends to get stronger, and the leaves tougher, as the plant ages. (For stages of use, see Mizuna, Use, above.)

For use, cooked and raw, see Mizuna. In Japan mibuna is used as a fresh vegetable and pickled. So far I have mainly used it in winter and spring salads, and in stir-fried greens.

more likely to bolt from spring sowings than mizuna, though of course the bolting shoots can be eaten when young.

Cultivation

Like mizuna, mibuna can be grown as seedlings, as semi-mature and as mature plants, adapting well to cut-and-come-again treatment at any stage.

When to sow

The following is based on recommendations in Japanese seed catalogues.

Large plants
Sow *in situ*, or in seed trays or modules for transplanting.

In temperate climates make the main sowings in late summer to early autumn. They can be grown outside or planted under cover. I have found the winter crop, grown under cover, one of the most prolific oriental brassicas in early spring.

Seedlings and small plants
Sow *in situ*.

In temperate regions outdoor sowings can be made from spring to late autumn. Earlier and later sowings can be made under cover. In areas with cool summers outdoor *in situ* sowings can be made from late spring until the end of summer. Earlier and later sowings can be made under cover.

Spacing

(See Mizuna. Large plants can be spaced up to 20 in (50 cm) apart.)

Containers

(See Mizuna.)

Pests and disease

Flea beetle, slugs and occasional caterpillars are the only pests I have found. (See also Part 2, Pests and disease.)

Harvesting

Mibuna can be cut at any stage, but is generally slower growing than mizuna. The first cut of young leaves is usually made within about a month of sowing.

Varieties

The Japanese have developed 'Early', 'Medium' and 'Late' varieties parallel with the mizuna varieties. The early varieties are said to be the most suitable for sowing in warm conditions.

F1 'Green Spray', though an early variety, has performed well here during the winter months.

Mustard greens

Latin name   *Brassica juncea*
Other names in use   Chinese mustard/greens; Indian mustard/greens; leaf mustard; mustard cabbage
Mandarin   Jie cai; gai cai
Cantonese   Kaai tsoi; gai choy
Japanese   Karashina; takana

Background

The mustards are a vast, fascinating group of plants. Seeds of some mustards species are the source of our 'mustard seed' spice and of important oils. Other species are grown as fodder crops and green manures. What concerns us here are the many mustards traditionally used as vegetables in the Far East, all falling under the botanical umbrella of *Brassica juncea*. Some are annuals, some biennials.

They are thought to have originated in the Central Asian Himalayas, spreading to China, India and the Caucasus. The earliest mention of mustards in Chinese literature was several centuries BC: this was probably a small, rather rough-leaved, annual plant. Just as the simple European wild cabbage evolved over the centuries into headed cabbage, kales, the flowering headed-cauliflower, sprouting broccoli, kohl rabi with its swollen stem and the multi-budded brussels sprouts, so natural evolution, combined with local selection carried out mainly in China and south-east Asia, resulted in an astonishing diversity of mustard types. Today we have mustards with cabbage-like heads, with knobbly and swollen stems, enlarged leaf stalks and roots, and all manner of leaves.

The evolutionary story seems to go like this. First the seed pod types developed—used for spice and oil. Then, in about the seventh century AD, the leafy types evolved in temperate and humid areas in China. Types with fleshy taproots came next (perhaps to store the products now manufactured by the larger plants), followed, in dry regions of

Use

Flavour The mustards are among the most highly prized vegetables in China and the Far East. They are characterized by a peppery flavour—though the degree of pungency varies enormously not just from one variety to another, but from one part of a plant to another. Stems can be mild and leaves hot, or *vice versa*. It also varies at different stages in the plant's development. Small and young leaves are usually milder than large and mature leaves. Leaves generally become much 'hotter' when the plants are about to run to seed; also in unduly dry conditions, or if the plants become starved.

In the kitchen

Mustards are not to everyone's taste. I once gave two people raw leaves to sample: one said 'superb flavour', and the other spat it out! While the flavour can be too strong raw, it is muted to a pleasantly mischievous   spiciness   when

China, by types with curly and finely dissected leaves, adapted to arid conditions. Sometime around the seventeenth century forms with thick, fleshy midribs and leaf stalks evolved, then types with 'heads' or 'hearts', flowering shoot types, and finally the 'tsa tsai' or 'za cai' type, with its grotesque fleshy stem used to make the famous sweet and tender Chinese pickle of that name.

The mustards are said to be very nutritious, more so than European or Chinese cabbage. They have high levels of vitamins A and C, and are a good source of calcium, phosphorus, iron and potash. Perhaps this explains their traditional use as a spring tonic among the Chinese. Incidentally, honey made from mustard flowers is said to be delicious.

Climate

The majority of the mustards thrive in the warm, humid conditions of south and south-west China, and grow well in warm weather. They tolerate high rainfall, and are susceptible to drought and dry conditions. Others display considerable tolerance to cold, surviving several degrees of frost.

Soil/site

Mustards should be grown in an open site. Provided the soil is reasonably fertile and moisture-retentive, they tolerate a wide range of soil types. There is some evidence that *Brassica juncea* mustards grown as green manures might be effective in reducing soil-borne root rots in pea crops; this is attributed to chemicals given off as the plants decay. So they could be useful crops to include in rotations.

Decorative value

The mustards are excellent plants for a decorative vegetable garden. The savoy-leaved 'Miike Giant' type, the various purple-leaved varieties such as 'Osaka Purple', and many of the curly-leaved types are exceptionally hardy, so can be used to provide colour and dramatic form in winter. A favourite combination of mine is blue-green leeks planted between purple mustards. I grow them together every year in my winter potager.

cooked. Creative cooks seem impressed by the culinary potential of these still relatively unknown plants.

Although the mustards are coarser than most oriental greens, Westerners are beginning to use their sharp flavour sparingly, but very effectively, in salads. In California I saw densely grown, purple mustard seedlings, the young rounded leaves about an inch in diameter, being cut for salads. They were served mixed with salad rocket and lettuce. Larger, strong-flavoured leaves are excellent shredded into a salad, adding not just a 'zing' but colour and texture. Several varieties have striking deep green and purple hues, while texture ranges from a bubbly, savoyed quality, to the prettily fringed curly-leaved varieties. In spring the flowering shoots from bolting plants can be used in salads. When young they are surprisingly sweet, but later they may become too strong for most people's enjoyment.

The mustards, especially the leafy types, are often used in soups, and are also lightly steamed (which makes them less hot), stir-fried, stewed and incorporated into a wide range of dishes. They give a wonderful kick to a stir-fry of mixed oriental greens, and can be substituted for chard to make an excellent quiche. Curly leaved mustards are traditionally used in crab dishes in China. Various speciality dishes are made with stem mustards. Flowering shoots can be cooked by any of the above methods used for leaves.

In the Far East the mustards are first and foremost pickling vegetables. All parts—flowering shoots, leaves, ordinary and swollen stems and roots—are made into pickles: salted pickles, vinegar pickles, wine pickles, fermented pickles, short- and long-term pickles. They are enormously popular. Somewhat confusingly, when sold in the West pickled and salted mustards are sometimes labelled 'pickled turnip'.

Mustard leaves and shoots are also dried for winter use. (See also Recipes, page 193.)

Cultivation

(For general cultivation see Brassicas, General introduction, page 8. For cultivation details see Different types and varieties, below.)

The mustards are naturally vigorous and robust plants. Provided they are sown at the appropriate time for the variety, they are relatively easy to grow. They are mainly grown outdoors, but in temperate climates plants grown under cover in unheated greenhouses and polytunnels in winter can be of excellent quality and highly productive.

The bolting problem

With a few exceptions, the *Brassica juncea* mustards tend to run to seed in spring and early summer instead of developing into sizeable plants.

Broad leaved giant mustard

Whether this is in response to increasing day length, or is caused by low temperatures in the early stages of growth, is a point scientists are arguing over. In practice this means it is best to delay sowing until mid- to late summer if a mature plant is required. Earlier sowings can be made for seedling or small plants.

Stages of use

The mustards *can* be harvested at various stages, but are generally less suited to cut-and-come-again seedling production than other oriental brassicas. This is partly because they are slower growing than, for example, Chinese cabbage or pak choi, and partly because they are coarser and less succulent at the seedling stage. (The exceptions will be covered under Varieties, below.) With some varieties the full flavour only develops when the plants are nearing maturity.

When to sow

Use these general guidelines for new or unfamiliar varieties. For established varieties see under Different types and varieties, below.
AUTUMN/WINTER/SPRING OUTDOOR CROP Sow mid-summer in temperate areas. Sow late summer to autumn in frost-free areas. Later sowings can be made of seedling crops for harvesting young.
WINTER/SPRING CROP UNDER COVER Sow late summer to early autumn for transplanting under cover. Later sowings can be made of seedling crops for harvesting young.
SUMMER CROP Curly-leaved mustards and headed types picked at an immature, leafy stage seem the best adapted to summer production. Otherwise confine sowings to seedling crops or plants cut very young.

Sow outdoors in spring as soon as the soil is workable. Earlier sowings can be made under cover.

Sowing method

Mustard seed is small, so should be sown shallowly.

Spring sowings are best made *in situ* and thinned to the required distance apart. For summer and autumn sowings either sow *in situ* or sow in modules for transplanting. (See also Part 2, Plant raising, Use of modules, page 153.)

Spacing

Space plants from 4–18 in (10–45 cm) apart, depending on the variety and the size they will be harvested, i.e.:
—Plants being harvested young: 4–6 in (10–15 cm) apart
—Average varieties grown to a mature size: 12 in (30 cm) apart
—Large spreading varieties: 18 in (45 cm) apart

Further care

See Brassicas, General introduction, page 8.

Mature mustard plants are deeper rooted than many oriental brassicas, so require less frequent watering. However they must not be allowed to dry out. Take special care to ensure that spring and summer seedling crops don't dry out, or they run to seed rapidly.

Containers

If you want bulky leafy greens for the table, the mustards are probably not productive enough to warrant growing in containers. A case can be made for growing some of the more decorative purple and curly-leaved varieties, especially during the winter months. Give them as large a container as possible: they will become skimpy and unattractive if starved or allowed to dry out. (See also Part 2, Containers, page 169.)

Pests and disease

The mustards are rarely seriously troubled by pests and disease. Occasional problems include flea beetle, cabbage root fly, aphids, caterpillars and slugs. (See also Part 2, Pests and disease.)

Harvesting

Plants take anything from 2–5 months to mature, depending on the variety and season.
Seedling crops Start cutting when a couple of inches high. There is far less regrowth than with most oriental brassicas.
Small plants Where varieties are grown fairly close with the intention of harvesting as young plants, cutting normally starts when they are about 6 in (15 cm) high. Either cut the whole plant, or harvest a few outer leaves at a time. Some further leaves will normally develop.
Large plants For ordinary domestic use it is normally sufficient to harvest a few leaves at a time—especially with the larger leaved varieties. Some further leaves will develop. With hearted and swollen stem varieties, the whole plant is often harvested at once.

Different types and varieties of mustard

The following notes attempt to distinguish some of the main types and varieties of mustard, and indicate how they are grown and used. Although the categories are by no means cut and dried, it should be possible to slot most new varieties into one of the categories below.

There is enormous scope for developing exciting new varieties within the mustard greens.

Broad-leaved group

Brassica juncea var *rugosa*
This group comes under the Chinese umbrella label of 'Da gai cai' or big mustards. It embraces the giant-leaved mustards, and various headed or hearted mustards. In seed catalogues any of these may simply be listed as 'large mustard'.

Giant-leaved types

These are large, prolific, handsome plants. The lower leaves are very broad and long; they can be 12 in (30 cm) wide and over 24 in (60 cm) long. The upper leaves are thinner and narrower. Leaf colour ranges from green, to green with purple veins, to deep purple, the colours tending to deepen as weather gets colder. The leaves often have a very characteristic blistered or crêpe-like texture; the leaf stalks are usually quite thick. The plants grow to about 15 in (38 cm) high—and much more when running to seed—with an average spread of about 15 in (38 cm). Both leaves and stems can be used, the leaves being hotter flavoured.

The giant-leaved mustards are very hardy, and are best sown in summer for use during the winter months. For harvesting as large plants sow from August to October in cool and temperate climates, and until November in warm climates. These are mainly harvested the following spring, though leaves can also be harvested during the winter months. Although they survive cold weather well, they grow fastest in warm weather. They take on average 3–4 months to reach maturity, and should be spaced at least 12 in (30 cm) apart.

Red-leaved varieties such as 'Red Giant' can also be sown from spring onwards for cutting as seedling crops, harvested very young to give colour to salads, or as slightly larger plants harvested 6 in (15 cm) high. (See Part 2, Plant raising, Cut-and-come-again, page 155.)

Varieties

'Red Chirimen'/'Crêpe' (Japanese: 'Aka Chirimen'); **'Osaka Purple'**; **'Red Giant'**, **'Giant Red'** (Japanese: 'Aka takana')

All similar ('Osaka Purple' is considered more 'refined' than 'Red Giant'), possibly different selections of same variety. Can become large plants 18 ins (45 cm) wide and high. Broad leaves, generally greenish with purple edges in warm weather; crêpe-like outer leaves of mature plants predomi-

nantly maroon purple in cold weather. Inner leaves greener, milder flavour. Stalks generally rounded. Leaves can be harvested from plants which are running to seed. Overwintered plants among slowest bolting in spring in Rodale (USA) trials.

'Green Chirimen' Similar to 'Red Chirimen'; attractively blistered leaves, completely green.

'King Mustard' Handsome Chinese variety, similar to 'Miike Giant'.

'Miike Giant' (Japanese: 'Miike Ohba Chirimen Takana') Very vigorous variety, resembling 'Red Chirimen' group, but flattish stalks. Green crinkly leaves with glossy sheen. Purple veins, especially towards leaf tips; whole leaf becoming more purple at low temperatures. Mature plants weigh up to 6.5 lb (3 kg). (One spring I dug up plants in the polytunnel to plant summer crops and replanted them outside; they continued to grow well.)

'Permagreen' New variety, crinkly green leaves with purple tints; 'Miike Giant' flavour. Nearly winter hardy in temperate climates; recommended for autumn and winter harvesting.

Wrapped heart and headed types

Mandarin: Bao xin da jie cai ('Wrapped heart big mustard')
Japanese: Kekkyu takana
In this group of mustards the leaves may curl inwards to form small loose or compact, conical or

Wrapped heart mustard

rounded hearts, which are highly prized both for pickling and for fresh use. The flavour develops with age, the leaf stalks also tending to thicken and develop a notable flavour as plants mature.

Getting good hearts to develop seems to be tricky in temperate climates, and may depend on there being relatively warm conditions after the plants are sown, normally in late summer.

The mustards can be sown earlier in the year, in this case the usual practice is to harvest the outer leaves before the plants bolt. Some varieties are being grown in greenhouses in Europe for summer mustard greens.

Sowing times

Mature crop Temperate climate: sow in mid-summer, to mature from autumn to early winter.
Warm climate: sow in autumn to mature in winter.
Harvest of outer leaves only Temperate climate: sow in late spring, to harvest early to mid-summer.
Warm climate: sow early spring to harvest in summer.

Varieties

'Amsoi' Famous pickling variety (Cantonese: moo tsoi); central shoot especially prized. Highly productive in temperate climates for general use. Fairly hardy. Sow as above; also all year round under cover. Space 18 in (45 cm) apart for large plants; 9 in (23 cm) apart for small plants.

'Big Heart' Vigorous, semi-heading; only sow late summer.

'Chicken heart' Vigorous, semi-heading; broad, bright green leaves, thick wide leaf stalks; good flavour.

'Swatow (Chaozhou) Large Headed' (Mandarin: Ge li da jie cai 'Elder brother biennial big mustard; [May be synonymous with 'South China Big Heart'])

Looks like giant cabbage; leaf stems curve gracefully outwards. In China light green outer leaves trimmed off leaving tight round head, about 6 in (15 cm) diameter, composed mainly of wide leaf stalks. Sold as expensive delicacy

'Amsoi' hearted mustard: young plant

Common or leaf mustard

for pickling or fresh use. Stems and outer leaves also used. All have strong, pungent flavour.

'Wrapped heart' Attractive, fairly upright plant; light coloured, broad, rather undulating leaves; short, wide, flat leaf stalks. Looser heart than 'Swatow' mustard, but crisp and tender. Promising winter crop in temperate climates. Late August sowing here, planted in unheated polytunnel late September in mild winter, started hearting December. Flavour mild initially; in later stages very pleasant 'kick'; delicious raw and cooked.

Common or leaf mustards

Brassica juncea var *foliosa*
Mandarin: Ye yong jie cai ('use leaf mustard')
Cantonese: Gai choy
Japanese: Ha karashina ('leaf mustard')
Often known as Chinese mustard or little mustard, this group has fairly coarse leaves, usually a dark, bright green with rather serrated, saw-like edges. They are sometimes roundish, sometimes long, in which case they more or less 'feather' the leaf stalk. They are not unlike the leaves of the large 'daikon' radishes in appearance. The leaf stalks are light green with characteristic longitudinal ridges. The plants generally grow up to 12 in (30 cm) high, and about the same spread, but occasionally they become very large.

They tend to bolt rapidly in spring, so are only worth sowing in the summer and autumn, when they grow rapidly, maturing usually within about 40 days. The Chinese like to delay harvesting until the tasty stems have developed. They stand cold weather quite well.

In some cases the flowering shoots, for example from overwintered plants bolting in spring, tend to thicken and are peeled as pickles or used fresh. They have a good flavour. On the whole these mustards are milder than the giant mustards, though they can become hot flavoured.

Varieties

'Bamboo gai choy' Popular Hong Kong mustard, sweeter than most. Used fresh and pickled. Plants rather skimpy.
'South wind' (Mandarin: nan feng gai; Cantonese: namfong) Popular Chinese variety: tall, fast-growing, light green, fairly broad, roundish leaves. Heat tolerant, possibly better adapted to early summer sowings than some varieties (though overwintered plants bolted rapidly in spring in Rodale USA trials). Pretty robust; reputed tolerance to wind and rain. Grew very fast here in October. Can become very large; probably best harvested 6–8 in (15–20 cm) tall.
'Taishona' Attractive, light green leaved hybrid, 'South Wind' type; reputedly improved resistance to adverse conditions; recommended for warm conditions.

Green-in-the-snow group

Brassica juncea var *multiceps*
Mandarin: Xue li hong (pronounced 'Sher lee hoong', meaning 'stem or stalk in the snow', translated and known as 'red in snow'.)
Japanese: Serifong (an approximation of *'xue li hong'*); setsu ri kon
This type was one of the first oriental mustards to be introduced to the West. It is characterized by dark green, jagged edged leaves, often deeply lobed. There are several forms (in China there are 'yellow' and 'black' varieties), the commonest growing into a plant about 12–16 in (30–40 cm) high. Green-in-the-snow mustard is very vigorous, fast growing, very hardy, and displays considerable resistance to pests and disease.

Young raw leaves are pleasantly spicy, but mature leaves can become overpoweringly hot when the plant is beginning to run to seed, though they are still good cooked at this stage. The Chinese preserve *xue li hong* in salt. Tender young leaves are washed, dried, laid flat and salted in layers. They are then weighted down and kept somewhere cool. There is an art in adding just the right amount of salt: too little fails to preserve, too much makes them over-salty, though it can be washed out just before use. The salted greens are cooked with sliced meat, usually pork, giving them a unique flavour. When the salted greens start to deteriorate in spring they are dried out completely so they will keep almost indefinitely, and are

Green-in-the-snow mustard

used in soup. These are known in Mandarin as 'gan cai' ('dried greens').

It is best sown in late summer. Either sow for a seedling crop, or thin to 4 in (10 cm) apart for small plants, 8 in (20 cm) apart for medium-sized plants, 12 in (30 cm) apart for large plants.

Curled mustard group

Brassica juncea var *crispifolia* (also *Brassica cernua* and *Brassica chirimenna*)
These are distinguished by their very curly, sometimes rather stiff, crisp leaves, not unlike curly kale. Many are handsome plants, well worth growing for their decorative value, particularly in the winter months. They tend to be rugged and hardy.

Curled mustard leaf

The flavour is distinctive, on the peppery side, becoming very hot as the plants mature. They are cooked or used raw in green salads. They are also grown for fodder crops.

These mustards are best sown in late summer for winter use. Plants which overwinter often stand well in spring without bolting, providing greens when they are at their scarcest. They can also be sown in spring and early summer, though in this case should be harvested young, four or five weeks after sowing. Sowing in very hot weather is not recommended.

New varieties are being developed in both Japan and the United States. There is marked similarity between these mustards and the traditional, flatter leaved, milder flavoured mustard greens of the American south such as 'Fordhook Giant' and 'Giant Southern Curled'.

Varieties

'Art Green' Relatively mild flavoured, fast growing, very curly leaved. Versatile, good resistance to high and fairly low temperatures. In temperate climates can sow throughout growing season, but spring-sown and overwintered autumn-sown crops must be harvested young before bolting. Also grown under cover all year round to get tender crops and for protection against very low winter temperatures. In warm areas sometimes grown as spinach substitute in summer, cutting 8 in (20 cm) high, 25–30 days after sowing.
'Green Wave' Very pretty light green, fairly broad leaves, frilled at the margins. Slower maturing than 'Art Green'.

Swollen stem mustard group

Brassica juncea var *linearifolia*, var *tsatsai* ('Zhacai'), var *tumida*, var *strumata*
Mandarin: Jing yong jie cai ('stem use mustard')
This group contains some curious types, some having very swollen stems or leaf stems, or protuberances of some kind on the stem. These 'growths' are normally used for pickles, the most famous being the pressed stem 'Zhacai' pickle, a speciality of Sichuan province, which is often sold in tins. The swollen parts can also be peeled and cooked, and are said to have a good flavour. Leaves can be used when young, but once the plants start to develop swellings the quality of the leaves deteriorates.

They are reasonably cold-tolerant, but need plenty of moisture. On the whole sowings in very hot weather should be avoided; the principal sowings are in late summer for an autumn to winter crop.

There are many varieties in China, but so far few have reached the West. When they do they may be listed simply as 'stem mustards', without indicating which type they are.

Types

Horned mustard
Japanese: Kobu takana
An elegantly shaped plant with bright green indented and frilled leaves. A blunt protruding 'horn' develops in the centre of the leaf midribs. The flavour has been described as 'excellent with garlic overtones'. It is said to have considerable resistance to low temperatures. Japanese seed catalogues recommend the sowings below.
Mature crop Temperate and warm climate: sow in late summer for mature plants.

Colder climate: sow in mid summer.

Mature plants take an average of 3–4 months to mature.
Young crop Temperate and warm climates: sow in spring and early spring respectively, harvesting just the outer leaves within 6–8 weeks.

Parcel and pocket mustard
A type in which small swellings develop on the inner sides of the leaf stalks. They are said to be soft and tender but I have not yet tasted or grown this type myself.

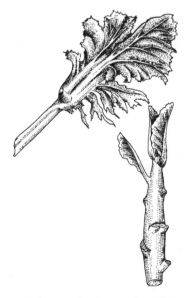

Horned mustard (*above*) and swollen stem mustard

Swollen stem mustard
A type with a thickened stem, which can be peeled, sliced and cooked.

Tsa tsai/Zhacai (Pressed stem)
The best known type, forming at least half a dozen curious lumps on the stem. Plants can be 6–8 in (15–20 cm) tall, 4–8 in (10–15 cm) spread, weighing 1–1½ lb (0.5–0.75 kg). I was given the following information on its cultivation in north China:

It is usually sown in September, ideally at a temperature of about 78°F (26°C), lowering the temperature to about 59°F (15°C) during the early stages of growth. The stems start to expand towards the end of October, and are ready about 110 days after sowing. The ideal temperature during the expansion phase is 46–55°F (8–13°C).

Root mustard

Brassica juncea var *megarrhiza*
Mandarin: Gen yong jie cai ('use root mustard')
This type is noted for its ugly-looking, fleshy tuberous root which is sliced and made into delicious salty pickles. The leaves are also edible. It is quite hardy, surviving temperatures of 25°F (−4°C).

Japanese turnips

Latin name *Brassica rapa* var *rapifera*
Japanese Kabu; kabura
Mandarin Wujing; manjing
Cantonese Mo ching

I won't dwell on turnips, for they belong as much to the West as to the East. But this book would be incomplete without mentioning some of the exciting turnips emanating from Japan: the unique long, thin, purple and white 'Hinona-kabu'; the little round white turnips of exceptional quality; and the round, red-skinned turnips.

The Japanese tend to treat turnips like their giant *daikon* radishes. They are munched raw, they are pickled, and they are cooked. The young green tops are cooked as greens, stir-fried, and used in soups. (For turnip greens and hybrid leafy turnips, see Komatsuna.) The Japanese often grow turnips instead of radish on heavy soils.

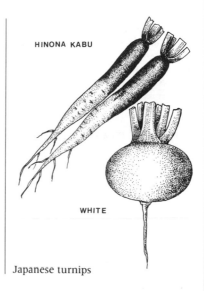

HINONA KABU

WHITE

Japanese turnips

Hinona-kabu turnip

Background and characteristics

This famous Japanese turnip is used to make the pretty *sakura zuke* cherry pickle, so called because of its cherry-blossom colour. The leaves, as well as the roots, are pickled.

The roots are 1–1½ in (3–4 cm) wide, and up to 10–12 in (25–30 cm) long. The top third protrudes above the soil and is a pretty purplish red, but the lower two-thirds are white. It bears a close resemblance to the old European turnip 'Long Red Tankard'—similarly coloured and much the same length, which, according to Vilmorin in 1885, was 'highly esteemed throughout Central Europe, from Poland to England . . .' Perhaps it was among European turnips known to have been introduced to Japan after the Meiji Restoration in 1867, and subsequently gave rise to 'Hinona-kabu'.

Climate

Turnips grow best in mild weather: the optimum temperature for growth is about 68°F (20°C). They

Use
In the kitchen

I was introduced to 'Hinona-kabu' in the United States, and grew it for the first time last year. The pretty, elegant roots we harvested were about 9 in (23 cm) long. We cut them into ½-in (1-cm) angled slices, parboiled them for 5 minutes, then glazed them in a frying pan with Chinese rock sugar (to add an authentic Eastern touch). They were tender, tasty and kept their colour beautifully when they were cooked.

are reasonably hardy, and will survive a few degrees of frost.

Soil/site

Turnips are best grown in an open site, on soil manured for the previous crop. Acid soils should be limed to bring the pH to between 5.5 and 7. The secret of producing really tender, sweet turnips is to grow them fast—so poor soils, and soils prone to drying out, should be avoided. 'Hinona-kabu' can be grown successfully on heavy soils.

Cultivation, harvesting
When to sow

Outdoors Although in theory 'Hinona-kabu' can be sown out-

doors in spring, and again in late summer and autumn, in practice spring sowings are very prone to bolting. Summer and early autumn sowings are a much safer bet.
Under cover Several sowings can be made:

- The first spring sowings can be made under cover very early in the year; these should be ready in early spring.
- A follow-on sowing can be made in polytunnels outdoors, removing the tunnels as soon as the weather warms up. These will mature in early summer.
- The last sowing of the year can be made in polytunnels or greenhouses in late autumn. These will mature during winter.

Thin in stages until the roots are

at least 2 in (5 cm) apart. The roots are at their best when the tops are about an inch (2–3 cm) in diameter, a stage reached on average 40–50 days after sowing. From late July sowings we pulled the first roots in early September. Once they pass this stage the core quickly becomes coarse and tough.

Pests and disease

There is some risk of attack from common brassica pests, such as flea beetle and cabbage root fly. In Japan turnips are often grown in unheated greenhouses in autumn, as this seems to give considerable protection against pests. (See also Part 2, Pests and disease.)

Small round white turnips
(Kobaku type)

Characteristics

Most of these are F1 hybrids, the Japanese having been the first to develop turnip hybrids in the late 1950s. They are usually round in shape, though some are slightly flattened. They are white skinned, and have white, crisp, flesh with a mild, very sweet flavour.

The mature turnips can be up to 6 in (15 cm) in diameter, but the beauty is that they can also be pulled when very small—anything from 1–2 in (2.5–5 cm) in diameter, depending on variety. This is when they are sweetest and most tender—at the munch-them-raw stage. The young tops tend to be bright green and well flavoured.

Climate, soil/site

See 'Hinona-kabu'.

Cultivation
When to sow

Outdoors Most of the small white turnips can be sown in spring, late summer and autumn; it is best to

avoid mid-summer sowings when temperatures are high. With some varieties there is a risk of bolting with spring sowings. Check the variety before sowing.
Under cover A sowing can be made in late autumn in unheated greenhouses, polytunnels or a solar frame for a late winter or early spring crop. In Japan late outdoor sowings were traditionally protected with windbreaks made of reeds.

Sowing method, spacing, further care

Seed is normally sown *in situ* about ½ in (1 cm) deep, and thinned to the required distance apart. However, late sowings for the under-cover winter crop can be sown in seed trays and transplanted when young. This has been shown to give higher yields.

It sounds extravagant, but thin to 6 in (15 cm) apart for small turnips, and up to 14 in (35 cm) apart if really large turnips are required. Be sure to keep the plants weed-free, especially in the early stages. Quality will suffer if there is

any check to growth, either from competing weeds or lack of water.

Containers

These small turnips can be grown quite successfully in containers. (See Part 2, Containers.)

Pests and disease

Although fairly disease-resistant, there is some risk of attack from common brassica pests. (See Hinona-kabu, above.)

Harvesting

Germination and growth are rapid, especially in spring and early autumn, when young turnips can sometimes be pulled within 25–30 days of sowing. Large, mature turnips normally take 50–60 days to develop, and up to 3 months for late autumn sowings under cover.

Turnips lose their crispness rapidly after being lifted, so wherever possible lift them just before use, especially for eating raw. They keep reasonably well in a fridge for a few weeks.

These tasty turnips could go a long way towards improving the low standing of turnips in Europe.

Varieties

Of several varieties becoming available in the West, 'Presto' and F1 'Tokyo Cross' have so far proved outstanding.

Ohno Scarlet

This could make a good companion to 'Hinona-kabu', being a roundish turnip with bright scarlet skin and white flesh. It is 3–4 in (8–10 cm) in diameter and about 2.5 in (6 cm)

deep when mature. It is sown in late summer and early autumn for harvesting in early winter. The roots should be thinned so that they are at least 10 in (25 cm) apart.

Oriental saladini (Brassica seedling mixtures)

'Saladini' is the name my husband Don and I have given to the mixtures of salad plants we grow for sale on our small market garden. The saladini is packed in lettuce bags, any one bag having up to twenty ingredients, including tasty young seedlings and colourful edible flowers like calendula or pansies.

The idea for saladini came from the traditional European salad mixtures, such as the French 'mesclun' and Italian 'misticanza', which are sown in patches to give a variety of salad leaves over a long period. The Italians call the small young leaves used in salads 'insalatine'. I misheard this as 'saladini'—hence the name we have adopted.

Seedling leaves of various oriental brassicas often found their way into our saladini—so why not an *oriental saladini* based on oriental brassicas? They seemed tailormade for the purpose: they germi-

nate fast and regrow rapidly after cutting, the young leaves look wonderfully fresh and healthy, and they taste delicious. So I started experimenting with various mixtures. I was delighted with the results. Not only are the mixtures highly productive, but they are a good way of getting to know and sample at least a few of the many oriental brassicas. I am hoping that seedsmen will develop 'off the shelf' mixtures, but there is no reason why we shouldn't mix up our own. (See Mixtures, below.)

Cultivation

Sow the saladini mixture as a cut-and-come-again seedling crop, either broadcast or in wide parallel drills. (See Part 2, Plant raising, Cut-and-come-again, page 155.)

Don't sow too thickly. As a rough guide a broadcast patch would require about ½ oz/sq. yd (12 g/sq. m). Wide parallel drills would require a little less. If the mixture looks too dense when it germinates, thin it out. Depending on when sown, the first cut can be made within 3–4 weeks, when the seedlings are a couple of inches high. In most cases a total of three cuts can be made over a couple of months. In mild winters autumn-sown outdoor crops can be cut through to the following spring—a wonderful source of greens.

When to sow

The best sowing times would be as follows:
Early spring, under cover
Late spring/early summer, outdoors

Use
In the kitchen

Oriental saladini is excellent for salads, either on its own, or combined with other salad plants. It can be dressed with a conventional French dressing, or a Chinese salad dressing (see Recipes, page 183). It can also be cut at a later stage, and cooked like any oriental greens.

Late summer/early autumn, outdoors
Autumn, under cover

Mixtures

The key to an evenly growing mixture is to select vigorous, fast-germinating species and varieties for the main ingredients. Avoid varieties which are slow to germinate, have a tendency to bolt, or would be unable to hold their own in a dense mixture. They must also be well-flavoured, pleasant to eat raw, and attractive looking. The main ingredients can be augmented with smaller quantities of other varieties to add extra colour, texture or flavour.

There is endless scope for experiment. Xotus Seeds in Holland are currently developing stir-frying mixtures, salad mixtures, oriental herb mixtures, and 'spinachy' mixtures, the latter consisting of spinach, amaranthus and ipomea.

If making up your own mixture, measure seeds by weight or by volume, shaking them together in a paper bag before sowing. Letter scales are convenient for weighing small quantities of seed. Or measure them in a tablespoon.

Oriental saladini

BASIC MIXTURE My basic 'recipe' uses 25 per cent of each of the following:

Green or white stemmed pak choi
Mizuna greens
Komatsuna
Non-heading Chinese cabbage (e.g. 'Santo' type)

They each contribute something to the mixture:

Pak choi provides crispy, attractive seedlings.

Mizuna adds a deeper green colour and a decorative feathery leaf.

Komatsuna supplies mild-flavoured bulk.

Non-heading Chinese cabbage adds a much lighter green leaf with a pretty frilliness.

EXTRA INGREDIENTS Smaller quantities of the following can be added to the basic mixture:

For colour
—Red lettuce, for example 'Red Salad Bowl', 'Red Lollo'.
—Red-leaved mustards (though they germinate more slowly and may bolt in spring-sown mixtures).

For texture
—Mibuna mustard (for its strap leaves).

—Edible rape F1 'Bouquet' (for its crêpe-like leaves)

For taste
—Salad rocket (*Eruca sativa*)
—Texsel greens (*Brassica carinata*)
—Spinach

These are only suggestions. There is endless scope for juggling both with the ingredients and with proportions. For example, any one of the 'extras' suggested above could be incorporated into the basic mixture as a main ingredient—reducing each to 20 per cent of the total.

Ornamental cabbages and kales

Latin name   Cabbage: *Brassica oleracea* var *capitata*; Kale: *Brassica oleracea* var *acephala*

Other names in use   Flowering cabbage/kale; variegated borecole; garnishing kale; salad savoy (in the USA)

Mandarin   Hua cai ('flower vegetable');* yu yi gan lan ('feather clothes cabbage'); ye mu dan ('leafy paeony')

Cantonese   Fa choy

Japanese   Ha botan ('leafy paeony')

* This is also used for other vegetables, e.g. cauliflower.

Background

The ornamental cabbages and ornamental kales are variegated forms of common cabbage and kale. Both in common parlance and in seed catalogues, they are often treated as one without differentiation, usually under the name of 'ornamental kale'. They

Ornamental cabbage

have been grown in Europe for centuries, primarily for decorative purposes; today their popularity has spread to the Far East, notably Japan, where the first of the high-quality hybrid varieties were developed.

Characteristics

The ornamental cabbages and kales have two outstanding features: wonderful colours and very decorative foliage. There is a nice account of the range of colours in curly kales in one of the earliest English gardening books, Parkinson's *Paradisus in Sole Terrestis*, written in 1629. Rendered in modern English this reads: 'either wholly of a green colour, or of diverse colours in one plant, as white, yellow, red, purple or crimson, so variably mixed, the leaves being curled on the edges like a ruff band, that it is very beautiful to behold.' He goes

Use

Cut flowers The ornamental cabbages and kales are often used in flower arrangements. A whole head or a small rosette of leaves can be floated in a bowl. The taller varieties of kales can be planted relatively close to get longer, more upright leaves and stems for use as 'cut flowers'. (See Planting, below.)

Pot plants They make ideal winter pot plants, provided they are kept in a cool greenhouse or in a cool situation indoors. (See Climate, below.) Not only are they decorative, but leaves can be picked off for garnish or salads throughout the winter. This doesn't seriously detract from their appearance as the plants will normally continue growing, producing more small leaves. (See also Containers, below.)

In the kitchen

The colourful and beautifully shaped leaves are a marvellous addition to salads. Use small leaves whole and larger leaves shredded, which makes them more tender. They are also ideal for garnishing, especially in autumn and winter when there is less choice of garnishing material. The texture of the leaves depends on the variety and the season. If they seem too coarse to eat raw, blanch them in boiling water for a minute to soften them.

Most people find the ornamental cabbages and kales coarse and poorly flavoured in comparison with ordinary cabbage and other greens, though they *can* be cooked by any recipe for cabbage or kale. Young kale leaves, for example, can be cooked as greens or used in soup.

on to describe a variety which is 'but a little curled on the edges, whose leaves are white, edged with red, or green, edged with white'. All these combinations, and more, can be found in modern varieties of ornamental cabbages and kales.

The leaf forms fall roughly into three categories:
• Rounded, but gently waved or slightly frilled
• Very finely frilled or crinkled, like a curly kale
• Deeply serrated, giving a feathery look
Most of the round-leaved forms are cabbages, while the highly frilled, curly and serrated forms are kales.

The ornamental cabbages and kales never form tight heads, but in some varieties form beautiful, very regular, flat-topped rosettes, up to 12 in (30 cm) in diameter. They could easily be mistaken for giant cabbage roses, the stiff leaves having an unreal, porcelain quality: the foliage could be hand-painted!

There are dwarf, medium and tall forms, height ranging from about 9 in (25 cm) for the dwarf forms to as much as 24 in (60 cm) for the tallest, serrated kales. Dwarf varieties occur mainly in the round-leaved and frilly types, tall varieties among the serrated-leaved kales.
Colour development The deep colours intensify and develop with the onset of cool weather, colour changes being triggered when night temperatures fall to 50–60°F (10–15.5°C). So, while the orna-

mental cabbages and kales are at their most spectacular in autumn, where cool summer nights are experienced they can provide a colourful display during the summer.
Longevity Strictly speaking, the cabbages and kales are biennial, but where picked continually, or where the heads are cut leaving the stalks to resprout, they become 'near perennial', lasting for a couple of seasons albeit in a rather straggly state. Older plants may become branched or develop side shoots. Rosettes of small secondary leaves may also develop, sometimes even on the main stem. These can all be used for garnishing or in salads.

Ornamental kale: leaf of frilled leaf type

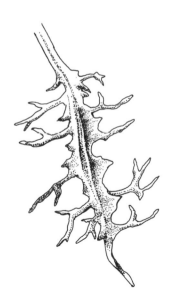

Ornamental kale: leaf of serrated leaved type

Climate

The ornamental cabbages and kales grow best in cool weather, at temperatures below 50°F (10°C). Most varieties can withstand some frost and snow, but will not survive many consecutive nights below freezing. They also deteriorate rapidly if heavy rain is followed by low temperatures. On the whole the serrated-leaved kales are the hardiest: indeed I have known varieties survive 14°F (−10°C) under cover.

Site/soil

Plants for use in summer and early autumn can be grown in an open situation. Plants for use in late autumn and winter will remain in a good condition longer if sheltered from wind. For these plants well-drained soil is very important. They can also be grown under cover (see below).

Ornamental cabbages and kales grow well in poorer soil than most brassicas; in rich soil they become too lush and will not colour up well. However the soil must be well drained and moisture-retentive: working in well-rotted organic matter will help to bring this about. (See Part 2, Soil fertility.)

Decorative value
Ornamental cabbages and kales are used all over the world as bedding plants, from the gardens of Versailles to hotel forecourts in China and Japan. At Kew Gardens a few years ago an inspired combination was the pink-centred, green-edged 'Pink Beauty' ornamental cabbage flanked with a thick band of soft-textured variegated mint. They are generally most effective when planted in clumps, but also look dramatic edging beds or lining paths. Colours are normally strongest in late summer and autumn, when many traditional summer bedding plants are going over. Where winters are mild they can be used for winter bedding schemes.

Cultivation

Propagation from cuttings

Although normally raised from seed, ornamental cabbages and kales can be propagated from cuttings. This is handy if you find a plant with colour combinations you want to perpetuate. Take cuttings of shoots, or young leaves with a piece of stem, and pot them up in small pots. Cuttings taken in spring root within 6 weeks.

When to sow

Plants should be sown early enough to develop into a reasonable size before night temperatures start to drop to around 50°F (10°C). Here in East Anglia we often have a few nights of 50°F as early as July, so I aim to make my first sowings in May and early June.

Main sowing in temperate climates Sow from early to late spring. This will be for plants maturing outdoors in late summer and autumn. The earliest sowings should be made in gentle heat indoors, the optimum temperature for germination being 68°F (20°C).

Late sowing in temperate climates Sow from late spring to early summer. This will be for:
● Plants which will be potted up for winter house plants.
● Plants transplanted into unheated greenhouses in late summer and early autumn. These should be usable from late autumn until the following spring and even early summer, unless indoor temperatures plummet.

Warm areas In areas with mild, virtually frost-free winters, sowings can continue into mid-summer. These plants will provide colour outdoors from winter through to the following spring. Germination is poor at very high temperatures, so seeds may need to be sown somewhere cool, and seedlings kept shaded.

Sowing method

Although ornamental cabbages and kales can be sown *in situ* and thinned to the correct distance, far better quality plants are obtained by sowing in seed trays or modules and transplanting. This is particularly true of the ornamental cabbages.

The recommended procedure if sowing in seed trays is to prick out soon after germination to about 2 in (5 cm) apart. A month later either space them out again about 6 in (15 cm) apart, or pot them up individually in 3–4 in (8–10 cm) pots. If sown in modules they can be planted out direct or, if planting is delayed, potted up into 3–4 in (8–10 cm) pots. (See also Part 2, Plant raising, Use of modules, page 153.).

The ideal stage for planting in the permanent position is when they have five to seven leaves.

Spacing

Plant 12–18 in (30–40 cm) apart, depending on the variety. Where the main requirement is to give a dense display, closer planting is recommended. Where kales are wanted for use as cut flower material, plants can be spaced 6 in (15 cm) apart.

Plant firmly, with a couple of inches of stem below soil level. This gives additional anchorage, and prevents plants from looking 'leggy'. Make sure plants are upright. The decorative effects of a group of ornamental cabbages and kales are completely destroyed if individual plants are lopsided.

Distinguishing between colours Sometimes one variety of cabbage or kale occurs in different forms: predominantly pink, or predominantly white for example. If sold in mixed packets you may want to separate the different colours for planting in contrasting patterns. I've found that most varieties can be identified at the seedling stage. Purple, pink and red varieties have pinkish stems, while green or white varieties have paler, greenish stems.

Further care

Some Japanese catalogues recommend removing some of the outer leaves about a month after planting to improve air circulation between plants. Cut the leaves rather than breaking them, leaving 1–2 in (2–5 cm) of leaf stalk; this heals, minimizing the risk of rots setting in. Where plants are grown in an exposed situation the stems can be earthed up around the base for 3–4 in (8–10 cm) to make them more stable.

An old technique, described in Vilmorin, was to select the best plants in autumn, dig them up, remove the tatty lower leaves, and replant them with their heads at soil level. Presumably they were replanted in a sheltered position to reduce exposure and increase their life expectancy.

Normally no extra feeding is required. Too much nitrogen, in particular, results in thin rather than sturdy plants. If growth is poor after planting, give a liquid feed before the plants start to colour. (See also Part 2, Soil fertility, Liquid feeding, page 144.)

Containers

Ornamental cabbages and kales are more suited to container growing than many brassicas, as they are undemanding about soil conditions. However, they must not be allowed to dry out.

Dwarf and medium-sized varieties are most suitable for containers. Dwarf varieties need a 5–6 in (13–15 cm) pot; medium-sized varieties an 8 in (20 cm) pot. Several plants can be grown closely in a pot or tub. The 'planters' I saw in the United States for ornamental cabbages as autumn house plants were 12 in (30 cm) deep and 14 in (35 cm) diameter; each contained three plants. (See also Part 2, Containers.)

Plant deeply to avoid a bare, 'leggy' look. No harm will come from burying the stem almost up to the head: it depends what kind of effect you are trying to create.

Pests and disease

In theory the variegated cabbages and kales are subject to any of the pests and diseases affecting brassicas, but in practice I've found the only serious problems to be mealy aphid and cabbage caterpillars. The latter are surprisingly hard to spot in the variegated and serrated leaves—the natural serrations being not unlike the ravages of hungry caterpillars. (See also Part 2, Pests and disease.)

Harvesting

The old varieties take four or five months to mature. The faster growing F1 hybrids mature in about three months.

Unless an entire head is wanted for decorative purposes, leaves can be cut a few at a time as required (see Further care, above). Plants resprout and continue growing over many months unless killed by frost.

Cut leaves shortly before required, as they wilt fairly rapidly. If heavy frost is threatened plants can be pulled up by the roots and hung in a frost-free shed for a short period.

Varieties

New varieties are continually becoming available, while some old ones are disappearing. On the whole it is worth paying the extra price for the more vigorous and uniform F1 hybrids. Be guided by seed catalogue descriptions for height, hardiness and colour combinations.

The following are favourites among those I have grown recently.

ROUNDED AND WAVY LEAVED 'Pink Beauty', 'Osaka' series

FINELY FRILLED 'Chidori', 'Red Wave', 'White Wave' ('White Christmas', 'Christmas Fringed White')

DEEPLY SERRATED AND FEATHERY 'Red Feather', 'White Feather', 'Red Peacock', 'White Peacock'

Alfalfa and Chinese clover

Alfalfa has recently become widely known in the West as a 'sprouting' vegetable, but is less well known as a green vegetable. In China a closely related species, known under a variety of names including 'Chinese clover' and 'bur clover' is cultivated. True alfalfa is probably also grown in China—for human consumption as well as a fodder crop—but such is the confusion over names it is hard to tell which accounts refer to alfalfa and which to Chinese clover. In China recently I saw only Chinese clover being grown.

As both are highly nutritious, easily grown and very tasty they deserve to be described briefly.

Alfalfa (lucerne)

Latin name *Medicago sativus*
Mandarin Mu xu
Cantonese Muk suk

Background

Alfalfa has been cultivated all over the world for centuries as a fodder plant, and was probably introduced to China from Central Asia about 100 BC. Several hundred years later the leaves of alfalfa (and/or Chinese clover) were being used as a vegetable.

Characteristics

Alfalfa is a deep-rooting, perennial plant, growing anything from 1–3 ft (30–90 cm) high. Growth is sometimes upright, and occasionally rather sprawly, plants growing low initially then curling upwards. It forms pretty, light green leaflets of three leaves typical of the clover family, and has beautiful purple flower spikes. It is very hardy, normally staying green throughout the winter in temperate climates.

Climate, soil/site

Alfalfa tolerates a wide range of climatic conditions from temperate to sub-tropical, providing, in the latter case, there is at least 14 in (35 cm) of rainfall during the rainy season. Otherwise it grows in drier conditions than most legumes. It does well on light soil.

Decorative value

Alfalfa is quite decorative, espe-

Use

In the West the young growths are used raw in salads or cooked—usually steamed or stir-fried. The young leaves are very nutritious, and are an excellent source of protein and vitamins. For this reason they are being widely used in 'leaf concentrate' nutrition programmes in Third World countries, where leaves are processed with simple equipment to make concentrates to supplement poor diets. The leaves can also be blended with mint to make a nutritious tea. The seeds can be sprouted. (See Seed sprouting, page 132.)

cially when flowering. It can be grown as a low hedge in a vegetable or herb garden, and cut back hard after flowering. After three or four years it usually becomes straggly, and it would be advisable to uproot it and start again.

Cultivation, sowing, harvesting

Sow *in situ*, outdoors in spring, and from late summer to autumn. In temperate climates a sowing can be made under cover in late summer or early autumn for a protected winter crop.

Either broadcast thinly in patches; or sow thinly in 4 in (10 cm) wide drills, the drills as close together as possible; or in rows 3–4 in (7–10 cm) apart. Further thinning is unnecessary. (See also Part 2, Plant raising, Broadcast sowing, page 151.)

Pick your growths when they are 1–2 in (2.5–5 cm) long: the first pickings can usually be made 3–4 weeks after sowing. The leaves become tough as the plants mature, but the plants can be cut back periodically to encourage fresh growth. Overwintered plants provide useful pickings early in the year. Plants will last several years, but once they reach the stage of producing only a handful of young shoots, they should be uprooted, as they will be tough to eat.

Chinese clover

Latin name   *Medicago hispida* (also *M. denticulata*)
Other names in use   Bur clover; toothed bur clover; hairy medick
Mandarin   Cai mu xu ('vegetable alfalfa'); jin hua cai ('golden flower vegetable'); huang hua mu xu ('yellow flowered alfalfa'); cao tou (Shanghai area)
Cantonese   Kam fa tsoi

Background

Chinese clover is a very popular crop around Shanghai, and was introduced to Hong Kong and Taiwan by Shanghai immigrants after the Communist takeover in 1945. On my recent trip to China we only saw it in Shanghai: barrowloads of fresh-looking shoots were a common sight in street markets.

It is a native of sandy and gravelly coastal sites in eastern and southern England, but has been introduced to the rest of Europe, North Africa and Asia, where it has become naturalized. Perhaps the time has come for us to take a leaf from the Chinese book and start to cultivate it.

Characteristics

Chinese clover is a creeping, annual plant, usually about 12 in (30 cm) high, though it can grow up to 2 ft (60 cm). The leaflets are similar in appearance to alfalfa, leaves being slightly oval in shape, and about ½ in (1.5 cm) long. They are smooth on top and hairy beneath. The flowers are yellow.

Cultivation/harvesting

Chinese clover is grown like alfalfa, and similarly is suited to light, well-drained soil. (For sowing times and methods, see alfalfa.)

From an evening chat with a straw-hatted grandpa, his daughter-in-law and the wife of his nephew working on their own plot on the outskirts of Shanghai, I learnt that the first cut can be made about a month after sowing, and a second cut about ten days later. In a good sunny year, they told me, a total of five cuts can be made; but in the current poor year only four cuts had been possible.

Harvest the shoot tips when they have no more than three or four full-sized leaves: the younger the tips the better the flavour. They must always be picked before the plants flower. The stems can be dried for use out of season.
Green manure Being a legume, Chinese clover can be used as a green manure, the root nodules being a source of nitrogen. After several cuts have been made it is ploughed or dug in to improve the soil's fertility.

Use
In the kitchen

Leaf tips, leaf stalks, and tender leaves are all usable. Chinese clover is cooked in various ways: in soups, boiled, steamed, and stir-fried. A Taiwanese recipe book suggests stir-frying with pork slices, or alternatively with bean curd, the dish being thickened with cornstarch. Both dishes are described as delicious. F H King, in his magnificent account of travels in Asia early this century, *Farmers of Forty Centuries*, describes a meal on a canal steamer where each passenger was brought a bowl of steamed rice and a tiny dish of Chinese green clover, 'nicely cooked and seasoned'.

Chinese clover

Amaranthus

Family *Amaranthacea*
Latin name *Amaranthus gangeticus**
Other names in use Chinese spinach; edible amaranth; edible
   amaranth spinach; bayam (Malaysia and Indonesia); calaloo
   (Caribbean); klaroen (Surinam)
Mandarin Xian cai
Cantonese Yin choi/in tsoi
Japanese Hi-yu-na, Java hohrensoh

* *A. tricolor* and *A. oleraceus* are synonyms of *A. gangeticus*. *A. dubius*, *A. mangostanus*, and *A. spinosus* are also species of leaf amaranth.

Background

The amaranth family is a large group of plants, originating in the American, African and Asian tropics, but now spread all over the world. They are exceptionally nutritious, and from ancient times seed and leaves of cultivated and wild forms have been used by man for food, medicine and animal fodder. Many exhibit striking colours in leaves and flowers, and have been grown as ornamental plants in the West.

For practical purposes the amaranths can be divided into the following groups according to their main use today:
—Leafy amaranths
—Grain amaranths
—Decorative amaranths
—Weeds
In fact the leaves of all the amaranths are edible so, from the vegetable point of view, *any* can be considered a vegetable. The 'leafy amaranths', however, are the species most worth cultivating for their leaves, though in many parts of the world the weed amaranths are eaten. (See also Weed amaranths, page 55. The grain and decorative amaranths are outside the scope of this book.)

Characteristics

There is tremendous variation in the amaranths grown as leafy vegetables, but all are erect, branching, short-lived annuals. The average height of mature plants is about 14 in (35 cm), though some grow up to 5 ft (150 cm) when flowering.

Amaranthus

The leaves are soft textured, and go limp quickly after being picked. They may be pointed or round, light green, dark green, green with a reddish centre or red markings on the leaves, deep red, or variegated. In the old garden variety 'Joseph's Coat', often grown as an ornamental plant, the leaf variegations are dark green, brown, red and golden yellow. Leaves also vary in size, the largest being fairly broad and up to about 6 in (15 cm) long. In some the leaves are very much smaller. Large-leaved forms seem to be more vigorous than smaller leaved. Stems are soft and juicy, very often blotched with red.

Many of the leaf amaranths have brilliantly coloured flowering spikes and leaves, and can double as decorative plants. The flower spikes are composed of many tiny flowers, colours ranging from yellow green to deep red. They are usually a few inches long, smaller than in the grain and decorative amaranths, and generally upright rather than drooping.

Use

Both the leaves and stems are edible, and delicious.
Flavour When picked young, amaranth has an excellent, distinct flavour. Friends have described it variously as 'like artichokes', and 'spinach with a bit of a twang'. The flavour becomes stronger and slightly hot in older plants. I find little difference in taste between the different-coloured leaves— but various communities have strong preference for one type or another. Indians, for example, prefer the green-leaved and Chinese the red-leaved. The leaves are very nutritious: rich in protein, iron, calcium and vitamins A and C.

In the kitchen

Very young leaves can be used raw in salads. Colourful red leaves look most attractive.

Young stems are tender and are used as they are; with thicker stems the ends may be tough, and the bottom inch or so should be cut off. If the stems are substantial they are best cut into 2-in (5-cm) lengths and cooked first. Older, thicker stems can be peeled. The Taiwanese rub the leaves to make them softer.

In cooked dishes amaranthus is used very much like spinach and can be substituted in any spinach recipe; it cooks faster than spinach, so take care not to overcook. It is best treated simply: steamed, stir-fried, mixed in meat or fish dishes. My first home-grown amaranthus was stir-fried with garlic chives and pronounced excellent. In China it is used very widely in soup— the leaves sometimes being eaten separately after being cooked in the soup. In southeast Asia amaranthus is often flavoured with mint.

(See also Recipes, page 186.)

Climate

The leafy amaranths only grow well at reasonably high temperatures—ideally 68–77°F (20–25°C). They will thrive at temperatures over 86°F (30°C). In northern latitudes they normally need to be grown under cover. In unheated greenhouses they may romp in good summers, but will linger rather miserably in poor summers. They will tolerate fairly dry conditions.

Soil/site

The ideal soil is light, sandy, fertile and well drained, though amaranths can crop well in heavier soil. The more fertile the soil, the better they crop. They will, however, tolerate fairly acid soils.

In northern latitudes a sunny, sheltered situation is essential; in warmer climates amaranthus can be grown in slightly shaded situations. In China it is sometimes intercropped between tall climbing crops such as gourds or beans.

Decorative value

The red- and green-leaved and variegated 'leafy' amaranths are decorative when growing. Provided they are in a warm situation, they would not look amiss in flower beds.

Cultivation

Amaranthus is normally grown from seed, but can be propagated from cuttings.

When to sow

There is never any point in sowing amaranthus too early. The minimum soil temperature for germination is 50°F (10°C), although germination is best at temperatures over 68°F (20°C).

In temperate climates sow indoors in late spring or early summer, after all risk of frost is over. In exceptionally warm summers it may be possible to sow outdoors in mid-summer, or transplant seedlings raised in modules. In heated greenhouses the first sowing can be made very early in spring.

In warm climates *in situ* sowings can be made outdoors from spring to late summer.

Sowing methods

The seed is very small, so to make sowing easier and speed germination it is sometimes mixed with dry sand, moistened, and put in a warm dark place for 24 hours before sowing. The seed/sand mixture is then sown normally. Amaranthus germinates best in the dark, so cover seed well after sowing. (NB: The seed is so small partly because commercial seed has been cleaned and de-husked. If you save your own seed it will be in a natural state and still have its husk, and will be easier to handle.)

Some varieties, especially the larger-leaved ones, are apt to flower prematurely when transplanted, so wherever feasible amaranthus is sown *in situ* and thinned to the required spacing. Alternatively, sow in modules or small pots. (See Part 2, Plant raising, Use of modules, page 153.) Sow several seeds per module, thinning to one when seedlings are about ½ in (1 cm) high and have 2–3 seedling leaves, a stage generally reached 2–3 weeks after sowing.

Propagation from cuttings

Amaranthus is also easily propagated from cuttings. Cuttings can be taken from non-flowering side shoots or young growths. Use plants bought in markets, or, if you simply want to increase stock, your own plants.

Spacing and harvesting methods

Amaranthus can be grown and harvested in the various ways given below, the harvesting method determining the spacing. Any amaranthus can be treated as a cut-and-come-again crop. (See also Part 2, Plant raising, Cut-and-come-again, page 155.)

HARVESTING AS LARGE SEEDLINGS I saw this method on a Taiwanese allotment. The seedlings are broadcast and cut when 4 in (10 cm) high.

For a continuous supply regular sowings can be made at two-week intervals, although there will be some regrowth of the seedlings.

PULLING THE YOUNG PLANT WHOLE Plants are grown fairly close together, and pulled up by the roots for use. They are often marketed with roots attached. Ideally, plants are spaced 3–4 in (8–10 cm) apart each way. They can either be sown in close rows, thinning to the correct distance or, if more convenient, sown in rows 10–12 in (25–30 cm) apart, thinning to 3 in (8 cm) apart in the rows. Alternatively they can be transplanted carefully. Thinnings can be eaten.

Plants are generally pulled when 8–10 in (20–25 cm) high, on average 6–8 weeks after sowing, but this will depend on temperature. They can be pulled younger if required.

CONTINUAL HARVESTING, SEMI-MATURE PLANTS Plants are spaced a little further apart, and young leaves and stems are cut continually over a long period. Average spacing would be 5–7 in (13–18 cm) apart each way; though plants could be as close as 2 in (5 cm) apart in rows 10 in (25 cm) apart. Precise spacing depends on the variety: larger-leaved, faster growing varieties need the more generous spacing.

Harvesting can start when plants are anything from 4–6 in (10–15 cm) high. Cut the whole plant back to about 1½ in (3 cm) above soil level, being sure to leave the basal leaves and some stem, or no new growth will be made. The plant regrows rapidly. Alternatively, cut the leaves and stem which form a cluster or rosette at the top of the plant. This encourages the development of side shoots along the main stem, which can be picked in turn.

Growth will depend on temperature, but using these methods harvesting can continue over several months for the smaller-leaved varieties, extending to the whole growing season for vigorous large-leaved varieties. Regular picking is essential to prevent the stems from becoming tough. Remove any flowers which appear.

LEAF AND SIDE SHOOT HARVESTING, LARGE PLANTS This is the system used in tropical countries, where there is a tradition of 'gathering' rather than cultivating vegetables. Plants are grown up to 2 ft (60 cm) apart each way, or spaced 16 in (40 cm) apart in rows 32 in (80 cm) apart. They are allowed to grow tall—even up to 6 ft (2 m) high, before harvesting starts. Any flowers which have developed are removed, and leaves and side shoots are harvested. Plants grown this way have strong reserves, and will continue producing into late autumn. The system has been used successfully in unheated greenhouses in Europe.

Further care

If the soil is reasonably fertile no feeding should be necessary. However, yields will increase if occasional nitrogenous liquid feeds are given. (See Soil fertility, Liquid feeding, page 144.)

Although amaranthus may bolt prematurely if allowed to dry out completely, my crop performed well in this summer's dry conditions.

Amaranthus seems to grow best in loose soil, so regular hoeing is advisable to prevent the soil from becoming compacted.

Never allow plants to flower and drop seed, as may well happen towards the end of the season. Amaranthus grown under cover, or outdoors in a warm climate, is liable to seed itself the following year and can easily become a weed.

Containers

Provided the soil is kept moist, leafy amaranthus can be grown in containers in conservatories or unheated greenhouses. Use a method where the plants are harvested young or semi-mature. The more decorative, green- and red-leaved varieties can look effective in containers.

Pests and disease

The most likely problems in temperate climates are damping off diseases affecting seedlings and young plants. (See also Part 2, Pests and disease.) In cold summers my plants have developed hitherto unidentified brown, rusty spots on outer leaves towards the end of the season. The only remedy seemed to be to strip off the affected leaves.

In warmer climates plants may be attacked by caterpillars and stem borers, and leaves and stems by the wet-rot fungus *Choenophora*.

Varieties

There is enormous confusion over both the Latin and English names of the different species and varieties of amaranth. Current seed catalogues and books use different names for the same variety and the same name for several varieties.

'Large-leaved Chinese' Light green variety; broad, rather lumpy leaves, often 5 in long and 4 in broad (13 × 10 cm). Can grow over 5 ft (1.5 m) tall. Considered a variety of *A. dubius*; widely grown in greenhouses in Europe.

'Small-leaved Indian' Small variety, averaging 3–4 ft (90–120 cm) high. Darkish green leaves on average 2 in long, ¾ in wide (5 × 2 cm), sometimes with purplish blotches. Considered a variety of *A. spinosus*; being grown successfully in Europe.

'Tampala' Very popular green-leaved, American cultivar. Name sometimes used generically for all leafy amaranths.

'White amaranth' Name used for several varieties with very pale green leaves and pale stems, grown and marketed by the Chinese and Japanese.

'Red amaranth' Used very loosely for both variegated green- and red-leaved 'leaf amaranth', and red-leaved forms of grain amaranth.

(The varieties 'Early Splendour', 'Red Stripe' and 'Joseph's Coat' are popular ornamental leafy amaranths, which can be cultivated for use.)

Weed amaranths

A. alba; *A. graecizans*; *A. lividus*; *A. retroflexus* (pigweed)

These are all edible, wild species of amaranthus, found in northern latitudes. *Amaranthus lividus* was cultivated in Europe in the sixteenth and seventeenth centuries, but was subsequently only used to feed pigs. There are a great many more species in warmer climates.

Basella

Family *Basellaceae*
Latin names *Basella rubra* (also *B. alba* and *B. cordifolia*, see below)
Other names in use Malabar spinach/nightshade; Ceylon spinach; climbing spinach; Indian/Surinam spinach
Mandarin Luo kui; mu er cai ('wood ear vegetable'); lu luo kui (green basella); zi luo kui (purple basella); ruan jian cai ('soft juice leaf'); yan zhi dou ('rouge bean')*
Cantonese San choi/shaan tsoi; lok kwai/lor kwai; hung tang tsoi
Japanese Tsuru-murasaki

* There are many other local names, referring graphically to its juicy, slippery and colourful properties.

Use

Leaves, leaf stalks and stems all have a very pleasant mild spinach flavour, at their best when young and fresh looking. An unusual characteristic of the leaves and stems is their mucilaginous quality. (See In the kitchen below.) They are very nutritious, being a rich source of minerals and vitamins. Young leaves and stems can be used raw in salads.

Basella

Background

Basella is probably Indian in origin, but has been cultivated for centuries in China. All over the tropics it is a very popular domestic vegetable, as it is one of the easiest of the 'spinachy' leaf plants to grow. It was probably introduced to Europe in the early nineteenth century, where it was cultivated as a stove house plant. In China it is also an important medicinal plant. All parts are used: cooked leaves and stems as a safe and mild laxative, the cooked roots as a remedy for diarrhoea. What more can you ask from one plant? Moreover, juice from the fruits has for centuries been used as a red dye, for colouring food, in rouge, in inks for official seals and so on.

Characteristics

Basella is a vigorous climbing vine. In humid tropics it is a perennial, the vines growing anything from 10–20 ft (3–6 m). The stems can become very thick. In cooler climates, where it is grown as a half-hardy annual, it is a much smaller plant, dying at the end of the season.

The leaves are thick and glossy, and are often described as fleshy or rubbery. There is considerable variation: they can be smooth or wrinkled, broad, oval, pointed or blunt. They are usually 4–5 in (10–12.5 cm) wide and about the same length, but can be as much as 10 in (25 cm) wide. The green forms are a beautiful bright green, the red forms an attractive coppery colour.

Small purple and white flowers are formed on spikes towards the end of the season. The colours tend to change from white tinged with pink to green, then to a reddish colour. The small, glossy berries are red initially, maturing to purplish black.

Types

There are three distinct forms of basella, with the inevitable argument about whether they are different species, or merely different varieties of the same species. The consensus seems to be to describe them as follows:

Basella rubra The whole plant is tinged with red, including the stems. The leaves are oval shaped. This is less popular and less widely cultivated than the green form.

Basella rubra* var *alba The leaves and stems are green. The leaves are oval or almost round. This is the most commonly cultivated variety.

Basella cordifolia The broad, dark green leaves have a somewhat elongated heart shape. Although allegedly a very productive variety, it is less commonly grown, and seeds are not often available.

In practice, packets of seed often seem to be a mixture of the first two types above.

Climate

A humid tropical climate is ideal for basella, but it will grow well wherever temperatures are high. It will not stand any frost. It is sensitive to daylength, in that it will only flower when daylength is less than 12 hours, i.e. after midsummer in northern latitudes. It grows much more rapidly when this point is

In the kitchen

Leaves and stems are cut into reasonably sized pieces for cooking. If the stalks have become tough remove the ends; similarly the midribs can be removed from older leaves. Never overcook basella or the texture becomes slimy. A little vinegar is often added when cooking to reduce the sliminess—though I have never found it necessary. Like spinach, the green forms retain their bright green colour when cooked.

Basella is cooked in various ways: by any method used for spinach; stir-fried; added to soups or stews, so ensuring no nutrients are lost. In China we had a simple but delicious dish of basella stir-fried with a little fresh garlic and salt. American friends enjoy it blanched and dipped in a little vinegar.

With its mucilaginous quality, basella is an excellent thickening agent. It can be used in meat stews and soups as a substitute for okra—another natural 'thickener'. The Chinese frequently make 'slippery soup' from basella, flavoured with ginger, bean curd, and hard-boiled egg.

(See also Recipes, page 187.)

reached. It tolerates high rainfall.

We are pushing our luck growing basella outdoors in northern latitudes—though it can be done in warm situations. It can be grown reasonably successfully in unheated greenhouses, and very successfully in heated greenhouses. Provided day temperatures remain above about 59°F (15°C) it will continue growing even in low winter light, and will tolerate night temperatures occasionally falling below about 50°F (10°C).

Soil/site

Basella grows on a wide range of soil types, but does best on a sandy loam. Compacted soils should be avoided. Although it tolerates fairly poor soil, it is far more productive in fertile soil rich in organic matter. Soil must be moisture-retentive, as the plant suffers badly if short of water.

In temperate climates only grow it outdoors in a south-facing situation, for example at the foot of a wall, provided there is adequate moisture. In hot climates it will grow in partial shade. When grown under glass, make sure the leaves don't get scorched.

Decorative value

Where it is hot enough to grow basella outdoors the red form looks very striking growing up bean poles or over a trellis. With its brilliant glossy leaves it can be an effective conservatory plant. Either treat it as a climber and tie it to piping or wires so the shoots can dangle down, or grow it as a trailing plant in pots on staging. Basella can also be grown in hanging baskets, provided it is cut fairly frequently to keep it within bounds.

Cultivation

Basella is normally raised from seed, though it can be propagated from cuttings, and grown as a perennial.

Sowing method

Sow in late spring or early summer in a heated propagator, at 65–70°F (18–21°C). (When basella was first introduced to Europe it was sown on a hotbed.) Seed normally germinates within 10–21 days, but germination can be accelerated by soaking seed for 24 hours before sowing.

Basella will establish itself faster after planting out if raised in small pots. So either sow in seed trays, eventually potting up in 3-in (7.5-cm) pots, or sow in modules. If they start to look starved in modules, it may be necessary to move them into small pots. (See also Part 2, Plant raising, Sowing indoors, page 152 and Use of modules, page 153.) After germination grow them on at temperatures of 60–65°F (15–19°C) if possible.

Planting

Plant them out when between 4–8 in (10–20 cm) high. Never plant into cold soil, or they are likely to be attacked by fungus diseases. If they are being grown outside, plant well after the danger of frost is past, after hardening off thoroughly.

Spacing and harvesting methods

Basella can be grown in the various ways given below, the harvesting method determining the spacing. The first harvest can usually be made about a month after planting.
AS DWARF, BUSHY PLANTS Space plants about 16 in (40 cm) apart. When they are approximately 12 in (30 cm) high, nip out the growing point to encourage the development of side shoots.

The Chinese delay harvesting until the side shoots are about 12 in (30 cm) long, but they can be picked at any length from about 5 in (13 cm) long. Cut the side shoots, leaving the two basal leaves on the stem. Plants need to be picked fairly hard to encourage the development of large leaves, but must never be stripped entirely. Either pick a few shoots at a time, or pick them all, allowing approximately 3 weeks between one picking and the next.
AS CLIMBING PLANTS Space plants 9–12 in (23–30 cm) apart. Once they are about 10 in (25 cm) high they will need support. They can be tied to canes, or twisted around string suspended from above. In Philadelphia I saw them happily growing up traditional climbing bean supports. Allow them to grow to the top of the support before nipping out the growing point, which will stimulate the production of more sideshoots.

Leaves develop on the main stem, and these can be harvested as soon as they are a reasonable size, but never strip the plant entirely. In due course side shoots develop: harvest these as for the dwarf plants above. The climbing system allows for continuous harvesting and is very productive, plants cropping over several months.

In warm climates basella is usually planted 9–12 in (23–30 cm) apart at the foot of a 3–6 ft (1–2 m) high trellis. Where several rows are grown they would be spaced at least 4 ft (120 cm) apart.
AS TRAILING PLANTS Space plants about 18 in (45 cm) apart each way, and allow them to trail over the ground like trailing marrows. Pick the longest shoots regularly to keep the plants within bounds. Plants can also be left to scramble over a fence.

Raising from cuttings

In Asia basella is usually raised from cuttings. It can be propagated from leafy shoots bought in a market. Use stem cuttings about 8 in (20 cm) long, remove the lower leaves and bury the cutting at least one node deep in sandy compost. Cuttings root faster if a hormone rooting agent is used.

Grown as a perennial

In the tropics basella is grown as a perennial, replanting the rootstocks or crowns each year, a method also used in Spain.

Further care

If growth seems poorly or leaves start to look yellow rather than a glossy green, apply a liquid feed. Where plants are being cropped heavily, they can be fed after each harvesting. (See also Part 2, Soil fertility, Liquid feeding, page 144.)

Containers

Basella can be grown in large pots at least 10 in (25 cm) diameter, in growing bags, or hanging baskets.

Pests and disease

Basella is rarely attacked by insect pests, partly on account of the thick cuticle (outer layer) of the leaves. Slugs may attack young plants.

In cold and damp conditions the plants are susceptible to damping off diseases and mildew, and botrytis may set in if they are harvested when wet. In these cases it is probably not worth growing the crop. (See also Part 2, Pests and disease.)

Beans

Family *Leguminoseae*

Several picturesque types of beans are grown in China, but with the exception of Asiatic forms of the European broad or fava bean, they are all much more sensitive to cold than the French and runner beans we already grow. For that reason it is unlikely that oriental beans will become major garden crops in temperate climates. So what follows is for the adventurous gardener wanting the challenge of something different. In areas blessed with high summer temperatures oriental beans can grow well; but where temperatures are lower they will have to be coaxed into bearing in greenhouses and sunny corners.

All the oriental beans can be cooked in the same way as French beans, when fresh, or like haricot beans when dried. Simmering them in stock gives added flavour. It is inadvisable to eat any beans raw, as they sometimes contain toxic substances. These are broken down in cooking.

Bean seeds display enormous variation in size, colour and markings, even *within* a variety. So don't be surprised if samples seem quite different from one year to the next: it is a very common occurrence.

Adzuki bean

Latin name *Phaseolus angularis* (*Vigna angularis*)
Other names in use Chinese red bean
Mandarin Hong xiao dou; ('red little bean'); chi dou ('red bean')
Japanese Azuki

Background and characteristics

Adzuki has always been an important bean in Japan, where it ranks second only to soya bean. It is an annual plant, making an upright bush about 2 ft (60 cm) high, rather like a dwarf French bean. The pods are short, from 2½–5 in (6–12 cm) long, containing up to a dozen roundish red (occasionally black) beans, about ¼ in (0.5 cm) long. The flowers are an attractive primrose colour.

Climate, soil/site

Adzuki beans are not frost-hardy, but show more adaptability to colder temperatures than some beans. They could be grown outdoors in a Mediterranean climate, but where summers are cooler, grow them in greenhouses or cold frames. Always choose a sheltered, warm position. They are short-day plants, flowering and forming beans from mid-summer onwards in northern latitudes.

Adzuki can be grown on light or heavy soil, provided it is well drained, but will not tolerate alkaline (chalky) soil. It is said to be fairly drought resistant, and relatively immune to pest and disease problems.

Cultivation

Temperate climate Sow in late spring, pre-germinating seed on moist paper towelling to give it a headstart. (See Part 2, Plant raising,

Use
In the kitchen

The young pods can be used like French beans, but in China and Japan are grown mainly for the bean seeds, which are exceptionally sweet. They are made into a paste which is used in deserts, pastries and even soft drinks. In various Indian recipes they are simmered until tender, puréed and mixed with spices. They are also used in soups. The seeds can be sprouted. (See Seed sprouting, page 135. Also, Recipes, page 186.)

Germination test, page 150.) Sow at a temperature of at least 60°F (15°C), in a heated propagator if necessary. Sow either in seed trays, potting on later into small pots if necessary, or in modules. (See also Plant raising, Sowing indoors, page 152.)

Harden off well before planting outside. Delay planting until the

soil temperature has reached at least 60°F (15°C), and there is no risk of frost. Space plants 10 in (25 cm) apart each way, or grow them about 3 in (7 cm) apart in rows 18 in (45 cm) apart.
Warm climates Sow *in situ*, about 1 in (2.5 cm) deep, spacing as above. Two or three seeds can be sown per station, thinning to the two best after germination.

Pests and disease

Adzuki beans are said to be relatively free of pests and disease.

Harvesting

Where small pods are required the plants should be picked frequently. To harvest the dry beans pull up the plant at the end of the season and hang it indoors, or in a greenhouse, to dry thoroughly before shelling the beans.

Varieties

'**Express**' Selected for northern climates by Johnnys Seeds (USA). Can be harvested 118 days after sowing: a most useful new variety.

Lablab

Latin names   *Lablab niger*, *Dolichos lablab* (also *Lablab vulgaris*, *Dolichos purpureus*)
Other names in use   Hyacinth bean; Egyptian bean; bonavist bean
Mandarin   Bian dou ('flat bean'); rou dou ('meat bean'); que dou
Cantonese   Pin tau; tseuk tau
Japanese   Fujimame

Background

Lablab has been grown in China for centuries, and is still a very popular plant, often grown scrambling over fences and trellises near the house. Because it is so prolific it has earned the nickname 'Seven Sons': one plant could keep a family supplied—in the days when Chinese families were large!

In the West the purple varieties are becoming appreciated for their decorative value: the purple and lilac flowers and gleaming dark pods are a wonderful sight. In 1987 I saw it romping in the famous Longwood Gardens in Philadelphia, entwined with rambler roses. A relative newcomer, it may have been introduced by Asian immigrants. I have also seen lablab growing outdoors (albeit struggling) in the Louvain botanic garden in Belgium, which suggests it could at least be grown in conservatories and greenhouses in cool climates. Breeding work is underway to develop varieties better adapted to cool conditions.

Characteristics

Lablab can be either an annual or a short-lived perennial. It is usually a climbing plant, growing up to about 8 ft (2.4 m) in temperate climates, but far more in the tropics. Sometimes it is allowed to romp into a sprawling bush. There is also a dwarfish form about 3 ft (1 m) high.

The lablab shows enormous variation in its flowers, pods and leaves. The flowers, borne in pretty spikes, vary in colour from white to rich purple. Leaves can be green or purplish green. The pods in the

Use

Lablab is used both fresh and dried as a fodder plant. Immature pods, young green seeds, leaves and tubers are all edible.

In the kitchen

The young immature pods are used whole or sliced (older pods may need stringing). They can be cooked by any methods suitable for French beans, and are good in curries. The purple varieties are considered the best flavoured, though they tend to be lower yielding than the green. Young leaves can be eaten raw, older leaves are cooked.

The Chinese dry the immature pods for winter use by putting them in very hot water for a few minutes, then drying them in the sun until they can be cracked into pieces. The mature seeds can also be dried. They must be cooked well before use, as they contain toxins. Rather like soya bean, they can be cooked for a very long time and made into a bean curd, which can be fermented, or ground into flour for baking or frying.

(See also Recipes, page 192.)

most common type (sometimes known as *seim*) are flat, blunt, slightly curved, fairly thick and on average 3–4 in (8–10 cm) long. There are green and purple forms. This type is mainly cultivated for the edible pod. So is the somewhat

Lablab bean

longer, thinner, round podded type (known as *valour* or *val*). Another type with shortish, flattish, inflated pods (known as *papri* or *popetti*), is mainly cultivated for the seeds.

Climate, soil/site

Although lablab will tolerate a mean annual temperature as low as 48°F (9°C), it is happiest at temperatures in the high 80s (28–30°C). Once established it has considerable drought resistance, and can be grown in areas of low rainfall.

Varieties differ in their sensitivity to daylength, some only flowering in long days of early summer, some in the shorter days of late summer and autumn.

It can be grown on relatively poor, acid or alkaline soil, provided it is well drained. The roots fix nitrogen well, and lablab is sometimes planted as ground cover to prevent soil erosion.

Cultivation, harvesting

For sowing, see Adzuki beans, above. Plants should be spaced 12 in (30 cm) apart.

Where grown in a greenhouse, make sure lablab has something strong to climb on. In hot climates it is often planted at the foot of a fence or a wall or even allowed to scramble up trees. As a field crop it is sometimes allowed to sprawl over the ground.

Lablab can take anything from 90–150 days before it is ready for harvesting. Pick the young pods continually.

Stop press! Plants grown in my polytunnel this summer showed remarkable resistance to red spider mite.

Soya bean

Latin name *Glycine max*
Other names in use Vegetable bean; vegetable soybean
Mandarin da dou (general term for soya bean). The different coloured beans are known as: huang dou ('yellow bean'); hei dou ('black bean'); qing dou ('green bean'). 'Mao dou' ('hairy bean') is used for the young, fresh green beans.
Cantonese Tai tau; wong tau; hak tau
Japanese Daizu; eda mame

Background

The ancestor of the modern soya bean grew wild in eastern Asia. The Chinese have cultivated soya for more than 4000 years, in the course of time developing a remarkable range of uses for it. For centuries soya oil fuelled the lamps and stoves of China. Today refined soya oil is used as a cooking oil, in margarine and in the manufacture of soaps, paints and plastics.

Due to its very high levels of protein, oil, calcium and vitamins soya bean has become one of the most widely grown crops in the world, aptly described as 'meat without the bones'.

Characteristics

Soya bean is an annual, upright plant 12–30 in (30–75 cm) high, prettier than most dwarf beans. The mature leaves form three-leaved leaflets; leaves, stems and young pods are rather downy. The white or lilac flowers are very small. The pods are 1½–3 ins (3–7 cm) long, and generally about ½ in (1 cm) wide. The seed can be green, black, yellow, or creamy white, depending on the variety.

Types

Green seeded These are the most tender and best flavoured, both fresh and dry. They are recom-

Use

The green beans from pods which are mature but not dry are used as a fresh vegetable (see also Harvesting, below), either simply steamed, or mixed into stir-fries, or cooked by any recipe suitable for lima or broad (fava) beans. They are excellent mixed with prawns.

The dried beans are used whole or split, are sprouted, and are ground into flour. They are also processed, both domestically and industrially, to produce soya milk and bean curd (tofu)—the latter in blancmangey slabs, sheets and strips. Then there are the fermented products: soya sauce, the paste miso, tempeh, and fermented black beans. Soya beans are also being converted into the meat substitute known so unappetizingly as 'textured vegetable protein'.

mended where soya is grown for the young shelled beans. Some of the green varieties are among those best adapted to northern climates. On account of their tenderness, they are becoming increasingly popular in China.
Black seeded These are used dried. They are tastier and easier to

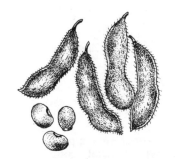
Soya bean pods and beans

cook than the yellow bean. Various products, for example black bean sauce, are made from black beans. **Yellow seeded** Yellow and light-coloured beans are mainly used to make soya milk, flour, bean curd, sauce etc. and for sprouting. If used as a vegetable they need to be soaked for 5 hours beforehand, preferably changing the water half way through, then boiled vigorously for 20 minutes.

Climate

Temperature and daylength are both important factors in growing soya beans successfully. They are warmth-loving crops, but can grow as far north as latitude 58 (north Scotland) provided the mean July temperature is within the 61–64°F (16–18°F) band.

TEMPERATURE REQUIREMENTS Soya has different temperature requirements at different stages, the highest temperatures being necessary at the flowering stage. As a rough guide, the following temperatures are considered 'sufficient'. Optimum temperatures would be about 5 degrees higher, but *some* growth will take place at somewhat lower temperatures.

Germination 53–57°F (12–14°C)
Flowering 66°F (19°C)
Seeds maturing 55–61°F (13–16°C)

DAYLENGTH The original varieties of soya bean only flowered and developed beans in the long days of early summer. The cold springs of northern latitudes did not give them enough time to reach the flowering stage. However, varieties have now been developed which flower in short days from midsummer onwards. These are more suitable for northern latitudes.

In the United States a range of varieties has been bred to suit the different latitudes encompassed by the country. Varieties are also being developed which tolerate lower temperatures and mature faster, so are suited to areas with a short growing season. Most require 3–4 months from sowing to maturity.

Soil/site

Soya beans need reasonably fertile, loamy, slightly acid soil. Always grow them in a warm, sheltered position. In cold areas grow them in frames or unheated greenhouses, or at least sow or plant under cloches to give protection in the early stages.

Cultivation

For sowing, see Adzuki beans above.

Spacing

Soya beans can be grown fairly close, and various spacing systems seem equally successful, i.e.:

- Single plants 3 in (8 cm) apart in rows 12–14 in (30–35 cm) apart.
- Two plants per station 8 × 10 in (20 × 25 cm) apart.
- Two plants per station 9–14 in (23–35 cm) apart each way.

Root inoculant

To stimulate growth and increase yields, seeds are sometimes treated with a bacterial root inoculate. This is unnecessary on acid soils with a pH of 5 or lower, but can be helpful on soils with a pH of 5.5 and above. The inoculum should be specific to soya beans, though sometimes a general legume inoculum is used. The beans are either treated before sowing or the inoculum is applied to the soil when planting.

Further care/pests and disease

Soya bean plants are naturally fairly erect, but benefit from being earthed up when the plants have about four or five leaves. Otherwise support them with small sticks or canes if it seems necessary.

Water enough to keep the soil moist. Over-watering, and too much nitrogen, can result in excessive foliage being produced at the expense of beans.

Soya beans seem to be relatively free of serious damage from pests and disease. Poor weather is the main enemy. They simply will not thrive in cold conditions.

Harvesting

Soya beans can be harvested at two stages.

1. GREEN SHELLING BEAN STAGE Wait until the pods are plump, but still green, then pull up the whole plant. To shell the beans, boil or steam the pods for 10 to 15 minutes, depending on the size. They will split open releasing the beans, which retain their pretty light green colour and have a delicious flavour.

2. DRY BEAN STAGE This would normally be anything from 25–30 days after the green shelling bean stage. Wait until the leaves have dropped and most of the plant has turned brown, then pull up the plants. Hang them in a warm place indoors or in a greenhouse to dry them completely. To extract the seed, Johnny's Seeds in the USA suggest holding a few plants by the roots and banging them on the inside of a barrel. Store them in jars in a cool, dry place.

Varieties

New varieties for northern climates are constantly being introduced. The following are currently recommended by Johnny's Seeds, who have done a lot of work on introducing soya beans to the gardening public.

(*Note:* The varieties of soya beans used for animal feed are different from those used for human consumption.)

'**Butterbeans**' Green-seeded; high-yielding; 90 days to green shelling stage.

'**Envy**' Green-seeded; very early, but lower yielding. Ideal for short seasons; 75 days to green shelling stage.

'**Black Jet**' Black-seeded; early maturing; 105 days to dry seed stage.

'**Fiskeby V**' Yellow-seeded; Swedish bred extra early variety; 91 days to dry bean stage.

Yard long bean

Latin names *Vigna sesquipedalis* (or *Vigna sinensis* var *sesquipedalis*; *Dolichos sesquipedalis*)

Other names in use Chinese long bean; Chinese pea; snake bean; asparagus pea or bean (see also note overleaf)

Mandarin Chang dou ('long bean'); cai dou ('vegetable bean'); jiang dou; chang jiang dou

Cantonese Cheung kong tau; dau kok

Japanese Sasage

Background

The yard long bean either originated in China or was introduced in prehistoric times. It is very popular there today. It is in the 'cow pea' group of vegetables, and is closely related to the common cow pea, *Vigna sinensis* var *sinensis*. This is the dwarf bean which was introduced into the southern United States by the slave trade, and is still grown, mainly for the famous dried beans known as 'black-eyed peas'.

Although the yard long bean is unlikely to yield heavily in cool climates it is fun to grow, not least because you can almost *see* the beans lengthen, inch by inch, day by day. In the warm summer of 1989 we picked many 18-in (45-cm) long beans in our polytunnel. Improved varieties more suited to cool climates may be bred in future.

Characteristics

The yard long bean is a climbing annual, growing up to 9–12 ft (3–4 m) high. The attractive, rather large flowers are generally a pale blue. The pods hang in pairs and justify their name by being anything from 1–3 ft (30–90 cm) long, though they are generally eaten when not much more than a foot (30 cm) long. They are narrow, round, and stringless; pale or dark green or purple coloured. The seeds are about ½ in (1 cm) long, and can be white, black or purplish red.

Climate, soil/site

This is another bean for areas with very warm summers, though not necessarily very long summers, as it grows fast and beans can be picked less than three months after sowing. Ideally, night temperatures should not drop below 65°F (18°C). In cool areas it needs a sheltered, sunny position, against a south-facing wall for example. Most varieties are short-day plants, so will not start to flower and form pods until after mid-summer.

Yard long bean tolerates acid soils and will grow in relatively poor soil, though yields are higher in fertile soil. It can be grown in areas with very low rainfall.

Cultivation

For sowing see Adzuki bean, above. Plant out when plants are 3–4 in (8–10 cm) tall, 6 in (15 cm) apart in rows 2 ft (60 cm) apart.

Supports

In temperate climates where growth is not very vigorous yard long beans can be grown up strings. As with climbing French beans, several plants can climb up the same support. In warm climates where growth is much more vigorous they will need strong supports such as climbing frames, canes, or trellis work, allowing for them to reach a height of at least 8 ft (2.5 m). In China they are often grown on poles straddling an irrigation ditch. They are sometimes interplanted between crops such as sweet corn, which give them the necessary support.

Root inoculant

In the United States the use of a legume root inoculant is recommended for yard long beans. (See Soya beans, page 61.)

Use

The young green or purple pods, the ripe seeds, the leaves and young stems are all edible. The pods have a mild flavour and, provided they are harvested before they become flabby, a wonderful 'melting' texture.

In hot climates the yard long bean is also used for green manure, as a forage crop, and for cover crops.

In the kitchen

The pods are usually cut into 1–2 in (2.5–5 cm) lengths for cooking. They should be stir-fried or boiled rather than steamed, which tends to make them soft. Being so slender they cook rapidly, and make excellent bean salads. In China the young pods are also pickled. The red-coloured form is almost unique among beans in retaining its red colour when cooked. The bean pods can also be dried.

The leaves and young stems are delicious steamed and served dressed with olive oil. (See also Recipes, page 197.)

Yard long bean

Harvesting

In temperate climates don't wait for the beans to grow a yard long. Pick them anything from about 10 in (25 cm) onwards, while the pods are still very slender with just a faint sign of bean seeds starting to swell inside.

Pests and disease

When grown under cover yard long bean is susceptible to red spider mite. (See Part 2, Pests and disease.)

Varieties

Varieties of light green, dark green and purple-podded yard long beans are currently available.

Note on other beans popularly known as 'asparagus bean' and 'asparagus pea'

TETRAGONOLOBUS PURPUREUS (previously *Lotus tetragonolobus*) This is an annual, dwarf bean, with beautiful coppery red flowers. The pods are about 3 in (7.5 cm) long, triangular in shape with protruding wings. It is European in origin, half-hardy, and easily grown in temperate climates. It is generally known as 'asparagus pea' though 'dwarf winged bean' might perhaps be considered a more appropriate name.

PSOPHOCARPUS TETRAGONOLOBUS This is a perennial, climbing tropical bean, sometimes hailed as a 'magic' bean, as it is has edible leaves, flowers, pods and tubers, all exceptionally good sources of protein. Oil can be extracted from the seeds, and the roots have excellent nitrogen-fixing properties. The flower colour varies from white to blue to purple. The pods are four-cornered, rectangular or square in cross section, with protruding 'wings' at each corner, and anything from 2½ in–2 ft (6–60 cm) long.

This bean grows only in very hot, humid conditions; moreover most varieties will only flower in daylengths associated with the tropics—south of latitude 20N. It is south-east Asian in origin. Its numerous names include asparagus pea, asparagus bean, winged bean, Goa bean, and four-angled bean. 'Climbing winged bean' would seem to be the most sensible name.

Yam bean

Latin name *Pachyrrhizus erosus*
Other names in use Jicama (pronounced 'Hi-ca-ma')
Mandarin Sha ge ('sand creeper'); di gwa ('earth gourd'); liang shu ('cooling tuber'); dou shu ('bean tuber')
Cantonese Sha kot; fan ko

The yam bean merits a brief note, as it is frequently listed in seed catalogues. An American plant in origin, it is very popular in southern China, where it is mainly grown for the large fleshy, four-lobed tuber. This can be crunched raw and has a very pleasant refreshing quality. It is also fried. The tubers were occasionally used for making starch. In the West the yam bean is recommended as a substitute for Chinese ingredients such as water chestnut, bamboo shoots and even daikon, on account of its blandness, its white flesh, and the crispy texture. The tubers have a low nutritional value.

The plant is a climbing annual vine with beautiful flowers. The young pods can be eaten, but mature pods contain the insecticide and fish poison rotenone, and are poisonous.

Yam bean requires high temperatures and a very long growing season before the tubers will develop. Moreover, the tubers don't develop until after flowering, which takes place in the short days after mid-summer. These factors combine to make it most unlikely that yam bean, as a food crop, can be grown successfully in temperate, northern climates.

Yam bean tuber

Burdock

Family   *Compositae*
Latin name   *Arctium lappa (A. majus)*
Other names   Edible burdock; great burdock; gobo
Mandarin   Niu pang; dong yang luo bo ('Eastern sea radish')
Cantonese   Ngao pong
Japanese   Gobo

Background

Burdock grows wild in many parts of the world, from Europe to Asia to North America, but it probably originated in Asia. For centuries the seeds and roots have been used in traditional Chinese medicine, and it is thought that the Chinese introduced it to Japan as a medicine about 1000 years ago. The Japanese are responsible for its use as an edible plant: beautifully packed boxes of elegant long burdock roots are a hallmark of Japanese markets, and are to be found wherever Japanese communities have settled overseas. It is popular pickled, often sold wrapped in perilla leaves, and is also used in the manufacture of soft drinks.

Edible burdock was introduced to France from Japan in the nineteenth century. The Vilmorin seedsmen, while far from being bowled over by the quality of the roots they tasted in the 1870s, were impressed by its hardiness, vigorous growth and the fleshiness of its long roots. They considered it had quite as much potential, if carefully selected, as wild carrot or wild beet. The Japanese, and to a lesser extent the Chinese, have since developed varieties which are a considerable improvement on the original wild forms.

Characteristics

Burdock is a hardy biennial plant, grown as an annual. The rather bare stems of mature plants are generally 3–4 ft (90–120 cm) tall, sometimes considerably taller. The large, almost heart-shaped leaves are rough in texture; they are dark green above, pale beneath, with pinkish veins. Short white hairs on

Burdock roots and young plant

the leaves and leaf stalks give them a whitish bloom. The plant has many insignificant little purple flowers which eventually become prickly burs. The flowers attract bees and butterflies, and are sometimes used to catch butterflies.

The fleshy tapering tap root can reach lengths of 4 ft (120 cm); in improved modern varieties they can be 1 in (2.5 cm) diameter at the top. The outer skin is usually brown, but whiter-skinned varieties are being developed. The flesh is white, but rapidly discolours when exposed to air. The root is covered with very characteristic, rather hairy rootlets.

Climate

As one would expect from such a widespread plant, burdock tolerates a wide range of temperatures. It does best at temperatures between 68–77°F (20–25°C) grow-

Use

Although grown primarily for the mature and nearly mature roots, the young leaves and young stems can be eaten in spring. They need very little cooking.

Burdock seeds can be sprouted, but care should be taken in collecting seeds. If doing so in any quantity a mask should be worn, as tiny hairs from the seeds can be inhaled, and are toxic.

In the kitchen

Highly prized as a delicacy in Japan, the burdock root has a flavour of its own, varying from mild to sweet to strong, depending on the age and quality of the roots. The best flavour is said to be just under the skin. Roots are at their most tender when young: they should snap when bent. Good, well-prepared roots have a pleasant, crisp texture. Thin and ageing roots can be coarse and woody, with a somewhat 'earthy' taste. The roots are nutritious, being rich in inulin, Vitamin B, and minerals.

Very young roots are peeled and eaten raw, but burdock is usually cooked. Burdock roots keep best if the soil is not washed off until they are about to be cooked. Then wash or brush them clean, and rub off the skin with the back of a knife, keeping the flavourful flesh beneath the skin intact.

According to how they will be cooked, cut roots into 1– 2 in (2.5–5 cm) lengths, matchstick julienne strips, or shavings—the technique usually described as 'like sharpening a pencil'. Then soak them in cold water for about an hour to remove the bitterness (caused by inulin) which is present in some roots. The water (which turns green) can be lightly salted, and/or acidulated with vinegar to prevent discolouration. After draining most recipes suggest simmering for at least half an hour before stir-frying, sautéing etc. Recipes quite often also suggest pounding the roots (like tenderizing steaks) to make them more tender. You will have to judge if this is necessary from your own roots. It is easiest to do this before cutting them into lengths for final cooking.

Burdock can be cooked in a number of ways, for example boiled, roasted, or stewed with other root vegetables. It is very often stir-fried like potato chips and served with soya sauce, or with a glaze made from dry wine, soya, hot pepper and sugar. Toasted black sesame seeds are frequently sprinkled over the burdock just before serving.

(See also Recipes, page 187.)

---

ing well in warm humid areas, such as Florida in the United States. The leaves die back a couple of degrees above freezing, but the roots survive temperatures well below freezing.

Soil/site

The ideal soils are deep sandy loams, enabling the roots both to penetrate easily and to be lifted easily. Burdock can be grown on heavier soils, but never as satisfactorily. Good drainage is essential. Where soil depth is limited or drainage in doubt, it is advisable to plant burdock on ridges. (See Part 2, The bed system, ridge and furrow system, page 148.) Dig over the soil well before sowing or planting: a low-nitrogen, high-phosphate fertilizer, such as bonemeal, can be worked into the soil to encourage root development.

Remember burdock grows tall, so site it where the plants will not overshadow a sun-loving crop. They make quite a good boundary for a vegetable garden.

Cultivation

When to sow

Burdock can be sown in spring or autumn.

SPRING Burdock can be sown very early in spring, provided the soil is warm enough for germination (see Sowing method, below). The roots will be ready in summer and autumn.

AUTUMN The autumn-sown crop overwinters in the soil, maturing the following spring or early summer. This seems to be the favoured option in Japan. Late autumn sowings can be covered with cloches or low tunnels in early winter, to bring the crop forward about a month. The autumn sowing must be done late, rather than early, in autumn or there is a risk of bolting. (See The bolting problem, below.)

Sowing method

The seeds are quite large—about ¼ in (50 mm) long. They can be sown *in situ*, but as germination is erratic better results are obtained by starting off seeds in a seed tray and transplanting them outdoors when young, before there is any sign of a taproot developing.

A minimum temperature of 50°F (10°C) is necessary for germination, but optimum temperatures would be 68–77°F (20–25°C). Germination is improved if seeds are either soaked in water overnight before sowing, or scarified (see Glossary). The seeds can be left uncovered, as they germinate best in the light. Once germinated, the seedlings grow very fast.

The bolting problem

For serious burdock growers the key facts about bolting in autumn-sown burdock are outlined below. Bolting occurs:
● With roots larger than ⅛ in (3 mm) diameter
● After exposure to low temperatures followed by daylengths greater than 12½ hours (as occurs in the lengthening days of spring).

In other words, a small plant is all that is required by the onset of winter. It will develop rapidly in

spring, whereas a larger plant will simply bolt in spring.

Spacing

Considering the size of the burdock plant and its leaves, it can be grown surprisingly densely. Close planting encourages the development of long, straight roots, rather than branched roots. Some of the new Japanese varieties have smaller leaves, enabling them to be grown even closer.

Japanese seed catalogues recommend spacing plants 4–9 in (10–22 cm) apart. They can also be grown in rows 12 (30 cm) apart, spacing plants 2–3 in (5–8 cm) apart in the rows.

Further care

Little attention is needed once the plants are established. They can be mulched to keep down weeds. Remove flowering shoots to concentrate growth in the roots.

Harvesting

Roots Spring-sown roots are ready for lifting 4–5 months after sowing; autumn-sown roots take about 9 months to develop. Although the roots can grow to enormous lengths, they are generally best lifted when about 12–18 in (30–45 cm) long while still immature: old and long roots are apt to become woody in the centre.

A market gardener in Japan showed me how to lift burdock, using a short-handled mattock. Seeing the enormous energy he devoted to the task convinced me that burdock will never replace parsnips in the West. If the roots fail to come up intact by inserting a fork or spade and wiggling, digging a trench alongside the plants, from which they can be excavated, is the only alternative.

Leaves and stems of young plants Pull the young plants with the very young thin roots intact.

Storage

Young roots can be kept for a few weeks in a fridge, wrapped in paper. They will become desiccated if kept in dry conditions. The Japanese keep roots for long periods in winter, buried underground.

The Chinese dry burdock root by cutting it into 2¼ in (6 cm) strips, about ¼ in (5 mm) thick. It is soaked in water, changing the water twice, before drying.

Varieties

Only a limited number of varieties is currently available in the West. Faster-maturing varieties, some adapted to spring or autumn sowing and some to different soil types, and varieties with improved resistance to bolting are being developed. Once these are introduced burdock may become far more widely grown than it is at present.

Chinese artichoke

Family *Labiatae*
Latin name *Stachys affinis* (*S. Sieboldii, S. tubifera*)
Other names in use Japanese artichoke; crosnes; crosnes du Japon; spirals
Mandarin Gan lu (zi) ('sweet dew'); cao shi can ('grass stone silkworm')*
Cantonese Kon loh
Japanese Choro-gi

* There are many other very picturesque Mandarin names.

Background

Chinese artichoke is a native of north China and Japan. It was introduced to Europe in the 1880s, when the plant collector Dr Brentschneider, a physician with the Russian Legation in Peking, sent some tubers to a Paris botanic garden.

In my old copy of the Vilmorin *The Vegetable Garden* a previous owner had pasted in a magazine article about Chinese artichokes published not long after their introduction to France. The information in the article was evidently supplied by the seedsmen Vilmorin. It tells how only half a dozen tubers from the original consignment survived the journey from Peking: all the others rotted. A Mr Paillieux planted these few in an old hot bed in his garden in Crosnes (hence the French name). They multiplied very satisfactorily, increasing 200–300-fold within two years . . . and subsequently became quite popular in France.

Characteristics

Chinese artichoke is a perennial plant in the mint family. It produces strings of small, white, edible tubers at the ends of underground stems. The tubers are rarely more than 2 in (5 cm) long and ¾ in (2 cm) wide, and are usually smaller. They are curiously segmented into a series of rounded ridges. In the past I've likened them to exceptionally chubby maggots, miniature Michelin men, Sumo wrestlers, and spiral sea shells. This gives some idea of their curious appearance. When freshly lifted they have a beautiful, pearl-like translucent quality, though this becomes dulled on exposure to air.

The plants grow about 18 in (45 cm) high, upright initially but tending to become sprawlier as the season progresses. The dark green leaves bear a close resemblance to mint. They have spikes of rather attractive pink flowers.

Chinese artichokes

Use

Chinese artichokes have a very delicate, slightly nutty flavour reminiscent of globe artichokes, new potatoes and water chestnuts. The texture is delightfully crisp and crunchy, similar to water chestnuts— indeed they can be substituted for water chestnuts in Chinese recipes. They are said to be nutritious, and are unusual in containing the carbohydrate stachyose.

In the kitchen

Prepare them by trimming off the remains of the stem and scrubbing them clean. The skin is very tender and can be eaten. Peeling would be an impossibly fiddly task: scrubbing is tedious enough if they have been grown in heavy soil. They can be used raw in salads.

Chinese artichokes demand simple, light cooking, for example steaming until soft; boiling in stock or water and serving with butter or cream; parboiling and then sautéing or frying. They remain crisp when stir-fried, mix happily with other root vegetables and can also be used in soups. Cooked artichokes are excellent in salads: mix them with a vinaigrette dressing while still warm, and allow them to cool.

In China and Japan they are mainly used for pickling. The Japanese pickle them in the 'plum vinegar' obtained after sour plums have been salted and pressed.

(See also Recipes, page 187.)

Climate

Chinese artichokes are adaptable plants, tolerating both high summer temperatures and low winter temperatures. The tops, however, are sensitive to frost.

Soil/site

They grow best in rich, light, sandy soil in an open, sunny site. They must not be short of moisture during the summer growing period. Plants appear to withstand even waterlogged soils during winter.

Chinese artichokes are in the ground for most of the growing season and make good ground cover plants in out-of-the-way corners. They are quite decorative when in flower.

Cultivation

It is easy to get a crop of small-sized tubers: the problem lies in getting sufficient numbers of reasonably sized tubers. The better they are treated, the larger they will be.

Planting

Select the largest tubers for planting, and plant them upright in well-prepared soil, as early in the year as the ground is workable. Tubers sprout naturally at temperatures above about 41°F (5°C). An early start can be obtained by planting a few tubers in moist peat in a pot or seed tray. Once they have started to sprout, they can be planted carefully outside.

Plant them upright in small holes. The average recommended planting depth is 1.5 in (3.5 cm), i.e. covered by at least an inch (2.5 cm) of soil. No harm seems to come from planting more shallowly or up to 6 in (15 cm) deep, the deeper planting being on light soils. Space them about 12 in (30 cm) apart each way, or 6 in (15 cm) apart, in rows 18 in (45 cm) apart. Two tubers can be planted together at each 'station'. They *can* be grown more closely spaced, but generous spacing will help the development of large tubers.

Further care

When the plants are between 1–2 ft (30–60 cm) high, they can be earthed up a couple of inches around the base of the stems. Keep them weed-free in the early stages; later the foliage forms a canopy over the ground. Mulching once the leaves are through the surface will help to retain moisture in the soil. Plants can be given a general liquid feed in summer to encourage good growth. (See Part 2, Soil fertility, Liquid feeding, page 144.)

If growth becomes rampant in summer cut back straggling stems hard. Flowers can also be removed. This helps to concentrate resources in the tubers.

Containers

Growing Chinese artichokes in containers is uneconomic in terms of time and space as they tend to be sprawly plants, with a relatively low yield. However, if you have only a few tubers and want to build up stock, single tubers can be started in small pots, then transplanted into a large, deep pot of rich, well drained soil. By the end of the season a considerable number of tubers should have developed near the surface. (See also Part 2, Containers, page 169.)

Harvesting

Tubers take 5–7 months to develop. They are not normally lifted until early winter, after the foliage has died back. They can be left in the soil until required, and will only need extra protection in very severe weather. They have been known to withstand waterlogging in winter surprisingly well. However, they can be covered with straw to minimize frost penetration and make them easier to lift.

Wherever possible lift just before required, as the small tubers quickly dry out, become wrinkled and lose their quality. If lifting beforehand is unavoidable, wash them, wrap them in paper and keep them in the fridge, or somewhere cool and dark. Alternatively, prevent them from drying out by storing them in moist sand or peat at temperatures between 32–36°F (0–2°C). They will keep for a few months, though some of the flavour will be lost after a few weeks.

When the ground is dug over again in spring, make sure even the tiniest tubers are lifted. Otherwise they can become invasive. Small tubers can be planted up in pots and used to increase stock. (See Containers, above.)

Chinese boxthorn

Family *Solanaceae*
Latin name *Lycium barbarum* (*L. chinense*; *L. halimifolium**)
Other names in use Chinese or common boxthorn; Chinese matrimony vine; tea tree; Duke of Argyll's tea tree; wolfberry
Mandarin Gou qi
Cantonese Kau kei
Japanese Kuko

* These were previously considered separate species, but are now recognized as synonyms for *Lycium barbarum*.

Background

Chinese boxthorn is a plant which grows wild throughout Asia, where it is still gathered from the wild. It was introduced to England in the 1730s as an ornamental plant, but confusion over labelling led to it being mistaken for the tea plant. It subsequently escaped from cultivation and become naturalized in Europe, where it is now common on waste ground.

In China the whole plant has a long history of medicinal use, both as a general, energy restoring tonic, and to cure a wide range of ailments from skin rashes and eyesight problems to diabetes. In China and Japan a tonic tea is made from the leaves, and a 'healthy' wine from the berries. The arching stems, especially when covered with berries in autumn, are very popular with Japanese flower arrangers. It is also grown as a bonsai plant in Japan.

Characteristics

Chinese boxthorn is a very variable plant, the many forms previously being considered different species. (See footnote to names above.)

It is a vigorous, medium-sized perennial shrub. Left to its own devices it grows rather untidily, scrambling over the ground and producing a lot of suckers. It can be anything from 3–10 ft (1–3 m) high.

The stems arch gracefully in free-growing plants, but when kept trimmed it is a far more erect and orderly plant, with straight, rigid stems. They are often spiny, though there are spineless forms. The bright green oval leaves are usually about an inch (2.5 cm) long. In summer Chinese boxthorn has reddish-purple or pink flowers, followed by orange or scarlet egg-shaped berries, which can be ¾ in (2 cm) long.

Climate

Chinese boxthorn is an adaptable plant, being both very hardy and tolerant of high temperatures.

Site/soil

It needs a sunny situation, and does well in maritime areas. It will grow on light sandy soil, and is often found naturalized on sandy cliffs. It is sometimes used to stabilize sandy banks. It will tolerate poor soil and rough ground. However, in China I saw it being grown on the highly fertile raised island beds in Guangzhou. Moreover, an old lady

Chinese boxthorn

was carefully tucking chicken manure around each plant, which would indicate that where being cut frequently for market it responds to higher fertility.

The Chinese often have a bush or informal hedge somewhere near the house, rather as Westerners have a bay tree.

Cultivation

Chinese boxthorn is either grown as single bushes or a hedge or, where considerable quantities are required, as a dense 'plantation'. It is almost always raised from cuttings, though it can be raised from seed, if obtainable. Cultivated plants normally last for about 10 years.

Propagation from cuttings

Hardwood cuttings 6–8 in (15–20 cm) long can be taken in autumn or spring and planted 2 in

Use

The soft young leaves are used mainly as a flavouring herb, but also as a vegetable. They have a pleasant flavour. I find it slightly reminiscent of cress, but it is sometimes described as a peppermint flavour. They are very nutritious.

In the kitchen

The leaves wilt rapidly once the stems are picked. They are stripped off the stems for use, and should be cooked for no more than 3–4 minutes. They are widely used to flavour soups, particularly Chinese soups made with pork or liver, but they can be added to any good stock for the last few minutes of cooking. They are also boiled with rice to flavour it.

The ripe berries have a sweet, mild, licorice flavour. Fresh and dried berries are used in speciality Chinese dishes, often to flavour meat and poultry.

(5 cm) deep. As they root easily they are often planted immediately in their permanent position, spaced about 12–15 in (30–38 cm) apart each way, the wider spacing when grown as a hedge. Otherwise they can be rooted in a sandy bed and transplanted later, in spring or autumn. Stems of Chinese boxthorn being sold for culinary use can be used for propagation.

Plants can also be propagated by layering in spring, or by cutting off and planting rooted suckers.

Protected cropping

GREENHOUSE PRODUCTION IN EUROPE Boxthorn has been grown experimentally in unheated greenhouses in northern Europe. Rooted cuttings were spaced 16 in (40 cm) apart, in rows 32 in (80 cm) apart. After planting the growing point was cut out to encourage a bushier plant. The first short stems were harvested 2–4 months after planting, cutting low on the plant but always leaving a few leafy stems on each plant to encourage fast re-growth. At the end of winter, in January or February, the plants were cut right back to 2 in (5 cm) above ground level. At this point leaves are yellowing and are unsuitable for marketing. Plants were being replanted every three or four years.

Pruning

Chinese boxthorn bushes should be pruned in winter, cutting out old and weak stems. They can be cut back hard, almost to ground level, as new growth will arise from old wood. In closely grown 'plantations' of Chinese boxthorn the plants are 'coppiced', i.e. kept about 2 ft (60 cm) high by regular cutting. This produces young shoots over a long period.

Harvesting

For culinary purposes soft young shoots or stems about 12 in (30 cm) long are required. Normally the first shoots can be cut about a year after planting, though where growth is very rapid, it can be sooner. For domestic use cut a few shoots at a time as required. Provided picking is moderate there will be a supply from spring to au-tumn, though the best quality shoots are obtained in spring.

Where bushes are cut for market, the main cutting is in spring, with a second cutting in autumn if growth permits. In South China we saw boxthorn being cut with a tiny blade slipped over the index finger.

Varieties

Apart from standard Chinese box-thorn, the following varieties with exceptionally decorative qualities can sometimes be obtained.

Lycium chinense var 'Carnosum' Pink flowers

Lycium chinense var aureomarginatum Gold edged leaves

Chinese celery

Family *Umbelliferae*
Latin name *Apium graveolens*
Mandarin Qin cai
Cantonese K'an tsoi \ kun choi
Japanese Seri-na

Background

Chinese celery probably evolved from a wild form of Asian celery. It bears a remarkable resemblance to the 'leaf', 'green', 'cutting', or 'soup' celery still grown in Europe as a herb—itself not far removed from the wild European celery. Both are hardier and generally more robust than the long-stemmed trench celery and self-blanching celery, which have usurped them as table vegetables in Europe and America.

In China celery has a long history of use as a flavouring herb and vegetable. When the newly discovered Han tombs in Hunan were excavated in 1972 – revealing extraordinarily well preserved food samples from the second century BC – the excavators found over 300 bamboo 'slips' inscribed with recipes. One was for 'dog meat and celery'!

Today celery is one of the most widely grown vegetables in China. On our autumn trip we saw the 'winter beds' in Beijing being prepared for celery, which would be overwintered and ready for Chinese New Year. (See Protected Cropping, Chinese solar frames, page 165). Further south, on the Long March Commune in Shanghai, girls were planting bed upon bed of celery with vegetable planting knives which looked like meat cleavers. Cauliflower plants which had yet to be harvested were carefully tied up to make room for the young celery plants – a good example of the Chinese reluctance to waste growing space. In Chengdu we saw the delicate, pale yellow-leaved variety growing on private plots.

Characteristics

Chinese celery is a biennial, grown as an annual. The plants make leafy little 'bushes' of erect stalks, anything from 10–15 in (25–37 cm) high. The stems are thin, hollow

Use

Both the leaves and stems have a strong celery flavour. The flavour is milder when the celery is growing lushly, but becomes stronger if the plants have been allowed to dry out. Stringy fibres may need to be peeled off older stems.

In the kitchen

As a flavouring herb Leaves and stems are used whole in cooking soups and stews. They can also be chopped finely and incorporated into meat and fish dishes, or sprinkled over them: the flavour is brought out best if the celery is stir-fried first.

As a vegetable The stems, sliced into 1–2 in (2.5–5 cm) lengths, are often used as a vegetable. A simple popular recipe is stir-fried celery stalks, flavoured with soy sauce, sugar and sesame oil. Stems can also be stir-fried with bean sprouts; or mixed into meat dishes.

Chinese celery is fairly strong to use raw in salad, but may be parboiled then added to a salad.

and crisp, coloured light green, dark green or white, depending on the type.

The leaves are jagged, flattish, usually shiny, and very similar in shape to those of European types of celery. Their colour varies from dark to light green to yellow.

Climate

Celery is a plant for cool climates. The ideal day temperature during growth is 59–73°F (15–23°C). It can survive temperatures of 23°F (-5°C) unprotected in the open, and 14°F (-10°C) in a sheltered position outdoors, or under cover in an unheated greenhouse. The green-stemmed varieties are the hardiest. In hot climates plants require shading in summer.

Soil/site

Celery is a marsh plant in origin, so needs moist conditions. It grows best in very fertile, moisture retentive soil, rich in organic matter.

Decorative value

The plants are neat and quite decorative in a garden, forming an even-textured patch when grown densely. Being fairly hardy, they retain their colour late into winter. The umbelliferous flower heads which develop in their second season have an attractive misty quality. A Chinese friend takes the base of a harvested plant and floats it in water. It re-sprouts to make an attractive indoor decoration.

Cultivation

With the use of protection in winter, it is possible to have a year-round supply of Chinese celery in temperate climates.

When to sow

It can be sown any time from spring to summer. For a continuous domestic supply it is advisable to make two sowings. Where plants are being uprooted for sale, successive sowings can be made at 4–6 week intervals throughout the growing season.

Chinese celery

TEMPERATE AREAS
Spring This is for the main summer supply. For the earliest crop, sow indoors about 5 weeks before the last frost in the area is expected. These plants may bolt prematurely in autumn.
Summer Sow from mid summer to early autumn (in warmer areas). These sowings can give fresh supplies from autumn until early summer the following year, a period when fresh green herbs are scarce.

Where celery is unlikely to survive winter outdoors, (see Climate above), sow *in situ* under cover in late summer for an indoor winter crop; or transplant a few plants in early autumn into an unheated greenhouse or cold frame. Plants will not grow much during the winter months, but will remain in good enough condition to use.
COLD AREAS
In cold areas restrict sowing to the summer months.
Self sowing If Chinese celery is allowed to run to seed it often sows itself, saving you the trouble next season. This is most likely to happen to plants grown under cover. Make sure the ground around them is kept moist, so the seedlings germinate. They can be transplanted to other situations if necessary.

Sowing Methods

As celery seed is small and germination can be erratic, the best results are obtained by sowing indoors in modules, or in seed trays, pricking out when seedlings are just large enough to handle. (See Part 2, Plant raising, page 152). Sow in gentle heat at temperatures of 50–59°F (10–15°C). Celery germinates badly at higher temperatures. Seed can be left uncovered, as it germinates best in the light.

Alternatively celery can be sown *in situ*, thinning to the required distance apart, or sown in a seedbed and transplanted.

Space plants 4–6 in (10–15 cm) apart. If they are going to be blanched (see below), grow them in rows 12 in (30 cm) apart.

Feeding, Watering, Pests and Disease, Further Care

Growth is normally slow in the early stages, but once established, Chinese celery grows well and can yield heavily in good conditions. Make sure plants don't suffer from lack of water. A nitrogenous liquid feed can be applied if growth is poor. (See Part 2, Soil fertility, Liquid feeding, page 144). Chinese celery is normally relatively free of pests and diseases, though celery fly (leaf miner), can be a problem. (See Part 2, Pests and Disease).

Blanching

Chinese celery is sometimes blanched to make the stems whiter, more tender, and better flavoured. The most common method is to earth up the stems when the plants are about 9–12 in (23–30 cm) high. The pale leaved varieties are more suitable for blanching than the dark leaved.

Protection

For a better quality and longer-standing crop during winter and early spring, cover outdoor plants with cloches or low polytunnels in early autumn.

'False plants' The traditional method of obtaining an early crop in North China was to transplant half grown plants, about 6–8 in (15–20 cm) high, into the 'cold beds' in autumn. (See Protected Cropping, Chinese solar frames, page 165). They were planted deeply so that most of the stems were earthed up. The cold beds protected them from severe frosts, so they could continue growing for harvesting in late January and February. Mature plants can also be 'stored' this way during winter.

Harvesting

The first cut can normally be made about 6 weeks after planting, when stems are 8–10 in (20–25 cm)

high. Either cut individual stems as required, or cut the whole plant an inch or so above ground level. For domestic use the plants can be left to regrow, though subsequent growth will be a little straggly. This enables the plants to be used over several months. In China the plants are pulled up by their roots for marketing, as this keeps them fresher.

DRYING Celery leaves and stems can be dried for winter use. They retain their flavour well.

Varieties

Chinese celery is not often listed in Western catalogues, but the following varieties are sometimes found:

Dinant Vigorous, green stemmed variety.
Yellow Heart/Chinese Golden (Huang Xin)
Popular Chinese variety; white to yellow stems, rather pale coloured leaves. There are early and late forms.

Where true Chinese celery is unavailable, use wild celery or European 'cutting celery', both of which may prove slower to run to seed. Recommended Dutch varieties are:
Amsterdamse fijn donkergroene (Amsterdam fine-leaved dark green) Prolific, attractive, dark green leaves.
Gewone snij (Common cutting) Lighter coloured, slightly coarser leaved, less vigorous.

Chinese chives

Family *Alliaceae*
Latin name *Allium tuberosum*
Other names in use Chinese leek; flowering leek; garlic chives
Mandarin Jiu cai (green chives); jiu huang (blanched chives); jiu cai hua (flower stem)
Cantonese Gau tsoi (green chives); gau wong (blanched chives); gau tsoi fa (flower stem)
Japanese Nira

Background

Chinese chives have been cultivated for centuries in China, Japan and other Eastern countries, where they have a long tradition of both culinary and medicinal use. A booklet I bought in China on Chinese chives described them as 'jewels among vegetables'. And it is true: they are very pretty, very useful, and easy to grow.

The pale tender leaves of blanched chives are one of China's culinary delicacies. The long yellow and white strands, sometimes decorated with bright red chillies, or draped over a line like mermaid's tresses, are a common sight.

Chinese chives: green leafy stage

Use

Almost all parts can be used: leaves, flower stems, flower buds and flowers. Whether used raw or cooked, all have a delicate, mild garlic flavour. The Chinese particularly appreciate the flavour of the whitened part of the leaf stem which develops below soil level.

In the kitchen

In China and Japan the flowers are ground and salted to make a savoury spice. Flower buds can also be dressed with sesame oil for a salad dish. Green and blanched leaves and flower stems are generally cut into pieces 1–2 in (2.5–5 cm) long and cooked very briefly so they keep their flavour and colour.

Like common chives, Chinese chives is mainly used as a seasoning herb in a wide variety of dishes: soups, fish and meat dishes; egg dishes—they are particularly good stirred into buttered or scrambled eggs; mixed with bean curd, bean sprouts and so on. It is sometimes cooked as a vegetable in its own right. For example, the leaves can be tied into bundles, dipped in batter and deep-fried for a tasty snack. The flower stems are particularly valued for their bright colour, which is retained when cooked. They are mostly used in meat dishes.

(See also Recipes, page 188.)

Chinese chive flower stems are becoming a sophisticated 'up-market' product all over the world. I also love to use them as cut flowers—both fresh and dried for winter.

Characteristics

Chinese chives is a perennial plant, living anything from about seven to up to thirty years, depending on the conditions. It grows in a neat, rather dainty clump, mature clumps being up to 12 in (30 cm) in diameter.

The narrow, flat leaves are from ¼–¾ in (0.5–2 cm) wide, growing 12–18 in (30–45 cm) high in mature plants. Their colour varies from dark green to a very pretty, fresh, light green. The parts of the leaf base which are underground become blanched to a paler colour. In summer Chinese chives produce beautiful inflorescences of star-like white flowers, up to 2 ft (60 cm) high.

Established plants have thick rhizomes, which enlarge a little every year, from which fibrous roots and shoots emerge.

Types

Chinese chives are usually divided into 'leaf' and 'flowering' types. In practice the distinctions between the two are blurred; many modern selections are considered dual-purpose, the leaves being cut in spring and summer and the flowers later.

The leaf type has tender leaves, is slow-bolting and is grown primarily for its leaves. There are allegedly broad-leaved and narrow-leaved forms (the latter flowering a little later) but growing conditions are probably more important in determining the size of the leaves.

In the flowering type the flower stems are more tender than in the leaf types, though the leaves may be tougher. It flowers earlier, and is recommended when growing primarily for the flower stems.

There is also said to be an exceptionally fleshy-rooted type, in which the roots are pickled, but I have not yet come across it.

Climate

Chinese chives are very adaptable, tolerating both extremely low and very high temperatures. In Manchuria the roots survive 40 degrees of frost, overwintering in the open.

The leaves remain green until temperatures fall to 39–41°F (4–5°C); they start into growth in spring at 35–37°F (2–3°C). The ideal temperature during the growing period is 64–75°F (18–24°C). If grown under much higher temperatures, especially in very dry conditions, the chives will be fibrous and of poor quality; this can be offset if they are shaded and kept humid.

Soil/site

Chinese chives tolerate a wide range of soils, from sand to clay, but do best in light fertile soils, rich in organic matter. They are not sensitive to pH. The roots of a well-grown 3-year-old plant can go down as much as 20 in (50 cm), so shallow soils must be avoided. Good drainage is essential.

An open site is preferred, but they tolerate light shade. Being perennial, they are best grown where they will not be disturbed, for example at the end of beds, or alongside a path. Ground should be well manured, weed free, and thoroughly dug before sowing or planting.

When grown on a large scale in China they are often treated as a semi-permanent crop, left in the ground for four or five years. They may be grown in wide strips, with the ground between the strips intercropped with short-term crops such as salads, spinach or quick-maturing greens.

Decorative value

Garlic chives rates highly as a decorative vegetable as it is attractive throughout the growing season. The young, bright green shoots provide some of the first signs of life in spring. In the months that follow the clumps retain their freshness with little of the unsightly dieback of ordinary chives. Later in summer the white flowers brighten up corners of the kitchen garden like dabs of sunlight. Clumps can be grown in flower beds, herbaceous borders and rockeries, and make effective focal points in herb gardens and decorative vegetable gardens.

Cultivation for green leaves

Chinese chives are a trouble-free crop, but be prepared for growth being slow in the early stages. In warm areas they will crop all year round. In temperate and cold climates the gap can be breached either by growing in unheated greenhouses or by forcing. (See Protected cropping below.) The average household would need no more than half a dozen plants.

Chinese chives are either raised from seed or by division of mature clumps. It is sometimes possible to buy young plants from good herb specialists.

(See also Cultivation of blanched chives and Cultivation of flower stems, below.)

Raising from seed

Chinese chive seed loses its viability fairly rapidly, so use fresh seed, certainly no older than the previous year's. Good seed is shiny black with a white hilum; older seed is dull, with a yellow hilum. If in doubt, do a germination test. (See Part 2, Plant raising, Germination test, page 150.)

Chinese chives is usually sown in seed boxes or a seedbed and transplanted, as this is more reliable and gives higher yields than the alternative of sowing *in situ*.

Transplanting methods

MAIN SOWING Sow from spring to early summer. The earlier the sowing, the sooner the first cut can be made the following year. Germination can be erratic, and is fastest at temperatures above 68°F (20°C). Sow in a heated propagator if necessary. Sow in one of the methods below. (See also Part 2, Plant raising, page 150.)

• In a seed tray, pricking out when seedlings are large enough to handle.

• In modules, with anything from about 6–15 seeds per cell. These are planted out as one clump.

• In an outdoor seedbed, in reasonably fertile, well-drained soil.

Seedlings can be transplanted into their permanent positions from 3–5 months later, in late summer or early autumn, when they are about 4 in (10 cm) high.

LATE SOWING A late sowing can be made in seed trays or modules in autumn. These can be overwintered in a sheltered place outdoors or in a cold frame, and planted out the following spring. The first cut could be made from late summer onwards, the following year.

Pre-germinated seed In large-scale cultivation in China seed is sometimes pre-germinated to encourage fast, even germination. It is soaked overnight in warm water, drained, then wrapped in wet cloth and kept at a temperature of 64–77°F (18–25°C), for 4–5 days. It is sown when the majority of seeds have germinated.

Spacing

As with ordinary chives, Chinese chives establish best if a number of seedlings are planted together in a clump. Recommendations vary from 4–5 seedlings to 40! A happy medium would be to aim for about 10 seedlings per clump. Leaves tend to become narrower in very large clumps, though the overall weight of leaf may be higher.

Plant clumps at least 8 in (20 cm) apart, and about 2 in (5 cm) deep. The leaf blades should be above the soil, and the top of the whitened part of the stem at soil level, so the lower part is buried and will become whitened.

Where grown on a large scale, rows can be anything from 1–2 ft (30–60 cm) apart, to allow for cultivation between the rows.

SOWING *IN SITU* OUTDOORS Sow as early in the year as the ground is workable. Sowings can be made into summer, but in temperate climates, sow no later than early summer. Seedlings develop slowly, and later sowings may not grow large enough to survive severe winter weather.

Sow seeds about ¾ in (2 cm) apart, about ½ in (1 cm) deep, in rows 1–1½ ft (30–45 cm) apart. As the seed is very small, germination will be better if the drills are lined with peat or sowing compost. They usually germinate in about two weeks. One traditional Chinese method is to sow in flat bottomed drills, 2–4 in (5–10 cm) wide and 4 in (10 cm) deep. Seed is scattered evenly in the drills, and covered with ½ in (1 cm) of soil. The drills are gradually filled in with soil as the plants grow so that the leaf bases become whitened.

Raising by division

This is a quick way of obtaining plants, sharing plants, or increasing your stock. Clumps can be divided in spring or autumn. It is probably best to wait until they are fairly large, say in their third or fourth season. Water the ground thoroughly beforehand if it is dry, dig out the clumps and pull them apart gently. Discard the older roots in the centre, and replant with several stems per clump. The Chinese trim the fibrous roots to about an inch to stimulate fresh root growth. Make sure the roots don't dry out while exposed.

Unlike ordinary garden chives which need to be divided regularly to keep them growing well, it is not necessary to lift and divide Chinese chive clumps *unless* they are losing vigour. However, where cropped

very intensively, the leaves tend to become narrow unless divided every few years.

Further care and harvesting

First season In the first season it is very important to keep the plants weed-free, as weeding is difficult once the clumps are well established.

Avoid watering unless conditions are very dry. Frequent watering encourages surface rooting, and it is far better to encourage plants to develop deep roots. However if the leaf tips start to die back in the middle of the growing season, extra watering is necessary.

Normally no leaves should be cut in the first year, so that plants can build up their reserves and develop good sturdy rhizomes. An exception is an early sown protected crop (see below).

Second season As soon as growth starts in the spring, rake over the clumps to remove debris and stimulate root activity.

Earth up or ridge up around the base of the stems for an inch or so. Where chives are grown in a furrow in China, soil from the edge of the furrow is eased around the lower stems. Alternatively, 1½–2 in (4–5 cm) of sandy soil is put into the furrow. According to the Chinese, this not only blanches the stems but covers the roots, which have a tendency to work up with time. 'Leaping roots' is the literal translation of the Chinese term.

The first cut can be made about 3 weeks later, cutting the whole clump when the leaves are 6–8 in (15–20 cm) high. The Chinese cut just below soil level, to get the flavoursome blanched leaf base. In the West plants are usually cut at ground level, giving a cleaner leaf. Two more cuts can be made, but plants should then be left to build up the root system. Or just pick a few leaves at a time as required. Any flowering stems which develop should be removed when young. In the third season they can be left to develop, then cut for use. However, in warm climates Chinese chives may self seed and become a weed. Where this is likely remove seed heads as they appear.

Plants will benefit from a nitrogenous liquid feed after each cut. (See Part 2, Soil fertility, Liquid feeding, page 144.) As in the first year, keep plants weed-free, and only water if conditions are very dry.

If cut frequently, Chinese chives may start to deteriorate after the third or fourth season unless looked after well. To summarize the Chinese recipe for chive longevity:
1 Rake clumps every spring.
2 Top-dress with sandy soil each spring.
3 Apply liquid feed between cuts.
This is a counsel of perfection for large-scale cultivation. In fertile garden soil with moderate picking, clumps will jog along happily for a good many years.

Protected cropping

FOR WINTER AND EARLY SPRING CROPS Chinese chives die back naturally in winter once temperatures are a few degrees above zero. In temperate climates the season can be prolonged by covering plants with cloches or low tunnels in early autumn. For very early supplies the following year, cover plants with cloches or low polytunnels during the winter: the earlier they are covered, the earlier they will come into growth. However, wait until the foliage has died down as they need a short dormant period before being forced into new growth. Alternatively, lift the dormant roots in winter and replant them in cold frames or greenhouses to encourage early growth. As a general rule, young plants transplant better than old plants.

Plants can also be potted up in mid-summer and brought indoors for small-scale winter supplies. Most of the leaves will remain green, though a few older leaves will die back. They will continue growing slowly.

In parts of north China with very severe winters elaborate systems have been devised to produce chives in winter as well as summer. One method involves constructing a greenhouse *over* the growing crop. The framework is put up in autumn, but it is not actually glazed until the ground has been frozen, allowing the leaves to die back first.

ALL YEAR ROUND GREENHOUSE PRODUCTION In Europe Chinese chives have been grown all year round in greenhouses. The first sowings are made in heated propagators in February, for planting in early summer, enabling the first cuts to be made in the same season. Greenhouses are slightly heated in winter, so the leaves remain green.

Cultivation of blanched chives

Blanching makes the leaves etiolated, yellow, softer and subtler in flavour. It is done by covering cutback plants, and allowing them to resprout in the dark. They are normally blanched immediately after harvesting the green leaves. In summer blanched chives would be ready for cutting in three or four weeks, depending on the temperature. It takes longer at lower temperatures.

Blanching inevitably weakens the plants, so is normally only done once a season. In the exceptionally good growing conditions of south China, where it is possible to get eight cuts of chives a year, it is common practice to alternate green and blanched crops. In north China, where the growing season is shorter, they take three cuts of green chives during summer, followed by one of blanched chives in the autumn. The same techniques are used for blanching outdoor summer chives and for winter crops grown under cover. Besides the various Chinese methods outlined below, any Western methods used for blanching endive or Witloof chicory can be used for Chinese chives. Whatever method is used, the plants must be dry when covered, or there is a risk of rotting.

Pots, boxes and tiles Cover clumps with upturned boxes, or large clay pots with the drainage holes blocked or covered with tinfoil to exclude light. They need to be at least 10 in (25 cm) deep. If you are lucky enough to have one, use a traditional seakale blanching pot. Or cover an ordinary cloche with black plastic film to make it light-proof.

The Chinese use special clay pots, about 12 in (30 cm) high, and 8–10 in (20–25 cm) in diameter. Some have a solid rounded top, others are lidded, in which case the lids are removed the night before the plants are cut for market, giving them one more night's growth. Typical Chinese ingenuity! A blob of mud may be put on the lid and slapped over the base of the pots when the plants are covered, to slow down evaporation and make the pots more stable.

The Chinese sometimes embrace the clumps with pairs of clay tiles to blanch them, in much the same way that tiles were used in Europe to blanch show leeks. With the chives the gap between the tiles is covered with mud to exclude light totally.

Low black plastic film tunnels This system is useful where chives are grown on a large scale. Rows of chives are covered with low tunnels of opaque black film. (See also Part 2, Protected cropping, Low tunnels, page 166.) I saw this system in operation in California. Here the black film was laid over wire hoops, and held down with nylon netting, anchored into the soil with steel pins. Because of the

Chinese chives: blanching under pots

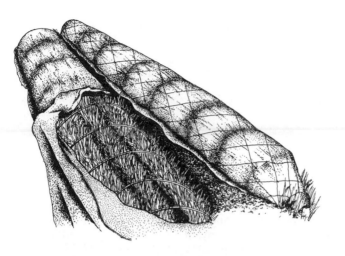

Chinese chives: blanching under plastic film tunnels

Chinese chives: buds and flowers

high temperatures, trickle irrigation had been installed under the tunnels.

Earthing up The cut-back plants can be covered with soil to make a ridge at least 6–8 in (15–20 cm) high over them. This is most successful with light sandy soil. Where this system is used in China the ground between strips of chives is intercropped until required for earthing up. (See also Soil/site, above.)

The Chinese have many other ingenious methods of blanching chives. There's even a 'five-coloured chive'—produced in early spring by blanching with different layers of straw, sand and other materials, to get a chive with white, yellow, dark and light green and purple bands—the last from exposing the tops to cold.

Cultivation of flower stems

The Japanese have led the field in developing varieties with good-quality flower stems. They recommend growing them as follows:
● Prepare the ground by working in an organic fertilizer.
● Sow in March or April, transplanting into permanent positions about 3 months later.
● Plant in groups of three or four seedlings, the groups 8 in (20 cm) apart. Alternatively, space groups 10 in (25 cm) each way.
● In the first season remove any flower stems as they appear, so the plants are not weakened. They can be cut in summer in their second season. Cut at the base of the stem, when they are 12–18 in (30–45 cm) long, before the buds lose their green colour. They open gradually after picking.

When grown for marketing the flower stems are often packed in long narrow boxes. The lengthy dark green stems and tightly closed white buds are most elegant.

DRY FLOWERS If you want to dry Chinese chive flowers for the winter gather the last of the flower heads at the end of the season. By then they are papery and harbouring dainty jet black seeds.

Containers

Chinese chives can be grown in containers. The containers should be as large and as deep as possible, with a minimum of 8 in (20 cm) of rich soil. Top-dress during the growing season with garden compost, or give dilute liquid feeds of a general fertiliser roughly every 6 weeks, or after cutting. Make sure the roots don't dry out. (See also Part 2, Containers.)

Being a well-behaved plant which keeps within bounds, Chinese chives is a good candidate for containers.

Pests and disease

In temperate climates Chinese chives are remarkably free of pests and disease. Aphids can be a problem at high temperatures. (See also Part 2, Pests and disease.)

Storage

Chinese chives are best used fresh, but will keep in a fridge crisper for up to a week in a plastic bag. The flavour becomes stronger during storage. Blanched chives will keep for no more than a day or two in the fridge.

Leaves can be dried for winter use. I have found it best to dry them fairly rapidly in gentle heat, then crumble them into a jar. Leaves (whole or chopped) and stems can be deep-frozen satisfactorily.

Varieties

In China there appear to be many distinct strains of Chinese chives. Western trials have revealed little difference between available varieties. Japanese companies list the following:

'Broadleaf' Wide-leaved variety for leaf production.

'Tenderpole' Early flowering variety, grown for the flower stem.

Chrysanthemum greens

Family *Compositae*
Latin name *Chrysanthemum coronarium*
Other names in use Garland chrysanthemum; chop suey greens;
  Japanese greens; crown daisy crysanthemum; edible
  chrysanthemum; cooking chrysanthemum
Mandarin Tung hao; hao zi gan (Beijing)
Cantonese Tung ho; tong ho choi; chong ho
Japanese Shungiku ('spring chrysanthemum'); shingiku; kikuna

Background

The edible chrysanthemum originated in the Mediterranean, spreading throughout Europe and into Africa and Asia, often becoming naturalized in the wild. Strangely it has only been adopted as a vegetable in China, Japan and south-east Asia. In the West it is grown as an annual garden chrysanthemum.

In China it is a vegetable of humble status, as its European name 'chop suey' greens implies. 'Chop suey' (the anglicized form of the Mandarin 'za cui') was the boiled up left-overs from restaurants, which were given to the poor. In Japan it is one of the most popular leafy vegetables, being widely used in many traditional Japanese dishes. Attractive bunches are available in markets all year round, from both open and covered production.

Chrysanthemum greens: serrated and broad-leaved type

It is undemanding, relatively hardy, tasty and nutritious, and deserves to be more widely grown in the West, especially during the cooler months of the year when fresh greens are scarcest. In some situations it obligingly seeds itself if a few plants are allowed to flower.

Characteristics

The edible chrysanthemum is an annual plant, growing about 1 ft (30 cm) high in its leafy phase, and sometimes over 3 ft (60 cm) when flowering. Its normal spread is about 6–8 in (15–20 cm) across, though it can become quite shrubby, especially when harvested repeatedly. The leaves resemble florist chrysanthemum leaves in size, colour, texture and smell, the largest being about 5 in (13 cm) long and 1½ in (4 cm) wide, though many are smaller. They vary in shape from a simple oval blade with slightly indented or saw-tooth edges, to a very deeply cut, jagged, and much thinner leaf. (See Types below.)

The flowers are typical single daisy flowers, 1½–2¼ in (3–6 cm) in diameter. The petals are variations of yellow, white and orange, often a pale creamy yellow on the outer edge, but a deeper yellow towards the centre.

Types

Traditionally, edible chrysanthemum was divided into several types, largely on the basis of leaf size and serrations. Now these distinctions are being eroded by modern selection and breeding.

Use

The edible chrysanthemum is mainly grown for its leaves and young stems, which are used both for flavouring and as a vegetable. The flowers can also be used (see below) and the seeds sprouted. (See Seed sprouting, page 136.)

In the kitchen

Not unexpectedly, the leaves taste 'chrysanthemumy'. It is quite a distinct, tangy flavour, pleasantly mild in young plants, becoming much stronger as plants mature, and bitter when they start to flower. They have a slightly succulent, pleasant texture, and are said to be rich in vitamins and minerals.

Young leaves are excellent raw in salads. They are best mixed with other leafy greens, or with tomatoes, bean sprouts or with finely chopped bean curd served with a sesame oil dressing. The Japanese sometimes blanch the leaves in boiling water for a few seconds, plunging them into cold water to cool before incorporating them in a salad. This gives them a healthy, dark green colour.

The leaves, either used whole or roughly cut, only need light cooking, becoming bitter if overcooked at high temperatures. As a vegetable they can be steamed, blanched as above, lightly boiled (like spinach, with a minimum of water), or stir-fried. They can also be stir-fried on their own—perhaps with the addition of a little sugar and a drop of wine or sherry—or combined with almost any other vegetable and/or with minced or finely sliced meat, chicken or fish.

The Chinese use the leaves to make soup, often with chicken stock flavoured with ginger. The Japanese add it to stews and their famous 'one-pot' dishes—*suki-yaki* and *yosenabe*. The leaves are also used in *tempura*, battered and deep-fried, and in *ohitashi*.

The flowers are edible, but as the centre has a bitter after-taste, normally only the petals are eaten. They are used fresh or dried, in soups, sprinkled over salads, and as a garnish. (See also Recipes, page 189.)

Chrysanthemum greens: flowers

Small-leaf type

This is the closest to the wild types, with very indented, thin, almost feathery leaves of a rather light green. The plants are small and up-right rather than branching, and low-yielding. They tend to be adapted to a wide range of climate. This is the most popular type in north China. The flavour is on the strong side.

Large, broad, round or spoon-leaved type

The leaves are thicker and darker coloured, with much smoother, only slightly indented and rather spoon-like leaves. The plants are larger, bushier, more spreading and higher yielding. They probably evolved in south and central China and are considered a Chinese type. The leaves are mild flavoured and very tender, especially when the plants are young.

Intermediate type

This is the most popular type today. The leaves are moderately thick, and moderately 'cut' or indented. They are fast growing and have a bushy, branching habit making them high-yielding. They tend to be dark green and, like the finer leaved types, are well adapted to both cool and warm climates.

Climate

The edible chrysanthemum is a cool, temperate-climate plant. It does not grow well at temperatures much above 77°F (25°C), tending to become bitter with heat. It will withstand light frosts in the open, and under cover will survive several degrees of frost. It grows well in low-light levels in the autumn to early spring period. Plants often continue flowering in autumn until cut back by frost. It doesn't like very wet conditions. The Japanese crop is often grown under protective netting or film to protect it from heavy rain.

Soil/site

The edible chrysanthemum is not fussy about soil, though it grows more lushly on fertile, moisture-retentive soil. It should be grown in an open situation in the cooler months of the year, but will tolerate light shade in summer. I was told in China that the roots, like those of the marigold *Tagetes minuta*, can be effective in controlling nematodes, which would make it a useful plant in rotations. As far as I know this has never been investigated scientifically.

Decorative value

With its attractively serrated leaves, the edible chrysanthemum is a pretty vegetable. If cut regularly it makes a neat edge; or let a few plants flower for a pretty patch.

Cultivation

The edible chrysanthemum is normally raised from seed. However, like most chrysanthemums it can be propagated from soft cuttings.

Cuttings taken in spring from over-wintered plants will root within a month—a quick way of replacing stock.

When to sow

For most households two or three sowings a year prove adequate. However, for a supply of exceptionally tender young leaves, successive sowings can be made at 2–3 week intervals throughout the normal sowing periods.

EARLY SPRING SOWINGS Make the first sowings under cover in an un-heated greenhouse, cold frame etc, as early in the year as possible. This will provide a very useful spring crop.

SPRING TO EARLY SUMMER OUTDOOR SOWINGS Outdoor sowing can start as soon as the soil is workable, after the risk of heavy frost has passed. Cutting can continue over several weeks or months, although plants are likely to bolt eventually in particularly hot weather.

LATE SUMMER TO AUTUMN SOWING OUTDOORS Edible chrysanthemum grows very well at this time of year in temperate climates, and will continue cropping until frost. Make the last sowing approximately 8–10 weeks before the first frost is expected.

AUTUMN SOWING UNDER COVER This sowing will provide an early winter crop, and in mild weather cropping may continue all winter. Where winter is more severe plants will cease growing in mid-winter, but are likely to sprout again in early spring, giving welcome early pickings.

Plants can also be sown in seed boxes etc. in late summer or early autumn and planted under cover in autumn for a winter crop. If unexpectedly hot weather strikes the seedlings should be shaded or they may bolt prematurely.

Hot weather sowing In most areas mid-summer sowings are best avoided, as they tend to run to seed rapidly, producing 'leggy' rather than leafy plants. In very hot climates edible chrysanthemum is generally grown in the winter months, from autumn to spring.

Sowing method

The seed is very fine, and should be sown shallowly, or only lightly covered with soil or compost. It is sometimes sown on the surface and just pressed in with a board, the ground then being covered with light mulching material to keep the surface moist until the seed has germinated. It normally germinates within about 10 days of sowing.

Edible chrysanthemum can either be grown as a cut-and-come-again seedling crop, or as single plants. Single plants are either pulled up and harvested whole, or are cut several times.

CUT-AND-COME-AGAIN SEEDLING CROP Seed can be broadcast in patches, or sown in rows, or in wide drills. Sow thinly, as the seedlings should be spaced about 1¾ in (4.5 cm) apart. They can be thinned out if necessary. This method of growing gives high yields and tender leaves. (See also Part 2, Plant raising, page 155.)

SINGLE PLANTS There are several alternatives:
- Sow *in situ*, thinning to the required distance apart.
- Sow in a seed tray or seed bed and transplant.
- Sow in modules for transplanting. (See Part 2, Plant raising, Use of modules, page 153.) This is sometimes done for the winter greenhouse crop to get a larger root system.

Spacing

Plants can be spaced 3–6 in (7.5–15 cm) apart each way, depending on the variety.

Catchcropping and intercropping

As edible chrysanthemum is normally in the ground for no more than two or three months, it can be a useful catch crop. In spring it is often grown before tender summer crops such as tomatoes, peppers or gourds, or before Chinese cabbage and other oriental brassicas which cannot normally be sown until mid-summer. (See also Part 2, Plant raising, cropping systems, page 155.)

The fact that it is shade-tolerant, and the plants are relatively small if kept cut regularly, makes it suitable for intercropping between tall or slow growing crops.

Protected cropping

Edible chrysanthemum lends itself to cultivation in unheated greenhouses and polytunnels from late autumn to early spring. It can also be grown very successfully in cold frames, low polytunnels and under cloches. In north China the first crop each year is produced in the 'cold beds' protected by windbreaks (see Part 2, Protected cropping, Chinese solar frames, page 165.) Similarly, in the West, the first outdoor crop can be sown under cloches or low tunnels, which are removed when temperatures rise. Conversely, a late summer crop can be covered with cloches or low tunnels in late autumn. Make sure any winter crops are well ventilated on warm sunny days.

Containers

Edible chrysanthemum is a suitable subject for containers, not least because it responds well to being trimmed back and so kept within bounds.

Further care

Edible chrysanthemum is remarkably free from pests and diseases, and requires little attention other than being kept weed-free. This is essential in the early stages when the young plants are easily suffocated by weeds.

If growth is thin and spindly after a few weeks, pinch out the top 2 in (5 cm) of the main stem to encourage branching and the development of side shoots. Nip off any flower buds as they form, as growth becomes coarser and more bitter-flavoured once the plants flower.

In dry conditions water enough to prevent the soil drying out. Extra feeding is normally unnecessary, though in poor soil plants may benefit from liquid feeding after being cut. (See Part 2, Soil fertility, Liquid feeding, page 144.)

Harvesting

Seedlings The first cut can usually be made 4–5 weeks after sowing, when 2–4 in (5–10 cm) high. The plants regenerate rapidly and several cuts can be made from them over a month or so.

Single plants These are normally ready to be cut 6–8 weeks after sowing, when 5–10 in (13–25 cm) high. Some small and intermediate leaved types may be harvested whole at this point, when they are at their most tender. Alternatively, pick off tender shoots a few inches long, leaving the plant to develop more shoots. It may continue to do so for up to 3 months. Never be afraid to cut back fairly hard; it almost always stimulates the development of further side shoots.

As the plant matures the stems become too tough to use, but individual leaves can still be stripped off the stems for use.

Edible chrysanthemum wilts rapidly after it is picked, so is best cut just before it is required. It will keep for about 2 days wrapped in a fridge.

Varieties

At present named varieties are rare in Western catalogues. If 'labelled' at all, it is simply to denote whether they are small (serrated-leaved) types, or large (round-leaved) types. No doubt some of the improved varieties being developed, mainly in Japan, will eventually become available. In the meantime I would suggest growing the more adaptable smaller-leaved types for winter crops. Where the main requirement is for salads the larger-leaved types, with their milder and more tender leaves, are probably more suitable.

Cucurbits

Family *Cucurbitaceae*

General introduction

Background

The term 'cucurbit' is used widely, albeit loosely, to include cucumbers, melons, marrows and pumpkins (summer and winter squash), and other closely related but more exotic fruiting vegetables generally considered to be gourds. No traveller to China can fail to be intrigued by the strange gourds seen in markets. These range from the mighty winter melons—sometimes upright, rock-like specimens standing a couple of feet high and weighing 100 lb (45 kg) or more—to the snake gourd, with its well-named fruits anything from 1–2 yd (1–2 m) long.

None of the cucurbits can stand any frost, and many of the oriental species require long hot summers and near-tropical conditions to ma-

Cucurbit shoot tips and flowers

ture, so are unsuited to cool temperate climates. The exception is the robust Japanese pumpkin. In temperate and cool climates the warmth-loving species have to be grown in greenhouses—and even so you will be urging them on. Where summers are hot they will flourish: the problem then is keeping them under control.

From the many warmth lovers I have selected those which, for one reason or another, have already aroused interest in the West and are fairly frequently listed in seed catalogues: luffa, wax gourd, hairy melon, bottle gourd, oriental pickling melon and bitter gourd, with brief notes on oriental cucumber and spaghetti marrow.

Certain aspects of cultivation are common to all the cucurbits.

Site/soil

Avoid cold sites and exposed positions, and allow the plants plenty of room to spread.

The cucurbits are hungry and thirsty plants. The roots need to be able to 'romp' deeply and freely in fertile, well-prepared and well-drained soil: the roots of some of the larger types can penetrate as much as 6½ ft (2 m) deep. Prepare the ground by making individual holes at least 1 ft (30 cm) deep and 1½ ft (45 cm) wide, or 18 in by 2 ft (45 × 60 cm) for larger cucurbits. Fill this with well-rotted manure and compost, mixed thoroughly with good garden loam. This will supply nutrients, make the soil moisture-retentive and ensure good drainage. Cover it with 4–6 in (10–15 cm) of good garden soil. Alternatively, dig a single trench, prepared the same way.

Cucurbits are often planted on mounds or 'hills', several inches above ground level, to improve drainage.

Cultivation
Sowing

Once germinated the gourds grow very rapidly, so they can usually be sown 3–4 weeks before the last frost is expected in the area.

Most cucurbits will not transplant well unless handled very carefully, so in warm conditions they should be sown *in situ*. The soil temperature should be at least 56°F (13°C). Seeds are large and are normally sown about an inch (2.5 cm) deep. Sow them on their sides, not flat. In temperate areas cover them initially with a jam jar or cloche to encourage germination and protect them in the early stages.

In cool areas, and for those cucurbits which need a long season, it pays to start them off indoors. Sow in small pots or modules to minimize transplanting damage. (See also Part 2, Plant raising, Use of modules, page 153.) A minimum temperature of 56°F (13°C) is necessary for germination: in fact the higher the temperature the faster they will germinate. The optimum temperature is 95°F (35°C).

Seed can be soaked overnight before sowing, to assist germination; or it can be chitted, and sown when sprouted. In north China all cucurbits are given an early start by chitting the seed, and sowing them 3 in (7.5 cm) apart, on a very fine seedbed, each covered with a cone of very fine soil 1 in (2.5 cm) high. (See also Part 2, Plant raising, Germination test and chitted seed, page 150.)

Planting

Plant them in their permanent position when they have from 3 to 6 true leaves, hardening off well beforehand if planting outside. The neck of the plant is particularly vulnerable to rots, so should never be buried. When raised in small pots plant with the top inch or so of the pot sticking out of the soil. After planting mulch the plants, either with an organic mulch, or with black plastic film. (See Part 2, Weeds, mulching and watering, page 157.)

Supports

Most cucurbits will either trail over the ground or climb or clamber over supports. They take up less space, and the quality of the fruit is better, where they are allowed to grow up supports. This is particularly true of long fruits, which are apt to become twisted and curved on the ground, but will be much straighter if they can hang freely. (The Chinese sometimes hang weights on fruits to make them grow longer and straighter.) Pergolas, posts, bean poles, trellises, netting, strings and wires can all be used as supports: but they must be strong enough to bear the not inconsiderable weight of the plants.

The cucurbits may need to be 'helped' to climb by tying them in to the supports, especially in the early stages, or when they show signs of wandering too far afield.

The weighty giant gourds have to be grown on the flat. The leading shoot can be trained round and round in a circle, at intervals either pinning it down or burying the stem. This both saves space and looks neat. Most of the cucurbits develop roots on the stem, and this encourages them to do so, incidentally increasing the plant's food supply.

Pollination

Male and female flowers are usually borne separately, and are insect pollinated. The female flower can be distinguished by the tiny bump behind the petals, which develops into the fruit after fertilization. If fruits are failing to set, it may be necessary to hand pollinate. This is normally best done in the morning. Either take a male flower and insert it into the female flower, or use a paint brush to transfer pollen from the male flower to the stigma of the female flower. One male flower can be used for several female flowers.

Some species cross-pollinate very easily. This will not affect the fruit you are currently growing, but if you want to save seed for following seasons, you may find it has been hybridized. To prevent this different species of cucurbits will have to be grown in different parts of the garden.

Training

Fruits tend to develop on laterals and sublaterals, as well as on the main stem. With the more rampant gourds and pumpkins, never hesitate to nip out the main growing point when the first stem is 1–2 ft (30–60 cm) long. This will encourage the development of laterals. When growth becomes too rampant, shoots can be cut back to within a couple of inches of the nearest developing fruit.

Where masses of young fruits are forming, and only a few medium- to large-sized gourds are required, remove excess small fruits.

Further care

The cucurbits must always be kept well watered, especially as the fruits start to swell, but they must never be allowed to become waterlogged. Where grown on the flat, mark the plant with a tall cane when planting. By mid-season it can be hard to spot the position of the original plant among the forest of growth. The larger plants will benefit from supplementary liquid feeds several times during the growing season. (See Part 2, Soil fertility, Liquid feeding, page 144.)

Bitterness in fruits

In some cucurbits fruits may become bitter, due to a combination of genetic factors and growing conditions. In cucumbers the bitter factor has largely been removed in new varieties. A contemporary Chinese textbook on vegetables cites very high and very low temperatures, very high and very low nitrogen, and poor irrigation, as factors exacerbating bitterness.

Pests and disease

Generally speaking, the cucurbits grow healthily in suitable weather conditions. In the early stages slugs can be a problem; in warm climates aphids, and in the USA cucumber beetle and the range of pests common on summer squashes. When grown under glass red spider mite can be serious.

In cold weather cucurbits may be attacked by downy mildew, and in hot weather or dry conditions, powdery mildew. They are also susceptible to various, mainly soilborne, root rots and wilts; wax melon is sometimes grafted onto resistant pumpkin rootstocks to overcome them. Virus diseases are sometimes a problem: aphids and other insects which transmit virus diseases must be controlled. It is important to practise rotation, and to burn diseased material. (See also Part 2, Pests and disease.)

Harvesting, use of flowers, leaves and shoots

It is not always realized that the flowers, young shoots and young leaves of the cultivated cucurbits are edible.

Pick the male flowers once the female fruits have set—or use surplus female flowers. They can be stuffed, or used in soups or salads.

Pick shoots from the top 6 in (15 cm) or so of the stems. New shoots will soon be produced. Remove any tough fibres on the stem. Shoot tips and young leaves can be boiled like greens.

Oriental cucumber
(*Cucumis sativus*)

The Chinese consider cucumber a 'Western' vegetable, and indeed, the ordinary Chinese cucumber is very similar to the traditional, stumpy, rough-skinned European 'ridge' cucumber. They probably share common ancestry. This type is notable for its robustness and disease resistance. The Japanese have used the Chinese cucumber to develop an excellent range of long-fruited outdoor cucumbers such as 'Chinese Long Green' and 'Kyoto Three Foot' which have become very popular in the West.

Besides using cucumbers raw, the Chinese use very ripe, yellowing cucumbers for making soup, cutting the skin and juicy flesh into cubes. It is also very popular as a pickling vegetable.

Oriental cucumbers are cultivated in the same way as Western cucumbers.

Spaghetti marrow/vegetable spaghetti (*Cucurbita pepo*)

Vegetable spaghetti is probably Chinese in origin. It is widely grown in China, and in recent years has become very popular in the West.

Sometimes classified as a vegetable marrow, sometimes as winter squash or pumpkin, the cylindrical, marrow-like fruits grow to about 12 in (30 cm) long and about 8 in (20 cm) wide. They are a pale, creamy colour when young, becoming yellow to orange when mature. It owes its popularity to the flesh taking the form of translucent threads, which after cooking for about 20 minutes bear a close resemblance to spaghetti. It can be scooped straight out of the shell on to a plate. I personally find vegetable spaghetti rather bland, but it has an enthusiastic following.

It is easily grown, early maturing and prolific. Fruits can be used young, or mature fruits stored for several months. The vines are trailing, and plants need to be spaced about a yard apart. Recently introduced improved varieties include 'Orangetti' and 'Gogetti'. For cultivation see Japanese pumpkin.

Luffa

Angled luffa

Latin name   *Luffa acutangula*
Other names in use   Chinese okra
Mandarin   Si gua ('silk gourd'); lin jiao si gua; you lin si gua (both mean 'angled silk gourd')
Cantonese   Sze/see kwa

Smooth luffa

Latin name   *Luffa cylindrica* (*L. aegyptica*)
Other names in use   Dish cloth/dish rag gourd; sponge gourd; vegetable sponge
Mandarin   Si gua ('silk gourd'); shui gwa ('water gourd'); pu tong si gua ('common silk gourd'); man gua ('wild silk gourd')
Cantonese   See kwa; shih kwa
Japanese   Hechima; ito-uri

Background

Luffas are a very popular vegetable all over China. They grow like weeds, dangling from upstairs balconies, scrambling over fences, and climbing up canes which straddle irrigation channels.

Two types of luffa are grown for use as a vegetable when immature: the angled luffa and the smooth 'sponge' luffa. Western gardeners

Use

Luffas can only be eaten when young. The mature luffas become very bitter, due to the development of purgative chemicals. The texture and flavour of young luffas is very similar to courgettes.

In the kitchen

The fruits are prepared and cooked much as courgettes, sliced, peeled or grated. Try them grated, lightly cooked, and folded into a crab omelette. When very young they can be used unpeeled, but the peel becomes bitter later, and should be removed. If the ridges are peeled off angled luffas, you get a pretty striped pattern.

The young shoots, young leaves and flower buds are edible, and are usually stir-fried or deep-fried.

In China and Japan the young fruits are sliced and dried for use in winter.

(See also Recipes, page 192.)

---

are often tempted to grow luffas in the hope of producing a home-grown backscrubber. Although both types *could* be made into sponges, the smooth luffa is used for the purpose as it is much easier to extract the fibrous skeleton of the mature, dried luffa—which becomes the sponge. (See drying mature luffas, below.) The best-quality sponge luffas are grown in Japan, and exported all over the world.

The 'sponges' have been put to many uses besides backscrubbers. Before the Second World War they were used as filters in the US navy steam engines; they are still used in Asia for cleaning dishes and scouring pots, and in the manufacture of a wide range of products including mats and shoes.

Characteristics

Luffas are climbing annuals, growing up to about 15 ft (4.5 m). They have large leaves, which in the smooth luffa are pale, with silvery patches, and deeply cut.

The fruits of the ridged luffa are usually 1–2 ft (30–60 cm) long, though they can grow very much longer. They are 1–2 in (2.5–5 cm) in diameter, dark green, and characterized by ten raised ridges running down the fruit. This gives a superficial resemblance to okra and explains the misleading name 'Chinese okra' often applied to ridged luffa.

The fruits of the smooth luffa are normally 12–18 in (30–45 cm) long, cylindrical and smooth, though they are sometimes very slightly ridged. They are green and often lightly striped, and generally much heavier than the fruits of the angled luffa. They tend to be larger at the lower end and are often described as bat-shaped.

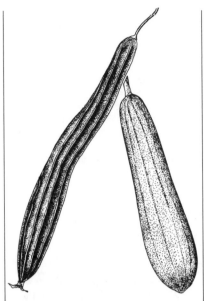

Angled (*left*) and smooth luffa (*right*)

Climate

Although luffas flourish in warm and tropical climates, they need a long growing season to mature, and can only be cultivated successfully outdoors in the *warmer* temperate regions. Elsewhere they must be sown in greenhouses—best of all, gently heated greenhouses. In conditions where greenhouse cucumbers are grown successfully, there is a good chance of succeeding with luffa, though they would ideally require slightly higher temperatures.

Some varieties are sensitive to daylength, and will only flower and fruit in the short days of late summer. For northern latitudes long-day varieties must be used. Some are being developed in Taiwan.

Cultivation

For site, soil and cultivation see Cucurbits, General introduction.

The seed coat is hard, so seeds should be soaked in water for 24 hours before sowing. Space plants about 2 ft (60 cm) apart, planting at the foot of supports. Tie them to the supports if necessary. It is advisable to pinch out the tips when about

5 ft (1.5 m) high to encourage fruit development.

In the past in England luffas were sometimes grown in frames, kept within bounds by pinching out the top after four or five leaves had developed, and later pinching out the tips of the laterals which subsequently formed. Even so, they only expected to be able to harvest immature fruits in September.

Pollination

There are usually far more male than female flowers. Once female flowers appear it is advisable to hand-pollinate them. This should be done in the morning where possible, but in the ridged luffa the flowers open in the evening. In cold climates the young luffas may drop off prematurely. (See also Cucurbits, General introduction.)

Harvesting

For use as a vegetable pick luffas between 4–6 in (10–15 cm) long, just before required as they do not store well. This stage may be reached two to three months after sowing.

Drying mature luffas The skeleton of immature fruits will not become rigid enough to use as luffa sponges, so fruits must be allowed to hang on the vine until they are mature, the skin hardens and the stems turn yellow. After cutting them down drying can continue for a few weeks, in a warm kitchen indoors if necessary, until the skin is brown. Then peel off the thin outer skin, and remove the pulp clinging to the skeleton by rinsing in running water. It may be necessary to soak them for several days before the job is completed. They can be bleached by soaking in weak household bleach.

Seeds extracted from the luffas can be saved for another season.

Varieties

There are several varieties, of different lengths and widths. For luffa sponges, the longer the variety the better.

Wax gourd

Latin name *Benincasa hispida*
Other names in use Winter gourd/melon; white gourd; Chinese preserving melon; Chinese squash; ash gourd/pumpkin; Chinese wax gourd
Mandarin Dong gwa ('winter gourd')
Cantonese Tung kwa
Japanese Tohgan

Note In the West 'gourd' and 'melon' are used loosely and interchangeably in describing various oriental cucurbits.

Background

These giant vegetables are the hallmark of Chinese communities all over the world. They are thought to have originated in Java, but have been grown in China since ancient times. Apart from its culinary uses wax gourd is reputed to have medicinal properties. In the past the waxy coat was used to make candles.

Characteristics

Wax gourd is a vigorous annual, which will climb or sprawl over the ground like a pumpkin. The stems are thick, furrowed and hairy; the

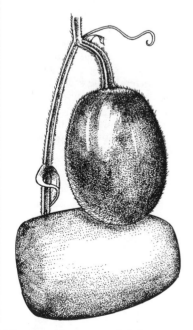

Wax gourd fruits: roundish form (*above*) and boxy form (*below*)

large, rather beautiful leaves are rough to touch.

In the immature fruits the skin colour can be various shades, from light or dark green to a purple blue—depending on the variety. The flesh is white. In the smaller-fruited varieties the young fruits are covered in downy hairs and are used as 'hairy melons'. (See Hairy melon, page 85.)

It is the mature wax gourds which are so remarkable. The mature fruits develop a distinctive waxy layer, which is sometimes chalky-white. This protective layer enables them to be stored for long periods. They vary in shape from truly spherical, to round with flattened ends, to a cylindrical sausage or 'Chinese pillow' shape.

There is also enormous variation in the size, both round and long types having small and giant forms. The smallest 'family size' winter melons weigh 5–10 lb (2.2–4.5 kg), and are roughly 12 in (30 cm) diameter or 15 in (38 cm) long.

The giant round gourds can be up to 20 in (50 cm) in diameter, and the long types 2–4 ft (60–120 cm) long. These can weigh anything from 25 to 100 lb (11–45 kg). I have been told of 1100-lb (5000-kg) monsters being produced by burying the stems so they produce extra roots, one plant eventually covering a whole acre of ground!

The roots have considerable resistance to various soil-borne diseases, and are sometimes used as a rootstock for other cucurbits, such as melons, which are grafted on to them.

Use

Wax gourd has a juicy texture and mild flavour, verging on the bland in mature melons, but stronger flavoured in semi-mature and young fruit. Its nutritive value is low.

In the kitchen

Whole wax gourds are stuffed and baked, but their best-known use is in making 'winter melon pond soup', a feature of Chinese banquets. For this the outer surface of the gourd is beautifully carved (after scrubbing off the waxy coat), and the melon itself is used as a vessel in which a multi-ingredient soup is steamed for several hours. It is served at table in the gourd, chunks of the flesh being scooped out and served with the soup. Even though the 'pond' is only made with 'smallish' wax gourds, the logistics of the steaming operation are formidable. Only firm-fleshed varieties can be used.

Wax gourds are also cut into sections, peeled, and cut into smaller chunks or slices for use in soups, or stir-fried with meat. The chunks take on an attractive translucent quality when cooked. Wax gourd is also used to make a rather strange tea.

(For use of very young wax gourds see Hairy melon, page 85.) Leaves and young flower buds are also edible. (See Cucurbits, General introduction, page 80.)

Wax gourd is widely used to make pickles, and sweet candied preserves, not unlike Turkish delight in taste and texture.

(See also Recipes, page 196.)

Climate

The optimum temperature when growing is 73–82°F (23–28°C). Wax gourds need a long growing season of about 5 months to develop to maturity, though they can be harvested at various immature stages.

Site/soil

See Cucurbits, General introduction, page 79.

Wax gourd is reasonably drought-tolerant. Where large fruits are wanted they are grown flat on the ground: otherwise they are allowed to trail over fences etc. or to climb up supports.

Cultivation

Sowing method, planting

See Cucurbits, General introduction.

The seeds can be chitted to get them off to a good start. For the first few weeks after germination try to maintain a minimum night temperature of at least 50°F (10°C)—higher if possible. They can be planted in their permanent positions when 6–8 in (15–20 cm) tall.

Seed can be sown *in situ* outdoors only in very warm areas, after all risk of frost is past. Mice are partial to the seeds, so set a few mousetraps when sowing. Sow several seeds per station, about 1 in (2.5 cm) deep, thinning to the one or two strongest when the plants are a few inches tall.

Spacing

Where grown upright, allow at least 2 ft (60 cm) between plants. Where trailing over the ground, space them 8–10 ft (2.4–3 m) apart.

Further care

Regular feeding, every three weeks or so, with a general liquid feed will be beneficial; such large plants naturally respond to generous feeding. (See Cucurbits, General introduction, page 80.)

Training

Plants may need tying to supports, especially in the early stages.

The growing points can be nipped out of climbing plants when they reach the top of the supports, unless there is space to continue training them horizontally. The first fruits are usually borne on the main stem, and later fruits on the laterals which develop. In the later stages the growing points of some of the laterals can be nipped off to keep plants in check. Some Chinese growers advocate nipping out the growing point on the young plant after about four leaves have appeared, allowing four branches to develop. This method has proved successful in greenhouse production in Europe. It may give earlier fruiting.

Once the fruits start to form on trailing plants a little straw should be tucked beneath them to keep them dry. Weighty suspended fruits may need to be supported by nets attached to something firm, so they don't pull down the vine.

Pollination

Plants usually start to flower 60–80 days after planting. In cold climates fruit setting may be a problem, with young fruits turning yellow and falling off instead of developing properly. In this case hand pollination is recommended. (See Cucurbits, General introduction.) One commercial grower in the British Isles keeps a hive of bees in the greenhouse to ensure pollination.

Harvesting

Immature fruit Very young 'hairy melons', a few inches long, can sometimes be picked as soon as a week after the flowers have been pollinated. (See Hairy melon, page 85.) From then on immature melons can be picked at whatever size they are required. They are used fresh as they will not keep in good condition for more than a week or two.

Mature fruit If wanted for storage it is essential to wait until the gourds are mature and the waxy bloom is starting to appear.

Storage

Mature wax gourds keep for at least six months, sometimes up to a year. They should be stored at 'cool room' temperatures, ideally at 55–59°F (13–15°C), in a fairly dry atmosphere. They can be suspended in nets or sacks, or placed on shelves, singly, not stacked, with the paler, lower side, facing down.

In south China fruits which mature in early summer are stored in open outdoor sheds for use in the height of summer. They are piled several deep and given a half turn every week.

Drying The pulp of wax gourds can be shredded and dried for winter use. (See Japanese pumpkin, page 89.)

Varieties

In China some varieties are considered best for certain purposes, i.e. for making 'pond soup', for sweet preserves, or for storage. As there is little choice of variety in the West at present, one has to assume, unless seed packets state to the contrary, that a given variety can be used both as a fresh vegetable when immature and, when mature, harvested for storage. Small round varieties tend to be earliest, and the most suitable for temperate climates.

'Jointed gourd/melon' is a variety of wax melon used primarily as a hairy melon, *qv.*

Hairy melon (Jointed gourd)*

Latin name *Benincasa hispida* var *chieh-gua*
Other names in use Hairy gourd; fuzzy gourd/melon; hairy cucumber
Mandarin Mao gua ('hairy gourd'); jie gua ('joint/node gourd')
Cantonese Mo kwa; tsit/tse/tsee kwa

* Strictly speaking, hairy melon is the immature young fruit of a variety of wax gourd known as the 'jointed gourd'. However young fruits of small fruited types of wax gourd described in the previous section are also grown as hairy melons. To add to the confusion, some varieties of bottle gourd are known in Chinese as 'hairy gourd'. (See Bottle gourd, below.)

Characteristics

Think of the hairy melons as oriental courgettes. Just as courgettes are 'baby' marrows—and usually far better tasting than a full-grown marrow—so the hairy melons are generally firmer textured and better flavoured than the adult gourds they would eventually become.

The common feature of all hairy gourds is the soft downiness on the skin, which they lose as they mature. Their texture is firm. The jointed gourd fruits are cylindrical, slightly narrowed in the centre, their length being two or three times their width. Those from ordinary wax gourds are long or round depending on the 'parent' variety. The mature fruit of the jointed gourd does not develop a wax layer like other wax gourds. The leaves are hard textured, like cucumber leaves, and the flowers are yellow.

Climate, soil/site, cultivation, training, pollination

See Wax gourd, page 83.

As the fruits are harvested young, hairy melon is a better bet than many gourds in temperate climates. Plants can be grown a little closer than the distances recommended for mature gourds. They are best trained up supports.

Hairy melon

Use
In the kitchen

Hairy melons have a pleasant flavour, much like courgettes. The fruits can be peeled or the hairs removed by scrubbing or rubbing with paper towelling. However, I found this unnecessary with home-picked fruits, as the hairs disappear in cooking. Cut the fruits into chunks, slices or matchsticks for cooking.

They can be cooked by any method used for courgettes, taking care not to overcook them, or the flavour is lost. They are frequently stir-fried, either on their own, thickened with cornflour and seasoned with sugar, garlic, soy or oyster sauce, or in mixed meat or fish dishes. A Taiwanese recipe suggests shredding and frying with chillies. They can also be steamed, used in soup, or hollowed out carefully and stuffed. The leaves and shoot tips can be cooked as greens.

(See also Recipes, page 191.)

Harvesting

The jointed gourd produces a good crop of fruits, initially on the main stem, and later on laterals. Pick fruits when still covered in silky hairs, anything from 4–8 in (10–20 cm) long, and up to about 1 lb (450 g) in weight. They are ready about 90 days after sowing.

Edible bottle gourd

Latin name *Lagenaria siceraria* (*L. leucantha*)
Other names in use Calabash gourd; dudi; white-flowered gourd
Mandarin Mao gua ('hairy gourd') (edible type); hu gua and hu lu gua ('bottle gourd') (hard-shelled type)*
Cantonese Po/poo gwa (edible type); oo lo/wu lo kwa (hard-shelled type)

* There are many other highly descriptive Chinese names.

Use
In the kitchen

Bottle gourds are a popular vegetable in China, and are used in soups and stir-fried in much the same way as courgettes or hairy melon. They are considered to have a good flavour. Leaves and shoot tips are cooked as greens. Hard seeds should be removed before cooking.

Japanese *kampyo* is made by paring bottle gourd flesh into long thin strips or ribbons and drying it. It is used to flavour *maki sushi*—vinegarized rice rolled up in a sheet of seaweed, or to tie bundles of food for steaming—once picturesquely described as 'edible string'. Before use *kampyo* is usually soaked, salted, rinsed, and boiled to soften it.

Characteristics and types

Bottle gourd plants are exceptionally vigorous climbing vines, with impressive strong tendrils which twine round strings, other plants and any object within grasp with unbelievable tenacity. The enormous leaves have a remarkably soft, felt-like texture, and a strange musky scent some people find repulsive. They have pretty white flowers.

The many varieties produce fruits of all shapes and sizes, of which only a few kinds are used as vegetables when immature. These include thin varieties up to 24 in (60 cm) long and no more than 2–3 in (5–7.5 cm) thick, with a slightly swollen, bat-like end; longer and wider varieties, up to 36 in (90 cm) long and about 8 in (20 cm) thick; and some round varieties growing to football size. Most round varieties are too bitter to eat. Bottle gourds have a smooth skin (some are slightly hairy when very young), and are light green.

In addition there are many varieties of bottle gourd which develop a hard wooden shell when mature and dried, and are used to make drinking gourds, bowls, musical instruments and so on. They often have a characteristic, indented 'waist'. Initials carved in the young fruits will swell as the fruits grow, marking the matured wooden shell. The majority of these varieties are inedible.

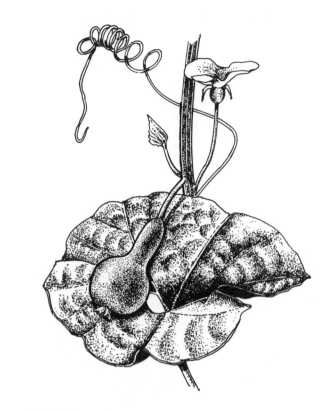

Young edible bottle gourd

Climate, soil/site, cultivation, training, pollination

See Cucurbits, General introduction.

In my experience the edible bottle gourds tolerate lower growing temperatures than some other oriental gourds. I have also found them remarkably pest and disease free, even displaying considerable resistance to red spider mite. The downy texture and strong smell of the leaves may act as a deterrent.

Bottle gourds are best trained off the ground so the gourds can hang straight. As the plants are so vigorous and all-engulfing, and the best fruits develop on laterals, it is advisable to nip out the growing point in the early stages and train shoots upwards. Hand pollination of the fruits is recommended. To keep plants within bounds have no hesitation about trimming back long shoots, and cutting off any growth a couple of leaves beyond a fruit.

Harvesting

For use, fresh fruits must be picked before the skin has hardened. Young fruits of round varieties are harvested at about 4 in (10 cm) diameter, and long varieties can be picked at any stage. The younger they are, the more tender they will be.

Varieties

The following are suitable for use as a vegetable.
'Early Long Green' Fruits 2 ft (60 cm) long, narrow, bat-shaped type.
'Large and Long' Longer, broader fruits, weighing up to 20 lb (9 kg).
'Calabash' Round fruits, growing to football size, mainly used for dried flesh.

Pickling melon

Latin name *Cucumis melo* var *conomon*
Other names in use Chinese white cucumber
Mandarin Yue gua
Cantonese ts' it kwa; uet kwa
Japanese Uri; shiro uri

Characteristics

The oriental pickling melon is a climbing annual, growing very vigorously in warm climates. Although it is a species of melon, in most varieties the fruits look far more like fat cucumbers than a typical rounded melon. They grow up to 12 in (30 cm) long, and usually about 3 in (7.5 cm) in diameter. Some varieties have round fruits. Skin colour varies: it can be white, light or dark green, mottled, or green with white, light green or golden stripes. The skin tends to turn white as they mature.

Pickling melon tub

Climate

Pickling melons are warmth lovers. The optimum temperature for growth is 77–85°F (25–30°C), and growth is very poor at temperatures below 55°F (13°C). My only attempt to cultivate them foundered in an exceptionally miserable English summer. They can however be grown successfully in many parts of the United States, and should do well in southern Europe.

Soil/site, cultivation, training, pollination

See Cucurbits, General introduction.

Seeds should be germinated at a temperature of 68°F (20°C). Pickling melon can be grown on the flat, spacing plants 5 ft (150 cm) apart each way, or trained up supports about 2 ft (60 cm) apart. Keep nipping back the tips of shoots to encourage the development of laterals. If the fruits are not setting well hand pollination is advisable.

Use
In the kitchen

Pickling melon can be stuffed, stir-fried with meat, chicken or vegetables etc., or made into soup. Young pickling melons can be sliced and eaten raw like cucumbers.

In China and Japan the fruits are mainly grown for pickling. In Taiwan I watched a family pickling melons, perched on tiny stools under a bamboo awning on the outskirts of a market. The foot-long melons were first sliced in half, then quartered, then deseeded before being put into large wooden tubs and salted. When the tub was full huge smooth stones were piled on top in a carefully balanced pyramid. The pickles were left for 24 hours before being drained and sold as fresh pickles.

Harvesting

The earliest maturing varieties are ready about 2½ months after planting. For use fresh pick them about 12 in (30 cm) long. For pickling harvest before they show signs of turning white.

Varieties

'Numame Early', F1 'Narita Green' and 'Tokyo Wase Shiro Uri' are early-maturing varieties.

Bitter gourd

Latin name *Momordica charantia*
Other names in use Bitter melon/cucumber; karella; balsam pear; alligator pear
Mandarin Ku gua ('bitter gourd'); jin li zhi ('bright beautiful lichee'); lao pu tao ('ugly grape')
Cantonese Fu kwa
Japanese Reishi; niga uri

Background

Until recently this strange-looking vegetable of tropical origins was little known outside south China, south-east Asia, India and the Philippines. It is now a familiar sight in the West, in the British Isles known by its Indian name, karella.

Characteristics

The plant is a very pretty vigorous annual vine, capable of climbing to well over 12 ft (3.6 m). The stems are thinner and woodier than a cucumber's. The attractive leaves are deeply indented; the dainty yellow flowers are fragrant.

The fruits are beautiful. Their waxy, warty skins look as if they rubbed shoulders with alligators in the primordial slime. Ten slightly smoothed ridges run the length of the fruit, with dozens of little blistered warty bumps packed between them. The immature fruits are either pale green, dark green or a silvery white when immature, all turning an orangy red when fully ripe. The mature fruits sometimes split open revealing an interior of dramatically red pulp.

Fruit size and shape varies considerably, depending on variety. They may be spindle-shaped, pear-shaped, or more or less oblong, almost always tapered towards the tip. The average length of mature specimens is 4–8 in (10–20 cm), but some are shorter, some much longer. Average width is about 2 in (5 cm), though some broad spindle types are 6 in (15 cm) wide.

Although high yields of bitter gourd have rarely been achieved in the West, the answer to better performance may lie in improved strains.

Climate

Bitter gourd prefers a warm, humid climate: the indications are that it requires more heat than the wax gourd and other gourds covered earlier. It has been grown fairly successfully in unheated greenhouses in the British Isles, but would fruit more heavily at higher temperatures. It does well outdoors in parts of the United States with warm summers.

Site/soil

See Cucurbits, General introduction.

Bitter gourd tolerates a wide range of soil types, but requires

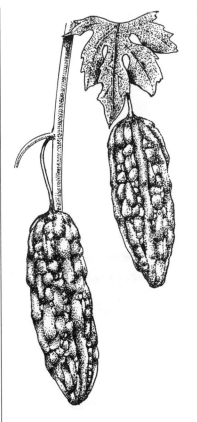

Bitter gourd

plenty of water throughout growth. In cool climates it makes an unusual greenhouse climber, in warmer climates a striking summer hedge or fence.

Cultivation
Sowing

As bitter gourd seeds lose their viability rapidly, germination problems are common. Unless the seed is very fresh, pre-germinating before sowing is recommended. Soak the seeds in water for 24 hours, then wrap them in damp paper towelling, put them in a plastic bag and keep them at a temperature of 80–85°F (26–29°C). They should germinate within a couple of days. Sow the germinated seed in modules or small pots. In very warm areas they can be sown *in situ* outdoors. (See also Cucurbits, General introduction.)

In India the germination problem is apparently solved by press-

Use

It is grown mainly for the immature fruits, though the young leafy shoots and leaves are edible. All parts are said to be very nutritious.

In the kitchen

In their natural state the immature fruits have a bitter flavour, due to the presence of quinine. It is a strong, unusual flavour, with perhaps a hint of okra or aubergine about it. Bitter gourd appears to bring out the flavour of other ingredients during cooking, and is in turn neutralized by them.

Bitter gourds are usually cooked unpeeled, though the rougher parts of the outer skin can be scraped off. Except in very young fruit, the seeds (which are purgative) and soft pith must be removed.

If the natural taste is considered too bitter, the flavour can be modified by blanching or salting before cooking. Either cut the fruits in half, remove the seeds and parboil for a couple of minutes, or make slits in the fruit or cut them into slices, sprinkle with salt, leave for at least 10 minutes before squeezing out the juice and rinsing thoroughly.

Bitter gourds are cooked in many ways. They are often stuffed and steamed, either in halves, or whole with the tops cut off to remove the seeds etc. Fish and meat stuffings are the most popular. They are also stir-fried with meat, such as crispy pork, or with other vegetables. They are frequently combined with black fermented soya beans, and used in curries. They can also be pickled and made into chutney. Leaves and young shoots must be parboiled for a few minutes, the water changed, then boiled or stir-fried like greens.

(See also Recipes, page 187.)

ing fresh seed into fresh cow dung, drying it, and storing until required for planting.

Growing on, planting

During the early stages of growth try and maintain minimum temperatures of 64°F (18°C); certainly the temperature should not fall below 50°F (10°C). If the plants are outgrowing the modules or small pots, pot them on, in good potting compost, in 4–5 in (10–13 cm) pots. Keep them well spaced out, so the young trailing stems don't get entangled with each other.

Planting, supports, training

Plant in their permanent positions in early summer, at the foot of supports, spacing plants 2 ft apart (60 cm) each way, or 1 ft (30 cm) apart in rows 3 ft (90 cm) apart. Watch out for slug damage in the early stages.

In the Indochinese community gardens I visited in Seattle, where the climate precludes very rampant growth, bitter gourds were trained horizontally over a low trellis of wooden slats on 2–3 ft (60–90 cm) high posts. The fruit was able to hang down freely. Otherwise it has a tendency to get 'lost' in the foliage.

When grown under glass in Europe they are usually trained up strings or up 6–8 in (15–20 cm) netting, hung vertically from the roof of a greenhouse to ground level. Bitter gourd more or less clings naturally to supports; however it may be necessary to tie or tuck in 'wandering' shoots, and to trim back excessive growth.

Further care

Bitter gourd needs plenty of water throughout growth. Provided the soil is fertile and plenty of organic matter was dug in initially, extra feeding is normally unnecessary. If growth seems poor occasional liquid feeds could be beneficial. (See also Cucurbits, General introduction.)

Pollination

See Cucurbits, General introduction. Bitter gourds normally need to be hand pollinated. When grown commercially under glass beehives are sometimes introduced to ensure pollination.

Harvesting

The first fruits are ready on average 8–9 weeks after planting. They can be picked at any length from a couple of inches (5 cm) to their full length. They must be picked before they ripen, while firm to the touch and before developing any orange tints. They are very sensitive to the ethylene given off by ripening fruit and once full-grown ripen rapidly within a couple of days. They must therefore be picked regularly. They will continue to ripen after picking. In Taiwan ripening fruits may be protected with a paper bag while still on the tree to shield them from the sun, which darkens the fruits and makes them more bitter. It also protects them from insect pests.

Varieties

Varieties are currently named according to their physical characteristics: light green, dark green, spindle-shaped etc. There is a need for improved higher-yielding varieties selected for short growing seasons in cool climates to make the crop more worth growing.

Japanese pumpkin

Latin names *Cucurbita moschata* and *Cucurbita maxima*, and some hybrids between the two
Japanese Kabocha
Mandarin Nan gua ('southern gourd')
Cantonese Nam kwa

Background

The many kinds of pumpkin (winter squash) already widely grown in the West are outside the scope of this book. In recent years several smaller varieties, developed mainly in Japan and generally known as 'Japanese pumpkins', have appeared and become very popular on account of their excellent culinary and storage properties. When mature they are more solid and less watery than most pumpkins, with drier, sweeter flesh with a nutty flavour.

Characteristics

There seem to be two main types. As with all pumpkins, there is enormous variation in appearance and hybridization between the two groups has occurred, blurring the distinctions between them.

The 'Green Hokkaido' type
These are flattish, round pump-

Use
In the kitchen

Pumpkins are much more nutritious than courgettes and marrows (summer squash), and can be used both in savoury and sweet dishes. As a vegetable they can be puréed, cut into chunks and stir-fried or deep-fried, made into soup, or cooked with mustard greens. The many forms of pumpkin pie are the best known desserts. They also make excellent sweet pickles, not unlike mango chutney. The ripe seeds can be roasted. (For use of flowers, growing shoots and young leaves see Cucurbits, page 80.) (See also Recipes, page 194.)

kins, to a greater or lesser degree ribbed. The skin is typically dark green, sometimes nearly grey, often turning yellow and occasionally brown or red on maturity. In some varieties the skin is mottled, striped or warted. (The variety 'Chirimen' is well known for its very warted skin—though the Japanese word 'chirimen' translates more elegantly as 'crêpe'.) The flesh is yellow, usually becoming orange on maturity. They are normally 5–10 in (13–25 cm) in diameter, with an average weight of 2–5 lb (1–2.2 kg). These kinds have probably been developed from Chinese pumpkins.

Some forms have a distinctive flattish cap or button, several inches in diameter, on the crown. The popular American-bred variety 'Buttercup' is very similar in appearance and character to these.

The 'Orange Hokkaido' type
These are 'tear drop' or pear shaped. They have a smooth golden skin, ripening to a beautiful orange, and yellow flesh. They average 6 in (15 cm) in diameter and weigh 5–10 lb (2.2–4.5 kg). There are also some blue-green

Japanese pumpkins: flat type (*above*) and tear-drop type (*below*)

skinned forms of this type. They have been developed from the famous American 'Hubbard' squashes, and in the United States are sometimes known as the 'Baby Red Hubbard'. The original 'Orange Hokkaido' is known in Japan as 'Uchiki kuri' or 'Red kuri'.

Climate

See Cucurbits, General introduction, page 79.

They require a growing season of 3–4 months, with mean monthly temperatures of 60–80°F (18–27°C).

Site/soil, cultivation, training

See Cucurbits, General introduction, page 79.

Japanese pumpkins are best grown on the flat. They are fairly robust and disease-free, powdery mildew and rots being the most likely problems. (See Part 2, Pests and disease.)

Harvesting

Although pumpkins can be used immature, flavour and texture are better in mature fruits.

Where pumpkins are grown for winter storage they must be harvested mature. Signs of maturity are:
● Skin colour changing from light to dark, and with some of the green pumpkins losing their glossiness.
● Stalks becoming corky and dry. About 50 per cent brown is a good sign of maturity.
● Skin cannot be pierced with a thumbnail.
● Flesh is orange rather than yellow, and seeds are hard.
Pumpkins should be left on the

vines as long as possible, but harvested before frost. Cut them with a 1–2 in (2.5–5 cm) stalk. Most varieties then need to be cured in the sun for about 10 days to allow the stems to seal and the skin to set. If necessary put them against a sunny wall or, in poor weather, in a greenhouse. Protect them from frost at night.

Pumpkins should be stored in well ventilated conditions at temperatures between 45–60°F (7–16°C). At higher temperatures they will dry out. On average they will keep 6 months, depending on the variety and storage conditions.
DRYING AND FREEZING Pumpkin flesh can be dried for winter use. A Chinese method is to cut the pumpkin into strips 1/8–1/4 in (2–4 mm) thick. These are boiled for 1–2 minutes before drying, so they retain their colour and do not smell.

Cubed, uncooked pumpkin and cooked pumpkin purée freeze well.

Varieties

'Green Hokkaido' type
F1 'Butterball', 'Buttercup', 'Chirimen', 'Delica', 'Green Hokkaido', F1 'Iron Cap', F1 'Kurinishiki', F1 'Sweet Delite' (improved form of 'Home Delite').
'Orange Hokkaido' type
Golden Debut, Onion Squash, Orange Hokkaido (Red Kuri), Blue Kiri (a flatter, blue-green form).

'Small Chinese Turban' (Hong nan gua 'red southern gourd') Small, 2–3 lb (1–1.5 kg) pumpkin. Many forms; often bright red with yellow and green stripes and small, bumpy 'top knot', resembling European 'Turk's Cap' or 'Turban' pumpkin. Firm, sweet, good quality flesh.

Garlic

Family *Alliaceae*
Latin names *Allium sativum*
Mandarin Suan; hu; hu suan (garlic plant); da suan (garlic clove);
   suan miao (garlic shoots/leaves); suan tai (flower stem); suan qing
   (green-leaved garlic with small bulb)
Cantonese Suen tau/tao; taai suan
Japanese Nin-niku

Background

To most Westerners 'garlic' is syn-onymous with dried bulbs and the sickle-shaped white cloves. The Chinese also use the young green leaves (fresh or blanched), the whole, immature plant of young leaves and an undivided bulb (sometimes sold in the United States as 'fresh' or 'baby garlic'), and the young flower stem.

True garlic is not found in the wild, but the ancestral garlic is thought to have come from central Asia. The Chinese are known to have cultivated it since at least 3000 BC. In many cultures garlic is associated with good health. Its antibiotic and antiseptic properties are well established, but it is also very nutritious, rich in minerals and vitamins.

My memories of our Chinese 'vegetable tour' are peppered with garlic scenes. There was the old lady with a garlic and ginger stall in Chengdu. Her stock included large pink and white bulbs, a range of cloves graded by size, 'rounds' (sold mostly for planting), and peeled cloves for the hard-pressed house-wife. While she ate her breakfast noodles out of an enamel mug, an elderly man in the background was patiently peeling cloves. In Shang-hai we visited a food processing factory where girls in the quality control department were sorting through huge piles of dehydrated garlic flakes. The rejected overhe-ated or poor-coloured flakes were made into spicy soy sauce or medi-cal preparations.

As for the garlic flower stems, I was completely baffled when I first saw these long, slightly twisted stems, with flower heads attached,

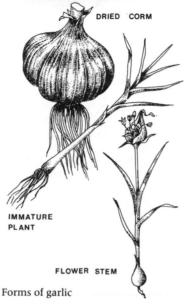

DRIED CORM

IMMATURE PLANT

FLOWER STEM

Forms of garlic

in a Beijing market. Later, in a Jap-anese supermarket, I sampled a 'taster' of garlic stems, dressed in oil and soy sauce. They make a deli-cious appetizer.

Characteristics

Garlic is a biennial, though if left in the ground it will perpetuate itself and behave like a perennial.

The leaves are flat and narrow, varying in width from ½–1 in (1–2.5 cm) depending on the type. They are mostly up to 1 ft (30 cm) tall but some forms grow up to 3 ft (about 1 m). The leaves are usually erect initially, but there are some forms with softer, more drooping leaves.

The garlic bulb, unlike the bulbs of other members of the garlic fam-ily, develops a couple of inches be-low ground. Anything from half a dozen to over thirty individual cloves develop within the encom-passing, papery, outer skins of the

Use
In the kitchen

Garlic, with its unique, sweet pungency, is one of the most distinctive and best known of culinary flavours. What is not always appreciated is the rela-tionship between the way garlic is prepared and the strength of the garlic flavour. The true garlic flavour is re-leased by chemical reactions which occur when the plant cells are broken. So the garlic flavour is strongest when cloves are squeezed and juice extracted, slightly less strong when grated or finely chopped, less again with sliced cloves and mildest with whole cloves. In addition, the longer garlic is cooked, the milder it becomes. Mildest of all are cloves cooked whole—whether boiled, baked or sau-téd.

Pink-skinned garlic is gener-ally considered better fla-voured than white-skinned; flavour is also influenced by climate and husbandry. To test the flavour cut a clove in half lengthwise and touch the cut surface with the tip of the tongue. The more it 'stings', the better the garlic.

Peeling garlic cloves is la-borious. Try the Chinese trick of bruising them with the side of a kitchen knife or cleaver: the papery skin then tends to break away.

In Chinese wok cookery sliced or chopped garlic is most frequently used to 'sweeten' the oil; it is cooked briefly in the oil and then removed. It is also incorporated in very many dishes. Whole garlic is made into a very pleasant sweet pickle.

(See also Recipes, page 191.)

bulb. The outer skins of the garlic bulb and the skins of the individual cloves can be white or a purplish pink. In poor growing conditions, or when very small cloves are planted, small, single, solid, rather round bulbs, known as 'rounds', form instead of the multi-cloved bulb.

Not all strains of garlic form an inflorescence (flower head). Where they do, the flower stalk is bright green, round, solid and smooth, and can be at least 18–24 in (45–60 cm) tall. Again, unlike other members of the onion family, the flowers almost never open beyond the bud stage, and only rarely set seed. Tiny bulbs or bulblets form among the flower buds. Sometimes the whole inflorescence is trapped within the stem, several inches above ground, making a rather curious swelling, out of which tiny bulblets burst.

Green forms of garlic

The various 'green' forms of garlic, that is the young leaves, the young flower stem, and the immature, 'baby' garlic plants, have a mild, refreshing flavour. They are used in much the same way as spring onion, are often cooked in meat and fish dishes, and lend themselves to use raw in salads. The flower stems retain their bright colour when cooked and are sometimes eaten with the fermented 'hundred-year-old' eggs.

Young leaves and stems can be frozen. The garlic stems are also tinned, and in some parts of China are peeled and dried for winter use. They are easily reconstituted in water.

Climate

Garlic is very hardy, surviving temperatures of 14°F (−10°C), and possibly lower temperatures. It benefits from reasonably warm temperatures during its growing period and when ripening, but needs a cold period in its early stages (see below). It does not grow successfully in areas of high rainfall, but needs moisture in spring, when leafy growth is at its height.
Ideal daylengths and temperatures Growth of the *leaves* is fastest in the short days of early spring, at temperatures of around 61°F (16°C). Development of the *bulb* takes

Green garlic in an 'improved' Chinese winter bed

place in the lengthening days of early summer, and is fastest at temperatures above 69°F (20°C). To develop into good bulbs the dormant cloves or young plants need a cold period, with temperatures of 32–50°F (0–10°C) for 1–2 months. For autumn-planted garlic this occurs naturally during the winter. Garlic planted in early spring is less likely to get the requisite cool period, unless the cloves have been stored in cool conditions.

Very low temperatures during growth result in poor-quality bulbs, the cloves sometimes sprouting prematurely. Conversely, if cloves are stored, or bulbs grown, at temperatures much over 77°F (25°C), there is a risk of them not bulbing at all.

Soil/site

Garlic grows well on a wide range of soils, the ideal soil being a deep, well-drained sandy loam. Where drainage is poor, or the soil very shallow, it is advisable to grow garlic on ridges. (See Part 2, The bed system, page 147.) Always grow garlic in an open, sunny position.

Garlic is not a very hungry crop, but the soil needs to be reasonably fertile. Freshly manured and very acid soils should be avoided. In poor soils a balanced dressing, giving moderate levels of nitrogen, can be applied before planting.

Garlic is susceptible to the pests and diseases which attack onions, so should be rotated with the onion group. Never plant on soil where onions have recently been grown.

Cultivation

Bulb cultivation

Garlic is grown by planting cloves or 'rounds' (see Characteristics, above). *Wherever possible, use stock that is guaranteed virus and nematode free.* If using home-raised garlic, select cloves only from very sound, healthy-looking bulbs. Garlic appears to 'acclimatize' after a period, so there are advantages in growing clones adapted to your locality.
Clove size As a general rule, the larger the clove, and the further apart it is planted (up to a distance of 8 in (20 cm) apart) the larger the bulbs will grow. Aim to plant cloves at least ½ in (12 mm) in diameter, or over 1 gm in weight. Reject the very small cloves from the centre of the garlic bulb. Where small cloves are used, plant them relatively far apart to compensate for their small size.

When to plant

Ideally, garlic should be planted from late autumn (i.e. late October and early November in the British Isles) to early spring. This allows the plants to get well established and make plenty of leafy growth before bulbing starts in early summer. The amount of leaf the plant has when bulbing starts determines how large the mature bulb will become: it can't 'catch up' later.

In light soils, and areas where spring is dry, plant in late autumn. This allows the plant to develop a good root system, enabling it to get sufficient moisture in dry periods. Short-storage types should always be planted in the autumn. In wet and heavy clay soils planting may have to be delayed until spring. In this case an alternative is to start off the cloves in modules. (See Part 2, Plant raising, Use of modules, page 153.) Plant them in the modules any time during the winter, and stand them in a sheltered place outdoors to get the necessary cold period. Plant the modules at soil level in early spring, planting only cloves which have sprouted. This method gives a very good quality crop.

Research in the British Isles indicates that autumn-planted garlic gives the highest yield, but spring planted is sometimes better quality.

Planting method

Garlic is normally planted on the flat. Experiments have indicated that growing garlic on ridges, a practice sometimes adopted in heavy or poorly drained soil, can result in higher yields even in normal conditions. In France garlic is often planted in shallow furrows, covered by soil.

It smacks of the obvious to say plant cloves straight and the right way up—but if planted crooked the necks may be bent, and if upside down they may die off altogether. It is not always easy to see which *is* the right way up, but a flat 'base plate' distinguishes the bottom of the clove.

Garlic cloves are apt to work themselves upwards after planting. For this reason they are traditionally planted at about twice their own depth—with at least an inch (2.5cm) of soil above them. Research has indicated that higher yields can be obtained by planting 4 in (10 cm) deep, though this would not be recommended on wet soils.

Spacing

Spacing cloves about 7 in (18 cm) apart each way gives the highest yield from any unit area. If you prefer planting in rows, make the rows 10–12 in (25–30 cm) apart, spacing the cloves 3–4 in (8–10 cm) apart in the rows. An alternative is to plant in double rows 6 in (15 cm) apart, the cloves 6 in (15 cm) apart, with 12 in (30 cm) between each pair of rows.

Further care

As garlic does not naturally form a canopy over the soil, it is important to keep it weed-free. Beds can be mulched after the shoots have come through the surface, to help keep down weeds. In spring it may be necessary to water in the early stages of growth.

Pests and disease

The most serious diseases are white rot, rust, onion yellow virus and garlic mosaic virus. Stem eelworm is sometimes a serious pest. (See Part 2, Pests and disease, page 172.)

Harvesting

Garlic bulbs are ready for harvesting anytime from mid-summer onwards. They should be harvested *before* they have died back completely, when the leaves are beginning to fade and are turning yellow. If harvesting is delayed the cloves may start to sprout, the bulbs can become stained, and there is a much higher risk of disease during storage.

Dig the bulbs out of the ground, handling them very carefully. They bruise easily, limiting their storage life. A French lady whose family had been garlic growers for thirty years, once told me they should be handled like peaches. It *hurt* her to see the way people threw garlic about. Cut any remaining stem with secateurs, leaving up to 2 in (5 cm) of stalk.

Garlic must be dried thoroughly for storage. In warm dry weather it can be dried in the sun and wind, lying on the ground. In less perfect conditions it should be raised off the ground on trays or wire racks. In really wet weather it is better to bring it under cover, ideally to a greenhouse where it can be given a good baking. It usually takes 1–2 weeks to dry.

Storage

Store the bulb whole, plaited in braids, or hung in bunches tied by the leaves. When harvesting conditions are very dry the bulbs may break apart; the cloves then have to be stored in nets. Garlic for domestic use should be stored in the driest conditions possible, such as in a dry room indoors. Garlic for planting should be stored in a cool, dry, well ventilated place, ideally at 41–50°F (5–10°C). Garlic will start to sprout if it becomes moist. Storage life depends on the type, but most garlic

will keep for at least 5–6 months, and often up to a year.

Varieties

A crop as ancient and widespread as garlic inevitably displays enormous diversity, with different regions developing types adapted to their conditions. The borderlines between types are blurred, and it is often hard to distinguish between so-called 'varieties' and 'selections'. At present the differences are largely of academic interest, as amateur gardeners are rarely in a position to obtain named varieties. For the best yields, use virus-free stock from clones adapted to your locality.

Green leafy shoot cultivation
Green garlic shoots are grown in China for use in winter or very early spring, when green vegetables of any sort are scarce. In Beijing, where winters are severe, they are grown in the sunken 'winter beds', which are covered with heavy insulating mats in the depth of winter. (See Part 2, Protected cropping, Chinese solar frames, page 165.) In more temperate climates they could be grown in ordinary garden frames or unheated greenhouses.

Plant cloves close together, 1¼–1½ in (3–4 cm) apart, in early autumn in a frame or greenhouse, ventilating them well on sunny days. The green shoots can be cut whenever they are a usable size; they will regrow to give a second cut. Alternatively, they can be left until they reach the 'baby garlic' size, with the young bulb just beginning to swell, and used whole.

I have noticed in England that garlic bulbs accidentally left in the soil instead of being harvested produce a mass of green, very usable shoots in December.
The plate method A Chinese friend told me that in winter in Inner Mongolia, a plate is covered with garlic cloves, which are threaded together with a very fine piece of bamboo. These 'sprout' into a mat of green shoots, to provide the first tasty fresh leaves of spring.

BLANCHED SHOOTS The Chinese also appreciate the sweeter flavour and whitened appearance of blanched garlic shoots. For this purpose growth should be fast and shoots tender, so they are not grown in the toughening conditions of the traditional cold frames, but in specially constructed, heated, lean-to greenhouses. They are then forced in darkness, in any of the methods used to blanch Chinese chives (see page 74). This was sometimes done at home, constructing a canopy of some kind over a *kang*—the traditional brick or clay platform beds heated with a brazier beneath. It can be done in a warm airing cupboard, putting the cloves on damp sand in a seed box. There is no danger of their becoming smelly, unless they are bruised or diseased.

Flowering stem cultivation

In China, garlic flower stems are a side product of garlic bulb production, using strains known to produce flowering stems. The bulbs are cultivated in the normal way, the flower stems being cut in early summer when green. They are harvested very carefully so the bulb is not damaged and can be left to mature. Methods of harvesting include pinching the stem low down and pulling gently, and slicing through the stem with a sharpened bamboo. The longer the stem, the better. For some reason bolted (i.e. flowering) garlic plants, unlike bolted onions, produce normal, sound bulbs.

In Europe, flowering strains of garlic are probably rarer, garlic having been selected over the years for non-bolting characteristics. So for anyone keen to savour garlic stems, it is a case of watching your crop and utilizing any bolters which arise. In variety trials carried out in England in 1982 the French variety 'Grulurose', when planted in autumn, invariably produced flowering stems without any impairment to the quality of the bulb. So should there be a demand for flower stems, varieties could no doubt be made available which would satisfy both the stem and the bulb enthusiast.

Ipomea (Water spinach)

Family *Convolvulaceae*
Latin name *Ipomea aquatica* (*I. reptans*)
Other names in use Water convolvulus; kangcong; swamp cabbage; engtsai*
Mandarin Kong xin cai ('empty heart/stem vegetable'); weng cai ('pitcher vegetable')
Cantonese Ong/ung tsoi, tung tsoi
Japanese Asagaona ('morning glory leaf vegetable')

* In the West it has usually been known by its Malaysian name 'kankong'.

Background

Water spinach is widely grown throughout Asia, often escaping from cultivation and growing wild on muddy banks. Because it can so easily become a weed in warm and watery areas its cultivation is forbidden in Florida. We saw it wherever we travelled in China: in the south it was among the most eye-catching crops on the 'island' raised beds. It is particularly popular in high summer, when it is too hot to grow leafy crops like cabbage and spinach. The leaves and stems are also used to feed chickens, ducks, pigs and cattle.

Ipomea has no relationship with ordinary spinach, but is closely related to sweet potato and convolvulus.

Characteristics

Ipomea is perennial in warm climates, but an annual in cooler climates. Its natural habitat is water or swampy land. It is characterized by long, jointed, hollow stems, which can float on water, or creep out over muddy ground, rooting at the nodes. They exude a milky juice, and are white or green, depending on variety.

The leaves are flat, and the shape varies, depending on variety, from slightly heart-shaped, to long, narrow and arrow-shaped. Narrow leaves are ½–1 in (1–2.5 cm) wide, and 6–10 in (15–25 cm) in length. Broader leaves are up to 2 in (5 cm) wide, but shorter than the long-leaved type. The attractive flowers

Use

The leaves, especially the young leaves which constitute the tip of the trailing stems, and the tender stems are eaten. The leaves have a very pleasant, mild, sweet flavour and slightly slippery texture, which contrasts when cooked with the crispness of the stems. The Chinese consider the white-stemmed forms better flavoured and more tender than the green. Like many water vegetables, the leaves are very nutritious, being rich in vitamins and minerals. They are also a mild laxative.

In the kitchen

Although normally cooked, ipomea can be eaten raw. It probably makes a better salad if cooked briefly first. Serve it with a garlic-flavoured dressing of soy sauce and sesame oil.

Ipomea deteriorates rapidly once picked, so must always be used very fresh. Cut off the bottom inch or so of the stem, if it is tough, and cut the remaining stem into 1–2 in

(2.5–5 cm) pieces. The leaves can be used whole, or cut into smaller pieces if necessary. Like spinach, they 'disappear' when cooked, so start with a panful. The stems require slightly longer cooking than the leaves.

It is cooked much like spinach: boiled, steamed, stir-fried, used in soups, creamed, and used in mixed dishes. Favourite Chinese combinations are with dried shrimps and chopped red chillies; sliced beef and shrimp sauce; and pork and fermented red bean curd. It almost always seems to be flavoured with garlic. The Japanese use it for *ohitashi*.

have the typical open, trumpet shape of convolvulus or bindweed flowers. They are usually white, sometimes with a pinkish centre. Wild forms may have purple or mauve flowers.

Types

There are generally considered to be two types:

Lowland or aquatic type
('Water' ipomea)
This is adapted to growing in very wet situations. The leaves are relatively broad.

Upland, or dry type
('Dry' ipomea)
This can be grown in beds, provided there is always plenty of moisture. The leaves are narrow, but tend to be more abundant. It sometimes grows quite tall.

Climate

Winter spinach is a crop for warm climates, growing best when mean temperatures are above 77°F (25°C), and growing slowly once temperatures drop below 50°F (10°C). It can't stand any frost. In warm, temperate climates it can be grown outside in summer. In cool and northern areas it can be grown

in unheated greenhouses in summer, but will require heated greenhouses for a spring crop. It will not grow well in low-light levels typical of European winters, even if temperatures are high.

Once daylength starts to shorten, from mid-summer onwards, it makes less vegetative growth and starts to flower—one reason for it failing to flourish in northern latitudes. The consolation for northerners is that the leaves are exceptionally tender when grown under cover.

It is a crop that tolerates very high rainfall.

Site/soil

Water spinach should normally be grown in full sun, though when summer temperatures are very high it is sometimes grown as ground cover beneath climbing plants. It should be sheltered from strong winds.

It needs very fertile soil, rich in organic matter. It responds well to nitrogen, but beware of overfeeding, which can lead to high nitrate concentrations in the leaves and stems. In Asia water spinach is either grown 'wet' on marshy land, even amongst watercress in watercress beds, or 'dry', in beds which are kept well watered. It is often grown on raised beds. (See Part 2, The bed system, page 147.)

Ipomea

Cultivation

The dry bed system is the most suitable for Western gardening.

Sowing and planting

TEMPERATE AREAS Wait until late spring or very early summer. Sow fresh seed, no more than 2 years old. The seeds require a temperature of 68°F (20°C) to germinate. They can be soaked for 24 hours before sowing to encourage germination. Sow in a seed tray, or, preferably, a module, to develop a good root system. (See Part 2, Plant raising, Use of modules, page 153.)

Transplant into the permanent position when plants are 4–6 in (10–15 cm) high, and have developed four true leaves. Large plants do not transplant well. It is usually grown in blocks or patches, highest yields being obtained by spacing plants 6 in (15 cm) apart each way. They can be spaced up to 10 in (25 cm) apart if more access between plants is required. This can be an asset under glass, where plants tend to sprawl uncontrollably. Closer spacing generally produces slender, single stems, rather than branching stems. Alternatively, grow them in rows about 12 in (30 cm) apart, spaced about 8 in (20 cm) apart in the rows.
WARM AREAS Seed can be sown *in situ*, about 1 in (2.5 cm) deep, at the spacing recommended above. In Taiwan broadcast patches looked very dense and healthy.

Cuttings

Ipomea can also be raised from cuttings, though the crop will be more uneven than if raised from seed. Take 12 in (30 cm) long cuttings from young growths, cutting just below a node. Remove the two lower leaves. Either root the cuttings in sandy soil, with the lowest node below soil level, or suspend them in water. Roots will normally form within about a week. Plant them about 6 in (15 cm) deep. To get an early start in China roots are sometimes lifted at the end of the season, stored carefully in winter, and shoots from them planted out in spring.

Further care

Plants must be kept well watered: an organic mulch is advisable to help conserve moisture. (See Part 2, Weeds, mulching and watering, page 157.) Regular liquid feeds with an organic fertilizer, every 2 weeks or so during the growing season, will be beneficial. (See also Part 2, Soil fertility, Liquid feeding, page 144.)

Pests and disease

In hot climates ipomea is vulnerable to the same range of pests and diseases as sweet potato. In cool climates low temperatures are the main enemy.

Harvesting

Ipomea should always be harvested before it flowers. The first pickings can usually be made about 2 months after sowing. Harvest in one of the following ways:
● Pick young leaves or the tips of the trailing stems. Where growth is very succulent the end 8–12 in (20–30 cm) can be harvested. Pick regularly to encourage further, tender growth; otherwise plants quickly become tough. Discard stems which have thickened.
● Cut across the plant about 2 in (5 cm) above soil level, leaving the plant to regenerate. Further cuts can be made at 3–4 week intervals. This method generally gives high yields of tender thin shoots. In unheated greenhouses in north Europe the last cuts are generally made at the end of September.
● Pull up the entire plant. This method is recommended where the growing season is short or where the ground is required for further crops. In favourable conditions several sowings can be made.

Varieties

At present few varieties are available. Where possible choose large-leaved varieties suited for dry cultivation. Green-stemmed varieties which produce few runners are said to be the fastest growing. There is a need for varieties selected for temperate climates and cultivation in greenhouses.

Lettuce (stem)

Family *Compositae*
Latin names *Lactuca sativa* var *augustana* (var *asparagina*)
Other names in use Asparagus lettuce; celtuce; Chinese lettuce
Mandarin Wo sun; wo ju sun; jing wo ju ('tender stem lettuce')
Cantonese Ngao lei shaang tsoi; woo chu; woh sun

Background

Stem lettuce is an oriental lettuce of Chinese origin, long cultivated in China for its tender stem. It is not a cross between celery and lettuce, as is sometimes claimed. It was introduced to the United States in the late nineteenth century, probably with missionaries returning from China. The name 'celtuce' was coined by the American seed company W. Atlee Burpee, presumably to convey the idea of a lettuce with a crunchy stem eaten like celery.

Characteristics

Stem lettuce is an annual. It never makes a compact head, but in its early stages forms a rosette of rather stiff leaves, which can spread to about 18 in (45 cm) in diameter. Later the central stem elongates and thickens, becoming 1–3 in (2.5–7.3 cm) thick and at least 12–18 in (30–45 cm) tall—sometimes considerably taller. The stem is usually greenish white, is covered with leaves and crowned with a tuft of small leaves. Under some conditions several thin branching stems are formed instead of a central thick stem.

Leaves display considerable variation. They can be narrow or broad, dull or glossy, smooth or crinkled like Swiss chard. Most are light green, but there is a red-leaved form.

Climate

Stem lettuce tolerates a wide range of temperature. At one extreme it can stand light frosts: at the other it tolerates temperatures over 80°F (27°C). It has good bolting resistance, but it may bolt prematurely in very hot conditions. (See Sowing method below.)

Use
In the kitchen

Stem lettuce has a very refreshing, crunchy texture and to my mind an unmistakable mild lettuce flavour; however it is often described as 'nutty cucumber'. It is excellent raw and cooked. Prepare stems by peeling off the slightly tough whitish, outer layer, which can be bitter. The flesh beneath is a delicate light green. Then cut them into thin slices or matchsticks for salads, or into larger pieces for cooking. It can be used raw, or cooked and cooled in salads, served with a spicy dressing.

Stem lettuce should only be lightly cooked, for 4 minutes at the most. It is usually stir-fried, either with white meat, poultry, fish or other vegetables, or on its own, seasoned with garlic, chilli or pepper, or soy or oyster sauce. It can be lightly boiled, then served with a creamed sauce or baked *au gratin*. The Chinese also use it in soup and pickle it.

Young leaves can be eaten,

though they are coarse compared with ordinary lettuce. In China they are cooked like greens, though Westerners sometimes use them in salads. Older leaves are usually too coarse and bitter to use: in China they are fed to livestock.

Site/soil

Stem lettuce needs well-drained, fertile soil. It is often said to have very shallow roots and to grow best on light soil; but experience has shown that in fertile, heavy soil it can develop a strong root system, supporting robust plants.

Cultivation

When to sow

In temperate climates stem lettuce is normally grown as a summer-to-autumn crop. Early crops can be obtained by sowing and planting under cover in early spring, and late crops by transplanting summer sown crops under cover in autumn. In frost-free areas it can also be grown successfully as a winter crop. In very hot areas midsummer sowings should be avoided.

Stem lettuce

Sowing method

HIGH TEMPERATURE DORMANCY Stem lettuce does not germinate well at temperatures above 80°F (27°C), so germination problems may arise with summer sowings. Even in England the top inch of soil can become surprisingly warm in midsummer. In these circumstances sow in seed trays or modules in a cool room or shady place. The Chinese sometimes moisten the seed, wrap it up, then hang it in a cool well for a couple of days until it has germinated. The germinated seed is then sown.

Indoors Wherever possible sow stem lettuce in modules to get good strong plants. Weaklings never develop good stems. (See also Part 2, Plant raising, Use of modules, page 153.) Alternatively, sow in seed trays.

Outdoors Either sow in a seedbed and transplant, or sow *in situ*.

Planting and spacing

Where sown *in situ* thin when about 2 in (5 cm) high. Where raised indoors plant out at the three or four leaf stage, generally 3–4 weeks after sowing. Don't leave it much later, as the plants need to get their roots down and develop a strong rosette before the stems start to elongate.

Plants should be spaced about 12 in (30 cm) apart each way, or if grown in rows, with at least 18 in (45 cm) between rows. Mulch after planting to help conserve moisture and keep down weeds, as roots are easily damaged by hoeing.

Intercropping

As stem lettuce is fast growing and fairly erect, it is often interplanted in China between slower growing crops such as cauliflower, self blanching celery, or Chinese chives.

Further care

In the early leafy stage the crop needs plenty of water. Once the stems are developing moderate watering is called for: they are liable to crack if the soil becomes too wet or too dry. A liquid feed can be applied every 3 weeks or so. (See Soil fertility, Liquid feeding, page 144.)

Crops can be covered with cloches or tunnels to extend the growing season in the autumn.

Pests and disease

Stem lettuce is susceptible to the same pests and diseases as ordinary lettuce, such as slugs and downy mildew. Leaf disease in the later stages is less serious than with ordinary lettuce, as the leaves can be stripped off when harvesting leaving the stem undamaged. (See also Part 2, Pests and disease, page 172.)

Harvesting

The stem is ready for harvesting 3–4 months after sowing, when roughly 12 in (30 cm) high, and at least 1 in (2.5 cm) in diameter. It can be left until just before flowering without becoming bitter—though occasionally the stems become hollow at that stage. Pull up the plant or cut it off at ground level, and trim the leaves off the stem. The 'topknot' of leaves is usually left on until the plant is used: it probably helps to keep the stem fresh.

Some young outer leaves can be picked from the rosette a month or so after planting—but don't denude the plant. Once the stalk starts to develop, the leaves tend to become bitter.

The stems can be kept for a few weeks in cool conditions. In autumn in north China the plants are uprooted, the leaves trimmed off apart from the central tuft, and the stems packed tightly in winter cold frames at temperatures of about 32°F (0°C). They keep for a couple of months. (See Part 2, Protected cropping, Chinese solar beds, page 165.)

Varieties

In China varieties generally fall into fairly distinct groups. Most seed sold in the West seems to be a mixture of the first two types, giving rather erratic results.

Narrow dull-leaved
'Zulu', Promising new variety suitable for cool climates.

Broad dull-leaved
Prone to branching in cool climates.

Broad glossy-leaved
Less vigorous.

Red-leaved
May be hardier. Suitable for autumn sowing; may bolt early from spring and summer sowings.

Indian lettuce (*Lactuca indica*)
This is a perennial lettuce, growing up to 4 ft (120 cm) high, which grows wild in southern China. The leaves, which are often reddish, are used as a vegetable.

Mitsuba

Family *Umbelliferae*
Latin name *Cryptotaenia japonica*
Other names in use Japanese honewort; Japanese wild chervil; Japanese wild parsley; trefoil
Mandarin San ye qin ('three leaf celery'); ya er qin ('duck celery')
Cantonese San ip
Japanese Mitsuba ('three leaves')

Background

Mitsuba is very much a Japanese plant. It grows wild in Japan and may have originated there. It is considered one of the most important native fresh vegetables, finding its way into many traditional Japanese dishes. It is closely related to *Cryptotaenia canadensis* or honewort, a north American wild plant which used to be gathered by the American Indians and used as a herb and vegetable.

Characteristics

Mitsuba is a hardy perennial, the average height of mature plants being about 12 in (30 cm). The flat, light or dark green leaves are slightly heart-shaped, up to about 3 in (7.5 cm) wide, with saw-tooth edges. They form pretty leaflets of three leaves at the end of long slender stalks, their general appearance being not unlike a flat-leaved parsley. The stalks are naturally white or green, depending on variety, but are sometimes blanched artificially to make them sweeter and longer. Insignificant little white flowers appear in summer. A few leaves grow on the flower stem.

Climate

Mitsuba is essentially a cool-weather crop. It is fairly hardy, and can stand temperatures of 14°F (−10°C) for short periods.

Site/soil

A woodland plant by nature, mitsuba grows best in damp, lightly shaded situations. In these conditions it can be a useful ground cover plant, spreading by self-seeding itself. It can be grown in the shade of taller vegetables, but I have also seen it making an attractive edge to a vegetable bed. In full sun the leaves tend to turn yellow.

Mitsuba leaf and young stems

Use

Mitsuba has a delightful flavour, often described as celery-like, but to me a unique blend of parsley, celery, and angelica, with angelica predominating. The leaves, the green stems and the highly prized blanched white stems are the main parts used. The roots are normally cut off and discarded, but some people eat the roots or use them for flavouring. The cress-like young seedlings are used in salads and are excellent fresh in soups. The seeds are occasionally used in cooking.

In the kitchen

Leaves and stems, fresh or blanched, are frequently used for seasoning clear and fish soups. The stems may be rubbed between the fingers until soft then tied into knots, which are dropped into the soup. Chopped blanched stems look beautiful scattered over soup.

Leaves and stems are also used to flavour a wide range of Japanese dishes, from savoury custards to *sukiyaki* and *ohitashi*: they should never be cooked for more than a couple of minutes or the flavour is destroyed. In Western cookery they can be chopped finely and used as a parsley substitute, giving a new dimension to commonplace dishes. They add a lovely flavour to rice dishes. Whole leaves make an attractive garnish, sometimes dipped briefly in boiling water beforehand to tenderize them.

Young leaves and tender stems are also cooked as a vegetable. They can be lightly boiled or stir-fried, either on their own, or in mixtures of vegetables, fish or meat.

It tolerates any garden soil, but it grows much more lushly in rich soil. Work in plenty of well-rotted compost to create a humus-rich, woodland-like spot. In Japan intensively grown mitsuba is rotated over a 5–6 year cycle.

Forms

In Japan and Taiwan mitsuba is marketed in various forms, which require different cultivation. Generally speaking, the young and blanched forms are eaten raw, and the older forms cooked.

Young green-stem mitsuba

The young green stems are harvested about 2 months after sowing from about 5 in (13 cm) high. They may be pulled up by their roots (in which case they are usually sold in bunches with the roots trimmed off) or cut off at ground level. This thin-stemmed mitsuba is available over a long period. When planted densely the stems naturally become somewhat 'blanched' and tender.

'Root' mitsuba

Spring-sown plants are overwintered and harvested early in their second season, after the new leaves and stems have grown. They develop stronger roots than the young mitsuba above, and are higher yielding. Stems can be harvested at any length before they run to seed.

Tenderized or blanched mitsuba

Plants are 'tenderized' by blanching in darkness or by earthing up to produce subtly flavoured tender white stems, 8–10 in (20–25 cm) long, topped by green leaves. These are generally sold with the roots trimmed off.

Mitsuba seedlings

See Seed sprouting, page 137.

Cultivation

Sowing (general)

Although a perennial, mitsuba is normally grown as an annual. The principal sowings are in late spring and early autumn, as mitsuba grows fastest in early summer and autumn. The ideal soil temperature for germination is 77°F (25°C), though seed will germinate at higher and lower temperatures.

Sow seed shallowly, making sure it never dries out. Mitsuba is usually sown *in situ*, thinning to the correct distance apart where necessary. It can also be sown in a seedbed, or in seed trays and planted out as young seedlings after hardening off.

Young green-stem mitsuba

In temperate climates sow from spring to early autumn. In cooler climates sow from late spring (there is a risk of bolting with early spring sowings) to late summer. For a continuous supply of young stems sow in succession every 6 weeks or so. The season can be extended by making early and late sowings under cover. (See Protected cropping, below.)

Either broadcast in patches, or sow, in wide drills so seedlings are eventually about ½–1½ in (1–3 cm) apart. (Commercial growers sow at a rate of about 1 oz (30 g) per sq. yd (sq. m).) If the stems are to be uniform in size, it is important to space the seedlings evenly. Where necessary start thinning when seedlings have 2–3 leaves.

Depending on temperature, they will generally be ready within 50–60 days. They can be left a few more weeks and harvested at a later stage. Either pick leaves and stems as required, or pull the whole plant. Stems should be harvested while still supple, before they become stiff or run to seed.

Green mitsuba grown as a perennial The crop is sometimes grown as a perennial. Sow *in situ*, in a seedbed, or in a seed tray, finally thinning or spacing plants about 13 in (32 cm) apart each way. The stems are cut

at regular intervals just above ground level, when 8–10 in (20–30 cm) tall, leaving the plants to resprout. Plants can be cut over several years provided they remain healthy, but if they become infected with virus should be uprooted.

EXTENDING THE SEASON WITH PROTECTED CROPPING The outdoor season for green mitsuba can be extended with earlier and later sowings in unheated greenhouses, cold frames or solar frames. Like parsley, mitsuba will remain in good condition and grow well at fairly low temperatures if protected from the elements. Greenhouse crops must be kept moist, and in sunny conditions will need to be shaded.

Crops will be ready for pulling within 2–3 months, depending on the season. A late-autumn sowing will provide the first cut early the following year, while a very early spring sowing will provide a successive crop.

In Japan mitsuba is grown all year round in greenhouses to provide a continuous, high quality crop. The plants are often grown hydroponically, and may also be blanched (see below).

Root mitsuba

Seed is sown in spring and planted 8 in (20 cm) apart in rows 12 in (30 cm) apart. Stems are cut during the first season, and again early the following season when they have regrown. In Taiwan they are transplanted in the second season, and pulled up by the roots when the new leaves develop.

Tenderized or blanched mitsuba

Commercial growers in Japan and Taiwan use various methods to tenderize mitsuba.

TRADITIONAL WINTER BLANCHING Plants are sown in spring, left to grow during the summer months, and blanched in relays during the winter months. In some cases the plants are lifted in autumn and early winter and replanted in special darkened tenderizing beds. Regrowth of the stems takes several weeks, the beds sometimes being heated to force growth. The leaves are exposed to the light shortly before harvesting, to allow them to green up.

Alternatively, the plants are left in the soil, and very early in spring either earthed up with 6–8 in (15–20 cm) of soil, or covered with straw and rice bran. The stems grow through, becoming blanched in the process; the leaves are exposed long enough to turn green. The process is sometimes forced by covering the plants with low film or muslin tunnels in spring.

SUMMER BLANCHING To satisfy the demands of the modern market mitsuba is now also sown in autumn and blanched during the following summer, by transplanting about 12 in (30 cm) apart in purpose-built darkened tenderizing beds. This is a highly specialized operation, requiring very careful control of temperatures.

Varieties

The Japanese recommend different strains of mitsuba for different purposes.

'Kansai' Greenish stems, used mainly for 'green' mitsuba.

'Kanto' Whiter stems, used for blanching and perennial culture.

Onions

Oriental bunching onion

Family   *Alliaceae*
Latin name   *Allium fistulosum*
Other names in use   Japanese bunching onion; Welsh onion
Mandarin   Cong (onion); qing cong ('green onion'; da cong (large and single stem types); feng cong; xiao cong (small and multistem types)
Cantonese   Tsung
Japanese   Negi (bunching onion); me negi (small leafy shoots); ko negi (leafy scallions); nebuka (white blanched stem)

* For the oriental bulbing onions 'Rakkyo' (*Allium chinense*), and *Allium ledebouriana*, see pages 105 and 106. For brief notes on the traditional European 'Welsh onion' and the overwintered bulb onion known as 'Japanese onion' see page 105.

Background

For centuries the most important onions in China and Japan have been white-stemmed types of the leafy green Welsh onion, *Allium fistulosum*, rather than the common bulb and spring onions, *Allium cepa*, which have always predominated in Europe and the West. They have become widely known as Oriental or Japanese bunching onions. They are not known in the wild and their origin is uncertain. White-stemmed onions were mentioned in Chinese literature as long ago as 100 BC, and were probably introduced to Japan a thousand years later. It is assumed that they reached Europe sometime during the Middle Ages. (The name 'Welsh' is thought to have come from the Anglo Saxon for 'foreign'; there is no connection with Wales). Their hardiness and general usefulness made them a good standby in European cottage gardens, though they were never widely cultivated.

It is a different story in the Ori-

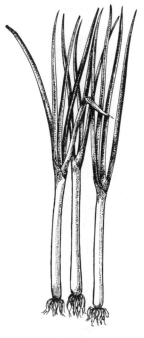

Oriental bunching onions: leaf and stem stage

Use

The leaves can be used as green onions at any stage from very small cress-like seedlings 2 in (5 cm) high, to the long leaves of the mature plant. Being available all year round, they are especially welcome as a source of fresh green onion in winter and spring. The thick stems are used more like leeks; indeed they are a good substitute for leeks or bulb onions and are excellent in soups and stews. They are both used young and harvested at a later stage after earthing up, which makes them more delicate and tender.

In the kitchen

The flavour depends on the variety, but is generally stronger than the traditional Welsh onion or Western spring onion or scallion. They are used raw in salads and for garnishing, and cooked lightly in any number of ways—in soups, fried dishes, omelettes, or made into the famous Chinese onion pancakes. The very small leafy shoots are used in a Japanese noodles dish. The leaves should only be cooked very briefly.

(See also Recipes, page 193.)

ent. If the long loaf epitomizes the French shopper, the long white-stemmed onion epitomizes the Chinese. Tied to bicycles, peering out of panniers, it is the most ubiquitous of Chinese vegetables. In Taiwan I drove through a famous 'onion village', where long onions were hanging to dry from every window and roof. In Japan the perfectly earthed up beds of blanching onions are a fine example of the art of horticulture. The bunching onion has followed the Chinese community overseas. Whenever I wandered into a Chinese market garden in Vancouver I disturbed someone—usually an elderly lady or young lad—bunching onions.

Stages of use

Bunching onions are harvested at several different stages of maturity and development. In practice the stages tend to merge into each other: onions sown primarily for use as leafy scallions, for example, could be thinned out and harvested later as leaves and stems.

Small leafy shoots
These are harvested no more than 2–6 in (5–15 cm) tall, before the stems develop.

Leafy scallions or small bunching onions
These are still almost all leaf, about 12–16 in (30–40 cm), tall and ¼ in (5–7 mm) in width. The leaf stems are very fine and slender, with only a hint of a white, slightly swollen base at ground level.

Leaves and stems
These are dual-purpose, the stem and leaf being almost two distinct vegetables. The white part of the stem has developed and thickened, but the leaves are still soft and usable. In the smallest types the stem is about 10 in (25 cm) long and the leaves about 14 in (35 cm) long. In the larger types the white stem can be up to 18 in (45 cm) long and nearly an inch (2.5 cm) thick, and the leaves 12 in (30 cm) long.

Long blanched stems
Varieties with straight white stems are blanched by earthing up to make them longer, whiter and very tender. The largest could have 20 in (50 cm) of blanched stem, up to 1¼ in (3.5 cm) diameter, with 12 in (30 cm) or more of shiny leaf. They

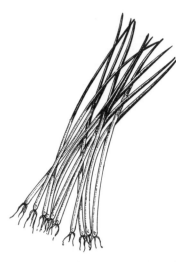

Oriental bunching onions: small leafy shoots

Onions: leafy scallions

are grown primarily for the stem, the leaves gradually becoming rather hard and coarse.

Characteristics

Oriental bunching onions are hardy perennial plants with long, hollow, remarkably round leaves. Most are evergreen, but some die back in winter. They do not form bulbs. They are generally more vigorous and substantial than the traditional Welsh onion.

They are loosely divided into two main types: multi-stem and single stem, indicating the extent to which the plants 'divide' into more or fewer stems. The *multi-stem* types

are closer to the traditional Welsh onion, tillering to form clumps of anything from a few to up to 20 leaves. The smaller types have leaves about ¼ in (0.5 cm) in diameter, and up to about a foot (30 cm) high, but others are larger. The white stem at the base of the leaves makes them look like very slender spring onions.

The *single stem* types are usually, as the name implies, single, though they sometimes split into more than one stem. Their main feature is that the lower part of the stem can develop into a straight, leek-like shaft, up to 18 in (45 cm) tall and an inch (2.5 cm) diameter, topped by about half a dozen green leaves perhaps a foot (30 cm) long. The shaft can be earthed up to get blanched stems.

In practice there are many intermediate forms between the two main types. There are also varieties in which the outer layers of skin are red, the colour varying from an insipid to deeper red according to the variety and the extent of exposure to cold.

Flower stalks The flower stalks are relatively short, round and hollow like the leaves, and can be eaten when young. The flowers are ivory coloured.

In their early stages the Japanese bunching onions look very similar to ordinary bulb onions, but in the latter the leaves are 'D-shaped' in cross section rather than round.

Climate

The bunching onions tolerate a remarkable range of temperatures and are very hardy: it is a common experience to harvest them from under the snow. They also tolerate high temperatures, and can be grown in the tropics.

Site/soil

Like all onions, bunching onions do best on fertile, well drained soils—rich sandy or peaty soils being the most suitable. Very heavy clays should be avoided. Acid soils should be limed to bring the pH to 6.5–7.5. (See Soil fertility, Very acid soils, page 145.) Never plant in freshly manured ground, as free ammonia is harmful to onions.

Although the bunching onions tend to have more resistance to pests and diseases then normal onions, it is advisable to rotate over at least a three-year cycle.

In China bunching onions are often intercropped between other vegetables such as mustards, pak choi and radishes. Their upright habit, and the fact that they can be harvested at any stage, makes them a convenient 'intercropper'. I often plant them as edges to vegetable beds. The multi-stemmed types, which are usually harvested young, make a neat, almost bushy short-term edge, while the single-stemmed onions act as stately sentinels for a longer period.

Cultivation (general)

For sowing times, sowing methods and spacing for different stages of use, see below.

Oriental bunching onions are normally raised from seed, though it is sometimes possible to increase stock by dividing clumps in their second season. Only do so if the plants look healthy.

Sowing

Although perennials, the oriental bunching onions are usually grown as annuals or biennials. They are either sown *in situ*, or sown in seed beds or seed trays and transplanted. They respond well to being multi-sown in modules, covered lightly with sand. Six seeds can be sown in a 1½ in (3.8 cm) module. (See Plant raising, page 153.)

Onions germinate over a wide range of temperatures but the higher the temperature, the faster they will germinate. Sow about ¼–½ in (6–12 mm) deep, keeping them moist until germination.

Planting

Bunching onions transplant well, growing vigorously after trans-

planting (especially in summer when their growth is fastest). Most crops are transplanted, the exceptions being those harvested as leafy shoots and leafy scallions, and some fast-growing summer crops. These are sown *in situ*. In China and Japan the slower-maturing varieties may be transplanted twice or more, both to save space and to develop very strong plants.

Transplanting can also be used to control harvesting times. Plants from one sowing, for example, can be transplanted over several weeks to give a succession.

The seedlings or young plants should be planted shallowly without burying the necks. The Chinese often plant in shallow furrows, sometimes washing the seedlings first, presumably as a precaution against disease. They are often planted in groups of two to four seedlings.

One disadvantage of transplanting from a market gardener's point of view is that the plants are more firmly rooted and harder to pull up quickly.

Containers

Onions harvested young can be grown satisfactorily even in shallow containers: all over China discarded washing bowls and disintegrating baskets, perched on doorsteps, window sills and any spare surface, can be seen sprouting crops of young leafy onions. Larger onions would give poor returns in containers.

Pests and disease

The most serious diseases are downy mildew, white rot, virus and sometimes rust. The most common pests are thrips (this is worst in dry areas) and stem and bulb eelworm. (See also Part 2, Pests and disease.)

Storage

In north China mature bunching onions are partially dried and stored for winter. They are dried in the sun, in the wind, sometimes even hanging outside in the frost,

until the outer layers are paper-dry. This dry outer layer preserves the inner layers of stem and leaves. The onions are piled in heaps 3–5 ft (1–1.5 m) high under shelters or in sheds, with the roots facing outwards. The heaps are covered with heavy mats to keep out the frosts and are worked through constantly to remove decaying plants. Even though the leaves may yellow, they remain usable. The plants are stored for 4–5 months, until spring. This technique is only practicable in a cold, dry climate.

Cultivation for different stages of use

Choice of variety

Wherever possible, choose the most suitable variety for each purpose. Some are suited to harvesting only at certain stages, while others are more flexible and can be harvested at several stages. They also vary in their tolerance of heat, cold, disease, and in their tendency to bolt. Quality deteriorates once they start to flower.

Varieties which die back in winter are used for the overwintered crop in areas with extremely severe winters, such as northern Japan. They start into growth again in spring. (See also Varieties, page 105.)

Small leafy shoots

Special varieties of single stem onions are normally used for this purpose, though multi-stem varieties can be used.

WHEN TO SOW

Outdoors The earliest sowings are made in spring under low tunnels, as soon as the soil is workable. Sowing can continue throughout the growing season. As the young plants are delicate they should if possible be protected from very heavy rain. (See Protected cropping, page 162.)

Indoors Sowings can be made all year round, though germination will be very slow in unheated houses in mid-winter. Sowings can be made in autumn in cold frames for harvesting in spring.

SOWING METHOD Sow thickly in wide drills or broadcast patches. (See Part 2, Plant raising, page 151.)

HARVEST Seedlings can be cut or pulled at any size from 2–6 in (5–15 cm). They are usually ready 30–40 days after sowing.

Leafy scallions

Multi-stem varieties are normally used. Some varieties are recommended for summer cropping, others for winter.

WHEN TO SOW
Outdoors The first sowings are made under low polytunnels, as soon as the soil is workable. The tunnels can be removed once the weather warms up. Sowings can continue until late summer or early autumn.

Indoors
See Small leafy shoots, above.

SOWING METHOD Sow thinly, *in situ*, in rows, wide drills or patches. The soil must be fertile and moisture retentive, to support the rapid growth. Plants can be thinned to about 1½ in (4 cm) apart.

HARVEST They are generally pulled when about 12 in (30 cm) high, a stage reached 60–80 days after sowing.

Leaves and stems

Single and multi-stem varieties are used. Where tender green leaf is required most single stem varieties must be harvested within about 70 days of sowing. Some multi-stem varieties remain tender in their second season.

WHEN TO SOW
Within this group onions can be ready for harvesting anything from 3–12 months or more after sowing. This depends on a) the variety, b) the stage of harvesting, and c) whether they are being harvested in the year of sowing, or overwintered for cropping the following year. Careful planning allows for continuous production.

Various options for sowing are outlined below. Choose the method best suited to the size required and the variety being grown.

Harvesting young in the same year

Sow *in situ* outdoors as soon as the ground is workable. These onions can be pulled within about 3½ months. An earlier crop can be obtained by sowing *in situ* under low polytunnels, which are removed when temperatures rise.

These early sowings grow rapidly and can only be harvested young for a fairly short period. (Note also that not all varieties are considered suitable for *in situ* sowing.)

Larger plants, for harvesting later in the year over a longer period Sow in spring or early summer, transplanting within 4–8 weeks for a late summer to autumn harvest. These can also be started under low polytunnels to get a slightly earlier harvest.

Sow late summer to early autumn, transplanting in early autumn or spring. These will be ready for use in spring and early summer the following year—i.e. providing the first crops of the season.

SPACING Several different spacings are used, to some extent depending on the variety, e.g.:

• Rows about 15 in (38 cm) apart, planting two or three seedlings together, 3–5 in (7.5–13 cm) apart in the rows.

• Rows 15 in (38 cm) apart, but plants at the wider spacing of 6–9 in (15–23 cm) apart in the rows.

• Rows 12 in (30 cm) apart, plants 3 in (7.5 cm) apart.

• Equidistant spacing, plants about 8 in (20 cm) apart in each direction.

HARVEST The earliest are ready within three or four months of sowing, at which stage they would have more leaf than stem. They are usually uprooted completely. The overwintered plants are in the ground very much longer, and have a greater proportion of white, leek-like stem.

Long blanched stems

This is the most demanding crop, and must be grown on very fertile, well drained soil.

Single-stem types are normally used. Multi-stem types are sometimes used, but if so they are divided into separate stems when planted out. Some varieties are

Earthing up single stem onions

considered more suitable for summer harvesting, others for harvesting during winter and early spring.

WHEN TO SOW Summer-harvested types are generally sown in late summer or early autumn, either *in situ*, thinning later to the correct distance apart, or transplanting in early winter or early spring. These would be ready during the summer, taking an average of 10–11 months to mature. The growing time is sometimes reduced to 8–9 months by starting them off under polytunnels in late autumn or early spring, thinning or transplanting later.

The winter types are normally sown in autumn and transplanted into their permanent positions in spring, for harvesting from autumn to winter. They are also sometimes started off under low tunnels in very early spring, for a slightly earlier harvest.

The large stem onions should always be sown thinly, as it is important to get large, strong seedlings.

SPACING AND BLANCHING The object with this type of onion is to earth up the stem, eventually to a height of 10–12 in (25–30 cm), so that it becomes very white and tender. To this end they are either planted in furrows about 12 in (30 cm) deep, which are gradually filled in, or planted on the flat, gradually ridging them up. The rows are 32–36 in (80–90 cm) apart, with plants

3–4 in (8–10 cm) apart within the rows.

The stems are earthed up two to four times during growth, a few inches at a time, starting generally about a month after planting. A direct sown crop would be earthed up about 7 months after planting.

FEEDING Onions grown this way are usually given a top dressing or liquid feed two or three times during the earthing up period. (See Part 2, Soil fertility, page 141.)

HARVEST The soil is pulled back to harvest the stems. They can either be uprooted, or cut about an inch (2.5 cm) above the base. In this case they will regrow to give a second crop. As they develop the soil is pushed back around the stems.

Red-stemmed onions

In a few varieties of bunching onion the two or three outer layers of the stem are reddish coloured, though the red colour doesn't develop fully until the plants have experienced low temperatures. Existing varieties tend to be of the multi-stem type, for example the variety 'Red Beard', which when mature is 28–32 in (70–80 cm) tall, with stems up to ¾ in (1.5 cm) thick. It is harvested in winter.

SOWING AND PLANTING Japanese recommendations are as follows. Either:

● Sow in early spring, transplanting in mid-summer for an early winter to spring harvest, or:

● Sow in autumn. In this case transplant in early spring and again in mid-summer, to obtain larger plants for harvesting from early winter to spring.

Plant in rows 28–32 in (70–80 cm) apart, plants 6–8 in (15–20 cm) apart.

Varieties

Japanese seed catalogues list a wide range of varieties of bunching onion developed for specific purposes, i.e. for use as small leafy shoots, leafy scallions, dual purpose leaf and stem, or for blanched stems. At present there is less choice in Western catalogues: it is a case of taking the available varieties and adapting them to different uses. A few guidelines are given below. Varieties mentioned are well-established, but others are likely to appear in future. European seed companies are currently developing milder-flavoured varieties.

FOR LEAFY SHOOTS, SCALLIONS AND FAIRLY THIN LEAF AND STEM ONIONS Use types listed as 'Small bunching onions', for example 'Kujo', 'Asagi', and 'Kyoto Market' multi-stem varieties.

FOR LARGE DUAL-PURPOSE LEAF AND STEM ONIONS, AND STEM ONIONS FOR BLANCHING Use single stem types. Most can also be harvested very young as leafy scallions.

VARIETIES USED MAINLY FOR SUMMER AND AUTUMN HARVESTING 'Kincho', 'Long White Tokyo'.

VARIETIES GROWN MAINLY FOR WINTER HARVESTING 'Ishikura', 'White Evergreen'.

Traditional European Welsh onion

This is a hardy, perennial, evergreen plant, with hollow, circular leaves usually 12–18 in (30–45 cm) high, and up to ½ in (1 cm) diameter. The bases of the stems are thickened into what could be considered a rather squashed elongated bulb. Flowering stems tend to be produced early in the season.

To propagate Welsh onion either divide established clumps or sow *in situ* in spring or late summer, in rows about 9 in (23 cm) apart, thinning to 8 in (20 cm) apart. Spring-sown plants would be ready by summer; summer-sown by spring the following year. The clumps gradually spread, and need to be divided every 2–3 years to maintain their vigour. Divide them in spring or autumn, pulling the clumps apart and replanting younger pieces in a different site.

'Top set' Welsh onions

There is evidently one rather small kind of Welsh onion which forms bulbils in its flower head. These can be used for propagation of small green onions. The variety dies back in winter and is used in cold climates.

Rakkyo (Baker's garlic)

Latin name *Allium chinense*
Mandarin Jiao tou; ku jiao
Cantonese Tsung tao
Japanese Rakkyo

Characteristics and use

This Asiatic onion grows like chives in clumps of 10–15 leaves. The leaves are slender and hollow, more sharply angled than chives and bright green. They die back during a dormant period which usually starts in mid-summer when temperatures reach about 77°F (25°C). It flowers in the autumn, after the dormant period, with striking pinkish-purple or lavender flowers, on very long stalks. The flowers rarely set seed. Rakkyo grows wild in north-east China.

It is grown for its bulbs which can be 1½–2 in (4–5 cm) in diameter. They develop underground and resemble shallots, with reddish-brown skins and pinkish inner flesh. Sizeable bulbs may not develop until the second or third season. They are usually harvested during the dormant period. They are said to be mild and sweet flavoured.

In the kitchen

Rakkyo is used raw or cooked, like bulb onions, but is most popular as a pickling onion. It is pickled in various ways, sometimes in salt, sometimes salted first then pickled in vinegar, sometimes in vinegar sweetened with sugar or honey. In the United States these pickles are sold under a variety of names—pickled shallots, pickled scallions, Rakkyo zuke and even pickled leeks.

Cultivation

They will tolerate poor soil, but grow best in light, sandy soil. Bulbs are planted in spring or summer. They can be planted either singly or in pairs, about 5 in (13 cm) apart in rows about 12 in (30 cm) apart. They are normally harvested in the dormant period, 8–10 months after planting. They can be left in the ground and harvested during the second or third season.

Breeding work is underway in Japan to develop more prolific varieties.

Allium ledebouriana
This is smaller than the traditional Welsh onion, and produces very small, fleshy onions sometimes

Rakkyo bulbs

known as 'fire onions'. It is cultivated in China and Japan by planting small bulbs.

Ever-ready onion (*Allium cepa* var *perutile*)
This is an evergreen perennial onion, with finer and flatter leaves than the Welsh onion. It is grown for the leaves, and is easily propagated by division of the clumps.

Japanese bulb onions
The term 'Japanese onion' is currently used for the hardy, early-maturing varieties of bulbing onion (*Allium cepa*) developed by the Japanese. They have become well established in temperate northern climates, where they are sown in late summer and early autumn. They mature in early summer, before the spring planted crop is ready. 'Imai Early Yellow', 'Express Yellow' and 'Senshyu Semi-Globe Yellow' are well known varieties.

Pea shoots

Family *Leguminosae*
Latin name *Pisum sativum*
Mandarin name Dou miao; wen dou miao
Cantonese Dau miu
Japanese Tohbyo

Background

Pea shoots are the tendrils and the top pairs of leaves at the tip of a pea stem. They are an exquisitely flavoured, extravagant delicacy. Although occasional references to eating pea shoots can be found in old European gardening books, the practice now seems to be confined to the Orient. It has spread from China to Japan, and has been introduced to south-east Asia by people such as the Hmongs.

I first saw peas grown for shoots in a village near Chengdu in south-west China, renowned for its use of biogas. All over the village there were little clumps of young peas—on the edges of paths, on banks, and in awkward corners in the fields. I watched an old lady delicately cutting the tips from these very small pea plants. In another Chengdu commune we saw neat little circles of peas on the workers' private plots: a good source of income as the Chinese are prepared to pay high prices for them. The low yields and light weight of the shoots account for the high price.

Use

In the kitchen
Pea shoots, perhaps not surprisingly, taste of fresh peas. They are exceptionally tender, and can be used raw in salads.

The Hmongs simply squeeze lemon or lime juice over them.

Otherwise, they are steamed or very lightly stir-fried, sometimes with ginger, sometimes with a little sugar and wine.

They may also be mixed in fish, chicken and pork dishes. Alternatively they can be cooked with sausages, or used in soup.

Climate

Peas are essentially cool weather crops. The ideal mean temperature for growth is 55–65°F (13–18°C). Most peas can stand a little frost when they are young, though frost will damage the flowers and pods.

Soil/site

Peas grow on a wide range of reasonably fertile, moisture-retentive soils, but not on compacted, poorly drained or waterlogged soil, or extremely acid or alkaline soil. They must not be allowed to dry out. Wherever possible members of the pea and bean family should be rotated, ideally over a 6-year cycle, to avoid the build up of soil diseases.

Peas do best in an open situation, though will tolerate light shade in mid-summer. Prepare the soil beforehand by digging it over and working in plenty of well-rotted manure to improve the drainage. Peas do not have high fertilizer requirements. Within 4–6 weeks of sowing, bacteria on their root nodules normally fix nitrogen from the soil to supply the plant's needs.

Cultivation

As far as I can ascertain, any variety of pea can be used for pea shoots. They are usually sown in spring or late summer, the first shoots being picked within about a month.

Sowing methods

The peas can be sown and cultivated by any method used for ordinary podded garden peas. The four methods below are used in China; in the first three the peas grow prostrate without any supports. These methods, which involve sowing peas very close, use a fair amount of seed, so in good seasons it could be worth saving your own. (See Part 2, Plant raising, Saving seed, page 154.)

Seed tray method Sow seeds closely in soil or potting compost in a seed tray. The seed trays can be started in the dark, and moved into the light when the seedlings are 4–6 in (10–15 cm) high to allow them to green up. Harvest the shoot tips as they develop.

Close sowing in situ Peas are sown so close they are virtually touching. In this case the whole plant is sometimes harvested for pea shoots. Seed can also be sown in little clumps about 12 in (30 cm) apart to allow for access.

Wider sowing Sow seeds 3–4 in (7.5–10 cm) apart, in rows or evenly spaced. When plants are 4 in (10 cm) high nip out the growing points. This encourages them to develop into bushy plants with plenty of tender shoots.

Shoots are picked between 2 and 4 in (5 and 10 cm) long, the first pickings being made when the plants are anything between 6–10 in (15–25 cm) high. Keep picking the tips of any side shoots to encourage further shoots.

Supported plants Grow plants as normal garden peas, supported by sticks, but harvest the shoot tips as they develop. Remove any flowers which appear, to prevent the formation of pods and concentrate energy on the production of shoots.
TIP AND TENDRIL STEALING FROM STANDARD GARDEN PEAS Where peas are being grown for pods, it is often possible to pinch out a few shoot tips for use without damaging the plant.

The tendrils of the leafless and semi-leafless types, which are far more numerous than the tendrils of ordinary leafy pea varieties, can also be cut and used as a vegetable. They are only tender enough to eat raw when very young, otherwise they should be cooked. Harvesting a few sparingly will not damage the plants.

Edible podded pea
The edible podded pea, also known as the sugar or mangetout, is the main type of garden pea eaten in China and Japan. Although in the West it is widely considered a Chinese vegetable, it originated in the Mediterranean, the Mandarin name being 'he lan do' or Holland pea. It is highly recommended, being easily grown and having an excellent flavour. The flat-podded types are 2–4½ in (5–12 cm) long, and up to an inch (2.5 cm) wide, sometimes smooth and straight, sometimes sickle-shaped with a slightly bloated look. They are eaten when the swelling peas can be seen within the pods, pushing against the skin. In the round podded types the wall of the pod is much thicker and fleshier, fitting so snugly around the peas the two seem welded together. These are best eaten when the peas have swollen to the size of ordinary shelling peas. When fully mature, pods can be shelled and peas used as shelling peas. The American-bred 'Snap Pea' is typical of this type.

Pea shoot

Perilla

Family *Labiatae*
Latin name *Perilla frutescens* *
Other names Beefsteak plant; shiso; tai to (Vietnamese)
Japanese Shiso; ao shiso (green perilla); aka shiso (red perilla)
Mandarin Zi su

* The green and red forms used as culinary herbs are often called *P. frutescens* var *crispa*

Background

Perilla is the quintessential Japanese herb for seasoning and garnishing. My first 'live' encounter with perilla was probably typical. It was one element in an elegantly arranged *hors d'oeuvre*: two thin slabs of raw pink fish, three of white fish, a 'blob' of wasabi (horseradish) sauce and a single green perilla leaf concealing a tiny mound of shredded radish. Each ingredient was dipped into soya sauce before being eaten—the perilla leaf wrapped round one of the pieces of fish. I've since learnt that the Japanese eat perilla with raw fish to counteract stomach parasites which may be in the fish.

Although perilla doesn't feature in modern Chinese cooking, it is mentioned in ancient Chinese recipes and was used as a vegetable and in soups. Oil extracted from perilla seeds was one of the first culinary vegetable oils. Perilla also has a long history of medicinal use, which extends to the present day.

Characteristics

Perilla is a tender, bushy, annual herb. The two most distinct types are green-leaved and red-leaved, but there are many intermediate forms. For example, the green-leaved forms may be speckled with purple, or have pinkish or red undersides to the leaves. The colour of red-leaved forms ranges from pinkish to deep red to a rich bronze, the underside sometimes paler.

The leaves can be up to 3 in (7.5 cm) long, and much the same width. Depending on variety, they can be round, oblong or pointed, but the leaf margins are usually

Perilla

serrated. The red-leaved forms are smooth or crinkled; the green-leaved are flat and soft textured and bear a close resemblance to nettle leaves. The crinkle-leaved forms are often confused with the crinkle-leaved 'Ruffles' varieties of basil. The red forms have square red stems, and long narrow spikes of tiny purplish red flowers, while the green have green stems and green flowers.

The size and vigour of the plants depends largely on the climate and growing conditions. The red form is usually the tallest, on average 18–36 in (45–90 cm) tall. The green form is usually not much more than 2 ft (60 cm) high. Some forms are more branching than others.

Climate

Perilla grows best at temperatures above 64°F (18°C). It is not frost-hardy, though I find it withstands cold conditions slightly better than basil. In areas where basil fails to

Use

Seeds, sprouted seeds, the tiny cotyledon leaves of seedlings, mature leaves and flowering spikes are all used for seasoning and garnishing. The ground seeds are one of the spices in the famous *Shichimi* 'seven spice' mixture, added to many dishes much as Westerners use salt.

Flavour The unique flavour of perilla defies description. Western palates find it strange initially, but quickly get to like its subtle qualities. To me it has the mustiness of coriander; others find it reminiscent of cinnamon or citrus. The green-leaved forms have a stronger, richer flavour than the red. The flavour is said to be best in leaves about 2 in (5 cm) wide and when leaves are grown in acid soil.

In the kitchen

In Japan tiny seedlings, flowering shoots and finely chopped leaves season and garnish raw and cooked fish, chilled bean curd and salads. It is especially good with cucumber and shredded cabbage. Red leaves not only add their distinctive colour to salads, but turn juices a beautiful pink colour. The highly decorative, tiny red seedlings could well become a prized salad ingredient in restaurants.

Grated radish and chopped perilla are often used as a garnish for beefsteaks (hence its name?). The leaves are often used to wrap pieces of cooked beef, pork or fish. In a Tokyo supermarket I saw burdock and pepper pickles wrapped in perilla leaves; a friend admits to a passion for whole, salted, boiled quail eggs wrapped in a perilla leaf.

Perilla is both used to flavour cooked dishes and cooked in its own right. Leaves and flowering shoots are fried in batter (the Japanese *tempura*) and used in soups. Leaves are also used in beef and barbecued dishes, and to give a wonderful flavour to rice and potato dishes. They are an integral part of the classical Japanese *shiso maki*, made from cold rice (*sushi*) and perilla wrapped in seaweed.

Red perilla leaves are widely used in making pickles, as they dye the vinegar pink. The famous Japanese sour plum pickle, *umeboshi*, is made with perilla leaves, as are fresh ginger pickles. I have used them to colour radish pod pickles. The leaves can themselves be pickled, by steaming for 10 minutes before covering with a mixture of soya sauce and vinegar. The seeds are salted to make a pickle; even the tiny cotyledon leaves are dried and salted.

thrive outdoors, grow perilla in a frame or unheated greenhouse. Perilla needs short days to produce flowering shoots.

Soil/site

Perilla does not require particularly fertile soil, and grows well in acid soils with a pH between 5.5 and 6. It will not tolerate waterlogging. In cold areas warm, light, well-drained soils are preferable to cold heavy soils.

In cold areas it should be grown in a sheltered sunny situation outdoors, or under cover. In warm areas it can be grown in full sun or light shade.

Decorative value

Perilla—especially the red-leaved form—was a popular summer bedding plant with the Victorians. They probably kept the shoots pinched back to prevent them becoming too straggly. In places with reasonably warm summers the plants are very eye-catching, worthy of inclusion in flower beds and in decorative vegetable plots.

Cultivation

For cultivation of seedlings and flower spikes, see below and page 110.

Perilla is normally raised from seed, though it can also be propagated from cuttings. In warm climates it often seeds itself in gardens. A few plants are sufficient for most households.

When to sow

In temperate areas perilla is sown indoors in spring, transplanting outside after all risk of frost. Sow 30–40 days before the last frost is expected. Outdoor sowings can be made in early summer, preferably under a cloche or in a warm spot.

Sowing method

It can be sown *in situ* or transplanted. Use fresh seed, as germination falls off rapidly and can be erratic. (Coleus seed is occasionally passed off as perilla. Beware!) The seed is very small, and must be sown on fine soil.
Sowing indoors Sow in seed compost on the surface. The ideal temperature for germination is about 68°F (20°C), though seed will germinate at slightly lower temperatures. Cover the sowing container with glass or plastic to keep in moisture until the seeds germinate.

Prick out when seedlings have 3–5 leaves; or pot them up in small pots. Plant outside after hardening off, spacing plants about 12 in (30 cm) apart each way, or 8 in (20 cm) apart in rows about 2 ft (60 cm) apart.
Sowing in situ In warm climates perilla can be sown *in situ* outdoors, thinning in stages to the distances above.

Further care

The growing points can be nipped off to keep the plants sturdy. (They can be used for flavouring.) Little other attention is needed, though plants should be kept well-watered.

Protected cropping

In Japan winter crops are obtained by growing perilla in greenhouses with artificial light. The earliest crop is obtained by sowing in summer, transplanting into a greenhouse in autumn. This is ready in winter and early spring.

This is followed by an autumn sowing, transplanting into the greenhouse in early winter. This is ready in late spring the following season.

Containers

Being an undemanding plant perilla can be grown well in containers. Nip back the growing points if necessary to keep them within bounds. Vietnamese immigrants in the USA often have a pot of perilla on the doorstep.

Harvesting

Leaves from mature plants can normally be cut within 2–3 months after sowing, and harvesting can continue over several months. Pick off individual leaves as required. In my experience plants die back suddenly towards the end of the season, the leaves turning brown and losing all flavour.

Perilla leaves wilt rapidly after picking. When packed for market they are often sealed into flat packs, sometimes lined with damp paper towel to keep them moist. They can be kept in a cool department of a fridge for several days. Stems can also be hung up to dry, and the leaves removed and stored in airtight containers once they are crackly-dry.

Cultivation for seedlings
In Japan red perilla is harvested as very small seedlings. For this purpose it is normally grown under cover in greenhouses, making successive sowings from spring to autumn. The seedlings are sown thickly on wide beds, covered with transparent film until germinated. They must have good light and adequate moisture. They are cut with scissors any time from about 40 days after sowing, either as tiny cotyledons, or at the 2, 3 or 4 'true leaf' stage.

Cultivation for flower spikes

The shorter varieties of perilla are used for flower spike production. The more compact the flower spike, the better. The following is based on Taiwanese practice. Seedlings are transplanted at the 3–4 leaf stage into groups of 3–4 plants, the groups 4–5 in (10–13 cm) apart. The flowering shoots are harvested when they are about 3 in (7.5 cm) long, pulling up the whole plant. As perilla only flowers in short days, the seedlings are sometimes covered with black plastic film in the morning and evening to reduce the daylength to 6–7 hours.

Varieties

Although perilla displays considerable variation, there seem to be few named varieties. The main choice is between green and red forms, and within red forms between smooth and crinkle leaved.

Perilla frutescens var *nankinensis* is sometimes sold as a particularly dark-leaved red form for bedding. It can presumably also be used for culinary purposes.

Radishes

Family *Cruciferae*
Latin names *Raphanus sativus* (sometimes var *longipinnatus* or var *radicola*)
Other names in use Daikon; mooli (mainly used for white types, derived from 'muli'—the Hindi for radish)
Mandarin Luo bo; lai fu
Cantonese Lo/loh bok/pak
Japanese Daikon ('big root')

Background

The radish occupies a far more exalted position in oriental cultures than it does in the West, and is much larger than its Western counterpart. It is the most widely grown vegetable in Japan, where, so I've been told, gift-wrapped radishes are a token of esteem. It is used mainly for cooking and pickling, but there are some unique and exciting salad types. Besides being used fresh, some types are stored for winter use, while others are salted and dried to preserve them. Radish leaves, stems, seed pods and seedlings are all valued as vegetables, cooked, pickled or raw.

Characteristics

Oriental radishes are annual or biennial, depending on the variety and how they are grown. The plants are usually 1–2 ft (30–60 cm) high, though they can shoot up to 6 ft (1.8 m) when flowering. They are much leafier than European radishes, the mature leaves being large and rather rugged and handsome, sometimes upright, sometimes sprawling. They tend to be deeply indented or lobed, although there is considerable variation in shape, and some are relatively smooth-margined. Texture ranges from smooth and glossy to rough and hairy, leaf col-

our from dark green to greenish-grey, sometimes with purple leaf stalks or purple splashes on the leaves. The flowers in cultivated varieties are white, pink or purple.

The roots display tremendous variation in size, shape and colour. The typical oriental radish is a long white root—anything from about 4 in (10 cm) to well over 2 ft (60 cm) in length. The roots are tapered, cylindrical or spindle-shaped, and pointed or rounded at the bottom. Some are quite stocky in shape. They can be 1–4 in (2.5–10 cm) in diameter. In addition there are a number of round types, typically about 6 in (15 cm) in diameter and 4–5 in (10–13 cm) deep. The world's largest radish, the famous Japanese variety 'Sakurajima', can reach giant proportions—a girth of 32 in (80 cm), and 5 in (12 cm) depth. Oriental radishes can weigh anything from 1–60 lb (0.5–30 kg).

The skin colour may be pure white, but many varieties are green-shouldered, or green-skinned for two thirds of the root. There are also red-skinned varieties, both round and long in shape, and completely green-skinned varieties. The internal flesh is normally white, but some of the green-shouldered varieties have green flesh, while others—for example the famous north Chinese 'Beauty Heart' radishes—have

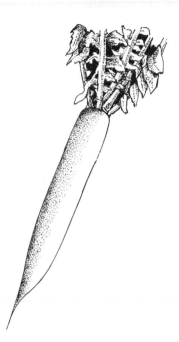

Typical Japanese 'Mooli' radish

beautiful pink, red and white flesh.

Many oriental radishes push several inches out of the ground as they grow.

Types of Oriental radish grown for their roots

Although there are no hard and fast divisions, it is easiest to consider the oriental radishes as falling into two main groups:

The white 'mooli' types
These are now widely associated with Japan and are often known as 'daikon'.

The 'coloured' types
This group includes the red- and green-fleshed northern Chinese varieties, and the various red-skinned varieties.

White 'mooli' radishes

Development of different types

The modern Japanese varieties originated in southern China, being introduced to Japan about 1000 years ago. Certain types are still referred to as 'Chinese' in Japan: these tend to be suited to tropical conditions, and to be rather short and thick. Though coarser than most mooli, they are said to keep their shape well when cooked.

Over the centuries, with generations of farmers selecting for their own purposes and conditions, the original Chinese radishes evolved into a number of very distinct types: a striking example of adaption to different soil types and climatic conditions. The root shape in particular, and the extent to which roots protrude above ground, has been very influenced by soil type. Take the 'Moriguchi' radish, which occasionally reaches a length of 4 ft (1.2 m), and lays claim to being the world's longest radish: its exceptionally long, thin, straight roots, entirely below ground, developed on very deep, coastal, sandy soils.

Very large, slightly spindle-shaped types, in which the top quarter of the root protrudes above ground, developed in deep volcanic soils. Here the richness of the soil contributed to their size, but the soil's lightness enabled the bulk of the root to swell below ground. These are vigorous leafy types. The giant roundish variety 'Sakurajima' mentioned above comes in this group.

In heavy clay soils it is almost impossible for roots to swell below ground, so these conditions led to the evolution of types with roots largely pushed up above ground. Sometimes they give the impression of being perched on the surface. There are both round and long types suitable for heavy clay soil. 'Shogoin' is a well-known round variety: three-quarters of its bulk is above ground. The same is true of the cylindrical 'Shiroagari' types. 'Small' by mooli standards—they grow only 12 in (30 cm) long—they are the best adapted to clay soils.

Intermediate types of radish developed on intermediate soil types, such as medium, loamy soils.

Some overwintering varieties have characteristics which indicate adaptation to low temperatures,

Use

Mooli radishes are crisp-textured, tender, and vary in flavour from sweet and mild to fairly hot and pungent. On the whole the stronger flavoured varieties are used for pickling and cooking, while the milder, sweeter varieties are eaten raw.

Flavour even within a variety is not always consistent: it can vary with soil conditions, temperature and the stage of growth, tending to become hotter in heavy soils, at high temperatures, and when the plant is about to run to seed. The hottest flavour is generally in the skin. Some varieties become sweeter if kept a few days after lifting.

In the kitchen

As the pungency is normally associated with the skin, mooli radishes are usually peeled before being cooked or eaten raw. They are also less hot if grated. In Chinese and Japanese cuisine radish is widely held to assist digestion.

Raw The size of the roots makes them a tempting proposition for deft-fingered cooks. Besides being cubed, sliced, cut into matchsticks or shredded, they can be carved into decorative shapes—usually flowers (see 'Beauty heart' radish below). The Japanese peel radishes into paper-thin sheets, which are then cut into long thin strips. These are traditionally either served with grilled beef, or salted, drained, and folded into whipped cream to make radish 'foam'.

Grated radish makes a fine garnish or salad, lightly dressed with soy sauce or sesame oil. It is a key ingredient in the dipping sauces served with Japanese *tempura* and other dishes, and can happily be substituted for grated onion in hamburgers and hot dogs. To

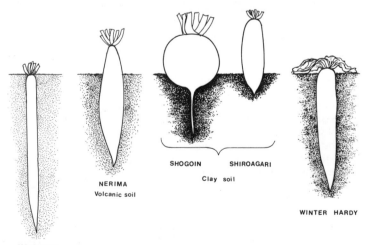

MORIGUCHI
Deep sandy soil

NERIMA
Volcanic soil

SHOGOIN   SHIROAGARI
Clay soil

WINTER HARDY

Evolution of different types of radish root (based on Shinohara)

make grated radish more colourful, the Japanese sometimes cut a root into sections, make two lengthwise holes in it with a chopstick, insert dried red chillies in the holes and then grate the radish—getting a red and white mixture. Where the radishes seem rather watery, they can be made crisper by slicing or grating, sprinkling with salt, and leaving them for up to twenty minutes before being drained and used.

Cooked In the East radishes are cooked in a surprising number of ways—in Western eyes being treated more like turnips than radishes. (We tend to forget the Victorians cooked radishes.) Indeed, any method used for cooking turnips can be used for mooli radish. They can be stir-fried, braised, boiled, steamed with peas, or grated into gravy or sauces to add piquancy. They are also used in stews and casseroles, the Chinese often combining radishes with pork. In addition they are made into all types of soup. I came back from China with recipes for vegetable, fish and meat soups all using radish. Another Chinese speciality is 'radish pudding'—a savoury dish in which batter made from rice flour is stuffed with radish and various ingredients such as Chinese sausage, shrimps, meat or

mushrooms. This is steamed, and then usually sliced and fried.

Dried and pickled
Until the advent of modern methods of vegetable storage oriental radishes were mainly grown for preserves. Sometimes they were simply shredded or sliced, dried in the sun, and salted—perhaps flavoured with sugar and spices such as hot peppers. These preserved radishes can be eaten immediately as snacks— sometimes to accompany breakfast porridge—or kept for long periods. They are used cooked or raw.

Innumerable methods of pickling have been developed: in soy sauce, in vinegar, in a mixture of wine and soy sauce. The Japanese *takuan* pickles are fermented in layers in a barrel; the famous Korean *kimchi* pickles, and some others, use leaves as well as roots. Some pickles are short-term, some long-term. Pickling bestows a distinct flavour, but a yellow dye is sometimes added to give an appealing colour. Among the many Japanese varieties of radish, some are considered best suited to one type of pickles, some to others. Standard Western recipes for pickling vegetables can also be used for pickling radish.

(See also Recipes, page 194.)

Climate

The mooli radishes are essentially coolish-weather crops, the ideal growing temperature being about 68°F (20°C). Well-established plants will continue growing when night temperatures are not much above 32°F (0°C), although if *sown* at low temperatures there would be a risk of bolting. In warm climates mid-summer sowings should be avoided, unless heat-tolerant varieties are used.

Mooli radishes are most likely to bolt in the lengthening days of spring and early summer, especially if sown at temperatures below about 53°F (12°C).

Soil/site

In general, mooli radishes do best on rich, light, well-drained soil; deep light soil is essential for the longer-rooted types. In China they are often grown on ridges to ensure good drainage. The soil should preferably be manured for the previous crop, rather than freshly manured. When grown on a large scale radish should be rotated carefully to avoid the build up of root nematodes. The plants are large and require an open site, not cramped or shaded by taller plants.

Cultivation
When to sow

The most important factor with mooli radish is to sow the appropriate radish for the season (see Varieties, below).

MAIN SUMMER SOWINGS The main sowings are made in mid- to late summer to mature in autumn, roots usually taking 2½–3 months, and more, to mature. These autumn-maturing varieties can withstand light frosts, but make the last sowings in the open roughly 3 months before the first frost is expected.

SPRING AND EARLY SUMMER SOWINGS Using appropriate varieties, earlier sowings can be made in spring and

such as roots forming entirely below ground, and leaves spreading out horizontally, giving additional protection on the surface.

During growth the root shape of any particular variety may be modified by the character of the soil in which it is growing. A heavy, long-rooted 'volcanic soil' type may become rather thin in poorer sandy soil or heavy clay soil and stumpier in ordinary loam. So if your radishes don't look quite like the picture in the catalogue, this could be the reason.

A radish for every season The mooli

radishes naturally run to seed in the long days of spring. So the 'natural' time for the *roots* to develop is during summer and autumn, maturing from late summer to early winter. However, and again it has been a story of patient selection over the centuries, a range of varieties has been developed which can be sown earlier and earlier, from spring onwards, with far less risk of bolting prematurely. There are a few very versatile varieties which can be sown over a long period, but for most mooli varieties there is an optimum season in which they

should be sown. (See Varieties, page 114.)

early summer, to mature during the summer. These varieties tend to be faster maturing, taking on average 1½–2 months to mature. It is unwise to sow until the average temperature is about 53°F (12°C).

In cold climates the first spring sowings need to be made under cover, or with protection from woven film. (See Part 2, Protected cropping.).

AUTUMN AND EARLY SPRING SOWINGS In mild areas cold-tolerant over-wintering varieties can be sown in autumn to provide early crops the following year. In areas where frost is expected they can be sown under cover. Most of these varieties can also be sown very early in spring—often under low polytunnels which are removed when temperatures rise. However, they are of better quality if autumn sown. These cold-tolerant varieties tend to be slow maturing, and generally somewhat poorer quality, than mooli grown in the summer months.

Sowing method

Radish is usually sown *in situ*, although young seedlings can be transplanted successfully. They can also be sown in modules and transplanted. (See Part 2, Plant raising, Use of modules, page 153.) This is most successful with round and oval varieties. With long-rooted varieties the ends of the roots tend to become misshapen when grown in modules. Transplanting may sound a rather elaborate way to raise a radish, but these large radishes respond to VIP treatment. One household doesn't require very many: it can pay to grow relatively few specimens really well.

Seed should be sown ½–¾ in (1–2 cm) deep. Seedlings grow very fast, tending to become 'leggy', and for this reason I usually sow in sunken drills—the drills being about 1½ in (4 cm) deep. Earth from the edge of the drill can be gently pulled around the seedling stems as they grow to give extra support. Always sow thinly, or station-sow in groups, to make thinning easier. (See Part 2, Plant raising, Sowing outdoors, page 151.)

Spacing

Spacing will depend on the variety. The smaller varieties, and varieties being pulled young, can be 3–4 in (7.5–10 cm) apart each way; large varieties need to be up to about 16 in (40 cm) apart each way. If growing in rows, space rows at least 14 in (35 cm) apart. Varieties with an upright leaf habit can often be grown closer than those more sprawling, horizontal leaves.

Thin in stages, starting as soon as seedlings are large enough to handle so their growth is never restricted or checked. The thinnings are often large enough to be used. INTERCROPPING Where radish is grown in widely spaced rows, a fast-growing seedling crop such as salad rocket or pak choi can be sown between the rows, provided it is harvested when 2–3 in (5–8 cm) high.

Further care

Transplanted radishes may need watering until established. Like many root crops, radishes require a steady supply of water, so watering may be necessary in dry weather if the soil is drying out. Take care not to overwater once roots are developing, or they may start to crack. Other than keeping the plants weed-free, little further attention is required.

Pests and disease

Radishes belong to the same family as the brassicas, and tend to be subject to the same pests and diseases.

In practice the most common pests are flea beetle and various cabbage caterpillars—both of which feed on the leaves—and early in the season cabbage root fly, which attacks the roots. Slugs and cutworm can also cause damage. Growing radishes under woven film until shortly before harvest is an effective way of preventing cabbage root fly attacks. Where radishes are grown continually in the same ground eelworm can become a problem.

Under good growing conditions in temperate regions the only likely diseases are clubroot and alternaria leaf spot. In hot climates fusarium wilt and various virus diseases can cause problems. Many modern Japanese varieties are bred with resistance to virus, fusarium wilt and root knot eelworm. (See also Part 2, Pests and disease.)

Harvesting

Most varieties of mooli can be pulled for eating at various sizes during the course of development. Spring and early summer varieties tend to become spongy or pithy after they reach maturity, so should be lifted and used before they deteriorate.

The autumn radishes can be left in the ground for 4–8 weeks after maturing without deteriorating. After that they tend to become tougher. However, most can be lifted and stored for a further 1–3 months, depending on variety.

Store them in boxes of moist sand or ashes in a cool, frost-free cellar or shed, or in the garden covered with soil and straw. In north China radishes are stored in layers in 6 ft (2 m) deep pits, each layer separated by a few inches of soil, and the entire pit covered with 12 in (30 cm) of soil. In parts of Japan where heavy snow is the norm, radishes were traditionally left in the field, insulated by a blanket of snow. They were much valued as fresh vegetables in the winter months.

Varieties

Below are some of the major types of mooli, and some of the varieties currently available, grouped according to their principal sowing season. In practice there is overlapping between the different categories. Days to maturity, where given, should be treated as approximations. Improved F1 hybrids of many of the traditional types are now being developed. The autumn and winter maturing group, which is much the largest and the most easily grown, has been treated in greatest detail.

Autumn/winter maturing

These are sown from mid-summer until autumn, for harvesting in autumn and early winter or—in areas with little frost—late winter. They tend to be vigorous, good quality varieties. If uncertain about the correct sowing time for any variety of mooli, it is safest to assume it belongs to this category.

F1 'Mikura Cross' Long, straight, white, cylindrical roots; mature rapidly, stand well without becoming pithy. Mild flavoured. (55–60 days.)

F1 'Mino Summer Cross' Long, white, tapered root; good heat and disease resistance; mild flavour. Roots harvested any stage from 6–14 in (15–35 cm) long. (45 days.)

F1 'Minowase Summer Cross No. 3' Long, white, tapered, good quality roots; good heat and disease resistance. Also suited to late spring sowing. (55 days.)

'Miura' types Large, stout, spindle-shaped white roots; require deep rich soils. Can harvest late, as slow to become pithy. Spreading, protective leaves; stand cold well. In areas with very mild winters sow in autumn for harvesting around Christmas or very early in spring; otherwise sow summer for early winter harvest. Sweet-flavoured. (90–100 days.)

'Miyashige' types Medium sized, white roots, adapted to wide range of soil types. Many forms: stump rooted, pointed, green shouldered, white shouldered, plus early and late varieties. Mild flavour, tender, crisp texture. The late varieties are sown in early autumn; suitable for storing. (50–60 days.) 'White Miyashige' grew well transplanted into solar frames in autumn.

'Nerima' types Vigorous, large, long, generally spindle-shaped roots, suited to deep rich soils.

Pointed and stump-rooted forms. Late maturing; crisp flesh. (70–100 days.)

'Okura' types Stump-rooted, white roots up to 18 in (45 cm) long; crisp and mild flavoured. Crop well in winter months. In areas with mild winters can sow autumn for February harvest. (65–75 days.)

'Sakurajima Mammoth' Originated southernmost tip Japan. Huge, round, white roots. Only grow successfully in frost-free winters and rich, deep, light soils. Sown mid-summer; requires 200 days to reach maximum size. Often harvested 150 days after sowing, when 10 in (25 cm) diameter, 12–18 lb (5–8 kg) weight. (If 5 in (12 cm) diameter not reached after 100 days' growth, roots become spindle-shaped and poor, fibrous quality.) Unsuitable for storage, but unique in that even if outer 3 in (7.5 cm) become pithy, inner core remains juicy and crisp. Normally cooked or pickled. Huge leaves fed to animals.

'Shogoin' types Round, medium-sized roots, develop largely above ground, suited to heavy clay soils. Average size about 7 in (18 cm) diameter, 5 in (13 cm) deep, up to 5 lb (2.2 kg) weight. Green necks; shape ranges from spherical to flattish. Mild flavour, excellent quality. Takes 70–100 days to mature; early varieties become pithy fastest. Later-maturing varieties keep in ground several weeks. Leaves protect roots well; tasty cooked.

Summer/early autumn maturing

These varieties have been selected for their resistance to bolting. Depending on the variety, they are mainly sown in spring and early summer, for maturing from mid-summer onwards. The majority are long, white, pointed varieties developed from the original slow-bolting, heat-tolerant variety 'Minowase'. They grow rapidly but don't stand well once mature. Generally speaking, they are more pungent than the autumn varieties, though much of the 'bite' is lost if they are peeled.

The most cold tolerant varieties can be sown in mild areas very early in spring and in late autumn, often under protection.

VARIETIES FOR EARLY SUMMER SOWING
F1 'April Cross'
'Mino Early Long White'
'Mino Spring Cross'
'Mino Summer Cross 3'
F1 'Tsukushi Spring Cross' (Green shouldered)

VARIETIES FOR EARLY SPRING SOWING
'All Season White'/'Tokinashi'
F1 'All Season Cross'/F1 'Omny'
F1 'Easter Cross'
F1 'Hi-Light'
F1 'Mino Spring Cross'
F1 'Mino Summer Cross 3'
F1 'Tsukushi Spring Cross'

VARIETIES FOR LATE AUTUMN SOWING IN MILD CONDITIONS OR WITH PROTECTION
'All Season White'/'Tokinashi'
F1 'All Season Cross'/'F1 Omny'

European long white radishes

'Rettich' or 'Ramanas' are types of white radish which have been developed in Germany and Holland from European types of radish. They were traditionally eaten with Bavarian beer. They grow to about 8 in (20 cm), are rougher-skinned than 'mooli' and probably inferior in quality. They may be found in markets masquerading as 'mooli', while in Germany 'mooli' are sometimes sold as 'Rettich'.

Coloured-fleshed radishes

There are several types of Chinese radish with coloured flesh, the colour ranging from pale to dark pink, to green, to purple.

'Beauty Heart' radishes

This unique radish comes from the Beijing area of north China. Its apt Mandarin name 'Xin Li Mei' (pronounced 'shin lee may') means 'heart inside beautiful'. On the outside it is rather rough-looking, with thick, nondescript green and white skin. But the interior of a good specimen is spectacular, with deep pinky-red rays on a white background radiating from the centre. The radishes weigh 1–2 lb (0.5–1 kg), and are either round or oblong in shape. (See Types, below.)

In north China the 'Beauty Heart' radishes are treated as fruits. The traditional street cry was 'radishes . . . better than crisp pears'—and north Chinese pears are exceptionally crisp! In the old days it was sold at night from gas lit carts, the colour of samples shown off by the light behind them. They are sometimes displayed by making longitudinal cuts inside the perimeter of the radish, then bending the cut sections backwards to look like petals. Samples are cut from the exposed 'beautiful heart'.

Exquisite 'radish flowers' are carved from 'Beauty Heart' as decorations for festive dishes. Just before leaving Beijing a lady chef demonstrated radish carving for us. I will never forget the agility with which she peeled and sliced, removing a sliver here and another there with a large kitchen knife. She created dahlias, paeonies, water lilies and chrysanthemums, but best of all an exquisite butterfly, its red-and-white-tipped wings delicately hinged slices of radish. We had to leave to catch a train before she had time to make us crickets and dragonflies, but she put the butterflies into a plastic bag filled with water to keep them fresh—and we took them away like goldfish won at a fair.

Types

There are two types: the large, oval or 'rectangular' type, and a smaller, rounder type. In both the shoulders and top third are green-skinned, but white below.

Large oval type

On average these are 4–5 in (10–12.5 cm) long and 2–3 in (5–8 cm) wide. Their chief merit is that they are less likely to bolt than the smaller type when sown in cool conditions. In north China they are mainly sown in spring, though they can also be sown in summer. They tend to be pale coloured in-

ternally. They do not store as well as the smaller round types, though they can be stored for short periods.

Small round type

These are shaped like round turnips, roughly 3–4 ins (7.5–10 cm) in diameter. The flesh can be very deep coloured. They are more prone to bolting than the long type, and are sown in summer. They store well, and in north China are sometimes stored from winter until the following spring. At present most of the varieties available in the West are of this type.

Climate

'Beauty Heart' requires higher temperatures than mooli radish, and is likely to bolt if subjected to temperatures below about 60°F (15°C) in its early stages. Ideally it needs at least three months of warm weather to develop, though mature plants can survive a little frost.

Soil/site, pests and disease

See Mooli radishes.

Cultivation

Sowing

As 'Beauty Heart' needs several months of warm weather, in areas with unreliable or short cool summers it is best grown under cover in an unheated greenhouse or tunnel. My best results in England have been obtained from July and August sowings in a polytunnel, though I have occasionally had good plants outdoors. In warmer areas it can be grown outdoors.

MAIN SOWING Delay sowing until early summer, when temperatures have reached about 60°F (15°C). (The colour sometimes fails to develop with premature sowings.) Sowings can continue until autumn; the last sowing will be transplanted under cover in late autumn.

Either sow *in situ* or sow in modules, transplanting seedlings at the 4–5 true leaf stage. Various spacings are used, depending on the size of root required:

Small roots: 4 in (10 cm) apart in

Use

When grown well and harvested at their peak 'Beauty Heart' radishes are crisp, mild and sweet-flavoured—though sweetness varies from one radish to the next. The hottest flavour is in the skin. If left in the ground too long they become tough and fibrous.

In the kitchen

They are mainly used raw as a salad. If cut into matchsticks the outer green or white skin gives a contrasting tip to the pink and white shaft. Poorer-coloured specimens are better grated, as even the slightest pinkish tinge in the root will show up through the white. The radishes are often served with sugar sprinkled on top. They can also be cooked by any methods suitable for mooli radishes.

'Beauty Heart' radish with a carved radish flower

rows 9 in (23 cm) apart, or 6 in (15 cm) apart each way.
Medium roots: 12 in (30 cm) apart each way.
Large roots: 12 in (30 cm) apart, in rows 2 ft (60 cm) apart, or 15–18 in (38–45 cm) apart each way.
EARLY SOWINGS For earlier crops

sow in late spring to early summer in modules, at a temperature of 68–77°F (20–25°C) to prevent premature bolting when transplanted. Transplant 4–5 weeks later at the 4–5 true leaf stage, hardening off well if growing outside.

Harvesting

Roots are generally ready for lifting from about 80 days after sowing. The Chinese say that a few cracks appearing in the roots is an indication of succulence and that they are ready. A clue to identifying a good coloured 'heart' before cutting open the radish is a pink tinge to the tiny root at the bottom of the radish. Roots will stand in the soil for a few weeks after maturing, but should then be lifted and stored. Some varieties can be stored for up to 5 months, until the following spring, if kept in conditions of high humidity. (See Mooli radishes.)

Variability

The sad truth has to be told: while it is possible to grow a really beautiful 'Beauty Heart', there is a large element of chance as the seed available at present is extremely variable. The odds are that some roots will have hollow instead of beautiful hearts, some may have so little colour they are virtually white, and there is a high risk of bolting. Bolting immediately leads to a loss of quality, though the roots are still passable if grated.

Plant breeders in China, Japan and Europe are working to improve 'Beauty Heart', and once they succeed I am sure it will sweep triumphantly through the gourmet restaurants of the Western world. In the meantime it is worth having a go: the law of averages will give you a few good roots each season. For several years now we have had an *hors d'oeuvre* of 'Beauty Heart' with our Christmas dinner.

Varieties

The following are varieties of 'Beauty Heart' radish:
'Aomaru-koshin', 'Green skin, red flesh', 'Misato Rose'/'Ten Ankoshin', 'Red Flesh', 'Red Meat'

Green-fleshed radishes

Like 'Beauty Heart', the green-fleshed radishes seem to have originated in north China. Some are broad like 'Beauty Heart', but most are long with stump-ended roots. The average length of mature roots is about 8 in (20 cm), but it varies from 4–14 in (10–35 cm). They are about 2 in (5 cm) in diameter. The largest weigh over a pound (450 g).

The extent to which they are green, both the outer skin and internally, varies considerably, as does the intensity of the green. In some the top third is a light pea-green, but the lower two-thirds is white; in others the top is deep green, the rest pale green—and all intermediate variations can be found. The radishes usually grow with much of the root pushed up out of the ground: it is at least 80 per cent in some varieties, known in China as the '80 per cent'. The exposed part is green.

Cultivation

The green radishes are much easier to grow than 'Beauty Heart', being more cold-tolerant and faster maturing. They are ready on average 60 days after sowing. Grow them like mooli radishes, sowing in summer to mature in autumn and early winter. A late sowing can be made in early autumn under cover for a late crop. Space smaller varieties about 5 in (13 cm) apart, larger varieties 8 in (20 cm) apart. The roots keep in reasonable condition in the soil, but before severe weather should be lifted and stored, as for 'Beauty Heart'. Most varieties will keep until spring in humid conditions.

The green-fleshed radishes will, I am sure, become very popular, once seed is readily available in the West.

Varieties

'Green Flesh', 'Green Meat Chinese', 'Shantung Green Skin'—all small varieties.
'Kochin': long, slightly hot when first harvested.
'Misato Green': long root, short tops so can plant close. Keeps well.

Use

The green-fleshed radishes are of exceptional good quality, juicy and usually very sweet. Some varieties are slightly pungent when lifted, but become sweet if kept for a day or two. Light frost may enhance their sweetness.

In the kitchen
They are used both raw and cooked. In the meal I described in my introduction we had them both grated raw and cooked with carrots (see page 195.) The Cantonese use green radishes for making soup; they are also pickled.

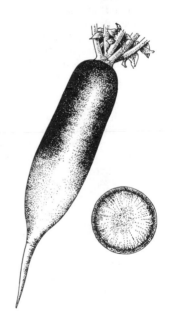

Green-fleshed radish

Red-skinned radishes

These red-skinned, white-fleshed radishes are medium-sized, weighing on average about a pound (less than 500 g). Most are round or oval, though there are long forms. The round ones are about 4 in (10 cm) in diameter and 2–3 in (5–7.5 cm) deep; the long ones up to 4 ½ in (12 cm) long, and about 1 ½ in (3 cm) diameter.

Cultivation

Sowing

In cool, temperate areas sow in early summer for autumn use, and in mid-summer for winter use. Earlier sowings can be made if seed is germinated at high temperatures. (See 'Beauty Heart', early sowings). In very hot areas sow in spring or from late summer to autumn, avoiding mid-summer sowings when temperatures are very high.

Sow *in situ* or in modules, transplanting at the 4–5 leaf stage. Thin to about 10 in (25 cm) apart each way; or grow in rows 15 in (38 cm) apart, thinning to 8 in (20 cm) apart within the rows.

Harvesting and storage

Roots are generally ready 10–12 weeks after sowing. Where winters are mild they can either be left in the soil or lifted and stored (see below). In my experience the flavour is better, as with so many root vegetables, if they are kept in the ground. This is more practical in light, well-drained soils. In heavy soils it may be difficult to lift them in mid-winter, and slug, mice and even rat damage can be severe. (I have a hunch that slug damage is more serious on long, rather than round, varieties. Do they lose their grip on a round radish?)

Cover radishes left in the ground with straw or bracken, to give extra protection, and to lessen the penetration of frost so lifting will be easier in frosty weather. Again this may attract the attention of rodents. My radish roots have survived temperatures as low as 14°F (−10°C) in the soil.

In areas with severe winters roots must be lifted and stored before the onset of severe weather. (See Storage of mooli radish, page 114.)

Use

These radishes tend to be fairly hot-flavoured, though milder when peeled. Their usefulness lies in their tolerance of cold temperatures, and the length of time they can keep in the soil without deteriorating. They have been known and grown in Europe for many years for this purpose, and can probably be equated with the old European winter varieties such as the black-skinned 'Black Spanish', and the violet-skinned 'Violet de Gournay'.

In the kitchen

They are used both as a winter salad radish and for cooking: one friend cooks them in the juice of a roast. The leaves can be eaten at the 2–3 leaf seedling stage. (See Leaf radish.)

Varieties

'Cherokee', 'China Rose', 'Long Red Chinese', 'Misato Red'.

Leaf radish

Today radish leaves are more appreciated in the Eastern than in the Western world, although our ancestors forced radish seedlings in hotbeds for winter and spring 'salading'.

Radish thinnings, at the 2–3 true leaf stage, are known in Chinese as 'wa wa cai' or 'baby vegetables'. Both the Chinese and the Vietnamese stir-fry them. Tender young radish leaves are used raw in salads, steamed, and even salted and dried for use in winter, often as an ingredient in dumplings. Somewhat coarser older leaves can be chopped finely and cooked in stock. The leaf stems of many kinds of radish are also used as a vegetable: little piles of neatly trimmed stems are sometimes seen in Chinese markets.

Choice of variety

Where radish is grown for leaves, the smoother and softer the leaf the better. (The small European radishes generally have smooth leaves, and most can be cut as seedling crops; they do not however produce much bulk.) Many of the large oriental radishes have tender leaves in the young seedling stage, but they may become hairy and coarse as they mature. Experiment with any varieties you are growing. Some varieties with smooth, almost hairless leaves have recently been selected for cultivation *primarily* for the leaf and stems, for example the Japanese variety 'Bisai' (see below).

CHARACTERISTICS OF 'BISAI' 'Bisai' is both heat- and cold-tolerant. It was originally developed as a substitute for leafy greens such as spinach, which cannot be grown in mid-summer in hot climates. However, it has also proved to be very cold-tolerant. It germinates and grows rapidly, is very vigorous, and gives high returns over several months from a small piece of ground. It can be harvested at various stages:

As a seedling crop The small seedling leaves have a very pleasant flavour and are best used raw. In summer the first cut of small leaves can be made 2–3 weeks after sowing, and several cuts can be made subsequently before the plants start to run to seed. Even then, usable leaves can be picked off the flowering stems. Growth takes 2–3 weeks longer at lower temperatures.

As larger leaves These are harvested when about 8–10 in (20–25 cm) tall. In summer they can be ready less than a month after sowing, and will normally resprout after cutting. As they are coarser than the seedling leaves they are best used cooked. They are excellent steamed or stir-fried with other greens.

As whole plants In this case the young plant is pulled up completely more or less at the 'larger leaf' stage, so that the leaves, stems, and young thin roots can all be used. They are prepared separately, the leaves requiring less cooking than the stems and roots.

Mature roots If 'Bisai' is left to ma-ture, intentionally or accidentally, it develops good white roots.

Sowing

Grow leaf radish as a cut-and-come-again seedling crop, sown in broadcast patches or in close parallel drills. (See Part 2, Plant raising, Sowing methods, page 151.)

'Bisai' can be sown almost all year round. Sow outdoors during the main growing season, and under cover in autumn and spring.

In cool temperate regions the most useful sowings are:
- In early spring, under cover initially, followed by an outdoor sowing.
- In late summer outdoors, and early autumn under cover. If a few plants from these last sowings are left uncut, there may be a surprise spring bonus of a fully mature white radish.

Leaf radish 'Bisai'

Radish sprouts

Japanese name: Kaiware daikon ('open shell radish')

Small punnets of radish seedlings are as commonplace in Japanese supermarkets as mustard and cress in the West. These highly nutritious, healthy-looking seedlings have crisp white, green or pink stems 3–4 in (7.5–10 cm) long, and a pair of deep green seedling leaves which resemble an opened shell—hence the Japanese name. They are mainly used raw in salads or as a garnish, but are also incorporated into soups and sauces. They have a very pleasant taste, ranging from slightly piquant to pungent depending on the variety.

Commercially, the sprouts are often grown on a foam base, to keep them fresh and moist as long as possible. Domestically, they can be grown in water (special containers are sold for the purpose) or on a base of sand, vermiculite, soil or sowing compost. (See also Part 2, Seed sprouting.) Very fast-germinating varieties are used for radish sprouts, '40 Days' being the most popular. 'Bisai' too can be sprouted very successfully. (See above.)

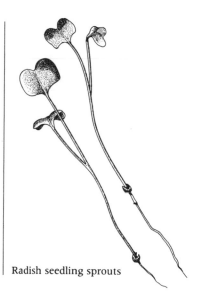
Radish seedling sprouts

Radish seed pods

In various parts of the world the young, immature seed pods of radishes are eaten. Long ago in Europe they were used fresh in salads or pickled, though the tradition has all but died out. In India they are still eaten raw, boiled and pickled. Provided they are picked while still green and crunchy, radish pods have a wonderful texture and deli-cious flavour, varying from mild to hot depending on the variety. They are excellent in a vegetable stir-fry. People with little liking for radishes often take to the seed pods.

Choice of variety

'Rat's tail radish' (*Raphanus caudatus*)

Traditional seed pod variety; virtually no taproot. Striking, reddish violet seed pods, up to 12 in (30 cm) long. Sow throughout growing season; thin to 12 in (30 cm) apart. Pods normally ready within 3 months.

'Münchner' ('München') Bier

Dual purpose German radish, grown for white root (the traditional beer drinkers' snack) and for huge crop of seed pods, up to 2 in (5 cm) long. Sow spring to summer, spacing 12 in (30 cm) apart.

Other oriental radishes

Many varieties could probably be grown for pods. The large-rooted oriental radishes produce huge crops of large seed pods if allowed to run to seed. As far as I know no trials have been done to ascertain which are the best-flavoured—so it is a question of trying out any varieties which have run to seed in your garden. Some will prove too hot for the average taste.

In my experience the over-wintering Chinese radishes, such as 'China Rose', produce very good pods when they run to seed early in spring. The summer mooli radish 'Minowase Summer Cross' produced excellent pods in September. These had been sown in May, and were unaffected by a slight frost.

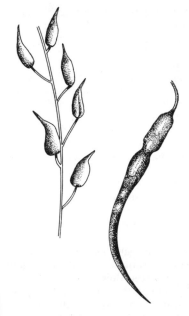

Radish seed pods

1. Green pak choi 'Shanghai' growing in unheated greenhouses for London's Chinatown

2. Creamy centred 'Eskimo', a 'fluffy top' type of loose-headed Chinese cabbage which makes a lovely salad plant

3. Pak choi grown for flowering shoots in Laguna Hills, California, showing the stage at which it is harvested

4. Making the beautifully constructed Chinese solar frames or 'winter beds' in October, on the Hua Xiang Commune, Beijing

5. Single-stem oriental bunching onions earthed up to blanch the stems, growing near Mobaru, Japan

6. Intensively used suburban allotment in Kaohsiung, Taiwan. The paths between the plots were growing medicinal herbs for the family

7. Early spring crop of brassica seedlings, including 'Minato Santo' Chinese cabbage, mizuna greens, komatsuna and pak choi, grown for BBC TV's *Gardener's World* at Barnsdale

8. Tender shoots of komatsuna resprouting after cut-and-come-again treatment as a semi-mature plant. Photographed in the author's unheated polytunnel in winter

9. Green and purple lablab beans on sale in Broom Street market, Nanjing

10. The picturesque bitter gourd, which turns orange-red when fully ripe. Here growing at Rokewood Nurseries, Wisbech

11. The vigorous hybrid komatsuna 'Savanna', growing on the Alf Christianson Seed Company trial grounds in Washington State

13. The Manchurian 'Beauty Heart' radish being deftly carved into a paeony by a chef in Beijing

12. Young edible bottle gourd with edible leaves, flowers and shoot tips. Here growing in the Danny Wu Indochinese Community Gardens in Seattle

15. Wax gourds being grown at Rokewood Nurseries for London's Chinatown. These will be harvested at 2–3lbs for use fresh. Giant specimens are for winter use

14. Ornamental kale 'Pink Beauty' offset by variegated mint in a bedding scheme at the Royal Botanic Gardens, Kew

16. Enterprising growers in the Napa Valley, California, have pioneered the use of seedling purple-leaved mustard to add colour and piquancy to salads

17. The curled mustards are both decorative in the garden and useful greens, especially in the winter months

19. A colourful form of the Japanese herb perilla or shiso (*Perilla frutescens* var *nankinensis*) perfectly at home in a flower bed

18. The yard long bean is cultivated widely in Korea, China and Japan and is harvested when 12–16in (30–40cm) long

20. Beautiful sample of flowering choy sum in a Guangzhou street market

21. A supervisor in a Shanghai market explaining the various stages in the use of pak choi to the author. The cabinet displays the day's 'Best Buys'

Tubers

Chinese yam

Family *Dioscoreaceae*
Latin names *Dioscorea batatas*; *D. opposita*; *D. japonica*
Other names in use Mountain yam; Japanese mountain yam;
  cinnamon vine
Mandarin Shu yu; shan yao
Cantonese Dai shue
Japanese Yamaimo ('mountain potato'); nagaimo ('long potato')

The yams are a family of climbing and trailing plants which produce a variety of strange-shaped tubers. Many of these are edible, and several attempts have been made to establish Chinese yam in the West as a substitute for potatoes. They have probably been defeated by the difficulties encountered in harvesting roots a yard long. It was introduced to France in 1848 by the French consul in Shanghai, and its cultivation is vividly described in Vilmorin's *The Vegetable Garden*. Never having grown it myself the following notes are based on the Vilmorin account and on the catalogue from the American Seeds Blüm who currently supply bublets for planting.

Characteristics

The Chinese yam is an attractive, hardy perennial plant. Its twining stems reach heights of 6–10 ft (180–300 cm) in cool temperate climates but can grow twice as high in warmer climates. In Japan I saw it trailing over fairly large trees on the edge of a wood. The green or violet stems are smooth. The leaves are very glossy, heart-shaped with a drawn out point, anything from 1–4 in (3–10 cm) in length, depending on the variety. The flowers are insignificant but highly scented (the scent said to be cinnamon-like), followed by small starchy fruits which are edible, and reputedly very good for your health. Tiny bulblets are sometimes produced on the stems in the axils of the leaves.

Plants normally produce two or three, ivory-coloured tubers. After a couple of seasons these can be well over 3 ft (1 m) long. They are very narrow and eventually swell at the far end to give a club-like appearance—the 'club' being 3–4 in (8–10 cm) thick. There are also forms which produce squat, heart-shaped tubers. The internal flesh is white or red.

Climate

Most of the yams are tropical and subtropical plants, requiring high rainfall and high temperatures, ideally 77–86°F (25–30°C), and a long growing season. This rules them out for cultivation in northern, temperate climates. The Chinese yam, however, is hardy and, moreover, good to eat.

Site/soil

These yams require deep, light, fertile, well prepared soil, moist

but well drained. Good drainage is most important, as all yam tubers are prone to rotting if they get waterlogged. They can either trail over the ground, or be trained up supports, over arches and arbours, where they make a decorative feature. Vilmorin recommends staking or some kind of support, to make it easier to cultivate around the plants.

Cultivation

They can be propagated by:
● Cuttings. These are the shoots which develop on top of the tubers in spring. They are cut off above the tuber and rooted.
● Planting small whole young tubers. Vilmorin recommends finger-thick tubers 8–10 in (20–25 cm) long.
● Planting the top third or so of mature tubers.
● Planting bulblets. These take up to 3 years to yield.

The heaviest yields are obtained by planting whole tubers. Plant after frost, spacing the plants about a foot (30 cm) apart. The longer the growing season the better, so tubers or bulblets can be started earlier in pots indoors, planting out after they have started into growth.

Further care

Chinese yams are apparently very pest- and disease-free, but need watering in dry weather. Keep them mulched to conserve moisture.

Harvesting

Smallish tubers weighing a couple of pounds should be ready by the autumn, about 6 months after planting. These first-season tubers are said to be the best flavoured. However the plants can be left in the ground to overwinter and enlarge over the next two or three seasons. They should reach about 2 ft (60 cm) by the end of the second season, but they become woodier with age. Small tubers can be lifted and used for planting.

The roots are brittle and harvesting, especially if roots have grown several feet in length, is tricky. They really have to be excavated, the only practical method being to dig a large hole around the plant. They can be stored for winter, in the same way as sweet potatoes.

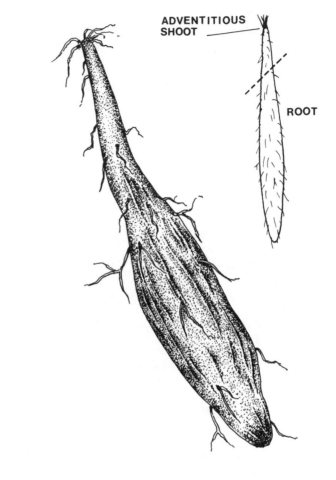

Chinese yam showing (*right*) how a shoot is propagaged from a tuber

Taro

Family *Araceae*
Latin name *Colocasia esculenta*
Other names in use Cocoyam; dasheen; edo; elephant's ear plant
Mandarin yu; yu tou (central tuber); yu nai (baby tubers)
Cantonese woo; wu chai; wu tau
Japanese sato-imo; kiomo (small taro tubers)

Characteristics

Taro is an elegant, perennial plant, growing at least 3 ft (1 m) tall, with beautiful light green, elongated, heart-shaped leaves—not unlike the shape of an elephant's ears. They are borne on long stalks.

About half a dozen types are known in Asia, the majority forming tubers. The principal types grown in China either form one large tuber, or have a central tuber surrounded by a mass of small tubers—'sons of taro' as the Chinese call them. Tubers vary in shape, but are roughly spherical, anything from tennis ball size to about 9 in (23 cm) diameter, and often covered in brownish hairs.

Climate

Taro is essentially a tropical or subtropical crop, requiring high temperatures, 77–95°F (25–35°C), and a season of at least 200 days (over 7 months). Originating in jungly tropical rain forests, it needs a lot of moisture during growth.

Cultivation of the tubers is im-

Use

The tubers are starchy, with a rather sweet flavour and doughy texture. They can be cooked like potatoes, and are sometimes used as a source of flour. They are often an element in mixed meat dishes. They must not be eaten raw.

In the kitchen

Leaves and young stems are edible, and considered more nutritious and better flavoured than the tuber. The leaves are best when young, and should be boiled twice discarding the water, to remove an acrid flavour. They are good puréed like spinach. The stems are cut into pieces, peeled, and boiled to remove the 'twang'.

Taro: leaf, mother tuber and 'sons of taro'

practical other than in frost-free areas with long warm summers. However, it is being grown in greenhouses in north Europe for its leaves (see below).

Soil, site, cultivation

In Asia taro is either grown 'wet' in paddy fields, or 'dry', using water and land types respectively. In dry culture small corms are planted in furrows or trenches about 15 in (38 cm) apart, about 6 in (15 cm) deep, covered by 2–3 in (5–8 cm) of soil. They are often grown alongside irrigation ditches or at the edge of fields and plots. They are harvested at the end of the growing season, when the leaves have turned yellow and almost died away. They can also be propagated by stem cuttings. The tubers can be left in the soil after maturing unless there is a risk of frost, in which case they must be lifted and stored in cool conditions.

Cultivation for leaf For leaf cultivation the Dutch company *Xotus* has selected varieties with insignificant tubers but very soft leaves. These are being grown all year round in greenhouses heated to a minimum temperature of 59°F (15°C) during the winter months; the soil is also heated. They seem to be tolerant of low winter light levels, possibly because of their shaded jungle origins.

Young leaves can be picked as soon as the first leaf is fully opened, but the plant should never be stripped entirely: one leaf should be left on the plant so that production will continue. The plants are left in the beds for two years.

Taro roots are sometimes forced in warmth in the dark, to produce blanched leaves, which are considered to be something of a delicacy.

Water vegetables

* For Chinese and Japanese names see Appendix page 210.

No book on oriental vegetables would be complete without some reference to the many water vegetables cultivated in the Far East. It is easy to understand their popularity. Travelling by train from Beijing to Nanjing across the eastern Chinese plains the landscape is dominated by water: flooded paddy fields, canals serving as highways, irrigation channels carving the land into a thousand segments, and countless ponds stocked with fish. The cultivation of aquatic vegetables has been a natural development—sometimes rotated with rice in the paddy fields, sometimes grown alongside the rice.

The water vegetables covered here briefly are mainly tropical or semi-tropical, requiring long hot summers to develop to a usable state. Nor do they lend themselves to Western gardening methods. Few of us have the swampy sites and ponds which are their natural habitat. Water-gardening enthusiasts sometimes succeed in creating the necessary conditions, harvesting a few water chestnuts or a lotus root for their pains. They generally use submerged containers, so the plants can be removed for harvesting or storage in winter. This also makes it easier to plant at the correct depth.

Arrowhead (Chinese potato, Swamp potato) *Sagittaria sagittifolia*; *S. sinensis*

Arrowhead is a hardy, perennial, water plant. It is naturalized in Europe, North America and Asia, growing in swampy situations, ponds, canals and slow-moving streams. It has striking, arrow-shaped leaves sometimes over 2 ft (60 cm) tall and up to about 6 in (15 cm) wide. The flowers are white, or white with black centres, depending on the species. It is grown for the tubers which form at the end of long creeping rhizomes. These tend to be egg-shaped, about 1½ in (4 cm) long and an inch (2.5 cm) wide, beige coloured, with a few small, brown, somewhat scaly leaves across them.

They have a slightly sweet, starchy flavour. Before use they are peeled and the sprout is removed. They can be cooked like potatoes, or Chinese-style, in mixed meat and vegetable dishes.

Arrowhead can be cultivated by planting the corms in spring, in fertile swampy soil or in mud, covered by 3–6 in (8–15 cm) water. In Vancouver the Chinese grow them in bathtubs. They grow best in warm weather, needing at least 6 months to develop.

Close related species which can be cultivated include *Sagittaria japonica*, which has larger leaves and is grown in garden ponds in Europe, and *S. latifolia* (wapatoo), a wild North American species.

Lotus *Nelumbo nucifera*

This well-known, perennial aquatic plant, with its beautiful white and pink water-lily flowers, is a native of Asia, growing mainly in shallow water ponds. Its large, rounded, waxy leaves, curling at the edges, are held clear of the water.

Leaves, flowers, flower buds, and seeds are all edible, as are the strange young fruits, shaped like a tea cosy, perforated like a watering can rose, and prized by flower arrangers for their curious elegance. Lotus is mainly grown for its equally bizarre-shaped stems or rhizomes. These buff-coloured, wooden-looking rhizomes are about 3 in (7.5 cm) thick and 2–3 ft (60–90 cm) long, divided into sausage-like segments, each up to 5 in (13 cm) long. Air passages run the length of the rhizomes, giving them a beautiful, paper-chain cross section.

The young rhizomes have a crisp texture and a mild, characteristic flavour. They are cooked in many ways: stir-fried, mixed with other vegetables such as red peppers, stuffed with pork, stuffed with rice and steamed, in soup, battered and fried, as well as being candied for special occasions. They are often cut in slices to make the most of their attractive appearance. They are also used as a source of starch and flour.

The seeds are harvested after the seed head turns brown. They can be eaten raw after removing the tough brown outer skin and the bitter green plumule within. They are roasted, candied, used to make a good chicken soup, and cooked slowly in mixed dishes. Leaves are eaten young, raw or cooked; and are also used to wrap and steam meat, rice and fish dishes.

Lotus is a tropical plant, requiring temperatures of 68–86°F (20–30°C) to grow well. Rhizomes with several segments are usually planted in mud at a 30-degree angle, the 'top end' in the mud, the

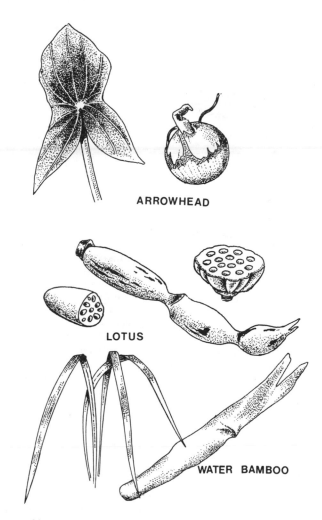

ARROWHEAD

LOTUS

WATER BAMBOO

Water vegetables: arrowhead, lotus and water bamboo

other end protruding out of the water. The water needs to be 4–8 in (10–20 cm) deep. Although the rhizomes can be harvested at any time, the best time is after the flowers have died down, but before the plants start to sprout again. In cold areas they must be harvested before the water freezes. Provided the rhizomes will not be frozen solid, they can be overwintered under water or submerged in the mud at the bottom of ponds. Otherwise the dormant tubers must be lifted and stored in winter in moist sand or peat, in cool conditions.

The roots and seeds of both white and pink flowered lotus are edible. The Chinese tend to cultivate pink flowered varieties for seed, and white flowered for the rhizome.

Water bamboo (wild rice)
Zizania latifolia

Water bamboo is a perennial, sedge-like aquatic plant which grows wild in Asia in pools and marshy areas. It is neither bamboo nor rice, though it has a superficial resemblance to both when growing. It grows with its shoots partly submerged below the water, and spreads by means of rhizomes.

The edible part is the swollen base of the stem. This swelling develops when the plant is attacked by a fungus, *Ustilago esculenta*. The fungus excretes the hormone indole acetic acid into the host plant, making the stem cells swell. The result is a highly prized delicacy, looking rather like a stubby bamboo shoot, about 7 in (17 cm) long

and 1¼ in (3 cm) wide. It is harvested with a couple of leaves around it.

The flavour is pleasant but mild; it reminds me of celeriac. Water bamboo is one of those Chinese ingredients used in a variety of dishes to absorb other flavours.

To grow well water bamboo needs high temperatures, 68–86°F (20–30°C), intensive light, and slightly acidic clay loam soil. Plants are propagated by division, planting pieces of stem or rhizomes. Cultivated forms are often used as, ironically, the wild species have developed resistance to the fungus. This is a unique case, in which man wants to cultivate disease *susceptible*, rather than disease *resistant*, plants. It is grown mainly in spring and autumn, being left in ponds during the winter months. Wild rice must be harvested at the right stage: the flesh deteriorates when the fungus starts to produce spores.

A closely related species, *Zizania aquatica* (*Z. palustris*), found in North America, was harvested for its grain by the American Indians.

Water chestnut *Eleocharis dulcis* (*E. tuberosa*)

Confusingly, two Asiatic plants are known in the West as 'water chestnut': this one is considered the authentic *Chinese* water chestnut.

It is a perennial reed-like plant, with long thin hollow leaves over 2 ft (60 cm) high, growing wild in shallow water. The edible part is the corm which develops under water. The mother corm produces long, horizontal rhizomes from the top of the corm, the fresh crop of corms forming at the end of these rhizomes. The corms look like horses' hooves (the literal translation of one of the Chinese names), or tufted sweet chestnuts. They are about 1½ in (4 cm) in diameter. The immature corms are pale; the Chinese prefer the mature, dark corms.

There are two types of this water chestnut: both sweet, nutty-flavoured and crisp-textured. They have to be peeled, but can be eaten raw (unlike the other water chestnuts) or cooked. Only light cooking is necessary: a very pleasant dish is a mixture of prawns and water chestnuts. These water chestnuts are the source of the authentic water chestnut flour.

It is a crop which requires rich, fertile soil and high temperatures, ideally 86–95°F (30–35°C) during the leafy stage, though about 10 degrees lower when the corms are forming. They need a 6-month growing season. In China they are grown in rotation with rice in the paddy fields. Tubers are planted in stagnant water in spring; or the young plants are raised in a nursery in spring, and planted out in the paddy fields when about 8 in (20 cm) high, after any risk of frost. They are normally spaced 2–3 ft (60–90 cm) apart. The fields are then flooded, and at the end of the season they are drained and the corms dug out of the ground. The corms must be kept in damp, frost-free conditions for replanting the following spring.

I have read accounts of water chestnuts being grown successfully in the warmer parts of the United States, using small plastic paddling pools with a cork fitted in the bottom so they can be drained. The growing season can be extended by starting the corms indoors.

Water caltrop (Water chestnut) *Trapa bicornis* (*T. bispinosa*); also *T. natans*

Also known as water chestnut, this vegetable floats on the water, its diamond-shaped leaves, about 1 in (2.5 cm) in diameter, being kept afloat by little inflated swellings in the leaf stalks which act as bladders. It produces a mass of filamentous green roots from the stems. The edible 'chestnuts' are the fruits or seeds—shiny black, two-horned nuts in the case of *T. bicornis*, but four-horned in the case of the closely related European *T. natans* or Jesuit's nut. They develop under the foliage in the centre of the plant after it has flowered.

Water caltrop is starchy, not unlike English chestnuts. It is used in much the same way as the 'horse's

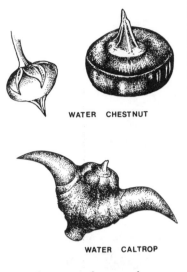

WATER CHESTNUT

WATER CALTROP

Water chestnut and water caltrop

hooves' nuts. They also need to be shelled, and similarly have a crunchy texture and somewhat bland flavour. However, because of toxins in them, they must not be eaten raw but should be boiled for an hour or steamed before being eaten. This may explain why the other type has become more popular.

They are not hardy and require high temperatures to grow well. The seeds, which have to be kept moist from one season to the next, are sown in still water, and harvested in late summer.

Water convolvulus

See Ipomea (water spinach), page 94.

Watercress *Rorippa nasturtium-aquaticum* (*Nasturtium officinale*)

A European crop in origin, watercress has spread to Asia and been adopted wholeheartedly by the Chinese. There are said to be some very hardy local cultivars in the Beijing area.

In Chinese cuisine watercress is normally cooked, rather than being used raw. I had an excellent watercress soup, flavoured with ginger and fish, in a Guangzhou restaurant run by the market 'company'. That afternoon we visited some watercress beds in the city suburbs, where cress was growing

in 'high quality' waste water piped from the city. When the beds are cut a small corner is left unharvested, these roots being pulled up, bunched, then replanted for the next crop. Most crops were cut four or five times.

Watercress is a hardy, perennial plant, growing naturally in springs or fresh running streams in limestone areas. It is a cool-season crop, in temperate climates growing best in spring and autumn. In warm climates it is cultivated mostly during the winter months. Ideally it needs clean-flowing, alkaline water, at a temperature of about 50°F (10°C), and good light. If you have these conditions in your garden, plant rooted watercress cuttings about 6 in (15 cm) apart along the banks of the stream in spring. The simplest way to obtain rooted cuttings is to buy watercress in a market and dangle it in a jar of water. Roots will develop very rapidly. Most crops can be cut two or three times, depending on the season. Winter crops need to be protected from strong winds and frost.

Commercial watercress is often raised from seed (see also page 216).

Watercress can be grown in pots kept standing in water. Use rich soil to which some ground limestone is added, change the water fairly frequently to prevent it becoming stagnant, and top-dress the pot from time to time with well-rotted garden compost.

Water shield (*Brasenia schreberi*)

A small-leaved floating plant in the water lily family, water shield is found in Asia, North America and Africa. The submerged parts of the plant are covered in jelly.

The 'delicious shoots', i.e. young curly leaf tips coated with jelly, were prized in ancient China for their nutritious and medicinal qualities. They are excellent with fish and in soups. The Japanese serve them with a dressing, and pickle them. They are usually gathered in the wild, the tender shoots being harvested before they emerge above the water. They are also cultivated in ponds, propagated by seed or offsets.

Herbs and wild plants*

* For Chinese and Japanese names see Appendix page 210.

Herbs

Many of the herbs we consider 'Western' are grown in Asia and have been absorbed into oriental cuisines—basil, coriander (sometimes known as Chinese parsley), dill, fennel, mint and parsley for example. They were introduced from the West centuries ago. For their cultivation consult a standard book on herbs. (See appendix.) Below are notes on a few herbs closely associated with Chinese cookery.

Ginger (*Zingiber officinale*)

This, the true ginger, is a perennial plant with narrow, strap-like, lemon-scented leaves, growing up to about 3 ft (90 cm) high. It is cultivated for its underground stems, or rhizomes, which form many knobbly branches. It very rarely flowers, so is always propagated vegetatively.

Use Ginger is used fresh, preserved and dried—the fresh being the best flavoured. Very young 'green' ginger is eaten raw, crystallized, and pickled. Mature ginger is stronger flavoured, and can be kept for long periods. It is used in many recipes, frequently coupled with garlic.

The young shoots of ginger, cut from about 3 in (7.5 cm) high, are a delicacy. They are sometimes marinated in vinegar, sugar and sesame oil. A few can be cut from a plant without harming it.

Cultivation Ginger is a tropical and sub-tropical plant, preferring temperatures of about 75°F (24°C) and high humidity. In temperate climates it can only be grown outdoors in frost-free areas with very hot summers. It needs fertile soil with plenty of moisture.

Young rhizomes with buds on them are planted in spring. One method is to dig a trench 10 in (25 cm) wide and 8 in (20 cm) deep, working manure into the bottom. Plant young rhizomes 5 in (13 cm) apart in the trench, buds uppermost, covering them with about 4 in (10 cm) of well rotted compost mixed with soil. Water them in before covering the trench with straw or hay, to conserve moisture and encourage shoot development. Remove this mulch about a month later.

Young ginger is harvested after 3–4 months' growth when the plants are still green, mature ginger after 7–10 months, after the leaves have died back completely. By then the skin on the rhizome will have set and they will store well.

Ginger makes an attractive house plant, and can be grown in pots or large containers indoors. It needs high temperatures, especially in the early stages. Use fresh pieces about 2 in (5 cm) long with bright-looking buds. Plant them 2–3 in (5–7.5 cm) deep in fairly rich compost in 5-in (13-cm) pots. Pot on into larger pots as they grow; a full-grown plant would need a pot at least 12 in (30 cm) deep and 15 in (35 cm) wide. Plants can be dried off in winter, and started into growth again in spring.

MYOGA/MIOGA GINGER (*Zingiber mioga*) This Japanese ginger is cultivated for its young inflorescence and leaves: the rhizome is inedible. It grows wild in Japan in damp situations in the mountains, and is cultivated in gardens. It appears to tolerate colder temperatures than most of the ginger family.

The flowers—seen first as conical flower clusters at ground level—appear in late summer. For culinary purposes they are harvested young before they open, and are used to flavour soups and various dishes. The mature flowers are pale yellow and very fragrant. The young leaves are blanched (presumably either by covering with a pot, or with straw to exclude light), and are widely used in flavouring.

Lemon grass (Citronella grass) (*Cymbopogon citratus*)

Although generally associated with Thailand and south-east Asia, this lovely plant has been absorbed into Chinese cooking in Malaysia. A perennial tropical grass, it makes

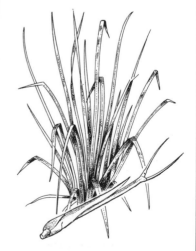

Lemon grass: leafy plant and leaf stalk

rather handsome clumps with its narrow leaves growing 2–3 ft (60–90 cm) tall. The stalks and blades of the leaves have a wonderful lemon flavour, sometimes described as 'sweet-sour'.

The white leaf stalk, sometimes slightly swollen at the base, is the part most used in cooking. It is usually removed just before serving. It is used to flavour fish, soups, salads and a wide range of dishes. The ends of the stems can be bashed and used as a brush to baste fish, adding their own lemon flavour in the process. The leaves are sometimes tied in bunches like a *bouquet garni*. They are also used to make a tea. In Thailand the leaves which form the inner heart are chopped and used in curries.

Cultivation Lemon grass needs fertile soil and plenty of moisture during growth. The true lemon grass very rarely flowers, so in areas where it is warm enough to grow, it is propagated by dividing established clumps, replanting young portions from the outer edges. Otherwise plant pieces of the root. Occasionally, fresh shoots bought in ethnic markets will root if planted. In cool climates it can be grown in greenhouses, provided temperatures don't fall much below 46°F (8°C) for any length of time during the winter.

Sesame (*Sesame indicum*)
An annual tropical herb, sesame is a rather attractive plant, growing 2–3 ft (60–90 cm) high, sometimes more; there are also some dwarfer varieties. It can be branched or single-stemmed. The flowers are white or pink, and the seed, for which it is cultivated, anything from a creamy colour, to black to red.

Use Sesame seeds are both crushed to obtain sesame oil (a very pure, pleasantly flavoured oil which keeps well at high temperatures), and used whole, crushed or ground, in cooking. The black seeds are generally more pungent. The seeds are often lightly roasted before use. Tahini paste is made from sesame seeds. The Koreans eat the leaves. Seedling leaves and thinnings can be chopped and used in salads.

Cultivation Coming from India and Morocco, sesame needs, and flourishes in, long hot summers. I have never grown it very successfully outdoors in England, though others have done so. In warm climates sow outdoors after all risk of frost, in drills about ½ in (1 cm) deep. Thin to 6–8 in (15–20 cm) apart. In cool climates sesame is best grown under cover. Sow in a heated propagator, potting up into small pots before planting. The seed pods form inside the faded flowers, bursting open when fully ripe: collect them before this stage.

'Sichuan' and 'sansho' pepper (*Zanthoxylum sp.*)
The Chinese Sichuan pepper ('hua jiao' in Mandarin), and the Japanese 'sansho' pepper come not from pepper plants, but from the berries of various species of the prickly ash shrub, *Zanthoxylum*. Known also as anise pepper and fagara, these rusty red little peppercorns are one of the ingredients in the famous Chinese 'five spice' mixture. They are widely used in Chinese cooking, often blended with hot pepper. Before use they may be toasted in a dry pan, to bring out the flavour, then ground.

As far as I can ascertain, the Chinese form is obtained from the following species: *Zanthoxylum alatum*, *Z. simulans*, *Z. planispinum*, *Z. armatum*—though some of these names may be synonyms. The Japanese pepper is obtained from *Z. piperitum*. In Japan the leaves are also used for flavouring, both fresh and dried then ground. Pestles made from prickly ash wood were used to grind the seed pods, which were kneaded into flour to flavour *kiri-sasho* cake.

Hot and prickly ash pepper are often used together in cooking.

The prickly ashes are very hardy, smallish shrubs, usually rather spiny though some spineless forms exist. They have beautiful autumn colouring, and can sometimes be obtained from Western nurserymen. The flowers, and hence the berries, are formed on old wood.

Wild plants

For centuries man has supplemented his diet by gathering local plants from the wild—many of them plants we consider weeds today. What is fascinating is that the same edible 'weeds' have traditionally been gathered in Europe, Asia, and the American continent. Chickweed (*Stellaria media*), dandelion (*Taraxacum officinalis*), fat hen (*Chenopodium album*), lady's smock (*Cardamine flexuosa*), shepherd's purse (*Capsella bursa-pastoris*), mallows (*Malva sp.*), purslanes (*Portulaca sp.*), various forms of polygonums, amaranthus and artemisias are some of the most common. Over the course of time some, such as dandelion, have been brought into cultivation. Shepherd's purse and mallow are two weeds commonly found cultivated in vegetable plots in China.

The Japanese islands are endowed with few native vegetables, so the Japanese have had an incentive to comb less promising habitats, from mountains to the sea, for edible plants. Few people have made such use of ferns, seaweeds, flowers and wild plants to supplement their diet. Many of these are now cultivated and commonly found in markets.

Wild plants should always be gathered very young, when they are at their most tender and tasty. Many have proved to be excellent sources of vitamins and minerals.

The following notes are on some of the wild plants I found being grown in China and Japan.

Aralia cordata

When I first saw the 2 ft (60 cm) long white stalks of this plant in a wholesale vegetable market in Tokyo I was completely mystified. They turned out to be blanched *udo*, sometimes called Japanese asparagus because of its distinct asparagus flavour. It is a large-leaved perennial plant, which grows wild in the mountains all over Japan, as well as in China.

The mild-flavoured, blanched young stalks are usually eaten raw, sliced into soups, salads, and various other dishes. Several cultivated varieties are grown in Japan, propagated by dividing the roots. The young stems are blanched by growing them in the dark, sometimes covered with rice husks, sometimes by earthing up the plants. They can grow up to 5 ft (150 cm) long, but only the young stalks are edible. Older stalks become large and hollow. (A large person without substance is called an *udo*!)

The young leaves of a related shrub, the Chinese aralia, *Aralia chinensis*, are also eaten as a vegetable.

Black nightshade (*Solanum nigrum*)

Western eyebrows tend to be raised at the idea of eating any member of the nightshade family, because of the very poisonous nature of the closely related deadly nightshade, *Atropa belladonna*. However, the young shoots, young leaves and young berries of black nightshade, which is found as a weed all over the world, are eaten in China, south-east Asia and elsewhere. Leaves and young shoots are made into soup, eaten with oysters, and sometimes boiled first then stir-fried. I was told it is cultivated in Taiwan.

The plant can grow up to 2 ft (60 cm) high but is usually smaller, has pointed leaves, small white flowers, and green berries which turn black when mature. Don't eat it unless you are 100 per cent sure of its identity—and avoid the very ripe black berries, which may be toxic under some circumstances.

Vilmorin reports that it was cultivated in France, sowing seed *in situ* in April in drills 12 in (30 cm) apart. Plants were thinned out: at a guess 6 in (15 cm) apart would be adequate. They are very tolerant of dry conditions.

Gynura bicolor (Velvet plant)

This intriguing plant is a perennial in the chrysanthemum family. It is usually 1–2 ft (30–50 cm) tall, has orange, daisy-like flowers and striking leaves, dark green above but purple beneath. The young leaf stalks are a deep purple colour. I saw it growing in allotments in Taiwan and it is most decorative in flower. It is sometimes grown in Japanese gardens as an ornamental.

The leaves, which are quite succulent, and leafy young shoots, are eaten in both China and Japan, in soups or as a vegetable. They are said to have a strange, 'laurel-like' flavour, which a Taiwanese friend describes as 'delicious'. It is also used medicinally, notably for curing goldfish diseases.

Being slightly tender, in cool climates it should be grown in greenhouses. Propagate it from cuttings taken in spring.

Mallows (*Malva verticillata* and *M. crispa*)

The tall-growing, slightly succulent leaved mallow is among wild plants which have been eaten since time immemorial all over the world. It is believed to have been one of the most important vegetables in ancient China, and cultivated clumps are common in the fields today. The main native oriental species are the flat-leaved *M. verticillata*, and *M. crispa*, which has crisply puckered leaves. This variety was cultivated in Europe in the past. Both are annuals, with smallish, pinky-white flowers. The common perennial European mallow, *M. sylvestris*, with its lovely large, rose-purple flowers, also grows in Asia and is used as a vegetable.

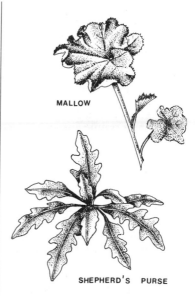

Mallow and shepherd's purse.

The young shoots, young stems and leaves of mallows are all used, either in soups, or boiled, steamed or deep-fried as a vegetable. They have a mucilaginous texture and, rich, pleasant taste. The flower buds and young leaves can be used raw in salads. Leaves and flowers make an attractive garnish.

Mallows are pretty hardy (one Chinese name means winter amaranth), remaining green after several degrees of frost. They are easily raised from seed. Sow *in situ* or in a seedbed, planting out seedlings when 2–4 in (5–10 cm) high, about 12 in (30 cm) apart. In practice I find established clumps perpetuate themselves by self-seeding. Growing up to about 3 ft (90 cm) high, with a mass of light green leaves, it is a pleasing plant in a flower or vegetable garden for much of the year.

Mugwort (*Artemesia spp.*)

Since ancient times several species of these widespread, perennial weeds have been used for culinary purposes in Asia. These include *Artemisia vulgaris*, the common mugwort of Europe and North America, and closely related Chinese and Japanese species (*A. princeps*), known as 'yomogi' in Japanese. Mugwort grows 2–3 ft (60–90 cm) tall, has finely cut foliage, the leaves dark green above but woolly white beneath. There is considerable variation within the artemisias, but they are all characterized by a strong, distinct flavour. They are closely related to absinthe, *Artemisia absinthium* or common wormwood.

The plants should always be used sparingly, discarding any tough portions of stem. The Japanese boil young leaves lightly and use them to flavour rice dumplings. In Taiwan they are stir-fried, as well as used in soups and stuffings.

Take care if cultivating artemisia in a garden. Common mugwort seeds itself very readily, while *Artemisia princeps* spreads rapidly by means of stolons and may become invasive. The roots can be divided if necessary to establish plants.

Polygonums (*Polygonum spp.*)

The polygonums (the knotgrass, smartweed and buckwheat family) are common annual and perennial weeds the world over. Several species have a long tradition of being collected from the wild, or cultivated for culinary use in Asia. One of the most popular in Japan is 'akatade', water pepper or smartweed (probably *Polygonum hydropiper* var *fastigiatum*), which is mainly grown for its tiny reddish, peppery-flavoured seedlings. (See Seed sprouting, page 137.) It is also found wild in Europe. It grows 10–30 in) (25–75 cm) high in damp situations, and has rather pointed leaves, 2–4 in (5–10 cm) long, which have an acrid, burning taste. It is used at every stage from seedling to flower spikes, primarily for flavouring. It is easily raised from seed, sown *in situ*, making sure seed keeps moist until it has germinated.

There is considerable confusion over the different species of *Polygonum* used in Asia. Occasionally they are found on sale in ethnic markets. They can often be grown from cuttings taken from these specimens.

Salsola (*Salsola spp.*)

Several species of *Salsola* are collected in the wild and cultivated in

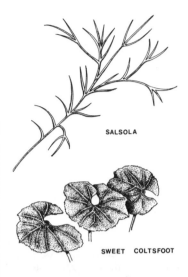

SALSOLA

SWEET COLTSFOOT

Salsola and sweet coltsfoot

Asia, including *Salsola soda*, *S. kali*, *S. asparagoides*, and *S. komarovi*. They are salt marsh plants, adapted to growing in soil or water with high levels of salt, and closely related to the European glasswort or marsh samphire (*Salicornia sp.*). The Japanese name, 'okahijiki', means 'land seaweed'. In the past several species of *Salsola* were used as a source of calcium carbonate in the manufacture of glass and soap. In Europe they have also been used as a food, raw and cooked.

Neat little packets of fresh *Salsola* are sold in Japanese markets. The pretty green, matchstick leaves are generally not more than 2½ in (6 cm) long. They have a crunchy tender texture: the flavour was described to me as 'green'! Salsola is usually made into soup or boiled for no more than a couple of minutes, then eaten with mustard or vinegar.

According to information on Japanese seed packets it can be grown on fairly poor soil; it grows more vigorously on alkaline soil. The first sowings are made under cover in spring as temperatures start to rise (this ensures a nice dark green colour). Seed is sown in rows or broadcast, then thinned to about 2¼ in (6 cm) apart. It is ready for harvesting within a month of germination. It can be cut from a very young stage, not much more than

an inch (2.5 cm) high. Later sowings are made in spring and early summer outdoors.

I have to add that I have attempted to grow *Salsola komarovi* several times, but have never succeeded in getting the seed to germinate. Whether this is because the seed loses its viability rapidly or for some other reason, I have yet to discover. However, a Japanese visitor recently told me that the seed loses its viability rapidly (so avoid old seed), and that in Japan seed is kept at a temperature of 41°F (5°C) before sowing in winter, and at 41–59°F (5–15°C) before sowing in summer.

Shepherd's purse (*Capsella bursa-pastoris*)

Shepherd's purse is a universal weed, long valued both as a vegetable and as a medicinal plant. Today it is cultivated on a small scale in much of China, and is becoming increasingly popular. It featured as one of the day's 'best buys' in a Shanghai municipal market we visited.

The ground-hugging rosettes of young leaves can be eaten raw in salads. Leaves from the taller, maturing stems, which grow well over a foot high, can also be picked for use raw or cooked. The Chinese use it boiled, stir-fried, and in soups and dumplings. Roots also are sometimes used. Shepherd's purse is rich in vitamins and minerals, its distinctive, likeable taste being due to mustard oils which contain sulphur.

It is easy to grow. When cultivated the leaves grow quite large, i.e. 2–4 in (5–10 cm) long and nearly an inch (2.5 cm) wide. The Chinese sow from spring to autumn, usually broadcast on a fine seed bed, occasionally sown in rows. It is harvested about a month later. I have found it grows best in the cooler months of spring and autumn. It is invaluable as an early spring salad crop, sown under cover in late autumn or very early spring, followed by a spring outdoor sowing. I either sow in wide drills and treat it as a cut-and-come-again seedling crop (see

Part 2, Plant raising, page 155) or space plants 4–6 in (10–15 cm) apart for larger plants. They run to seed fairly rapidly.

Sweet coltsfoot (Japanese butterbur) (*Petasites japonicus*)

The 3–4 ft (90–120 cm) long, slightly greenish stems of the Japanese butterbur (*fuki*), are an astonishing sight in a Japanese supermarket, often displayed alongside the long thin roots of burdock.

Closely related to common coltsfoot, butterbur is a perennial woodland plant, growing to huge dimensions in damp, shaded situations. The stems of the largest plants can reach a height of over 6 ft (2 m), with leaves over 3 ft (1 m) wide. The densely packed heads of whitish flowers appear in early spring before the leaves. The flower stems are up to 12 in (30 cm) long. Sweet coltsfoot grows wild in Japan, but is also found naturalized in the United Kingdom, as a garden escape.

Several parts of the plant are used. At an early stage the young flower stems are eaten, battered and fried. The flower buds ('fuki-no-to') have a bitter but 'agreeable' taste, and are used to spice soups and fish dishes. They are usually prepared by being boiled briefly, then dipped in cold water. The leaf stalks are used as seasoning or as a vegetable, boiled, dipped in cold water and peeled. For use as a vegetable they are subsequently baked or fried. They have a pleasant, fragrant taste.

Sweet coltsfoot is sometimes cultivated in gardens, making a good ground cover plant in damp shady places with humus-rich soil. It can be grown under fruit trees, spreading easily by means of underground runners. Propagate it by dividing plants after the leaf stalks have been harvested in late spring or early summer, or by planting pieces of the underground runners. Plant them shallowly. Cuttings taken from sweet coltsfoot bought in markets can sometimes be rooted. It can also be raised from seed, but this takes much longer.

GIANT SWEET COLTSFOOT (*Petasites japonicus* var *giganteus*) This really is a giant, with 6 ft (180 cm) leaf stalks and leaves 5 ft (150 cm) in diameter. It is less well flavoured than the smaller form, but even so is cultivated for use. The leaf stalks are sometimes thinned in spring to get better quality stalks. The best yield is obtained the third or fourth year after planting. Clumps are usually replanted every 7–8 years. Apparently the leaf stalks can be made into walking sticks.

Wasabi (Japanese horseradish) (*Wasabia japonica*)

A perennial plant growing wild in the Japanese mountains, in wet ground beside streams, Japanese wasabi is valued for its rhizomes, which have much the same flavour as western horseradish. The plants grow 12–16 in (30–40 cm) high, and are characterized by glossy, more or less heart-shaped, coarsely toothed leaves. The rhizomes are finger-thick and generally grow up to 7 in (18 cm) long.

The whole plant has a very pungent flavour. The rhizomes are normally used fresh, as the flavour lasts at most 4 hours after grating. It should be grated on a very fine grater—the grated root, incidentally, being bright green. It is a very popular accompaniment to raw fish, is also grated into soup just before serving, or mixed with soy sauce to make a dip for grilled fish or meat dishes. It is also dried and made into a paste. The leaves, leaf stalks and rhizomes are sometimes pickled to preserve them.

Wasabi sometimes succeeds in the relatively dry conditions of gardens. The Japanese have evolved fairly complex systems for growing it commercially—for example planting the rhizomes under stones, in a situation where they will constantly be kept cool by running water. The flavour is said to be best the second year after planting, deteriorating thereafter.

Water dropwort (*Oenanthe stolonifera*; *O. javanica*)

Also known as water celery and water parsley, this is another wild plant which causes alarm bells to ring with Westerners: it is closely related to other, highly poisonous species of *Oenanthe* or 'water dropwort', such as the water hemlock, *O. crocata*. The Asiatic species have a long history of being gathered wild and cultivated throughout Asia, and are found in markets today. Never gather it from the wild unless you have positive confirmation that it *is* an edible species. The red-leaved forms are most easily confused with poisonous plants.

The oriental water dropwort is a perennial plant, growing in water or in very wet conditions, spreading by means of hollow creeping stems. It grows up to 2 ft (60 cm) high, and has umbels of small white flowers, typical of the carrot and celery family. The leaves are shaped like celery leaves, and are not unlike watercress, though with longer, hollow stems.

Although it can be picked all year round, it is most valued in warm climates as a winter vegetable. Young shoots which sprout from the creeping stems are picked from autumn to spring. The flavour—depending on your point of view—is reminiscent of parsley or carrots. It is used raw in salads or cooked, in which case it is boiled for no more than a minute, cut into lengths and used for flavouring soup, chicken or fish dishes. In Japan finely chopped leaves are used in 'one pot' dishes such as *sukiyaki*.

It thrives in warm wet areas. Most forms are not frost hardy, but in some the roots survive frost. In China it used to be grown in paddy fields, in Japan in shallow plantations, harvested from flat-bottomed boats. It is sometimes grown in garden ponds or at the edge of streams, though there is a risk of it becoming invasive. It can be raised from seed but, as seed germination is erratic, it is normally propagated by dividing healthy plants in spring, or by cuttings from small pieces of stem, which root easily in the soil. Stems sold in markets can be used as cuttings. Space plants 4½ in (12 cm) apart. Harvest plants young, before they flower.

Seed sprouting

The Chinese were sprouting seeds for home use 5000 years ago, but if ever there was a gardening technique designed for the health-conscious twentieth century urban dweller, this is it. It requires minimum space, is almost instant (you may well sow on Monday and reap by Wednesday), it can be done all year round even in the depths of winter, and the end product is highly nutritious, absolutely fresh and very tasty.

What is sprouting?

Sprouting is the process of germinating seed and eating the very young shoots, or 'sprouts'. The stage at which they are eaten varies according to the seed, but essentially there are two distinct categories:

Seed sprouts

These are used at any point from immediately after germination until just before the development of the first tiny leaves. The sprout length could be anything from ¼ in (0.5 cm) to about 1½ in (4 cm) long. Most beans are used at the 'seed sprout' stage.

Seedling sprouts

These are allowed to grow into seedlings 2–3 in (5–7.5 cm) long, with the first small leaves developed. The traditional 'mustard and cress' is harvested at this stage.

What can be sprouted?

The seeds of many species can be sprouted successfully: peas and beans; brassicas and radish; onions and leeks; herbs such as alfalfa, fenugreek and mint; grains such as rye, barley and buckwheat and many more besides. Here we will confine ourselves to those with 'oriental' connections.

SOURCE OF SEED It is essential to avoid seed that may have been treated with chemical dressings, as is frequently the case with seed sold for garden use. Either use seed sold by seed companies *expressly* for sprouting, or seed from wholefood or ethnic shops, intended for human consumption. Remember the seed is viable: keep it in a dry container somewhere cool until required for use. (See Plant raising, seed storage, page 150.)

Sprout quality

NUTRITIONAL VALUE Sprouts are highly nutritious. The process of germinating initiates a frenzy of chemical activity in the dormant seed, so the sprouted seeds and seedlings are generally exceptionally rich in vitamins, minerals, high quality protein and enzymes.
FRESHNESS Sprouts develop very rapidly and soon pass their peak, from both the nutritional and flavour point of view, so *use them in their prime*. If a constant supply is needed, sprout small quantities at regular intervals. Rather than allowing them to continue growth after they are ready, harvest them and keep them in a fridge for a couple of days, wrapped in film or in a jar. Bean sprouts are easily infected by bacteria and, to be on the safe side, should be kept for no more than 24 hours, at a fridge temperature of 39°F (4°C).

Sprouts can also be deep-frozen, though much of the fresh flavour will be lost. Blanch or steam them for a minute before freezing. Some recipes call for dried sprouts, in which case dry them in a slow oven and store in airtight jars.
TOXICITY IN LEGUME SPROUTS A word of warning is necessary on eating raw legume sprouts—that is, members of the pea and bean family, including lentils, alfalfa, fenugreek and clover. In varying degrees raw legumes contain toxins. To some extent these are broken down by soaking the seed, by sprouting and by cooking, but it is a highly complex situation. (For example, mung and soya beans are much less toxic than french and broad beans.) The point is that one shouldn't eat *large* quantities of raw sprouts on a regular basis, though no harm will come from small quantities. So if you find yourself hooked on legume sprouts, eat them boiled, steamed or stir-fried.
DARKNESS V LIGHT Most seeds can be sprouted in the dark or the light: it is largely a question of personal preference. When sprouted in the dark, seedlings are white and usually crisper in texture. The greener sprouts obtained by sprouting in the light are more nutritious. Sprouts are often started in the dark but then moved into the light to 'green up'.
SPROUT USE Sprouts are used raw in salads, and incorporated into a wide range of cooked dishes.

Bean sprouting

For characteristics, uses, and recommended sprouting methods for specific beans see below.
THE COOLING FACTOR Beans are ger-

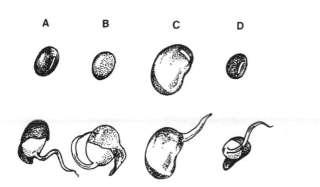

Beans for sprouting: (a) adzuki, (b) soya, (c) horse bean, and (d) mung

minated in moist, warm conditions, generating an enormous amount of heat as they do so. As a result they have to be cooled constantly to prevent them from going mouldy and rotting. Unfortunately the perfect conditions for sprouting are equally perfect for the development of moulds. So the aim of all bean sprouting systems is to provide the ideal conditions for growth, along with a simple 'cooling' system to keep them fresh, such as rinsing with cold water.

Traditionally in China mung and soya beans were sprouted in large earthenware jars, covered with a cloth or rice straw to keep them humid and exclude the light. Fresh water was poured in and out of the containers several times a day to cool them, the beans being held back with a long strainer. Sometimes they were sprouted in woven bamboo baskets or in pots with drainage holes in the bottom, which allowed the water to drain through. Nowadays semi-automatic systems are used for large-scale sprouting. We visited a modern beansprout workshop in Shanghai, which supplies bean sprouts to half a million people. Here the beans were grown in square concrete tanks, roughly 3 ft (90 cm) wide and 2½ ft (75 cm) deep in a dark basement. They were cooled by overhead sprinklers which came on automatically every 4 hours—a great leap forward from the traditional work-

shop, where families would work 4-hour shifts through the night, sloshing cold water over the sprouting beans.

I later saw bean sprouting on an even larger scale at the Fuji Farm on the outskirts of Los Angeles. These were being sprouted in 3-ton wagons, moved around on railway tracks.

MUNG BEANS AND THE PRESSURE FACTOR A common feature with all these systems is that the beans are subjected to enormous pressure, whether from the curved sides of the traditional pots, or the rigid sides of modern bins. I was amazed at how much effort was required to pull out a handful of mung beans from one of the Shanghai sprouting tanks. Recent research in Taiwan has shown that this pressure is a key to growing fat, crispy sprouts. Pressure leads to the production of the gas ethylene, which causes the sprout cells to swell and grow 'fat'. Grown without pressure, sprouts are longer, leaner, and far less crunchy. My own experience confirms this. For many years my mung bean sprouts, although edible, never had that fat, crispy texture of the authentic Chinese restaurant beansprout. I now put a weight on my sprouts (see Method, 5, below). This exerts the necessary pressure and—eureka—lovely crunchy sprouts.

Home sprouting

There are several methods of sprouting beans, and it is worth

experimenting until you find the system which suits you best. The essential requirements are a suitable container, the correct temperature and hygienic conditions. They can be grown 'loose' or on a 'base'.

LOOSE SPROUTING
This is the simplest method. As implied, the seeds are grown loose in the container. There is no wastage as the entire sprout can be used.

Growth is probably slightly faster than when grown on a base, but the sprouts will spoil fairly rapidly after reaching their peak.

Containers The container must be deep enough to allow for the expansion of the seeds as they germinate. Most beans will increase their volume 7–10-fold while sprouting. The most convenient sprouters are self-draining, as they minimize the disturbance of the sprouting seeds.

For a cheap, home-made sprouter, take any plastic carton or container and make holes in the bottom, effectively converting it into a sieve. This makes an excellent sprouter. (On a larger scale, sprouters have been made by puncturing holes in the bottom of a rubbish bin: the principal is the same.)

Any jar can be converted into a draining container by replacing the lid either with a mesh top, or with muslin kept in place with a rubber band. (Mesh tops which fit standard size jars can sometimes be purchased.) Water can be poured in and out of the mesh or muslin, though it doesn't flow easily through muslin, which has the added disadvantage that it is apt to stain.

There are many seed sprouters on the market. Most are self-draining, with a system of pouring water in and out to rinse the seeds. Some consist of a series of perforated dishes stacked on top of each other, so that several different kinds of seed can be sprouted simultaneously.

Temperature The ideal temperature varies with the type of bean, but is generally 55–65°F (12–18°C). Avoid temperature extremes: poor quality sprouts result from germination at very low and very high temperatures. In summer most sprouts can be grown satisfactorily at room temperature. In winter they may need to be grown above a radiator or in an airing cupboard.

Method

1 Examine seeds carefully, removing any which are damaged or off-colour as they will be likely to rot.

2 Soak seeds overnight or for several hours so that they swell. This 'primes' the seed, enlarging the embryo and leading to faster germination.

3 Rinse them with fresh water. (Tip them into a sieve and run water through, or use your sprouter if it is self-draining.)

4 Put the moist but drained beans in a layer at least ½ in (over 1 cm) deep in the bottom of the container. The layer can be any depth, provided the container is deep enough to allow them to expand anything up to 10 times their original volume.

5 (Mung beans only) Where a home-made container is used, cover them with a moist cloth and a weight. How heavy a weight is largely a matter of trial and error under your own conditions. As a rough guide, I use a 2-lb (approx 900-g) weight in a 5-in (13-cm) diameter container with about ½ in (1 cm) of sprouts in the bottom. However, considerably less weight can be effective. Unless the weight fits snugly on the container, put it on a saucer to distribute the weight more evenly.

6 Put the container somewhere to sprout at the correct temperature. Beans are best sprouted in the dark, for example in a cupboard. Alternatively, cover the container in tinfoil or black film to make it light-proof. Don't enclose it too tightly: the seeds must have air and 'room to breathe'. An opaque container can be made completely light-proof with a lid.

7 Rinse the seeds night and morning by running cold water through, disturbing the beans as little as possible so they grow in a compact mass. (The weight will have to be removed for rinsing.) Drain thoroughly, so the seeds are moist, but not submerged in water. In very hot weather rinsing may have to be more frequent.

8 Sprouts will be ready for use within a few days, depending on the temperature. Give them a final rinse before use, partly to remove any ungerminated seeds.

SPROUTING ON A BASE

The sprouts are grown on a dish or in a container, lined with a moisture-retentive base (see below). They will root into the base and stand upright. There is some wastage, as they normally have to be cut just above the base.

Growth is a little slower, but the sprouts remain in good condition longer by rooting into the base. They can be allowed to develop into seedling sprouts where required. The method is useful for those sprouts which can be eaten either as seed or seedling sprouts. Sprouts can be grown in attractive dishes, and served in them at table.

Container The container is usually solid, rather than self draining. Almost any type of container can be used, from shallow dishes and plastic cartons to seed trays.

The base Line the container with any moisture retentive material. I often use a piece of thin sponge or foam rubber, cut to fit the base, covered with a couple of layers of paper towel. This allows the foam to be reused several times. Alternatively use several layers of paper towel or blotting paper, any kind of cloth or flannel, or foam rubber.

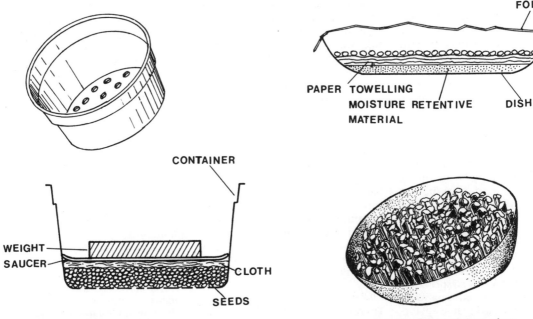

Home-made mung bean sprouter

Seed sprouting on a base

Sprouts can also be grown on a thin layer of sowing or potting compost, peat, or light sandy soil. This supplies a few nutrients so enabling them to grow to a more advanced stage or to stand longer without deteriorating. Cover them lightly with the soil or whatever medium is used. Although this system can be used for bean sprouting, it is more frequently used for seedling sprouts such as radish.

Method

Stages 1–3 as for loose sprouting, above.

4 Spread the seeds closely but in a single layer over the base.

5 As the base retains moisture it is not usually necessary to cover them with a cloth; nor is a weight necessary.

6 As above.

7 Rinse the seeds by pouring water gently into the container, and swilling it around before tipping it out. The seeds may need to be held in place with the back of the spoon until they have rooted in the base. On the whole, less rinsing is necessary when grown on a base. Where soil or compost is used, water sufficiently to keep it moist.

8 If the medium is very clean the sprouts may be used whole. Normally they will have to be cut just above base level.

Mung beans (*Phaseolus aureus*)

Mung beans (also known as green gram) are probably the most widely sprouted vegetable in the world. The beans are usually olive green, though occasionally brown or mottled in colour. They are very small, approximately ¼ in (½ cm) long. Not unexpectedly, the smaller the bean, the smaller the size of the individual bean sprout. However for a given volume, smaller beans give higher overall weight than larger beans. On average, the weight of the beans is increased sevenfold by sprouting – 1 lb (450 g) beans yielding approximately 7 lb (3 kg) sprouts.

Mung beans are best grown in the dark. They can be grown by any of the methods outlined above, but are most commonly grown by one of the 'loose' methods. The ideal temperature for good quality plump sprouts is about 68°F (20°C); the quality deteriorates if the temperature is much higher. They are normally ready in 3–6 days.

USE The optimum stage for use is at 2–3 in (5–7.5 cm) long, before the seed leaves develop. The sprouts should be pure white; the root tips and the neck of the sprout start to brown as they age.

The seed coats sometimes cling to the head of the sprouts as they germinate, looking rather unsightly. No harm will come from eating them, but they are easily removed by soaking the beans in water. The seed coats float to the surface and can be skimmed off. For aesthetic reasons Chinese restaurants 'top and tail' beans sprouts, removing the remnants of the bean seed and the tip of the root. Sometimes they even remove the *head* to make a delicate dish known as 'silver sprouts'. Trimmed sprouts don't keep as long as 'natural' sprouts. I once watched a pair of old ladies diligently topping and tailing on a pavement in Hong Kong: it's a job that requires infinite patience. (The Taiwanese have invented an automatic domestic bean sprouter, which not only keeps the sprouts constantly bathed and cooled, but also removes the seed coats.)

In the kitchen Mung bean sprouts have a delicious flavour and texture. The Chinese consider them 'cooling' and use them mainly in summer, unlike soya and horse bean sprouts which are 'warming' and used in winter.

Mung bean sprouts can be used raw or *very* lightly cooked. They should never be used in stews or baked dishes as long cooking destroys the vitamins and the flavour. They blend well with other vegetables, egg, meat, chicken or fish, and are frequently incorporated into stir-fried dishes in the last minute or so of cooking. They are also used to stuff pancakes, egg rolls and tortillas, in fried rice dishes and omelettes, and are excellent added to soup, again just for the last minute or two of cooking.

Soya bean (*Glycine max*)

Soya beans are rounded, larger than mung beans, and usually yellow though there are green, black and white varieties. The sprouts are considerably larger and more substantial than mung sprouts, and are eaten when 3–4 in (7.5–10 cm) long, often with the remains of the bean still attached. They tend to be yellow rather than white, and should be used before there is any greenness in the first small leaves. In China they are often sold neatly bunched—whereas mung beans are sold in untidy heaps. They are more nutritious than mung beans, having a higher protein level. They are also more strongly flavoured, less tender and more fibrous, and require slightly longer cooking. In general they are probably more suited to use in cooked dishes and soups than to consumption raw in salads.

They can be sprouted in the dark by any methods used for mung beans. They generally take longer to develop than mung beans (4–8 days), and are best sprouted at higher temperatures, about 70–77°F (21–25°C).

Adzuki bean (*Phaseolus angularis*)

These small red (occasionally black) beans are about the same size as mung beans. They have a nutty flavour and are best used about ½–1 in (1–2.5 cm) long. In general use them like mung beans. Try them raw, mixed with finely shredded cabbage and yogurt; or very lightly fried and worked into a cheese and potato casserole.

They can be sprouted loose or on a base. They sprout best at higher temperatures—up to 86°F (30°F)—and are normally ready to eat in 4–8 days. Very frequent rinsing is necessary.

Horse bean (*Vicia faba*)

This small-seeded form of the broad or fava bean is sprouted in China under the picturesque name of 'silk bean sprouts'. The main purpose of sprouting is to soften the bean, which is used when just sprouted in speciality dishes, and in the winter months, to supplement vegetables in short supply.

In the Shanghai sprouting workshop horse beans were being sprouted in very large jars, in the light, with no covering. They were ready in about 5 days.

Sprouting other seeds

Besides beans, quite a number of oriental vegetables can be sprouted indoors, for use either as seed or seedling sprouts according to taste (see below). They are very nutritious and invaluable during the winter. Think of the seedling sprouts as oriental forms of 'mustard and cress'. With their delicate stems and tiny fresh leaves, they provide an exciting range of flavours for salads, sandwiches and garnishing. Or incorporate them into cooked dishes and soups at the last minute.

Sprouting methods

See below for the characteristics, uses, and recommended sprouting methods for different species.

Seed sprouts

Use any of the loose seed methods for bean sprouting (see page 133). Where jars are used seeds can be rinsed by tipping them out into a strainer, and running water through them, rather than pouring water in and out through mesh or muslin. The tipping out does not disturb growth as it would with beans. Most will sprout at temperatures of 55–70°F (13–21°C), and can be germinated in the dark or the light.

Seedling sprouts

Seedling sprouts are normally grown in the light, but full sun should be avoided. They can however be started in the dark to develop tall, elongated seedlings. A couple of days after germination they should be moved into the light to 'green up'.

There are two alternative methods of sprouting:

Sprouting on a base See bean sprouting, page 134.

Where an inert base such as

foam or paper towelling is used the seedlings can normally only be cut once. Where grown on a base of soil etc, where there are some nutrients, they may resprout after the first cutting to give a second cut, provided they are cut *above* the first pair of seed leaves.

Raft method This is an excellent way of growing seedling sprouts. Seed is sown on a small 'raft' of rigid nylon screen, floating on water in a container. When the seedlings germinate their roots penetrate the screen and dangle in the water. They develop into a dense mat of upright seedlings, and keep in good condition for as long as 2 weeks, depending on the temperature. Change the water at least every 2 days to keep it fresh.

Several types of sprouter are marketed. Mine is a Japanese rectangular plastic container about 2 in (5 cm) deep and 5 in (13 cm) wide. A nylon screen fits onto a ridge inside the container, about ¾ in (2 cm) from the top. The container is filled with water up to the level of the screen, on which seeds are sown in a single layer. Cheap sprouting rafts can be made from any rigid screening material (it must be fine enough to prevent seeds falling through), attached to a frame to make it buoyant. It can then simply be floated in a bowl of water. It is easiest to put the seeds onto the dry raft, then to float it into the water.

The perforated dishes or trays in seed sprouting kits can be converted into *seedling* sprouters by placing them over a dish of water. The seedling roots grow through and dangle in the water.

Alfalfa (lucerne) (*Medicago sativus*)

Alfalfa sprouts have a fairly bland, sweetish flavour, and are rich in protein and vitamins. They are used at any stage from ½ in (1 cm) long seed sprouts to seedlings 1½ in (4 cm) high.

The seed sprouts are usually grown in a jar. Seed, which is very small, should be in a layer no more than ³⁄₁₀ in (½ cm) deep. They grow much faster if the jar is on its

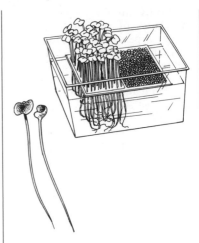

Japanese raft sprouter

side rather than upright. Seedling sprouts are grown either on a base or suspended in water. Commercially, alfalfa is grown (and sold) both in self-draining plastic punnets and in small containers lined with sponge. It germinates well at temperatures of 68–70°F (20–21°C), being ready in 3–7 days, depending on the stage harvested. The quality of alfalfa seed varies enormously, poorer quality seed germinating very erratically. The best seed comes from California.

Brassicas (*Brassica spp.*)

As far as I know all brassica seeds can be sprouted, and used either as seed sprouts ½–1 in (1–2.5 cm) long, or as seedlings up to 2 in (5 cm) high. Their flavour varies: Chinese cabbage, the spinach mustards (komatsuna) and turnip are mild flavoured; mustards such as 'Green-in-the-Snow' are spicy.

Brassicas are mainly grown as seedling sprouts, either on a base or suspended in water. Most germinate rapidly at temperatures of 55–60°F (13–15°C), though Chinese cabbage will germinate faster at somewhat higher temperatures.

Chrysanthemum greens (*Chrysanthemum coronarium*)

Seedling sprouts have a pleasant, interesting taste. When grown by the raft method, starting them off in the dark, they were ready within two weeks.

Mitsuba (*Cryptotaenia japonica*)
Mitsuba makes attractive, dark green seedling sprouts, which have a pleasant, angelica-like flavour. I have grown them very successfully by the raft method at ordinary room temperatures.

Onion (*Allium spp.*)
In China and Japan onion seed is sprouted. The Japanese use single-stem varieties of bunching onion, harvesting as seedlings about 2 in (5 cm) high. They are sometimes dressed with vinegar and used to flavour noodles. I have grown them successfully by the raft method, but found growth fairly slow.

Peas (*Pisum sativum*)
Any type of pea can be sprouted, including yellow fodder peas, red-coated peas and ordinary garden peas. They can be sprouted to the stage when the first small green leaves are apparent. Sprout in the dark using any of the mung bean methods. At temperatures of about 77°F (25°C) they take 6–8 days. They have a very pleasant, raw pea flavour.

Perilla (*Perilla frutescens*)
Perilla sprouts have the unique, musty flavour of the parent plant, and can be eaten from a fairly large seed sprout to the seedling stage. There are red and green varieties of perilla (see page 108), the red perilla sprouts having a purplish hue. Germination and growth is slower than for most sprouts.

Polygonum (Akatade/tade)
(*Polygonum sp.*, possibly *hydropiper*)
In Japan a member of the knotgrass or smartweed family is grown for its peppery seedlings, known as *akatade* or *tade*. The small seedlings are pink to bright red in colour and have a peppery taste. Traditionally used to flavour the fresh fish dish *sashimi*, they could add a pleasant piquancy to salad dishes. When I sprouted them on a paper towelling base, I found they took over a week to germinate.

Radish (*Raphanus sativus*)
See Radish sprouts, page 119.
Radish seed germinates and grows rapidly, and can be used at any stage from about ½ in (1 cm) onwards, a stage sometimes reached within 2–3 days of sowing. Any method can be used for growing at home. The jar method is very convenient for short sprouts; for larger seedlings use a base, or grow them by the raft method. In all cases they can be started off in the dark.

In my experience many varieties of radish can be sprouted, but the larger the seed the bigger the sprouts. For example, the large winter radish, 'China Rose', makes better sprouts than ordinary small summer radishes. The variety *Bisai* sprouts well (see Radishes, page 118). In Japan fast germinating varieties such as '40 Days' are used.

Mixtures
If you feel adventurous try sprouting different seeds together—alfalfa, for example, can be combined with radish. In theory the slower germinating seed (in this case alfalfa), will have to be sown first, if the end result is not to be uneven. Alfalfa, fenugreek and fennel is another recommended mixture.

A final word on sprouting
Once you have the sprouting habit, it becomes second nature. But beginners sometimes have failures. The commonest causes of failure are:
- Temperatures too high or too low.
- Seeds allowed to dry out or swamped by water.
- Insufficient rinsing.
- Dirty equipment.

I would advise anyone new to sprouting to start with one type of seed, and to grow it by several methods until you find the best for your conditions. Armed with confidence, it will be easy to move onto others. Radish is probably a good one to start with.

Part 2

Gardening techniques

Introduction

I am sure that most people venturing into oriental vegetables already grow 'ordinary' vegetables. Broadly speaking, of course, the methods used are the same. With almost all vegetables the better the soil and growing conditions, the better the crops will be. This is doubly true where the oriental brassicas are concerned: they are fast growing and very demanding.

These final chapters are not intended to be a comprehensive guide to vegetable growing. (See the Appendix, page 215 for recommended further reading.) Their purpose is:

● To explain the concept of soil fertility and summarize methods of creating it.
● To summarize basic methods of soil preparation, plant raising, weed, pest and disease control, watering and container growing.
● To describe some less common techniques—for example, bed systems, cut-and-come-again methods, protected cropping, the use of plastic film and woven film mulches—which I feel are particularly appropriate to the cultivation of the oriental vegetables in modern gardens.

As mentioned in my main introduction to this book, for many years I have gardened 'organically', without using chemical fertilizers or weedkillers, or chemical pesticides and fungicides, other than the safe products approved by the organic standards authorities in the United Kingdom. So the methods outlined here are essentially 'organic' or 'biological'. This is appropriate for the cultivation of oriental vegetables, for in China, where the majority of these vegetables originated, they have traditionally been grown under some of the most productive organic systems the world has known.

Soil fertility

Soil fertility is the cornerstone of successful vegetable growing (though other factors, such as shelter, have very important roles to play). So what *is* soil, and what is a fertile soil?

What is soil?

Soil looks solid, but the average garden soil is roughly half solid and about half air and water. The solid part is about 95 per cent mineral and 5 per cent humus. The *mineral* element has been formed by the weathering of rocks over the centuries, and depending on the nature of the original rock, consists of anything from tiny particles of clay to large grains of sand. The typical garden loam is probably a mixture of several types. The *humus* is derived from organic matter, that is decaying plant and animal remains, converted into humus by the army of bacteria in the soil. The minerals and humus are both sources of plant foods (see below).

Besides being a source of plant food, the soil has to be a reservoir of air and water. Air and water are essential both for the plant roots and for the many creatures which live in the soil—earthworms, soil fungi, bacteria and so on.

Plant foods
The foods or nutrients a plant needs to grow come from two sources. Carbon dioxide is taken in from the air through the leaves, where it is converted into sugars and starches. All the rest comes from the soil, absorbed in dilute solutions through the plant's roots.

The most important of these plant foods are nitrogen, phosphorus and potash: they are needed in relatively large amounts. Calcium, magnesium and sulphur are required in smaller quantities, while a host of trace elements, though vital, are needed only in tiny quantities.

Some of these nutrients are found in the mineral particles of the soil (especially in clays) but most come from humus. They exist in very complex forms, and have to be broken down into simpler forms which the plant roots can absorb. This is done by micro-organisms, mainly bacteria. To function effectively these micro-organisms need air, water, soil conditions that are neither too acid nor too alkaline, and a plentiful supply of organic matter.

Nitrogen is *the* most important nutrient for leafy green vegetables. It comes both from decaying organic matter, and from the air in the soil, where it is 'fixed' for use by plants by some of the soil bacteria. Nitrogen is very soluble and easily washed out of the soil during heavy rain, especially in winter.

What is a fertile soil?
A fertile soil is one which can supply all the plant nutrients required, air, water, and optimum conditions for the soil micro-organisms to function. Whether it can meet these requirements depends very largely on what is known as the *soil structure*. So what is soil structure? SOIL STRUCTURE In the ideal soil the mineral particles and the humus join together to form soil 'crumbs', tiny lumps which are almost impossible to break down when you try and crush garden soil in your hand. The crumbs, which vary in size, are separated from each other by air spaces: these spaces link together to form a network of aeration and drainage channels of the soil. The crumbs are remarkably stable, and don't disintegrate when the ground is very wet or very dry. It is the combination of the crumbs themselves and the air spaces between them which makes the soil structure.

The structure determines the amount of water and air in the soil. When heavy rain falls on a fertile soil, water drains off through the larger spaces, which quickly fill with air. However it remains in the small spaces, forming a vital reservoir of moisture. If the water didn't drain off, soil would become waterlogged. This would drive out the air and oxygen, plant roots would die, earthworms would die or migrate, soil organisms would be unable to break down organic matter to release plant nutrients, and plant life would grind to a halt. Good drainage and soil fertility go hand in hand.

A poor soil is one with a poor crumb or soil structure. There can be several reasons, the extreme cases being a very heavy clay soil and a very porous sandy soil. When a clay soil is very wet it forms great impenetrable sticky lumps of waterlogged and airless soil. A clay soil is basically a rich soil, but the nutrients are locked up in the large lumps. In a pure sandy soil, on the other hand, water drains right through, taking most of the plant foods with it. In dry conditions there is no moisture reserve—so, again, soil life ceases, this time starved of moisture.

Creating good soil structure is

the essence of creating fertile soil. To do so (considering again the extreme soil types of clay and sand) clay lumps have to be *broken down* into crumbs, and sandy particles 'glued' together, to *make* crumbs. In both cases this can be done with *humus*.

HUMUS Elements in humus both help coat sandy particles so they join together, and help in the breakdown of clay lumps. In addition humus also acts like a sponge, holding water and plant nutrients in the soil, and is a source of plant foods itself. Humus comes from the breakdown of organic matter, so the first step in building soil fertility is to feed the soil with organic matter, which in gardening terms is any kind of manure or compost. (See below.)

The role of earthworms

In almost all garden soils, the activities of earthworms play a crucial role in building up soil fertility. In ploughing through the earth, soil and organic matter passes through the worm's stomach, where it is mixed with gums and lime. This constitutes the first stage in breaking down organic matter: the bacteria then take over. At the same time many types of worms produce worm casts, which are deposited not just on the surface, but also within the soil. These casts can be seen as concentrated nuggets of soil fertility. For one thing they are very stable and play an important role in the formation of soil crumbs; as well, they are an extraordinarily rich source of plant foods, already conveniently broken down into forms which the plant roots can absorb.

The cement-sided burrows made by some worms is another bonus from earthworm activity. These act as permanent drainage channels, often doubling as channels for roots, so enabling roots to penetrate more deeply into the soil.

Finally, worms can be a rich source of fertilizer themselves. When *they* die and their protein-rich bodies are broken down, an enormous amount of nitrogen is eventually released to the soil—in

the order of 100 lb (45 kg) an acre!

So, for a variety of reasons a soil rich in earthworms is well on the way to being a very fertile soil. Anything which increases the worm population increases soil fertility. Worms feed on organic matter: there's a direct relationship between the amount of organic matter in the soil and the number of worms. Adding organic matter to the soil is the fastest method of increasing the worm population.

Feeding the soil with organic matter

To summarize, organic matter benefits the soil by:
● Supplying food for earthworms, which eventually is converted into humus and food for plants.
● Improving soil structure, drainage, and moisture retention.
Organic matter is the main agent for creating 'fertile, well-drained, moisture-retentive soil'—the somewhat contradictory sounding phrase used to describe the ideal soil for many vegetables.

In the long term almost any soil can be brought into a state of fertility, and kept that way, by continually working in organic matter. The majority of vegetables can then be grown perfectly satisfactorily without using any supplementary fertilizers. However it takes time to bring a poor soil into a state of fertility—it cannot be done in one season—and in the early years of doing so, it may be necessary to use supplementary feeds. It may also be necessary to take steps to improve poor drainage, or to correct acidity by liming. These problems will be dealt with later.

What can be used as organic matter?

It is well known that the extraordinary fertility of Chinese soils—and the same is true of Japan and other Oriental countries—has been based on the recycling of human manure or 'night soil' as it is euphemistically known. In addition, all forms of animal and vegetable wastes are composted and returned to the land, green manur-

ing is practised, and many crops are kept mulched with organic materials. Western gardeners are unlikely to convert to the wholesale use of human manure. But in growing oriental vegetables the Oriental approach to utilizing all possible forms of organic matter should never be far from our minds.

Finding organic matter is one of the most difficult problems facing the Western gardener today, especially the urban gardener. There is still a great deal of organic material around—often thrown away by our profligate society—but it is not always simple to track down, collect and utilize it.

Organic manures

Anything which was once living and will rot down can be used as organic matter. For improving the structure of the soil, the bulkier it is the better.

Making your own compost

A row of compost heaps is the hallmark of an enthusiastic gardener, either supplementing supplies of bulky manure, or a substitute for it. There are many (conflicting) theories about the best way to make compost. Don't let them deter you: however the compost is made it will benefit the soil.

HEAP METHOD The simplest method is to build a heap of domestic and garden wastes, finally covering with an inch (2.5 cm) of soil and insulating material such as old carpet or heavy duty plastic film. The heap can be of any size: it will shrink considerably while decomposing. Depending on the climate it may take up to a year before it has decomposed into soil-like material which is easy to handle. However, it can be applied to the soil before this stage. The drawback to this simple method is that temperatures may not rise high enough to kill disease spores and weed seeds.

COMPOST BINS The traditional compost heap is made in a well-insulated bin built on soil, with a drainage layer of bricks, sticks etc. in the base. Ideally, garden and household wastes should be ac-

Some examples of organic manures

Any kind of animal manure
It should be mixed with as much stable litter as possible. Generally speaking manure is best stacked in a covered heap for about 6 months before use.

Bird and rabbit manure
These are more concentrated than most animal manures, so are best worked in small quantities into a compost heap.

Spent mushroom compost
The chalk fragments in it help to break down very heavy clay soils.

Seaweed
It can be used fresh, dried or composted.

Recycled urban waste and treated sewage sludge
These products are becoming increasingly available. Use them as advised by the suppliers.

Straw and hay
This is also best stacked into a heap in layers about 6 in (15 cm) deep, watering each layer well. Sprinklings of poultry manure and lawn mowings can be added to each layer, to enrich it and hasten decomposition. Stack it if possible for about 6 months.

Leaves
These rot very slowly, so only work small quantities into a compost heap. Gather large quantities into black plastic bags or bins, and allow them to rot for a season into leafmould, for use in potting compost or as a mulch.

Garden and household compost
See 'Making your own compost'.

cumulated, so that the heap can be built up one layer at a time, rather than in dribs and drabs, in layers about 6 in (15 cm) deep. The material should be as mixed as possible. It is unwise to make a single layer of any one material, such as lawn mowings, which will form an impenetrable mass.

Although anything 'biological' can be used in the heap, tough and woody material should be shredded, and diseased plants and seeding weeds are best omitted. To accelerate decomposition each layer can be covered with a proprietary compost activator, or a thin layer of animal manure, or human urine diluted 1:4. However, this is not essential.

When completed, cover the heap with an insulating layer of, for example, straw or soil, and finally with a piece of old carpet or heavy plastic film. The decomposing heap should warm up to a high temperature, ideally 140–158°F (60–70°C), but will cool down after a few weeks. If it is turned at this point temperatures will rise again, making it decompose faster. In warm summer weather a heap will be ready for use within two or three months. The high temperature should have killed off the majority of disease spores and weed seeds. Recent research indicates that a temperature over 158°F (70°C) needs to be held for 30 minutes to kill most weed seed and disease organisms.

Worm compost

An excellent system for making compost in small households has been developed by the American biologist, Mary Appelhof (see Bibliography). Garden and domestic waste is put into a box or bin and fed to small redworms or brandling worms. The worms convert it into a very rich material, of peaty consistency, which can either be used as a fertilizer or made into a potting compost.

On a domestic scale a wooden box approximately 18 in × 24 in and 9 in deep (45 × 60 × 23 cm) will suffice. This is filled with about 3½ lb (1.5 kg) shredded newspaper as bedding, moistened with a gallon (4.5 l) of water. A handful of worms are put in, the box is covered to keep it moist, and small quantities of domestic wastes are fed regularly to the worms. Such a bin can be kept in a kitchen; there is no odour, and no risk of the worms escaping. When the food supply is exhausted the worms die, but before that point is reached, the box can be emptied and filled with fresh bedding, transferring a few worms into it to keep the system going.

Green manuring

Green manures are crops which are grown and then dug in to improve soil fertility. They are an excellent way of supplementing the supply of organic matter and/or nitrogen in the soil. Green manuring is an old-fashioned practice, but one organic gardeners are turning to increasingly.

In gardens green manures are either:
• Sown as catch crops between one crop being lifted and another sown, whenever a piece of ground becomes vacant during the growing season. These are dug in a few weeks to a month later, as appropriate. Buckwheat, mustard and fenugreek are typical summer green manures.
• Sown in autumn and dug in in spring. These crops, which must be winter hardy, have the additional merit of protecting the soil during winter. They also take up nitrogen and other nutrients, preventing them from being washed out of the soil in winter. These nutrients are returned to the soil when the crop is dug in in spring. Grazing rye grass, winter tares, and red clover

are examples of winter green manures.

Most green manures are broadcast on the surface (see Part 2, Plant raising, page 151), or sown in close rows. Green manures are dug in at different stages, but in almost all cases before they start to flower. It is sometimes necessary to cut back the foliage first, to make it easier to dig in the crop. (The foliage can, of course, be added to the compost heap.) Green manures are usually dug into the top 6 in (15 cm) or so of soil.

CHOICE OF GREEN MANURES There is a very wide choice of green manures, and it is important to choose crops which grow fast and well under your conditions, and suit your purposes.

Green manuring is a complex subject, though one well worth experimenting with and mastering. (For further reading, see page 216.)

Applying manure

Manures and compost can either be spread on the surface or dug in when the soil is being prepared. Again, there are many theories, climate, soil type, type of compost all having a bearing on the best course of action. As a rough guide, *well rotted manure or compost* is probably best worked in in spring, or spread as a surface mulch around plants after planting. *Fairly raw manure or compost* is best spread on the soil in the autumn. This is an excellent practice in areas with heavy winter rains which wash nutrients out of the soil. It protects the soil and you will find that, by spring, worms will have worked most of the manure into the soil, creating a beautiful layer of crumbly soil just beneath the surface. It is almost impossible to put on too much organic manure: think in terms of a layer at least 2–4 in (5–10 cm) thick, deeper if possible.

(For digging, see Part 2, The bed system, page 147.)

'Concentrated' organic fertilizers

Once your soil is very fertile, most vegetables can be grown without applying any extra fertilizer. However, there are cases where concentrated, i.e. non-bulky, organic, fertilizers have their uses to supplement the regular application of organic manures:

● To compensate for low soil fertility.

● To give plants an extra boost of nutrients during growth, to obtain higher yields.

● To correct nutrient deficiencies in the soil (See Common soil problems).

The non-bulky organic fertilizers are generally sold as granules or powders. They supply plant nutrients but, not being bulky, have little effect on soil structure. The nutrients become available to the plants relatively slowly compared with inorganic artificial fertilizers, which are fast-acting and may result in lush, soft growth. They can be applied before or during sowing or planting and during growth. They are generally scattered on the ground around the plants when the soil is moist, or made up in liquid form and watered on, according to the instructions.

Liquid feeds

There are various organic liquid manures, which supply nutrients rapidly to plants. They are invaluable for 'boosts' during growth. While some are commercially prepared, others can be made cheaply at home. They are usually diluted and watered on the plants. As a general rule, the younger the plant, the weaker the solution used. The following are some of the most common liquid feeds.

LIQUID MANURE ('Black Jack', 'Manure Tea') It is made by suspending a sack of animal manure in a barrel of water. The animal manure can be mixed with lawn mowings. (In the past soot was another common component.) It is usually diluted to the colour of weak tea before application.

COMFREY MANURE It is made from the deep rooted, perennial plant comfrey (*Symphytum officinale*). Although wild strains can be used, the most effective is the cultivated variety 'Bocking 14'. This is easily cultivated in the garden, though plants have to be purchased initially as it does not set seed. To make the comfrey manure a barrel is filled with leaves and water added. It is covered and left for about a month to ferment before use. Be warned: it becomes rather smelly in the process! It can be used concentrated or diluted at the rate of one pint in a gallon of water.

NETTLE MANURE This is made from young stinging nettles (*Urtica sp.*) in much the same way as comfrey manure.

Types of green manure

Fast-growing leafy crops
These give a quick release of nitrogen when dug in.
Examples: Mustard; rape (a rich source of nitrogen and phosphorus); fodder radish. Note that these are all brassicas (cruciferous) crops, so should not be grown where there is any clubroot in the soil.

Leguminous crops
Their root nodules fix the atmospheric nitrogen in the soil, releasing it slowly to following crops. Their leaves also rot producing nitrogen.
Examples: various types of clover; alfalfa; lupins; winter field beans; field peas; winter tares; fenugreek. Note that fenugreek will not fix nitrogen in all soils, and initially seed may need to be treated with the correct rhizobium to increase its efficiency.

Crops which produce a lot of root fibre
This both helps to improve the soil structure when growing, and increases the organic matter in the soil when dug in.
Examples: grazing rye grass; buckwheat.

Some organic fertilizers and the principal nutrients supplied

Bonemeal	phosphorus, nitrogen, calcium
Calcified seaweed	small amounts main elements; trace elements
Dolomite	calcium, magnesium
Magnesium limestone	calcium, magnesium
Gypsum	calcium, sulphur
Hoof and horn	nitrogen
Rock phosphate	phosphorus
Rock potash	potash
Seaweed meal	nitrogen, potash, trace elements
Proprietary organic fertilizers	various

SEAWEED EXTRACTS The various seaweed based products on the market appear to contain some nutrients, a wide range of trace elements, and other substances which seem to promote healthy growth. No-one is quite sure why, but plants appear to respond rapidly to a seaweed based 'pick-me-up'.

Common soil problems

Although most soil problems can be remedied within 3–5 years by the application of generous quantities of organic matter, gardeners sometimes take over gardens with more fundamental problems which require special treatment. The following are the most common soil problems.

Poor drainage

If water lies on the soil surface for several days after heavy rain, or is encountered within a foot (30 cm) of the surface when digging, there is a drainage problem. There are a number of causes of poor drainage. Sometimes there is a 'hard pan' or impermeable, compacted layer in the soil, perhaps caused by previous building operations. This has to be broken physically with a spade, pick axe etc. to improve the drainage.

Where poor drainage is caused by the nature of the subsoil or the slope of the land, it can often be improved by digging a number of soakaway trench drains—usually across the lower end or low-lying sections of the site. Dig them 2–3 ft (60–90 cm) deep, and about 1 ft (30 cm) wide, and half-fill them with stones, rubble etc. to absorb water. Fill the rest with soil.

Where there is a more persistent problem it may be necessary to lay a system of piped drains, draining to an outlet such as a ditch or an artificial soakaway. It is probably worth seeking professional advice on the layout, gradient and design of the drainage system.

Very acid soils

The acidity or alkalinity of a soil is, broadly speaking, a reflection of the amount of calcium in the soil. It is measured on the pH scale, which runs from 1–14. The neutral point is 7. Soils with a pH below 7 become progressively more acid, and those with a pH above 7, more alkaline. The soil pH can be measured with simple soil testing kits. In humid climates there is a tendency for soils to become more acid all the time, as the calcium is washed out of the soil.

Most vegetables grow best on slightly acid soils, with a pH of about 6.5. If plants are growing healthily in your garden, assume the pH is more or less correct. However, if plant growth seems very poor, if the soil has a somewhat 'sour' look with moss growing on the surface and weeds like sorrel and dock are common, the situation needs to be remedied. Extreme acidity has a number of adverse effects, one of them being that soil bacteria, on which the breakdown of organic matter depends, cannot work in very acid conditions.

Acidity can be corrected by liming the soil. This may have to be done in stages over several years. It is usually done in the autumn, dressing the soil with ground limestone or dolomite. The amount used varies with the type of soil, being lightest on light sandy soils, heaviest on heavy clay soils. An average dressing would be in the region of 1 lb per sq. yd (roughly 0.5 kg/sq. m). Limestone should never be applied at the same time as animal manure, as chemical reactions will take place. Care should be taken not to over-lime, which can in itself be very damaging to plants. On a small scale calcified seaweed, which is also a source of trace elements, can be used to raise the pH. It is rather expensive to use on a large scale.

Once over-acidity has been corrected, organic gardeners rarely find it necessary to lime again. Working in plenty of organic matter seems to keep the soil at the correct acidity level.

Very alkaline soils

Soils which are too alkaline, i.e. too chalky, to grow vegetables are uncommon—which is fortunate as it is less easy to correct excess alkalinity quickly. However, over the course of a few years the pH will naturally be lowered by the application of manure and compost. Alternatively, grow the vegetables in specially-made raised beds.

Mineral deficiencies

Occasionally, growth is very poor in gardens for no obvious reason, and the fault may lie with specific mineral deficiencies in the soil. Identifying deficiencies is a matter for professional help, the starting point being a laboratory analysis of samples of the soil.

In the long term deficiencies can

be corrected by the use of fertilizers, but it is a slow business. Organic growers use natural fertilizers—rock potash, for example—to correct a potash deficiency. In the short term liquid feeds of seaweed extracts, applied to growing crops, often help to overcome the deficiency. They can be watered in, or applied as foliar feeds sprayed on to the plants. These sometimes seem to act more quickly.

Maintaining soil fertility

Once soil has been brought into a state of fertility, it is important to keep it that way, mainly by continually replenishing the soil's larder with organic matter. In my own garden I aim to add some organic material to every bed every year: either digging in manure or compost when the soil is being prepared, or mulching growing crops with organic material, or sowing a green manure crop. Needless to say I don't always fulfil these good intentions!

ROTATION The rotation of crops has a part to play in maintaining soil fertility, by preventing the build up of harmful diseases and pests. (See The bed system, Rotation, page 149.)

PRESERVING THE SOIL STRUCTURE Good soil structure is usually a hard-won prize: few of us have naturally fertile gardens. And it is a fragile commodity. The soil structure is easily destroyed by working the soil when it is very wet or very dry, by heavy rain beating on bare soil, and by treading on the soil, especially when it is wet. Several practices, such as organizing a garden in narrow beds and keeping the surface mulched, help to conserve soil structure. They are discussed in the following chapters, and are well worth adopting in the interests of creating a highly productive vegetable garden.

There is doubt that creating fertile soil is the key to success with the majority of oriental vegetables.

The bed system

I am firmly convinced that the most efficient way of growing vegetables is in some form of 'bed system', in which plants are grown intensively but evenly spaced in highly fertile, relatively narrow, permanent beds. The beds are separated by narrow paths. Throughout Asia the centuries-old bed system is the principal method of vegetable growing. Interestingly, it was used in the West until the advent of the horse-drawn hoe, when plants were spaced farther apart to allow for cultivation between them. Gardeners also embraced the 'new' field system, inappropriate though it was for hand cultivation on a small scale, and the majority have clung to it ever since.

So the typical modern Western vegetable garden is a large plot where vegetables are grown in widely spaced rows. The whole plot is dug and manured (a waste of resources and energy), much of the soil is trodden in the course of cultivation and harvesting (destroying the soil structure), and weeds spring up in the spaces between plants.

Types of bed

In addition to the standard narrow bed, there are several types of bed designed to create exceptionally fertile ground: raised beds, deep beds, intensive beds, the Chinese flooded furrow system.

Raised beds

Most narrow beds gradually become raised slightly above ground level, simply through working in organic matter and not treading on the soil. Some, however, are purposely constructed so they are anything up to about 12 in (30 cm) above ground level. They are often tapered with sloping sides. Typically, the width across the top of a raised bed would be about 3 ft (90 cm), widening to 4 ft (120 cm) at the base. The top can be levelled flat or rounded.

Rounded beds have a special advantage in northern latitudes. When orientated in an east-west direction, the south-facing side and the top attract increased sunlight and radiation. Experiments at the University of Davis in California have demonstrated that a slope of 5 degrees is equivalent to the benefits of moving 30 miles south. Rounded beds also create a larger working surface.

Intensive and deep beds

These beds are prepared with exceptionally deep digging, working in a great deal of organic matter. (For further reading, see page 216.)

Advantages of the bed system

- All work is done from the paths, eliminating the need to tread on the soil.
- All manuring and all digging is concentrated on the precise area where plants will be grown, and not wasted on ground that will become paths.
- The two above factors, combined with the permanent nature of the beds, result in the soil becoming much more fertile than average garden soil.
- Because of the fertility plant roots penetrate more deeply, enabling them to withstand drought.
- Because of the fertility plants can be grown more closely, and overall yields and productivity are higher than normal.
- When equidistant spacing is used competition between plants for light, water and nutrients is minimized, leading to even and balanced growth.
- When mature most vegetables will form a leafy canopy covering the soil, which more or less prevents the growth and even the germination of weed seed. (Note that very narrow-leaved plants, such as onions, will not form a canopy.)
- Narrow beds are easily covered with long low polytunnels for protected cropping (see Protected cropping, page 166).
- The paths between the beds become hardened through use, so there is less soil splash and crops are cleaner. Well trodden paths seem to encourage worm activity and discourage weed growth.
- It is easier to work out a rotation system for a number of narrow beds rather than one large plot.
- *Raised* narrow beds warm up quickly and have improved drainage.

Chinese flooded furrow beds

Also known as 'island beds', these remarkable beds are typical of areas with very high rainfall. The beds are as much as 2 ft 6 in (75 cm) high, surrounded by water-filled ditches 1–2 ft (30–60 cm) deep and maybe as wide. They serve as drainage channels in the rainy season, but subsequently double as irrigation channels and paths, workers wading in them, barefoot or in wellies, to carry out the cultivation. Miniature 'boats', resembling floating trugs, are used to collect weeds, distribute manure and so on. The beds are remarkable for their intensive cultivation. In the summer months a network of canes is erected, straddling the ditches, for climbing crops such as beans and gourds. Not an inch is wasted, either at ground level or above.

Making a standard narrow bed

DIMENSIONS Beds can be any length though, if they are very long, there is the temptation to take short cuts by stepping over the middle rather than walking round, which leads to trodden edges. They are normally rectangular, but there is no reason why they should not be curved. Serpentine beds would look very attractive in a garden.

Width generally ranges from 3–5 ft (90–150 cm). The narrower the bed the easier it is to reach the centre from either side, but the higher the ratio of path to bed. It is largely a question of personal convenience. A factor worth considering is the dimension of any hoops you use for protective cropping. The more closely they match the bed width, the better.

PATHS Path width is also variable. The narrowest practical width is about a foot (30 cm). Occasional wider paths make it easier to handle wheelbarrows with wide loads. Paths can be bare earth, grassed and mown, concreted, or laid with gravel, stones, brick, wood bark, sawdust etc. In our own garden we have begun to lay

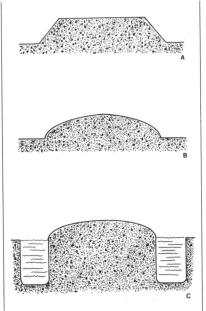

Types of raised bed: (a) flat-topped with angled sides, (b) rounded top, and (c) Chinese flooded furrow bed

old carpet on the paths. Disguised with a covering of sawdust, lawn mowings or reeds, it keeps down weeds very effectively and makes a firm walkway.

ORIENTATION If beds are orientated north to south, sunlight falls evenly on the surface. Where beds are orientated east to west the south-facing side receives more sunlight. As explained above, this has advantages with raised beds.

EDGES Narrow and raised beds are sometimes edged with tiles, brick, or timber. This gives a very neat effect, but there is the risk of pests being harboured under the wood.

PREPARING THE SOIL When the beds are initially being made, it is worth double-digging, i.e. working the soil to a depth of about two spades. The procedure is as follows:
- Mark out the boundaries of the bed with string.
- Working across the bed, remove a spade width, to the depth of a spade, across the bed, putting the soil in a barrow. Wheel it to the far end of the bed.
- Fork over the lower spit, breaking up any hard pan.
- Turn the soil from the adjacent

top spit into the first row. At the same time work in some bulky organic matter, trying to distribute it evenly through the soil.
- Continue to the far end of the bed in this way, filling the last row with the soil in the barrow.

Subsequent cultivation Once this has been done, single digging—forking over the top spit of soil only—should be all that is required in future. Digging can be done between harvesting one crop and sowing and planting the next, or when the ground is empty, in the autumn, or in the spring. As a general rule, heavy soils are best dug over in autumn: exposing heavy clods to frost helps to break them down. Light sandy soils, on the other hand, are best left undisturbed until the spring. Both benefit by being protected with a mulch of organic matter during the autumn.

WINTER RIDGING My own soil is a heavy clay, and I have found the narrow beds benefit from being ridged up in the autumn. To do this I fork the soil down the centre of the bed, then spade the soil from either side onto the central strip, making a ridge about a foot (30 cm) high. The ridge is then covered with manure or compost. Ridging the soil both keeps the bed well drained (level soil can become very waterlogged in winter, even if mulched) and exposes a greater area to the action of winter frost. It is a simple matter to break down the ridge in spring, just before the ground is required for sowing or planting.

RIDGE AND FURROW SYSTEMS In the past it was a common practice to ridge entire fields and vegetable beds. This was to overcome poor drainage, to increase the soil depth for long-rooted vegetables or to create miniature south-facing slopes for early spring crops. An old European practice, for example, was to sow early peas on the south side of a little ridge. The practice can still have a place in gardens with very poorly drained or shallow soil, and is quite frequently encountered in Asia. Make the ridges as for winter ridging above.

Making a raised bed

- Start by cultivating the whole area to a depth of 6–8 in (15–20 cm).
- Mark out the beds.
- Spade soil from the paths on to the bed area to raise it to the required level.
- Standing on the path, first on one side, then the other, rake up the soil from the sides to the middle to shape the bed.
- Firm the sides with the back of a spade.

As the structure and shape of a raised bed makes it awkward to dig deeply without damage, fertility is usually maintained by applying thick layers of mulch to the surface. (For further reading, see page 216.)

Rotation

The need for rotation

Some of the more common serious pests and diseases which live in the soil attack a range of plants within the same botanical group or family—but no others. If the sort of plants they attack are continually grown in the soil, the pests and diseases are liable to build up to serious proportions. If, however, there is a break of several years in which other crops are grown, their numbers will diminish and they will eventually disappear al-together. This is the main reason for rotating crops.

Unfortunately some of the more serious pests and diseases—clubroot and some nematodes (eelworm), for example—require a break of as much as six or seven years. Rotating over this period is obviously impractical in most small gardens but, wherever possible, rotate over at least a three- or four-year cycle, and avoid following any crop with another from the same group. Rotation is particularly important for organic growers, who cannot use chemicals to kill soilborne pests and diseases.

If you can work a green manure into the rotation to improve fertility, all to the good. (See also Soil fertility, Green manuring.) In China and other countries where rice is grown in flooded paddy fields, vegetable growing is often rotated with rice growing. The practice of flooding the fields as part of the rotation cycle is believed to kill many pests and diseases.

Principal rotation groups

Brassica (crucifer) family
All oriental and European brassicas, for example cabbage, cauliflower, kales, turnip, swede, radish; green manures such as mustard, rape and fodder radish.

Cucurbit family
Courgette, cucumber, gourds, luffa, melons, pumpkins, squashes.

Legume family
Peas and beans; green manures such as alfalfa (lucerne), fenugreek, clovers.

Onion family
Onions, leeks, garlic, Chinese chives.

Solanaceous family
Potatoes, tomatoes, peppers, aubergines.

Umbellifer family
Carrots, celery, mitsuba, parsley, parsnip.

Plant raising and cropping systems

The majority of vegetables are raised from seed. The few exceptions include corms and bulbs, such as garlic, and plants that are raised by division or cuttings. This may be necessary where the plants are sterile and don't set seed (as is the case with lemon grass), or because the seed is very variable and there is no knowing what you will get (e.g. globe artichokes). In some cases it is simply easier and quicker to raise the plants from cuttings or a rooted offshoot—Chinese box-thorn and watercress are two examples. These exceptions are dealt with where appropriate: this chapter is concerned with various aspects of raising plants from seed.

Seed

Seed storage

Seed is living material. Like all living things (sadly), it deteriorates with age, gradually losing its 'viability' or ability to germinate. The rate at which this happens depends on the species and how the seed is kept.

Seed is best stored in cool, dry conditions—the colder and drier the better. Seed firms store seed at low temperatures in a dry atmosphere. The ideal storage temperature is below freezing: for every 9°F (5°C) rise above zero the storage life of seed is halved.

Once purchased, keep seed packets in an airtight tin or jar in a cool room. (A domestic deep freeze is an excellent place to keep them.) Ideally, put a bag or dish of silica gel in the container to absorb mois-

ture, preferably cobalt-treated silica gel which turns from blue to pink when moist. When it has turned pink dry it out in a gentle oven until it returns to blue. A handful of cooked and re-dried rice grains in the jar will also absorb moisture.

Never store seed in a damp shed or steamy kitchen, and avoid buying seed which has been displayed in a hot shop window.

Today seed is often packed in hermetically sealed foil packets. These increase the life of the seed and should be used wherever possible. Once the packet is opened, however, the seed deteriorates normally.

Germination test Most seed remains viable for at least a couple of years. With older seed it is worth doing a quick germination test before sowing. Scatter a small sample on several layers of moist paper towelling on a saucer inside a polythene bag, or in a petri dish, putting it somewhere warm to germinate. Keep the paper moist: one way of doing so is to lay it over a moist sponge or small square of foam rubber. If there is no germination within about ten days, or germination is very erratic, start again with fresh seed.

Types of seed

Ordinary seed is known as 'naked' seed. Other forms are sometimes available.

Pelleted seed Each seed is coated with a protective layer, making it into a small ball. Developed to enable commercial growers to sow

seed precisely with mechanized seed drills, they are very easy to handle and sow. The coating breaks down in the soil, but it is important to keep the soil moist until the seeds have germinated, or they may fail to do so.

Chitted/pre-germinated seed Seed is sprouted to the stage when the tiny root appears, using the methods for testing germination suggested above. Seed companies despatch chitted seed in small containers, the seeds then being sown carefully in the normal way.

Chitting gives seed a head start. It is a useful practice where seeds need high temperatures to germinate—cucumbers, for example. It is also recommended for slow-germinating seeds which are liable to rot or become diseased if sown in cold soil. Once germinated, they will 'get away' in spite of adverse conditions. Peas and beans fit into this category.

In practice, large seeds are easier to chit and handle than small seeds. With small seeds take care not to damage the delicate root. The germinated seeds can be mixed with a gel, which acts as a carrier, and sown outdoors in the method known as 'fluid sowing'. (For further reading, see page 216.)

Seed tapes and seed sheets As a 'convenience' form of modern seed packaging, seeds are embedded in tapes or sheets, which disintegrate after sowing. They are sown in the normal way, lightly covered with soil, but, like pelleted seed, must be kept moist until they germinate. Their advantage lies in the seeds being well spaced out, so there is no overcrowding and no need for early thinning.

F1 hybrid seed Many of the most productive varieties of vegetables now being introduced are F1 hybrids. They are bred by crossing two pure-breeding inbred lines. The resulting plants have exceptional vigour and quality, and are very uniform, tending to mature at the same time. The involved process needed to produce F1 seeds means they are expensive, but in most cases worth the extra price. Seed should normally not be saved from F1 hybrids, as it will not come true. (However, it may be worth doing where you simply require a plentiful supply of seed for *seedling* crops.)

Sowing outdoors
Preparing the seedbed

To prepare the ground where seed is being sown, rake the surface to remove stones, break down lumps, and to work it into a crumb-like tilth. The secret is choosing the moment when the soil is 'just right' to work. Heavy soils must be allowed to dry out, so the soil does not stick to your feet and tools as you work. Light soils must be worked *before* they have dried to a powdery surface. Small seeds need to be sown in a soil with a fine tilth, but large seeds like peas and beans can be sown in a lumpier, coarser surface.

The seedbed can be prepared just before sowing, or several weeks in advance. This allows time for weed seeds to germinate: weed seedlings can then be hoed off before sowing the vegetable crop.

Soil temperature Soil temperature can be measured with a soil thermometer. Seed germinates at different temperatures, but few seeds germinate at soil temperatures below 41°F (5°C). It is *never* worth sowing in cold wet soil; the seed will rot or be attacked by pests or disease before it germinates. Better to wait until the soil has warmed up, or if necessary, to start seed off indoors. Soil can be warmed by covering the seedbed for several days in advance of sowing with plastic film, cloches,

or low polytunnels. Or make the sowing drill and cover it with a cloche to warm it up.

Sowing methods
Sowing in a drill

A drill is a narrow slit made in the soil with the corner of a hoe or blade of a trowel, to whatever depth is necessary for the seed. As a rough guide, seeds need to be sown at a depth of at least twice their diameter.

Spacing seed Sow seed thinly, spacing it evenly along the drill. Seed can also be 'station sown', sowing groups of three or four seeds together at regular intervals. If the plants will ultimately be spaced 8 in (20 cm) apart, station sow them in groups 4 in (10 cm) apart, thinning eventually to the required distance. Station sowing economizes with seed and makes thinning easier. A fast-growing crop, such as radishes, can be station sown between a slower-growing crop— making good use of the ground.

Thinning Seedlings generally grow very fast and need to be thinned to prevent them becoming overcrowded. Thin in stages so that seedlings are just not touching their neighbours. Water the soil beforehand if it is dry. Rather than pulling up the seedlings, which tends to damage the roots of the remaining adjacent seedlings, nip off unwanted seedlings just above ground level. Remove 'prunings' rather than leaving them on the ground, as their smell can attract the plant's pests.

Broadcast sowing

This method is used for crops which require little or no thinning, such as seedling and cut-and-come-again crops of pak choi and other oriental greens, which are cut at a young stage. The seedbed is prepared as above, and the seed is then scattered smoothly over the surface. To cover the seed rake it over first in one direction, then at right angles to the first direction. In hot weather cover the area sown with black plastic film to conserve moisture until the seed germinates, but remove the film as soon as there is any sign of the seedlings, or they will become pale and drawn. They can germinate within two days in hot weather.

It is difficult to weed broadcast areas, so only use this technique where the ground is weed-free. Or prepare the seedbed several weeks before it is required, hoeing off the first crop of weeds before sowing.

Wide drills

Wide drills can be seen as broadcasting on a small scale. It is a useful way of growing seedlings and cut-and-come-again crops, being easier to weed, sow and water than large broadcast areas. I like to make shallow parallel drills the width of a hoe, with adjacent drills as close together as possible. Sow seed evenly across the drills, covering them with soil from the edge of the drill. If sowing in dry weather water the drill as suggested for ordinary drills above. Seedlings sown in wide drills quickly 'spill over',

---

Sowing in adverse conditions

Sowing when the soil is very wet or very heavy
- Line the drill with a little peat, sand, or sowing or potting compost
- Sow the seed on this 'bed'.

Sowing in very dry conditions
- Make the drill, and water it very heavily without wetting the surrounding soil.
- Sow the seed in the wet soil, press it in, and cover it with *dry* soil from either side of the drill. The dry soil acts as a mulch preventing the soil moisture from evaporating. This keeps the seed moist until it germinates.

giving the impression that the whole area is sown, often forming very attractive patches in the process.

Seedbeds for transplanting
Traditionally, many vegetables were started in a 'seedbed' and later transplanted, when several inches high, to their permanent positions. This was partly to save space, as the ground they would eventually occupy could meanwhile be used for some other crop. Seed was sown in the seedbed in conventional drills, with the rows closer together than normal. Seedlings grown in seedbeds are known as 'bare root transplants'.

One disadvantage of seedbed sowing is that, except in very light sandy soils, the roots of the plants are likely to be damaged when being lifted for transplanting. And unless sown very thinly (and even the best of gardeners have an aversion to sowing thinly) the fast-growing plants are soon competing for light, water and nutrients and become straggly and drawn. On the whole I am convinced far better vegetables are grown by raising them in individual modules (see Sowing indoors, below.)

If a seedbed is used, site it in an open position, not in an out of the way, shaded corner as is sometimes done. The soil should be on the light side: it does not need to be rich. It is better to transfer seedlings from poor to rich soil, rather than *vice versa*. Sow as thinly as possible. Before transplanting water the soil if it is at all dry, to minimize the damage to roots.

Sowing indoors

The term 'sowing indoors' is used to describe any method of raising plants in a protected environment. This is usually in a greenhouse or cold frame, sometimes literally indoors on a window sill or in a warm spot, sometimes outdoors under some kind of shelter, but in a container rather than in the soil.

Sowing in wide parallel drills

Why sow indoors?
In cold climates plants are started indoors to get earlier crops and a longer growing season. This makes it possible to grow some of the tender crops which would not normally mature in a short or cool summer. Many of the warmth-loving oriental vegetables—basella, the gourds, amaranthus, water spinach—need to be started indoors if they are to succeed in cool temperate climates.

Plants which are liable to bolt if subjected to low temperatures in their early stages—oriental brassicas such as Chinese cabbage and pak choi for example—can be sown indoors to get them past their most vulnerable stage.

Occasionally, plants are started indoors to avoid high temperatures. Lettuces and onions will not germinate at temperatures above 75°F (24°C). If sown outdoors in summer upper soil temperatures can easily exceed 86°F (30°C), so preventing germination; indoors they can be kept cool during the critical germination period.

Indoor sowing techniques
Seeds are either:
• Sown in a container such as a seed tray or small pot in a light, porous 'sowing compost', and 'pricked out' into a larger container when large enough to handle, or
• Sown direct into 'modules' (see below) in which they remain until large enough to plant out, or pot up. They can also be sown in a seed

tray and later pricked out into modules.
Sowing compost Very confusingly, the term 'compost' is used both for the material made in a compost heap, and for the medium in which seeds are sown and grown. 'Compost heap' compost is too rich to be used in concentrated form for raising plants.

For sowing compost either use a commercial proprietary compost or mix up your own. A typical formula is a mixture of two parts of peat with one part of coarse sand. Or use sieved leaf mould, or sieved, light soil mixed with peat and sand. Currently most commercial composts are still peat-based, but in view of the concern about exhausting peat supplies, use alternatives, or soil-based composts, where available.

Heated propagators Seeds germinate faster if the soil temperature is at 55–60°F (13–16°C). In cool conditions raise the soil temperature by putting the container into a propagator after sowing. Domestic propagators range from units in which the heat is supplied by a light bulb beneath the seed tray, to electrically heated plates and coils placed beneath or within a seed tray. Propagators can be built on greenhouse staging using insulated electric cables buried in sand. Whatever system is used, the seed tray or container must be covered with a sheet or dome of plastic or glass to retain moisture and prevent the soil from drying out.

Sowing method

• Sow on moist compost evenly and thinly, seeds at least ½ in (1 cm) apart. Brassica seeds germinate and grow so fast they can be spaced as much as 1 in (2.5 cm) apart.

• Sow on the surface. Very small seeds do not need to be covered; larger seeds can be covered with a thin layer of fine compost or sharp sand, which seems to reduce the risk of seedlings being attacked by fungal diseases. As a general rule, seeds need to be covered by about twice their depth. Firm the soil after sowing.

PRICKING OUT When the seeds have germinated and are large enough to handle, or have developed their first true leaves, transplant individual seedlings into a larger container with richer, coarser compost, spacing them 1–2 in (2.5–5 cm) apart to allow them room to develop. At this stage most seedlings can tolerate a lower temperature, but it is important to have an airy, well lit place to accommodate them until they are ready to be planted outside or they will become lanky and drawn. They will, of course, take up much more space at this stage than when in the propagator.

For pricking out, either use a proprietary potting compost, or mix up your own. Use approximately 6 parts of good sieved garden soil, 3 parts peat*, 2 parts of sand, and work in some garden compost. The addition of dilute liquid manure (I use liquid seaweed for the purpose) will supply additional plant nutrients. (In practice many proprietary composts available are dual-purpose sowing and potting composts.) *See note on peat above.*

POTTING ON Most seedlings can be grown in this container until planted out. Plants which need to be held longer before planting out, or will eventually be grown in large pots or containers, may need to be replanted into individual pots of an intermediate size in potting compost.

HARDENING OFF The Japanese use an alternative method of hardening off. Seedlings are brushed back-wards and forwards with a piece of paper, cardboard, or a special brush. This is done for up to a minute a day, or sometimes simply twice a day twice in each direction, over the normal hardening off period. It saves moving the seedlings outdoors.

Don't feed seedlings before planting them out, as this makes them lush and soft. They can, in fact, also be hardened off by starving them a little.

Use of modules

The pricking out stage can be by-passed by raising plants in 'modules'. A module is any kind of small pot, container, cell, or soil block, filled with or made from dual purpose sowing and potting compost, in which the seeds are sown individually and grown until planted out.

The key factor with modules is that plants are able to develop individually within their 'cell' without competition. So they form excellent root systems, and there is the minimum root disturbance when they are planted out. It is an excellent method of producing top-quality plants. The main drawback is that, in the early stages when extra heat is required, they take up more space than seedlings sown in a small seed tray or pot. This is why seeds are sometimes sown in a seed tray and transplanted into a module.

TYPES OF MODULE

Moulded plastic and polystyrene cellular trays (cell packs) These are pre-formed units with tapered holes, anything from ½–2 in (1–5 cm) diameter, which are filled with compost.

Jiffy 7's These are compressed peat blocks encased in netting, which expand when soaked in water. The plant roots grow out through the netting.

Soil or peat blocks Potting compost is compressed into discrete blocks with a blocking tool which makes an indentation in the top in which the seed is sown. Block sizes range from tiny 'miniblocks' about ½ in (1.25 cm) square, to blocks 2 in (5 cm) in diameter. It is easiest to make blocks with a proprietary blocking compost which contains an additive making it adhesive, but with skill blocks can be made from ordinary soil- and peat-based composts.

Small pots Any small pot, made of clay, peat, plastic film or any other material, can be used as a module. People sometimes make their own open-ended pots out of newspaper or papier mâché, or use pieces of cardboard. The central cardboard spool of a toilet roll can be cut into two 'modules'!

Divided seed trays Seed trays can also be divided into sections with interlocking plastic dividers, so giving each plant its own 'compartment'. Makeshift dividers can be

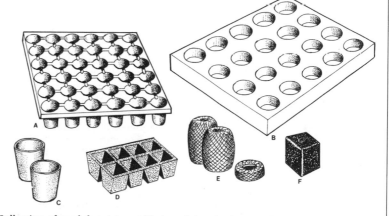

Collection of modules: (a) moulded modular plastic tray, (b) polystyrene cellular tray, (c) small pots, (d) fibre pots, (e) expanded and compact 'Jiffy 7's', and (f) soil block

made of plastic or cardboard.

SOWING IN MODULES Normally one only wants one germinated seedling in each module. To achieve this, either sow one seed in the module, or sow several seeds, nipping out all but the strongest once they have germinated. (This requires willpower. It is terribly tempting to leave several seedlings rather than 'waste' seed—but this defeats the purpose of raising in modules.) If doubtful about the viability of the seed, do a germination test first (see page 150).

Large seeds are easily sown individually in the modules, but it is harder with small seed. They can be pushed carefully off a piece of paper. An alternative method is to put the seeds on a saucer, and to use the moistened tip of a piece of broken glass to pick them up individually. They drop off when the glass is touched on the compost.

Multi-sowing in modules There are a few cases where several seeds can be sown together in a block and left unthinned, later planting out 'as one', though at wider spacing than normal. They are unaffected by the competition from close neighbours. Multi-block sowing can be done successfully with onions, leeks, round beetroot, round-rooted carrots, and with brassicas which will be harvested young. This enables them to be planted very rapidly.

Planting

When planting or transplanting, aim to disturb the plant's roots as little as possible. Water the seedbed or modules several hours in advance, and if the soil is dry, water the ground being planted. It is particularly important to water any modules or plants in *peat-based* compost: if it dries out in the ground before the roots have started to grow, it can become almost impossible to re-wet it.

Wherever possible plant in cool, dull conditions, preferably in the evening. handle bare root transplants by their leaves, rather than by the roots, and in most cases plant so that the lower leaves of the

plant are just above ground level. It is good practice to water and mulch plants immediately after planting. In very hot weather plants may benefit from being shaded (make a cone out of newspaper) until they have got established. With leafy plants such as spinach, the leaves can be cut back to within a couple of inches after planting, to help them 'get away'. On commercial holdings where ground is constantly watered, soil blocks are sometimes simply placed on the surface. The roots soon grow out of them and into the ground. Where watering is intermittent they are better planted in the soil, the top of the block just below soil level.

In the West planting is mainly done with a trowel. I was surprised in China to see that most planting was done with a 'vegetable planting knife' which looked uncommonly like a meat cleaver. A slit was cut in the soil, the plant slipped in, and the soil around the plant firmed with the handle of the knife. I brought one back, and have found it a good tool (see illustration on page 157).

Spacing As explained earlier (see The bed system, page 147), plants were traditionally grown relatively closely spaced in rows which were spaced far apart. However it is more productive, especially where growing in the bed system, to abandon rows and grow plants evenly

spaced each way. Convert standard recommended spacings to equidistant spacing by taking an average, i.e. if plants were spaced 6 in (15 cm) apart in rows 12 in (30 cm) apart, space them 9 in (23 cm) apart each way. When mature, plants want to be just about touching their neighbours.

Saving seed

Most seed crops need dry weather when maturing, so that the seed pods develop well and are disease-free. In areas with wet, unreliable summers saving your own seed is something of a gamble and it is hard to match the quality of bought seed. However, as there is still restricted choice with some of the oriental plants, it may be useful to save from your best plants, and hence to acquire seed more closely suited to your climate. Or you may want a plentiful supply of seed for cut-and-come-again sowings. Some commercial seed packets have far too little seed for this purpose!

In many cases it is necessary to isolate plants from others in the same genus to avoid cross pollination. Any oriental brassicas (crucifers) which are members of the *Brassica rapa* genus, for example Chinese cabbage, pak choi, mizuna greens, and turnip, will all cross pollinate. They will not however

---

Guidelines for saving seed

- Always save from the best plants, never from diseased plants, or plants which have bolted prematurely.
- Never save from F1 hybrids, which will not breed true.
- If necessary, isolate plants from others in the same genus to avoid cross pollination (see above).
- Keep plants well watered when flowering and when the seed heads are forming, but cease watering when the seed pods are turning from green to yellow.
- Stake or tie tall plants, to prevent them falling on the ground and becoming soiled.
- Where possible, allow the seed pods to dry naturally on the plant. If they are in danger of being spoilt by rain, or eaten by birds, pull them up and hang them upside down under cover, say in a greenhouse, to dry off completely. Place newspaper beneath to catch any falling seed.
- When the pods are brittle shake out the seed onto newspaper, and keep it in cool dry conditions, in a jar or paper envelope.

cross with members of *Brassica oleracea*, which include ordinary cabbage, cauliflowers, and Chinese broccoli. Any variety of radish is likely to cross pollinate with other radish varieties. For practical purposes in a garden context 'isolation' means growing things at least 100 yards (90 m) apart, with a couple of hedges between.

Cropping systems

Cut-and-come-again seedling crops

Many leafy crops will grow again after being cut, giving two or three, occasionally more, cuts from one sowing. It is a highly productive form of cropping—invaluable where space is short. Moreover, young seedling leaves are very tasty, fresh and appetizing looking and nutritious, often with twice the vitamin content of mature leaves.

Seedling crops should be grown fairly densely, so are best sown in wide drills or broadcast (see page 151). Try to sow at a rate of approximately ½ oz per sq. yd (12 g/sq. m). (See also Saladini, page 47.). The first cut can be made when seedlings are anything from 1–3 in (2.5–7.5 cm) high, using scissors or a knife. If the seedlings are to regrow they must be cut *above* the first, tiny seed leaves. This does not matter if the crop is only being cut once. Cut ¼–1 in (0.5–2.5 cm) above soil level.

Being grown so closely, seedlings require plenty of moisture, and should be watered if there is a likelihood of drying out. Seedling crops tend to run to seed fairly rapidly in hot weather, quickly becoming coarse and, in some cases, hot-flavoured. On the whole they are best value i) in spring and early summer, ii) for quick maturing, late crops in autumn, and iii) in winter under cover. In this case they can either be sown in the ground or in boxes.

Cut-and-come-again: semi-mature plants

Most of the oriental brassicas, and a number of other oriental vegeta-

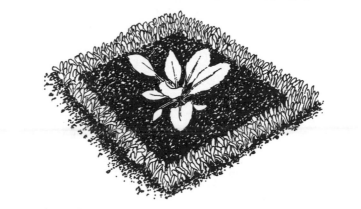

Intercropping seedlings around brassica plants

bles such as shungiku and amaranthus, have a remarkable capacity to regrow if cut at a semi-mature stage, i.e. when the plants are a substantial size but before hearting up or becoming fully mature. Cut them about an inch (2.5 cm) above ground level.

This form of cropping is very productive. It tends to delay bolting and so gives a constant supply of pickings over a long period. It also increases a plant's resistance to frost. I have found that a smallish, 'cut back' plant and stump will survive low temperatures which would have killed a fully developed leafy plant. This is most valuable for brassicas grown during the winter months under cover. It enables them to *survive* winter, albeit in a dormant state if temperatures are low; they then burst into renewed growth very early in spring, providing leaf when vegetables are most scarce.

Chinese cabbage can be given 'cut-and-come-again' treatment at both a mature and semi-mature stage, as the stump will resprout after a mature head is cut. Where a plant seems unlikely to form a head (perhaps because it is late in the season or it is showing a tendency to bolt), cut the existing leaves an inch (2.5 cm) above ground level. The plant will normally resprout, producing a useful crop of fairly crisp leaf, though not a dense head, over a long period.

The Rodale trials in the United States successfully grew Chinese

cabbage in winter in their solar frames, spacing plants 8 in (20 cm) apart, harvesting the outer leaves but leaving the five inner leaves to grow.

Intercropping

Intercropping is a space-saving measure where two crops are grown in close proximity, normally one being harvested some time before the other. On the whole, intercropping is most practical where crops are grown in widely spaced rows, but it can be practised in closely spaced bed systems. The best candidates for intercropping are slow- and fast-growing crops, or tall- and low-growing crops.

Seedling intercrops Seeds from different crops are sometimes sown together, though harvested at different stages. The Chinese, for example, mix carrots and pak choi. The pak choi is harvested young, leaving the carrots to develop more slowly.

Fast-growing seedlings which will be harvested as a seedling crop can be sown around and between fairly widely spaced brassicas when the latter are first planted. Sow in drills 2–3 in (5–8 cm) wide, depending on the available space. Seedling crops of oriental brassicas, mizuna greens, pak choi, non-heading Chinese cabbage, can be grown this way, as well as salad seedlings such as salad rocket, or ordinary radish. There may be time for no more than one, or at the most two, cuts before the space is required for the primary brassica crop.

Double cropping within rows Similarly, fast-growing seedlings, radishes or turnips can be sown between slower-maturing station-sown plants (see page 151). The classic combination is fast-germinating radish between slow-germinating parsnips.

Relay systems Young plants can be planted alongside a maturing crop, ready to 'take over' as soon as the maturing crop is harvested; or fast-growing crops can be planted between rows and harvested before the main crop develops fully. Many examples of this type of culture are found in China. I noticed a raised island bed in Guangzhou with a lettuce crop maturing on the outer edges, two wide rows of peas recently sown beyond the lettuce rows, and two rows of choy sum planted down the centre of the bed between the peas. The lettuces and the choy sum would be harvested before the peas would require the whole of the bed.

Tall and dwarf combinations Low-growing plants can sometimes be grown among, beneath, or alongside tall or climbing plants. Sweet corn is one of the most useful from this point of view, as its foliage is not dense so light reaches plants beneath. I often underplant it with mizuna greens, which will continue to crop long after the corn has been harvested and uprooted. (See illustration on page 8.) There are many other possibilities.

Where gourds and climbing beans are trained up tepees or rows

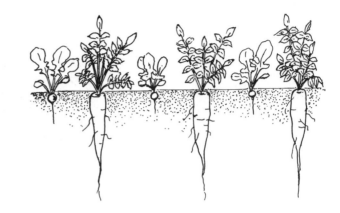

Double cropping in rows: fast-growing radish sown between slower-maturing parsnips

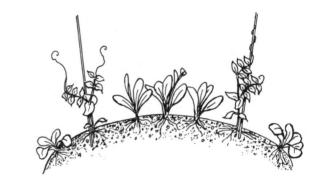

Intercropping: Chinese relay system. *From outside to centre*: lettuce, peas and choy sum

of intersecting canes, a quick-growing 'catch crop' can be taken from the central ground between the canes before it is completely shaded by the climbing crop. Dwarf crops can also be grown at the foot of climbing crops. Plants which benefit from light shade in hot summer conditions, such as peas, can be grown in their shade. (For further reading on Chinese inter-cropping, see Appendix page 216.)

Weeds, mulching and watering

Weed control

Weeds are fast growing, vigorous plants. If allowed to get out of hand they will smother vegetables and prevent their healthy growth by competing for water, nutrients, air and space. They also harbour pests. But they have their good points. Many, such as nettles, make excellent compost; several are edible (see Herbs and Wild Plants, page 127); many have medicinal uses; and in China many weeds are fed to livestock. 'Chickweed' (*Stellaria media*) is fed to rabbits and geese, its Chinese name being 'gosling weed'. *Plus ça change. . . .*

Types of weed

Perennial weeds These remain in the soil from one year to the next. Typical perennials have deep tap roots, or creeping runners which spread with alacrity, or roots which can resprout from small fragments left in the soil.

Annual weeds These are the commonest garden weeds, germinating, flowering, seeding, dying within a year, in some cases having several generations a year. Most are prolific seeders, producing maybe tens of thousands of seeds in a season. Seed can remain viable for many years if undisturbed in the cool depths of the soil, ready to germinate when exposed by cultivation to light and moisture. This explains the huge crop of weeds which appear when neglected land is first dug over. Rest assured it will diminish with time.

Oriental hand tools: (a) Japanese 'hori hori' knife, (b) Taiwanese combined rake and hoe, (c) Taiwanese banana knife, and (d) Chinese vegetable planting knife

Controlling perennials

Most perennials can be eliminated by digging them out. Hard work initially, but once it is done it is done. Try to remove every piece of root from perennials with easily regenerating roots such as bindweed, ground elder and couch grass—to name the trio I am plagued with. If the weeds are still triumphant and you don't want to use chemical weedkillers to eliminate them, mulch the affected area with heavy duty black plastic or old carpeting. You may have to leave this in place for as long as twelve months before the roots die off.

Never put the roots of perennial weeds on a compost heap unless you have killed them off first by allowing them to dry up in the sun. Burn them instead.

Controlling annuals

The important thing with annual weeds is to prevent them from going to seed. Provided this is done, the 'bank' of weed seed in the soil will be eroded gradually every year that a garden is cultivated—unless of course it is replenished by using weed-ridden compost. As mentioned earlier, where plants are grown on the bed system at equidistant spacing, their leaves eventually form a canopy over the soil, suppressing weed development. If weeds *have* gone to seed, confine them to the bonfire rather than the compost heap, unless your heap is large enough to reach and maintain high temperatures. (See Soil fertility, Compost bins, page 142.)

However, it is necessary to weed:
● Before the canopy stage is reached.
● Between narrow leaved plants such as onions which will not form a canopy.
● Where plants are widely spaced, and between drills.

On a small scale weeding can be done by hand, or with some kind of hoe which will cut off or uproot the weeds. Everyone has their favourite hoe: just choose the type you feel most comfortable with. My personal favourites are a small, swan-necked onion hoe, and a Taiwanese hand hoe with a 4-in

(10-cm) wide blade. One side of the blade is serrated and can be used as a rake, the other is a straight hoeing blade—ideal for making wide drills. The dagger-like Japanese 'hori hori' knife, which also has one serrated edge, is another excellent weeding tool.

Hoeing is useful where there is a large area to clear of annuals, or around very small plants. However, there is always a risk of damaging the roots, and, in dry conditions, hoeing breaks the 'crust' on the soil and increases the moisture loss. In the long term, mulching the soil is a more productive and beneficial method of controlling weeds and keeping ground weed-free.

Mulching

A mulch is any material laid on the surface of the soil, be it organic material such as straw or compost which eventually rots into the soil, or modern plastic films.

An aversion to bare soil is a common thread running through traditional Oriental methods of cultivation and twentieth-century organic growing in the West. In China and Japan mulched vegetable crops are a common sight, utilizing a wide range of materials from rotting weeds to rice straw to plastic films. The most productive organic gardens in the West are usually deeply mulched. In my experience oriental vegetables respond well to being kept mulched: I am always happiest to see mine in mulched rather than bare soil.

Organic mulches

MULCHING MATERIALS Many different materials are used for mulching; some are a better source of nutrients than others and contribute more to soil fertility. Others are more effective as weed suppressors or to conserve moisture. Most organic mulches should be applied in a fairly well rotted state, or nitrogen is taken from the soil in the early stages of decomposition. This is particularly true of materials derived from wood—such as sawdust and shredded bark—

Benefits of mulches

- Suppress weeds and prevent weed germination.
- Conserve soil moisture by preventing evaporation.
- Protect the soil surface during heavy rain and minimize erosion.
- Lessen compaction when the soil is walked upon.
- Add organic matter and nutrients to the soil.
- Insulate the soil, keeping it cooler in summer and warmer in winter.
- Encourage earthworm activity and soil life. (Rather surprisingly, earthworm activity seems to increase both with organic mulches and plastic film mulches.)
- Lessen the need to cultivate, sometimes eliminating it completely.
- Deter pests. There is evidence that shiny and chequered plastic mulches deter aphids and some other insects. (See Pests and Disease, page 172.)
- Help to control diseases by keeping plants cleaner.
- Keep fruiting crops such as tomatoes and courgettes clean.

Organic mulching materials

Mulches which increase soil fertility

Garden compost
Well rotted animal manure
Spent mushroom compost
Wilted comfrey (*Symphytum sp.*)
Well rotted lawn mowings
Well rotted straw
Seaweed
Salt grass, salt hay or salt meadow grass (*Spartium patens*).
 (This marsh plant is used in the United States, either whole or shredded.)

Mulches which control weeds and conserve moisture but have little nutrient value

Newspaper laid several layers thick
Cardboard
Old carpets and mats
Pulverized and shredded bark
Sawdust

---

which are generally unsuitable for vegetable beds unless a couple of seasons old.

WHEN TO MULCH A mulch always maintains the *status quo* of the soil. The ideal time to mulch is when the soil is moist but warm. Never mulch when the soil is very cold, very dry, or very wet. In spring wait until it has warmed up to a temperature of at least 42°F (6°C), but mulch before it has dried out completely.

With plants of a reasonable size it is sound practice to water and mulch when planting. If necessary the mulch can be built up around the stems of plants as they grow. Where seed has been sown, wait until the seedlings are several inches high before mulching, or they may be swamped. (Birds can cause disarray in a neatly laid mulch, scattering it all over young seedlings.)

DEPTH OF MULCH On the whole, the deeper the mulch the more effective it will be: aim for at least 1–2 in (2.5–5 cm) depth. To suppress weeds completely an organic mulch probably needs to be at least 4 in (10 cm) deep, but it is relatively easy to pull out any weeds which make their way through a more shallow mulch.

Plastic mulching films

Various films are used to control weeds, to warm up the soil before sowing or planting in spring, and to conserve moisture. They may also help to control the spread of disease. Many types are now available, each best for a specific purpose. (For perforated films, 'floating cloches' or 'row covers', and fibrous films see also Protected cropping, page 167.)

When to mulch

(See Organic mulches, above.)
HOW TO MULCH
Anchorage Films must be anchored well. Gaps at the edges and large planting holes let in wind, which can rip or lift the films. In warm weather film softens and can 'creep' over plants, damaging them in the process. The following are two common methods.

- Lay the film over the bed or areas to be covered, make slits several inches deep with a spade or trowel in the soil along the sides and edges of the bed, and bury the film edges in the slits. Push back the soil to keep them in place. This is probably the neatest and most effective method.
- Lay the film flat over the area, and anchor the outstretched edges with bricks, clods, pieces of timber etc., placed at least 3 ft (90 cm) apart.

It is much easier to lay films over slightly domed beds, which have the added advantage of not puddling after rain.
Sowing and planting Films can be laid either *before* or *after* sowing or planting. In most cases it is easiest to lay and anchor the film first. Once this is done make holes or slits in the film with a knife or the point of a dibber at whatever

---

Types of plastic film

Black unperforated film
- Suppresses weeds; helps retain moisture and warmth in the soil; does little to warm up the soil.
- Fairly thin film 150–200 gauge (40–50 microns) normally used.

Black perforated film
- Allows some rainfall into the soil; used for weed suppression on perennial or long term crops.
- Fairly thin film 150–200 gauge (40–50 microns) normally used.

Clear film
- Warms up the soil; to some extent helps retain moisture; does little to suppress weeds.
- Lightweight film 60–150 gauge (15–38 microns) normally used.

Opaque white film
- Reflects light up to plant; used to mulch fruiting vegetables such as tomatoes, peppers and melons; suppresses weeds to some extent. (In my experience oriental brassicas grown under cover in winter appear healthier if mulched with opaque white film.)
- Films about 280 gauge (70 microns) normally used.

Black and white film
- Combined film: the black underside suppresses weeds; the white top surface reflects light on to the fruit, accelerating ripening. Also warms soil.
- 340 gauge (48 microns) film normally used.

Chequered and shiny films
Used primarily to deter aphids; may also suppress weeds and conserve moisture.

Brown film
Combines the properties of black and transparent film; warms up the soil like transparent film; suppresses weeds.

Thermal film
High quality films. Warm soil, suppresses weeds. 280 gauge (70 microns).

---

spacing is required and sow through them. This method is most suitable for relatively large seeds which are spaced fairly far apart. Smaller seeds are best raised separately and transplanted as young plants. To plant through the film, make a criss-cross cut in the film no larger than is necessary to edge the plant through.

When film is laid over a *sown* crop slits or holes must be made in the film as soon after germination as possible to allow the seedlings to emerge. Where transparent films are used, seed may be sown in the bottom of shallow furrows, which allows seedlings to grow an inch or so before brushing against the film. For some reason lettuce seed does not grow well if sown in furrows. Where covering a *planted* crop roll the film over the crop, cut slits or holes in the film where appropriate to allow the plants through, and then anchor the film in either of the methods given above.

On a large scale film laying, coupled with seed drilling or planting, can be completely mechanized.

WATERING MULCHED CROPS If it proves necessary to water mulched crops, water carefully through the planting hole. Alternatively, place perforated seep hose beneath the film when it is laid. (See Watering guidelines, below.)

Plastic films tend to attract slugs, so watch out for them. (See also Pests and Disease, page 172.)

DISPOSING OF PLASTIC FILM Wherever possible avoid burning scrap plastic, as poisonous gases are given off in the process. It can be buried or laid beneath paths where it slowly degrades. Photodegradable films, which eventually break down in the light, are gradually becoming available. With currently available films breakdown is not guaranteed in areas with unpredictable sunshine. Nor do film edges buried in the soil break down.

Stone, gravel and sand mulches

In various parts of the world with hot climates stone, sand and gravel have been used very effectively to mulch vegetables, primarily as a means of conserving moisture. In southern Spain stone mulching is done inside polytunnels. The stones absorb heat during the day which is radiated at night.

Watering

The amount of watering necessary depends on the soil, the local rainfall and, of course, the crop in question. Many of the oriental vegetables thrive on plenty of water: a feature of Asian vegetable growing is the constant irrigation. In general, watering tends to encourage *leafy* growth, and fast-growing but shallow-rooted oriental brassicas are typical of vegetables which respond to plenty of water, and may need watering if optimum growth and maximum yields are to be obtained. Closely planted crops need more watering than widely spaced plants.

Watering guidelines

Aside from the work involved in watering, it makes sense to minimize the need for watering. Constant watering washes nutrients out of the soil, and encourages plants to develop shallow root systems near the surface, rather than a deep root system which will sustain them in periods of water shortage. Overwatering fruiting plants like tomatoes can diminish the flavour.

As mentioned earlier, working plenty of organic matter into the soil and keeping the surface mulched are measures which help to conserve moisture in the soil. Light soils, which dry out faster than heavy soils, particularly benefit from mulching.

Soil becomes wet layer by layer, and until the top layer is saturated, the soil beneath remains dry. The implication is that heavy, thorough, albeit infrequent watering is far more beneficial than frequent but light watering. The exception to this rule is newly planted transplants: these need frequent, light watering until they are established and have developed a good root system. The same is true of very shallow-rooted plants. In hot weather water in the early evening to minimize evaporation.

Plants should be watered as gently as possible. If watering with a can, use a rose when plants are small. Perforated plastic hose (such as 'layflat tubing' or 'seephose') is an excellent system for vegetables. The hose is attached to a tap or ordinary hose and laid between plants, water percolating slowly out of the holes. It can be laid permanently between vegetables, down the centre of a narrow bed, for example. It is easily moved from one part of the garden to another. Where automatic sprinklers are used, adjust them so the spray droplets are fine rather than coarse.

CRITICAL PERIOD All plants require moisture to germinate, and when first planted. Many plants have a *critical* point during the subsequent growing period when lack of watering is most damaging. Where watering is a problem, concentrate resources on these periods.

WATERING IN GREENHOUSES Greenhouses tend to dry out rapidly, and if the top ½ in (1.25 cm) of soil is dry, should be watered. In cool weather and during the winter months water in the morning, so that the foliage has time to dry before nightfall. This helps to prevent disease.

Watering guidelines

Leafy crops
E.g. brassicas, salads, spinachy greens
• Require moisture throughout growth; in hot weather benefit from 2–3 galls per sq. yd (11–16 l/sq. m) per week.
• Critical period: 10–20 days before maturity. One very heavy watering at this stage will to some extent compensate for lack of water earlier. The more closely leafy crops are grown, the more water they require.

Fruiting vegetables
E.g. peas and beans, cucurbits, gourds, tomatoes
• Need a steady supply of moisture throughout growth. Water sufficiently to prevent the soil drying out.
• Critical periods: when flowering, when fruit is setting; when the fruits start to swell. At these stages heavy watering (4 galls/sq. yd/week (22 l/sq. m) results in much higher yields.

Root crops
E.g. radish, turnips
• Only need enough water for steady growth during the early stages: overwatering encourages leaf rather than root growth.
• Once the roots are starting to swell they can be watered moderately if the soil is dry. Excess watering after a dry period can cause the roots to crack.

Protected cropping

'Protected cropping' and 'growing under cover' are terms used to describe methods of growing plants in a sheltered environment. It embraces greenhouses, 'walk-in' plastic film tunnels (polytunnels), frames, cloches, low level polytunnels or row covers, and various types of film mulches. Even the use of windbreaks can be considered a form of protective cropping.

The benefits of protection

In northern latitudes, cool climates, and in high and exposed areas some means of protection is of enormous benefit to vegetable growers. It enables them to increase their yields and quality, to extend the growing season (sometimes by as much as two months in the year), and to extend the range of crops they can grow successfully. Where oriental vegetables are concerned the value of 'protection' in cool temperate conditions is concentrated in two areas:

Summer With protection the more tender, warmth-loving crops, such as amaranthus, ipomea (water spinach), and the various oriental gourds, can be grown in cool climates. Even so, don't expect them to romp as they would in a really hot climate.

Winter With protection the potential of the hardy oriental brassicas can be maximized during the winter period. *Not only do they tolerate low temperatures, but they grow well in the low light intensities of the winter months.* Moreover, under these conditions the leaves and stems are often thinner, more tender and less fibrous than when grown outdoors in summer, making them among the most delicate of the vegetables available in winter.

Extensive trials into protected winter cropping at the Rodale Research Center in Pennsylvania, northern USA, concluded that the oriental cold season vegetables were *far* better value than traditional vegetables (spinach, winter lettuce) for this purpose. My own experience confirms this. I have often marvelled at the green jungle of oriental vegetables in my *unheated* polytunnel in winter, when the garden outside was almost bare and the ground frozen solid or covered with snow.

The effects of protection

Temperature

Plants normally start growing when day temperatures rise above 43°F (6°C) in spring, and stop when they fall below that point in autumn—the number of days between being known as 'growing days'. (In England the number of growing days ranges from about 250 to 300.) Under glass or plastic film daytime temperatures rise dramatically when the sun shines, even in winter, increasing the number of 'growing days'. This means that growing can continue at least three weeks later in autumn and start three weeks earlier in spring, and in addition there will be days in mid-winter when temperatures under cover are warm enough for plants to continue growing.

Summer temperatures, of course, are also raised under cover. This is not always an advantage, as insects multiply much faster at high temperatures.

The rate at which heat is lost at night is slowed down under cover, but more so under glass than under plastic.

Frost

Vegetables can be grouped according to their response to frost:

Tender Completely killed by frost, e.g. gourds, amaranthus.

Frost susceptible The leafy parts are damaged and become inedible, though the plant itself may survive, e.g. many varieties of lettuce, less hardy varieties of Chinese cabbage and pak choi.

Some frost tolerance The whole plant survives light to moderate frosts, but the leaves will often become tougher and inedible unless cooked, e.g. edible chrysanthemum, hardier forms of pak choi, some varieties of Chinese cabbage.

Considerable frost tolerance Plants survive several degrees of frost without damage, though they will not of course *grow* in frosty weather, e.g. oriental mustard greens, komatsuna.

With all vegetables on the borderline of frost tolerance or liable to be damaged to some extent by frost, it is the combination of frost *and wind* which is lethal.

Tender, frost-susceptible and frost-tolerant vegetables can only be protected from heavy frosts by being grown in heated greenhouses or heavily insulated structures, such as solar greenhouses or solar frames.

Glass and plastic film offer only slight protection from frost: indeed the air temperature on cold clear nights can be as low under cover as outside, though soil temperatures will probably be higher. However, they give protection from wind, so preventing the lethal wind + frost combination. Frost penetrates less deeply under cover, and does not remain so long in the soil. Fibrous films laid over crops will give protection against 2–4 degrees of frost. (See Film covers, page 167.)

The value of glass and plastic cover lies in *minimizing* the damage done by frost, in enabling frost-susceptible plants to survive so that they can start into growth when temperatures rise and allowing frost-tolerant plants to grow more lusciously.

SPRAYING TO MINIMIZE FROST DAMAGE
Frost damage is mainly caused by the rapid thawing of frosted plants. The damage can be lessened by spraying plants with water the following morning, before the sun reaches them. This allows them to thaw more slowly.

Wind

The benefits of protecting plants from winter gales and cold spring winds are obvious: less risk of frost damage, less wear and tear on the leaves from wind-borne grit and so on. Wind damage is particularly important with any crops eaten raw. No-one wants to chew tough, weatherbeaten leaves.

What is less appreciated is the gain from protection under 'normal' conditions. Experiments have shown that by protecting plants from even light winds yields are increased by a remarkable 20–30 per cent—more than they would be by increasing fertilizers or water to their optimum levels. So virtually all vegetables will give higher yields in sheltered conditions. In coastal regions there is the additional bonus of protecting plants from the damaging effect of salt spray carried in the wind.

Heavy rain and hail

Heavy rain and hail can cause a lot of damage, washing seeds out of the soil, flattening seedlings, damaging leaves, panning the soil surface. Plants grown under cover are spared such damage. In parts of

Asia which experience monsoon rains, vegetables are often sheltered in the fields with overhead nets, or temporary low tunnels covered with netting or fibrous film. Even in my garden in England we have lost so many seedlings in spring hailstorms that we now harden them off beneath a shelter made with windbreak netting.

In winter heavy rain can physically destroy the structure of the soil (unless it is mulched), and will also wash nutrients out of the soil. It is far easier to build up and preserve good soil structure in the protected environment of a greenhouse or some form of protected cropping.

Windbreaks

In China and Japan windbreaks are very much a feature of vegetable growing—especially off-season. Autumn- and spring-planted beds are often protected from the prevailing wind with fences made from reeds or bamboo canes, or mats of sorghum or corn straw. These fences may be erected at an angle over the crop to increase the protection: the angle may be changed according to the season, the direction of the wind, or the angle of the sun.

In any cold or exposed vegetable garden it pays to erect, or grow, some kind of windbreak. The ideal windbreak is 50 per cent solid. This allows the wind to filter through gently. With a completely solid windbreak such as a wall the wind swoops over, creating an area of destructive turbulence on the leeward side.

A windbreak is considered effective for a distance roughly six times its height. So in very exposed gardens 3-ft (1-m high) barriers can be erected at 18-ft (6-m) intervals across the garden, the crops being grown in the strips between them.

Hedges, lath fences, wattle hurdles, and windbreaks made by battening windbreak netting to posts are the most popular forms of windbreak in gardens. The draw-

back to hedges is that they compete for nutrients and moisture in the soil so plants cannot be grown too near them. Supports for net windbreaks need to be very substantial: they take terrific force when strong winds are blowing.

Urban gardens sometimes fall victim to the unpleasant, destructive draughts which funnel through the gaps between tall buildings, or between house and garage. Where this is the case, erect a windbreak which will extend across the gap and several feet beyond the gap on either side. This will 'trap' winds which sneak round the corner.

Protective structures

Heated greenhouses
Heated greenhouses are a luxury outside the scope of this book, though anyone fortunate enough to have a heated greenhouse can put it to excellent use, increasing the productivity of oriental brassicas in winter and the range of vegetables grown in summer.

Solar greenhouses
In northern latitudes there is now considerable interest in the use of solar greenhouses in winter. Skilfully designed to make maximum use of winter sunlight, they enable high temperatures to be reached during the day, and by releasing stored energy they allow minimum temperatures to be kept above freezing at night and in cold periods. In good solar greenhouses the number of winter growing days can be double that of a conventional greenhouse or polytunnel. Some are equipped with a means of back-up heating.

The degree of success depends on the design and construction of the greenhouse and on the weather, but there is no doubt they have great potential for growing useful crops of oriental greens in winter in cold climates. The Rodale Research Center has carried out a lot of work in this area. (For further reading see Appendix, page 215.)

Features of solar greenhouses

While there are many designs, the following are common features:

- Often built as lean-tos on existing buildings.
- Built in an east–west orientation, facing south, as most winter sunlight falls on south walls.
- The south-facing side is high pitched, at angles of between 45 and 69 degrees to the horizontal, to catch low-angled winter light. In summer these angles reflect some light away, so helping to prevent overheating. The south-facing side is sometimes curved.
- The south-facing side is usually double glazed. Various patented materials are used for the purpose.
- The north, back wall is painted with high gloss white paint, or mirrored, or covered with aluminium foil or foil covered cardboard to reflect light onto plants.
- North, east and west walls are heavily insulated, for example with 5 in (13 cm) fibreglass, or several inches of polystyrene. In some cases the foundation is also insulated. Good insulation is the key to preventing heat losses through cracks.
- Insulating curtains are used to cover the glazing, internally or externally, at night or in cold weather. Thermal screens or curtains are sometimes lowered over individual beds at night.
- Tanks of water, and/or 12 in (30 cm) deep layers of gravel on the floor, are examples of 'thermal mass' used to collect and store energy during the day and release it at night.

INSULATION METHODS: EAST AND WEST
Good insulation is one of the keys to making winter greenhouses more efficient, whether heated or unheated. Insulating materials, such as bubble insulation film, can be attached to the inner or outer surfaces of greenhouses, to keep warm air in and reduce the chill from cold wind. Where used on heated greenhouses, heating costs can be cut by as much as 45 per cent.

The Chinese are very ingenious when it comes to insulating winter greenhouses. A booklet I have on growing Chinese chives cites a greenhouse developed by a commune in Manchuria for forcing chives in mid-winter. To save on heating costs they built a low back wall along the length of the house about 16 in (40 cm) thick. This was backed by a second, insulating, 'keep-warm-wall' stretching from the ground to the eaves of the greenhouse. It was over 3 feet (a metre) wide at the top, spreading to nearly 5 ft (1.7 m) at the base, consisting of about seven layers of different materials: several of rice straw 'glued' together with clay, fine straw, corn straw, and finally heavy matting. A low wall ran along the front of the greenhouse, reinforced with a 'protection from cold' ditch filled with straw and weeds and covered with soil.

I don't expect structures like this to spring up in Western gardens. But anyone attempting to grow oriental vegetables in winter in very cold climates should bear this industrious example in mind.

Walk-in polytunnels

The modern polytunnel—a small version of the tunnels widely used by commercial growers—is to me the ideal form of protection for gardeners in cool temperate climates, giving the maximum covered area at the lowest cost. Shaped like a giant semi-circular cloche, it consists essentially of a sheet of wide plastic film stretched over heavy-gauge galvanized steel tube hoops.

The polytunnels currently available for amateurs are on average 8–10 ft (2.4–3 m) wide, about 6½ ft (nearly 2 m) high, and up to about 35 ft (10 m) long. If longer than this they would require additional ventilation in the centre. They are simply erected by sinking the hoops into foundation tubes knocked into the ground. To anchor the film a shallow trench is taken out around the edge of the tunnel. The edges of the film are laid in the trench which is then filled in with soil.

It is advisable to use fairly heavy film (500–600 gauge), which has been treated with ultra-violet inhibitor. This slows down the breakdown of the film, and gives it a life of at least 2–3 years. After that it will need replacing.

Polytunnels are easily erected, and equally easily dismantled and moved. This is an advantage over conventional greenhouses if 'soil sickness' develops where, for example, tomatoes have been grown continuously for several years. In fixed greenhouses the soil has to be sterilized, or changed, or the crop grown in containers. A polytunnel can simply be moved to a fresh site.

HINTS ON ERECTING A POLYTUNNEL

- Site it on good, well drained soil to maximize its potential.
- Put it up on a warm day. This makes the film supple, so it can be pulled much tighter. Friction, which eventually leads to tears, always develops first at points where the film is slack and so flaps in the wind.
- It is easier to tighten the film when it is weighted down. So when the film in the trench is half covered with soil, line your friends along the edge of the tunnel, each grabbing the outer edge of the film and get everyone to heave together. This removes most of the wrinkles in the film.
- Before putting the film over the frame cover all steel hoops, especially on the more exposed rounded sections, with insulated anti-spot foam-based tape. This acts as insulation between the metal and the film, and can prolong the life of the film by at least a year.
- Insulate any rough corners, at the top of doors for example, by binding them with tape or even rags.

- Build as much ventilation into the tunnels as possible. One of the drawbacks of basic polytunnels is the lack of a simple means of ventilation. Unlike even a small greenhouse, there are no windows. On all but the smallest models of tunnel it is advisable to have doors at both ends, and ventilation panels inserted into the doors. This helps to prevent the build-up of pests and diseases in summer. The panels can always be covered over in winter if necessary.
- Under very hot conditions dinner-plate size 'portholes' can be cut in the film at intervals, a foot or so above ground level, to increase ventilation. They can be taped over in winter if necessary.
- Plants can be grown along the outside edge, in the soil anchoring the film, to soften the appearance. They need to be fairly robust, as the soil will sometimes be very dry, sometimes very wet. I have found parsley, *Calendula*, and *Bellis perennis* among those which do well.

HINTS ON MANAGING POLYTUNNELS

- Build up the soil fertility as much as possible with plenty of organic matter. Not only will this increase the yields, but it will make the soil more moisture retentive. With the high temperatures reached under plastic, soil dries out very rapidly. However, I avoid using farmyard manure under cover, as I have found it introduces too many pests. I rely on spent mushroom compost and home-made garden compost.
- Keep the plants mulched as much as possible, both to keep down weeds and to conserve moisture. I have found straw mulches especially beneficial under cover: they encourage a good earthworm population.
- Repair any tears in the film as soon as they are spotted with the special strong tapes made for the purpose. Plastic film is much more rugged than it might seem, and can stand a great deal of patching.
- Discolouring green algae may develop on the film, initially on the north-facing side. This can be scraped off carefully; it is easiest to do when the film is wet.

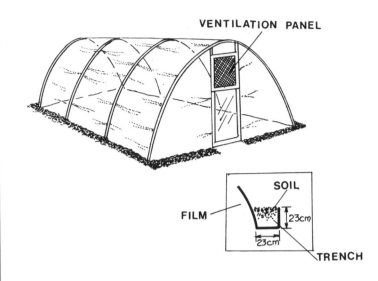

Walk-in polytunnel showing (*below*) how the film is anchored

Other plastic structures

Plastic film can be used to cover any structure to make a cheap greenhouse. Our largest 'greenhouse' is a dismantled wartime nissen (quonset) hut. We removed the corrugated iron and replaced it with film, giving us a wonderfully high structure for growing climbing beans and gourds in summer and a large expanse for oriental greens and winter salads in winter. Very large ventilation panels have been built into the structure at either end. We also have a much smaller, timber-framed greenhouse, now covered with plastic film battened to the original framework.

All kinds of useful, low-cost structures can be made using plastic film or one of the rigid plastic materials now available.

Traditional cold frames

The traditional garden frame provides a relatively small area of protected cover, primarily offering protection from the wind. It can still play a useful role in small gardens, where there is insufficient space for a polytunnel.

Frames can be permanent or portable, freestanding or lean-to.

Traditional frames had brick, concrete or wooden sides, and were covered with a 'Dutch light', a removable glass panel in a wooden frame. Modern frames are more commonly made from aluminium and glass, or some form of rigid plastic panelling.

Frames are normally built in an east–west orientation, with a sloping, south-facing side. They can be of any size, the traditional frame being governed by the dimensions of the 'Dutch light', roughly 5 ft × 2.5 ft (150 × 75 cm). A typical shallow frame for growing lettuce would be about 7 in (17 cm) at the front, rising to 9 in (23 cm) at the back, while a deeper frame for taller summer crops would be at least 12 in (30 cm) in front and 18 in (45 cm) at the back. Frames are easily ventilated by removing or propping up the top in summer. In severe winter weather they can be covered with matting for extra protection.

They are easily adapted to growing oriental vegetables, being particularly suitable for frost-tolerant brassicas, seedling and cut-and-come-again brassicas in the autumn-to-spring period, and for the more tender vegetables in summer. In spring they are useful for starting seeds and for hardening off plants raised indoors. Where this is done in solid-sided frames, the seed trays may need to be raised on upturned boxes to bring them closer to the light.

As with all forms of protected cropping, make the soil, especially the top 6 in (15 cm) or so, as fertile as possible. When watering in winter water the *soil* but try to keep the leaves dry, to cut down on the risk of moulds developing in the relatively enclosed space.

Solar frames

These are well-insulated frames in which natural sunlight is used to keep the temperature several degrees above zero during the winter months.

CHINESE SOLAR FRAMES Also known as 'sun beds' or 'winter beds', various types of frames are extensively used in north China to extend the growing season and protect plants during the severe winters. We were fortunate enough to visit the Beijing area in October, when many of the sun beds are made, constructed afresh each autumn on ground from which the summer crops have just been harvested. The long rows of freshly dug beds are works of art: they must be the world's most elegant frames.

The traditional type is a slightly sunken pit. The edges are built up into low walls raised above ground level, the sides are carefully angled to face south and catch the maximum winter sunlight, while the depth varies according to the crop to be planted. Bamboos are laid across the top of the frames to support the protective cover. Previously covered with glass, they now use plastic film, anchored in the soil. As the winter temperatures become lower the frames are covered at night and on cold days with progressively heavier and heavier layers of insulating matting made from bamboo, straw and reeds. In addition the frames are often sheltered by windbreaks.

A newer type of 'improved sun bed' is built as a lean-to against a mud back wall several feet high. Short concrete posts and pillars are set down the middle of the frames. Curved bamboos run from the wall to the ground, supported in the middle by the pillars. Film covers, and later additional mats, are laid over the framework. These higher frames are less humid than the old type, with the added advantage of allowing people to walk inside.

So well insulated are the Chinese sun beds, that the soil temperature can be as high as 41–50°F (5–10°C) when outside soil temperatures are 4°F (−15°C).

Use of the frames In autumn, celery, brassicas, lettuce, and garlic (for the leafy green New Year crop) are transplanted into the frames for a late harvest; later mature vegetables (known as 'false plants') are transplanted as a means of short-term storage; seed crops and brassicas such as western cabbage and cauliflower are overwintered in them. In spring they are used for plant raising and early crops of pak choi etc. In fact their use is very similar to that of the intensive

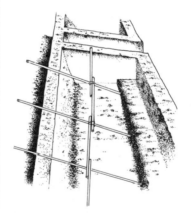

Chinese solar frame. The raised area on the right is permanently shaded and used as a walkway

Rodale solar frame, see text

French hotbeds, heated with fermenting manure, once so widely used in Europe (see page 201).

THE RODALE SOLAR FRAMES In the early 1980s the Rodale Research Center designed a relatively inexpensive, small, well-insulated 'solar grow frame' for growing vegetables on a family scale in cold northern latitudes during the winter months. In Pennsylvania the average number of growing days is 194, winter temperatures can dip below 0°F (−18°C), and the average snowfall is 28 in (71 cm) a year.

Features of the solar grow frame (For further reading see Appendix, page 215.)

• The frames are approximately 8 ft (2.4 m) long × 4 ft (1.2 m) wide. Where possible they are built in a sheltered position or against a building.

• They are east–west orientated, facing directly south. The south-facing side is at a 40-degree angle (it could be steeper), and is double-glazed. It is made of panels which slide open horizontally. They are covered with insulation at night.

• The walls are made of timber, north, east and west walls insulated with 2 in (5 cm) of polystyrene foam. The frame must be well built, painted and sealed so that it is absolutely airtight. Any cracks create draughts which would rapidly offset the benefits of insulation.

• The frames are built above ground on a concrete base, insulated *beneath* with 2 in (5 cm) polystyrene foam. This proved to be an important feature, though would be unnecessary in areas with less severe winters.

• A night shutter, made from 1-inch (2.5-cm) thick insulation board, is positioned directly over the crops at night. During the day it folds on hinges and is tucked out of the way against the back wall. This is considered a very important feature.

• The frames are filled with 8–12 in (20–30 cm) very fertile soil. The average minimum air temperature in the frames in the coldest months, between December and early March, was below 40°F

(4.4°C); the average maximum temperature 60°F (15.6°C). These were much the same as the temperatures achieved in the Rodale solar greenhouse. Vegetables were picked from the frame throughout the period from October to March. *Cropping in the solar grow frame* Oriental brassicas proved the most productive crops in the frames. Not only did they stand up to low temperatures well—they 'bounced back' after night temperatures of 22°F (−5.6°C)—but they coped with temperatures soaring into the 80s F (over 26°C) on spring days.

Fast-growing, frost-susceptible crops, such as pak choi, and heading and semi-heading varieties of Chinese cabbage, which would be damaged by heavy frost, were transplanted into the frames in early autumn, and were harvested before winter set in.

With slower growing hardy brassicas, such as mustards, komatsuna and mizuna, some harvesting could continue in mid-winter, even when average daytime temperatures were around freezing. These hardy overwintered crops, as well as spring-sown varieties of pak choi and non-heading Chinese cabbage, provided pickings in early spring when growth picked up as temperatures started to rise.

The most productive use of the frames was to mix different types of vegetables together, planting the smallest at the front of the frame. When plants bolted in spring, they were replaced with 2–3-week-old transplants raised in the solar greenhouse. However, judging from the behaviour of overwintered oriental brassicas in my polythene tunnel, the bolted shoots could equally well have been cut and used, leaving the plants to produce more edible shoots over several weeks.

As temperatures can rise very rapidly in frames, they must be ventilated by opening the front panels on warm days.

Cloches

For many years cloches were the most popular form of protected cropping in the kitchen garden. Though less popular today, they can, like all forms of protected cropping, be used with oriental vegetables to extend the growing season in autumn and spring, and to grow the more tender vegetables in summer. They are also very handy for warming up the soil in spring.

They provide little protection against frost, but good protection against wind. Temperatures will rise high under cloches in sunny weather.

The main advantage of cloches is their flexibility: they are easily moved from one crop to another. They can, for example, be moved over a mature crop in autumn so that it will stand longer into the winter. The other side of the coin is that cloches require a lot of handling, good cloches are fairly expensive, and they only cover relatively small areas of ground.

There are many types of cloches, from the original bell-shaped glass cloches to tent and high-sided barn glass cloches, to the many made from modern plastic materials. Cloches can usually be lined up end to end to make a low tunnel over rows.

When selecting cloches choose the strongest, the most stable, and the largest available, as leaves which touch the glass on cold nights will become frosted. In exposed situations cloches may need to be anchored, either with sticks or stakes pushed into the ground beside them, or with strings run through the top handles and tied to stakes in the ground at either end. Rows of cloches should never be left open-ended, as this creates wind funnels which will damage plants. Block the ends with small panels of glass or rigid polythene. In hot weather gaps can be left between adjacent cloches to provide ventilation.

Low polytunnels

Low polytunnels or row covers are an inexpensive form of protection. At its simplest a low tunnel consists of lightweight plastic film (usually about 150-gauge though heavier film can be used) stretched over galvanized steel wire hoops placed about a yard (90 cm) apart. At each end of the row the film is either buried in the soil or knotted around short posts in the ground. Along the length of the tunnel the film is kept in place with strings or wires, looped over the top and tied to the base of the hoops. In winter, when there is less need for access and ventilation, the film can be dug into the soil on one side to give added protection and to prevent the sides blowing up. While the hoops last many years the film needs replacing every one or two years. The height depends on the size of the hoops. A typical low tunnel would be about 18 in (45 cm) high and about 3 ft (90 cm) wide. As a general rule, the larger the tunnel, the more effective it is for crop protection.

In warm weather, ventilation is essential as temperatures and humidity can build up rapidly, encouraging pests and disease. The film can be pushed up on one or both sides for ventilation and access. Low tunnels can also be covered with perforated film (see below) which allows for better ventilation.

Low polytunnels are a fairly flimsy form of protection, liable to be flattened by heavy snowfall. However, they give protection from wind and heavy rain. They are used in early spring and autumn for early and late sowings, in summer for tender crops, and in autumn to protect mature crops. They can also be used *inside* a walk-in polytunnel, for extra protection in very severe weather.

IMPROVED FORMS OF LOW TUNNEL More substantial low tunnels can be made which will withstand colder conditions and provide improved growing conditions. The following model was designed by the Rodale Research Center. It covered a 5 ft (150 cm) bed, was 3 ft (90 cm) high at the ridge, and used 6 ml (600 gauge) clear plastic sheeting. (See diagram opposite.)
● Supports made from ½ in (1.25 cm) diameter PVC pipe.
● Supports sunk into ¾ in (2 cm) diameter pipe lengths in ground.

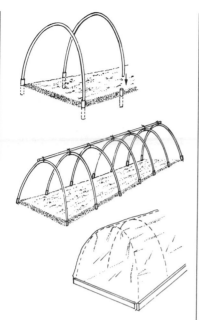

Improved low plastic film tunnel, see text

- Firm ridge made with 2 × 2 in (5 × 5 cm) timbers tied along the top of the hoops.
- Ends and edges of plastic film nailed between 1 × 2 in (2.5 × 5 cm) pieces of timber laid on the ground along the outer edges and ends of the tunnel. These could be lifted and rested on the ridge when working in the tunnel.

Under this kind of row cover soil temperatures could be 10–20°F (5.5–11°C) higher and air temperatures as much as 20–30°F (11–16.5°C) higher than outside. Frost-tender plants were killed in mid-winter, but the tunnels proved very useful for covering mature outdoor crops in autumn, for late autumn sowings, and for early spring sowings.

Film covers (floating mulches, crop covers, floating row covers)
These are lightweight films laid directly on the crops after they have been sown or planted. Because of their 'elasticity' they can to some extent expand over the crops as they grow, supported by them. They provide useful protection from wind and the elements, resulting in earlier, heavier and better quality crops, early and late in the year. They are invaluable where no other form of protected cropping is available.

TYPES OF FILM COVER There are two main types: the transparent, clear perforated films made from plastic, and the much softer, fibrous or fleecy films made from poly-propylene combined with other compounds.

This is a rapidly changing field, and new, improved products are continually coming on the market. As far as I know there has been little research on their use specifically for oriental vegetables, so keen gardeners will have to rely largely on trial and error, applying what *is* known about the films to their own situation and crops.

Although essentially used directly on crops without any supports, these films *can* be laid over supports when growing taller crops such as tomatoes or peppers, which would become too constricted or eventually puncture the films.

Characteristics of clear perforated films
- The most popular films are perforated with numerous small holes of 10 mm diameter, with anything from 200–500 holes per square metre. They are only 25–40 microns thick, and are relatively cheap. Types of film perforated with a multitude of tiny slits are generally much more expensive, but more 'elastic'. Perforated films will last for two seasons if handled with care.
- They offer very little protection against frost but the ground warms up rapidly beneath them. In sudden spells of hot weather temperatures can rise very high and be damaging.
- They are relatively impervious to rain and irrigation, so if left on too long plants can become short of water, and may also be chafed and damaged.
- For every crop there is a critical point at which the film should be removed, either because of chafing or temperature rises. For this reason they are generally used in the first few weeks or months of growth.

Characteristics of fibrous films
- There are several types. The best known are spun fibre, 'non woven' films manufactured from polyesters and polypropylene. They have a soft, cheese-cloth texture and drape easily over plants. 'Agryl P17' and 'P34', 'BASE UV17' and 'UV40' and 'Reemay' are products currently available. They are made in various thicknesses; the numbers indicate weight in grammes per square metre, so the higher the number the thicker the film.

Another type are 'woven films' made from polypropylene and polyamides. These are transparent, and take the form of a filmy net. They are much more durable. 'Agronet' is an example of this type.
- Fibrous films are more expensive than perforated clear films, but gentler in action, so there is less chafing of plants. They will normally last for two seasons if handled carefully; woven films can last several seasons.
- They are more permeable to air and water, so less subject to temperature fluctuations. The ground is less liable to dry out.
- They give some protection against frost, the degree of protection depending on the thickness of the film. Heavier films protect against 2–4 degrees of frost.
- They can be left on plants much longer than perforated films, sometimes until harvesting. They are especially recommended for early and late sown crops, and overwin-

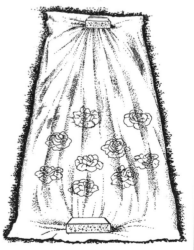

Floating row cover

tering leafy crops. They improve growth and quality.

- They give protection against birds and flying insect pests such as aphids, cabbage root fly, carrot fly, flea beetle, and butterflies and moths *provided* they are securely anchored at soil level with no gaps, and there are no holes. Japanese radishes, for example, can be covered with fibrous films until shortly before lifting for protection against cabbage root fly.

HINTS ON USING FILM COVERS

- The soil must be very well prepared. Film covers will not improve poor soil, though they will help *conserve* the structure of the soil from the damage of heavy winter rains.
- Covers are most easily managed on gently mounded raised beds, where they fit snugly over the surface.
- The edges of the covers can either be buried in the soil, making slits with a trowel, or simply weighted with soil, stones, clods, pieces of wood etc.
- Only cover crops that are free of pests and disease.
- Make sure the ground is weed-free before being covered.

Weeding is very difficult once covers are in place, and any weeds will flourish in the protected environment under the covers, smothering the crop. The fibrous films are sometimes lifted carefully on three sides, leaving them anchored on the fourth, for weeding, and then replaced. This is more difficult with perforated films as leaves grow into the perforations.

- As most covers offer relatively little protection from frost, frost-susceptible plants should not generally be planted any earlier than normal. Once planted, however, they will grow much more rapidly than they would in the open. Covers are a good method of cap-italizing on the advantages of naturally early sites. They should be considered a means of shortening the growing season.

- The growth of plants under covers will be rather soft, so they must be 'weaned' carefully if and when the covers are removed and they are exposed to the elements. This applies particularly to the perforated plastic films. Ideally, remove covers towards the evening on still, overcast or damp days. Weaning can start by slitting the covers several days beforehand. Make intermittent slits in lines along the bed, subsequently slitting the entire length.
- Water gently shortly after the covers are removed if the ground is dry, as it will often prove to be.
- Covers must be removed from insect-pollinated crops such as courgettes when the flowers appear.

Growing in containers

People turn to containers for vegetable growing when they have no garden or only a 'concrete' garden—or when the garden soil has become diseased. The most common example of the latter is greenhouse soils which develop 'tomato sickness' after growing tomatoes for a number of years.

City dwellers have always grown flowers in containers, but now many people seek the special satisfaction of producing something edible from their window boxes, patio pots, or 'growing bags' on the roof. It's a universal urge: time and again in China I noticed old bowls and dilapidated baskets perched on doorsteps, roofs, balconies, even on the pavements, sporting a little crop of green onions or garlic.

It is not easy to grow lush, demanding vegetables to maturity in the harsh confines of a container. But with ingenuity and skill it can be done. (See also Suitable plants for containers, page 171.)

Types of container

All sorts of ordinary—and extraordinary—things can be made into plant containers. For vegetable growing they must be:
- Strong enough to withstand the weight of wet soil and the mature crop.
- Stable enough not to topple over when crops grow tall.
- Have some means of drainage
- Be as large as possible.
It is an advantage if they can be moved easily.

Pots and boxes made of clay, wood or plastic, troughs, barrels, sinks, bathtubs, old wheelbarrows, tyres cut in half, cans, baskets, window boxes, hanging baskets, wooden drawers . . . these are just some of the items used as containers. Then there are various forms of 'growing bag'. These originated in the 70s and are essentially plastic bags filled with some kind of potting compost. DIY enthusiasts make their own from empty sacks by filling them with potting compost or soil, and tying them at the neck. They are then treated like commercial growing bags, cutting slits or squares along one surface for planting.

Size Containers need to be as large as possible to allow room for roots to develop, but also to minimize the drying out which is the bane of container growing. The larger the volume of soil in relation to the surface area, the less vulnerable it is to the drying effects of sun and wind.

The minimum practical size would be 6 in (15 cm) width and depth. There will be far more scope with containers of 8–10 in (20–25 cm) width and depth. Undemanding herbs can be kept in pots of 4–5 in (10–12 cm) width and depth. The average growing bag is about 6 in (15 cm) deep, 3 ft (90 cm) long and 1 ft (30 cm) wide.

Growing medium

The soil in containers needs to be very 'open' and well drained. Ordinary garden soil is usually unsuitable, as it tends to become compacted with the heavy watering in a confined space. A choice normally has to be made between a peat-based or a soil-based growing medium, although other types are sometimes available. I find a soil-based medium more satisfactory than peat-based for growing vegetables. All have their pros and cons. Either purchase a proprietary brand of soil- or peat-based compost or make up your own mixture (see below). See also Plant raising, sowing compost, page 152, on using peat alternatives wherever possible.

Characteristics of composts

Peat based
- Light weight. This is an important factor with containers on roofs and balconies. However containers filled with peat compost are more likely to topple over with a heavy crop.
- Dry out very rapidly.
- Do not hold nutrients for long, so more supplementary feeding will be required.
- Drain rapidly, so there is no risk of waterlogging.

Soil based
- Relatively heavy.
- Hold moisture longer.
- Have a reservoir of nutrients so less supplementary feeding is necessary.
- Are less well drained, so there is some risk of soil becoming stagnant.

Home-made soil-based mixtures For vegetable growing it is advisable to make up a fresh soil mixture every year. Gardeners have many favourite 'recipes', and much will depend on the quality of the ingredients. The final mixture must be very free-draining and very well mixed together. If plants then fail to grow well the most probable cause will be a lack of nutrients: this can be remedied by regular liquid feeding. (See Soil fertility, page 144.)

A typical mixture could consist of:

1–2 parts best garden loam
1–2 parts well rotted compost or leaf mould
1 part peat, sand or vermiculite, or a mixture of the three
1 part well rotted animal manure

or mushroom compost could be added if available. In areas with high atmospheric pollution a little lime can be added to prevent the soil becoming too acid.

SEAWEED-BASED MIXTURES I have seen excellent vegetable crops growing in the following mixture, which was prepared 3 months before planting and allowed to rot down in the containers:

1 part seaweed
1 part straw
1 part garden compost

Fertility

EARTHWORMS There used to be a school of thought which advocated excluding worms from containers, but it has now been demonstrated that they are beneficial. The problem is keeping them there! They need fairly fresh organic matter to feed on, and cool conditions. As soon as the soil gets uncomfortably hot, they will make a getaway: you can often find them 'cooling off' underneath the pot.

MAINTAINING FERTILITY Top-dress the containers from time to time with a handful of well-rotted manure or compost, worked into the top of the container. Once plants are well established they can be given a weekly or twice weekly watering with a dilute liquid feed. (See also Soil fertility, Liquid feeding, page 144.) Because the roots are con-

fined in a small area, containerized plants should never be fed with a concentrated or strong feed.

DRAINAGE A balance has to be found between good drainage (waterlogged roots soon die) and conserving moisture in the soil. Drainage is particularly important with soil-based composts: peat-based composts are naturally very free draining.

WATER CONSERVATION As mentioned earlier, exposure to wind and sun makes containers dry out rapidly. Once the top ½ in (1.25 cm) of soil has dried out watering is necessary: in dry weather it may be necessary to water twice a day. Watch out for containers placed against a wall, which may shield them from natural rainfall.

Management

SITING CONTAINERS The 'ideal' situation depends on the climate and the crop. Windy and draughty

spots should always be avoided, unless it is possible to erect some form of shelter which will not block the light. In cool climates containerized vegetables need as much sun as possible: in warm conditions they may need to be shaded for part of the day. Containers which are mounted on castors can be wheeled from one position to another as need dictates.

PLANT SUPPORTS Where tall and climbing plants such as peas, climbing beans, cucumbers or gourds are grown some means of support has to be erected. Containers can be placed at the foot of a trellis or wall, to which the plants are attached. Metal and plastic supporting frames can sometimes be purchased for growing bags. Alternatively, strings can be slipped under the bag and tied overhead, providing support for the plants. Where containers are deep enough canes can be inserted in them; or, if

---

Measures to improve drainage in containers

- Make drainage holes in the bottom of impermeable containers which have none. Make them about 5 in (13 cm) apart and about ½ in (1.25 cm) diameter. If they are angled they are less likely to get blocked. Drainage holes can also be made in the side about an inch (2.5 cm) above the bottom.
- Where appropriate stand the container on bricks or wooden blocks so it is clear of the ground.
- Line the bottom inch or two (2.5–5 cm) of the pot with material such as broken crocks or stones. They can be covered with a layer of dried leaves.

Measures to conserve water in containers

- Site containers in places sheltered from the wind.
- Line the container with heavy duty plastic film or foil, punching a few holes in the bottom so water can seep out.
- Mulch the surface with stones or gravel: it can be up to 2 in (5 cm) thick.
- Where practical, stand containers in shallow trays containing gravel, moisture-absorbing granules, vermiculite, or even bark. These help create a moist atmosphere, but prevent the plant becoming waterlogged. In very dry conditions keep a little water in the tray.
- With growing bags only cut small holes or squares in the top for the plants, rather than removing a large area.
- Where practical, pack soil or insulating material around the containers.

appropriate, pushed into the ground alongside the bag.

I have never tried it myself, but have read of vegetables like peas being grown successfully in hanging baskets, simply allowed to hang down.

SOWING AND PLANTING To make optimum use of a container transplant plants rather than sow direct. Preferably raise them in modules or small pots so that you get top quality plants. (See Plant raising, Use of modules, page 153.) Large-seeded plants such as beans can be direct sown if the space is available, but if started in a small pot and transplanted when a few inches high, something else can be growing in the container in the meantime. The exception is seedling cut-and-come-again crops, which are direct sown.

INDOOR CONTAINER GROWING IN WINTER Vegetables, like house plants, can be grown indoors in containers during the winter months. In northern latitudes they will normally require supplementary artificial lighting.

The ordinary domestic incandescent bulbs are unsuitable for the purpose, as they throw out too much heat, resulting in spindly unbalanced growth. A range of fluorescent lights have been developed specifically for plants. Various types are available, including mercury, metal halide and sodium lamps, which in differing degrees supply the correct red and blue light bands for plant growth. For further technical information and current sources of suppliers, consult recent editions of gardening magazines.

In trials at the Rodale Research Center in the USA the cool-weather, leafy oriental brassicas appeared to respond well to winter cultivation indoors. Rodale recommend 6 hours of sunlight (or the equivalent), and cool night air temperatures of 40–50°F (4–10°C).

They suggest spacing containers at least 4 in (10 cm) apart as a precaution against pests and disease. They harvested leafy greens both as whole plants, and cutting only the outer leaves.

Suitable plants for containers

If you are prepared to take trouble—in some cases a great deal of trouble—most oriental vegetables could probably be grown in containers. On the whole though, avoid extremely robust plants (such as winter melon), very deep rooted plants (long Japanese radishes and burdock), and plants susceptible to bolting (Chinese cabbage and pak choi sown early in the year).

For most of us it is more a question of finding what grows easily and what is most *worth* growing.

The relatively undemanding herbs and short-lived vegetables are easier to succeed with. Among oriental vegetables I would suggest the best returns would come from growing seedling crops of brassicas, chrysanthemum greens and leaf radish using cut-and-come-again techniques. Or try summer sowings of the cold-tolerant brassicas such as loose-headed Chinese cabbage, green-stemmed pak choi, komatsuna, mizuna and mibuna greens, and the mustards. Grown in a sheltered spot, they could give useful pickings well into winter.

Where containers are near the house the decorative qualities of the vegetables might influence the choice. Chinese chives, ginger, edible chrysanthemum, mizuna and mibuna greens, lablab beans, and the ornamental cabbages and kales are all vegetables with attractive features.

Plants for containers

Easily grown plants
Note: They may not attain the size they would in open ground

Amaranthus	Mitsuba
Brassica seedling crops: e.g.	Mizuna
loose-headed Chinese	Onions
cabbage, komatsuna,	Ornamental cabbage and kale
purple mustard, pak choi,	Pak choi (cut fairly small)
mizuna, mibuna	Pea shoots
Chinese chives	Perilla
Chinese celery	Radish, leaf
Chrysanthemum greens	Rosette cabbage
Coriander	Sesame
Garlic	Shepherd's purse
Ginger	Soya beans
Mibuna	

Plants requiring deep containers with fertile soil

Bitter gourd	Pak choi (grown to maturity)
Chinese artichoke	Peas
Chinese cabbage	Stem lettuce
Lablab beans	Yard long beans

For further reading on container growing see Appendix, page 216.

Pests and disease

The better the growing conditions, the fewer losses there will be from pests and disease. It is weak plants, overcrowded plants, and plants being forced in unfavourable conditions, which succumb to pest and disease attacks. On the whole, well grown, 'happy' plants can survive and outgrow most attacks.

There is of course an element of luck as well, with external conditions influencing the incidence of certain pests and disease. In hot dry weather insect pests seem to emerge from nowhere and multiply rapidly; many diseases flourish in cold, dank weather; agricultural crops in the vicinity may import pests and diseases which were previously no problem. These are factors beyond our control.

Why use organic methods of control?

As mentioned earlier, in common with many gardeners today, I grow organically without using toxic chemicals. So only organic or 'biological' methods of control are discussed in this chapter. My main reasons for avoiding toxic chemical sprays are:

● Most are strong, lasting chemicals, killing beneficial and harmless insects and other organisms as well as pests. Left unharmed, these beneficial creatures keep a natural check on many pests and diseases . . . the good old-fashioned 'balance of nature'.

● The long-term effects of chemical residues, in plants and in the soil, and hence their effect on various creatures in the food chain and on human beings, are still unknown. DDT is only one of many chemicals which was used for years before it was pronounced dangerous and banned.

● They are a risk to children and domestic animals.

● Their manufacture, use, and eventual disposal create environmental hazards and problems.

Chemical sprays undeniably provide a lot of short cuts, although they are expensive. Organic gardeners who forgo them have to tolerate a certain level of pest and disease damage, must be prepared to use physical rather than chemical methods of control, and to invest time and energy in creating a very healthy, fertile garden. The outer leaves of a Chinese cabbage may have to be discarded because they are riddled with slug holes, but if grown in fertile soil there will be plenty of crisp usable leaf in the heart.

Where a pest or disease does get the upper hand spraying may be the only means of saving a crop. In this case use one of the safer, organically approved chemicals. These are mainly derived from plants, and compared with standard chemicals are less potent and shorter lasting in their effectiveness, treating only one or two pests instead of a broad spectrum. They break down rapidly into non-harmful products, and are therefore far less damaging to the environment.

Integrated control . . . and the Chinese example

Insects, and various organisms which cause disease, rapidly develop resistance to specific chemical sprays. The chemical then has to be discarded and new chemicals developed—but eventually resistance develops to the new chemicals, and so it goes on. Keeping one step ahead is an expensive, self-defeating circle, which has led many commercial growers in the West to adopt a minimum-use policy known as 'integrated pest control'.

Integrated control embodies many of the principles of the organic approach. The idea is to monitor and predict the build up of pests and disease, and to delay using chemicals until they reach potentially damaging levels. Warnings are sent to farmers at this point. The build up of pests may be gauged by trapping insects (hormone traps are one method used), while diseases can be forecast by analysing recent weather data. As part of an integrated approach, alternative non-chemical methods of control are used wherever possible to minimize the use of chemicals. These range from physical barriers to biological control—where a natural enemy is harnessed to control the pest or disease.

The Chinese could claim to be the best practitioners of the integrated approach. Western visitors to China are often surprised at the relatively low levels of pest and disease in the intensively cropped fields. Much of this can be attributed to scrupulous hygiene, clearing away all the debris from crops as soon as they are harvested and composting it, feeding it to animals or ploughing it in deeply. Traditional Chinese practices such as ridge and furrow irrigation rather than overhead watering, and incorporating flooded crops into rotation cycles, may also account for fewer soil pests and diseases than would be expected. There also seems to be a high level of natural resistance to pests and diseases in Chinese vegetable varieties. This may stem from the widespread practice of saving seed locally, strains with the best natural resistance having been selected over the years.

As for controlling pests, the Chinese are masters of the art of forecasting. Almost every town has its forecasting station using various types of traps to monitor the build up of pests so that control measures can be applied when most effective. Take one example, the cutworm moth, whose caterpillars damage a wide range of crops. Initially black light traps are used to catch the night flying adults. When the numbers reach a certain level traps made of wilted twigs, baited with wine and sugar and incorporating a chemical, are suspended above the crops in the fields. These catch the moths before they lay their eggs.

Aphids, which are attracted to yellow objects, are caught on yellow sheets or boards smeared with grease (precursors of the greased sheets now available in the West) or in shallow yellow bowls filled with water. Not *all* the aphids are caught, but such methods, it is claimed, enable the use of chemicals to be halved.

Biological control is a highly developed art in China. There are many examples: magpies are reared to control the pine caterpillars; lacewings are bred to kill aphids (they lay their eggs into coils of newspaper, which are distributed in the fields); ladybirds are netted and transferred to aphid-infested crops; both bacteria and naturally occurring viruses are used to infect and kill caterpillars. My favourite example is the use of predatory ants to control a range of pests in citrus orchards. A few ant nests are collected and placed in the citrus trees, which are connected with little wooden bridges so the ants can migrate from tree to tree. But each tree trunk is surrounded by a trough of water to prevent the ants wandering further afield. The method died out when DDT was introduced, but as insect resistance to DDT developed it was re-introduced.

The success of some of these methods depends on the pest and disease 'literacy' of the rural population. Manuals illustrating the different stages of a pest's life cycle are cheap and commonplace: enormous numbers of Chinese are said to be able to identify pests. So quite frequently a peasant will spot a diseased caterpillar, and this will be used as a starting point, either for raising diseased caterpillars and releasing them in the field, or for making a spray to infect caterpillars. This particular method only works successfully above certain minimum temperatures. But back to the West . . .

Preventive medicine in the garden

The following practices, many of which are no more than applied common sense, all help prevent pests and diseases.

SOIL
- Good drainage, high levels of fertility, and high levels of organic matter are essential. High levels of organic matter may help to reduce clubroot.
- Practise rotation to limit the development and increase of soil pests and diseases. (See The bed system, page 147.)
- Digging the soil exposes pests to birds.

PLANT QUALITY
- Never plant diseased material. This is especially true of bulbs.
- Wherever possible, use varieties with resistance or tolerance to pests and diseases. Even partial resistance is a great help in obtaining a useful crop.
- Grow appropriate crops for your area. Attempting semi-tropical plants outdoors in cool areas is asking for trouble.

PLANT RAISING
- Aim to raise strong sturdy plants with a good root system. Wherever practical, raise plants in individual pots or modules. (See Plant raising, Use of modules, page 153.)
- Germinate plants rapidly, sowing in well drained, sterile compost in heated propagators where necessary.
- Never sow or plant in very cold, very wet or very dry soil.
- Thin early to avoid overcrowded and leggy seedlings; steady growth is healthy growth.
- Where feasible adjust sowing times to avoid or minimize pest attacks. Knowledge of local conditions is necessary. For example, in some areas flea beetle attacks are serious in spring, but far less severe in autumn.
- Grow plants 'hard' rather than overcoddling and overfeeding them. Soft growth is vulnerable to pest and disease attack. Too much nitrogen leads to soft growth; similarly, plants grown under cover tend to become soft. Give them plenty of ventilation, and in hot weather damp down greenhouses by spraying with water in hot periods. This also discourages greenhouse pests such as red spider mite which thrive in hot dry conditions.
- Avoid monocropping. As far as is practical, intercrop plants, or grow them in small plots between different vegetables. This lessens the likelihood of a pest or disease sweeping through a crop.
- Never allow plants to suffer from lack of water. Limp plants are most vulnerable to aphid attack.

HYGIENE
- Burn all diseased material, especially plants affected with virus diseases. Remove diseased leaves from plants.
- Dig up old brassica stumps at the end of the season, as they harbour overwintering pests. Bury them in the ground or deep in the compost heap. If there is any sign of clubroot swellings either burn the roots, or bag them and put in a dustbin.
- Clear away rubbish in the vicinity of vegetable beds, and keep paths weed free. Rubbish and weeds provide cover for overwintering pests and slugs.
- Keep propagating equipment clean to avoid 'damping off' diseases. Wash pots and seed trays

after use. Use sterile composts, stored in dry places.

● Keep water tubs covered: they provide breeding grounds for pests and disease.

● Eternal vigilance! Keep a constant watch on plants, so that you can spot the early signs of trouble and nip it in the bud. Look out for caterpillar eggs, young caterpillars, and early aphids and squash them. Investigate any wilting plant: perhaps it has been uprooted by a mole, or a leatherjacket may have started to nibble through the stem. It may be saved if you dig it up and replant it. Removing diseased leaves early on prevents infection spreading.

ATTRACTING BENEFICIAL CREATURES

● *Not* spraying with toxic chemicals is the most important step in creating a healthy environment. Beneficial insects such as lacewings, hoverfly, ladybirds and parasitic wasps; the various useful predatory beetles; the many beneficial organisms in the soil; frogs, toads, and birds all multiply in the absence of spraying. They all help keep down pests and disease.

● Plant flat open flowers, such as dwarf convolvulus, calendula (pot marigold), limnanthes (poached egg plant), nemophila (baby blue eyes) to attract hoverfly in particular. Their larvae feed on greenfly.

● In some part of the garden, though not in close proximity to vegetables, leave a few untidy corners sporting wild plants and weeds which provide food for beneficial insects, birds etc. Leave a few logs or piles of wood to provide overwintering hiding places. A pond will encourage frogs and toads, which help keep down slugs.

● Plant native species of trees and shrubs, which support a far more diverse range of insect life than foreign species.

Non-chemical methods of pest control

The following are examples of non chemical methods of pest control currently in use in the West. The hope is that future research into organic gardening will lead to the development of further controls. Organic methods sometimes involve anticipating a pest—as in the use of discs against cabbage root fly. More usually it is a case of taking action after the first damage has occurred. It may be necessary to combine several forms of control.

HAND PICKING Caterpillars, and colonies of green, black and mealy aphids are pests which can be picked off by hand. Slugs, snails, cutworm and chafer beetle larvae are among night-feeding pests which can be collected by torchlight at night. Celery leaves affected with leaf miner can be picked off.

BARRIERS

Nets Very fine agricultural netting, not unlike mosquito netting, can be laid on plants to protect them from birds and flying insects such as aphids, whitefly, flea beetle, pollen beetle, cabbage and carrot root fly, butterflies and moths. They must be carefully anchored at the base so there are no gaps, and be free of holes or tears.

Fibrous films The very lightweight fibrous films laid on plants as 'floating' row covers give protection from birds and the same range of insects as above, provided they are carefully anchored and free of holes. (See also Protected cropping, Fibrous films, page 167.)

Heavier plastic or net materials can be laid over low hoops over the plants, anchored carefully to avoid gaps, to protect against birds and, to a lesser extent, insects.

Cages Wire netting, nylon or plastic net cages are sometimes erected over vegetable plots to protect against birds, rabbits and animals such as deer.

Cabbage root fly discs Discs of about 5 in (13 cm) diameter, made from rubberized carpet underlay or similar material, with a slit in one side to a central point, can be laid on the ground around the stem of a brassica when it is planted. They prevent the adult cabbage root fly from laying her eggs at ground level, give cover to beneficial predatory beetles, and also keep the plant mulched.

Plastic pot barriers They can be used for the same purpose. Poke a hole in the bottom of the pot large enough to slip a cabbage plant root through from above; plant it, then bury the rim of the pot at least ½ in (1 cm) into the ground. This also offers some protection against slug damage. The pots may need to be cut away later to allow the cabbage stem to expand.

Bottomless bottle barriers Slice the bottoms off plastic bottles and use the tops to cover young plants, pushing them well into the soil. Although unsightly, this protects plants in their most vulnerable stages from slugs. Remove the bottles once the plant is well established.

STICKY YELLOW GLUE TRAPS Bright yellow pieces of rigid plastic coated on both sides with a sticky glue are hung in greenhouses and among crops to catch a variety of flying insects. They should be hung slightly above the plants. Although designed to monitor insects, they are used to help control aphids, whitefly, thrips, leaf miner flies, leaf hoppers and mites. For controlling whitefly, hang them in the greenhouse early in the season so they catch the first flies to appear. Small traps are 3.5 × 10 in (9 × 25 cm); large ones 10 × 15 in (25 × 40 cm).

FLEA BEETLE TRAPS Flea beetles can be trapped by a piece of wood coated with heavy grease. If held an inch or so above infected plants, the flea beetles will jump on to the board and stick in the grease.

REFLECTING MULCHES Various types of shiny, reflecting films can be laid around and among plants to deter insects such as aphids and thrips. In experiments in the USA aluminium film deterred over 90 per cent of aphids; to a lesser extent black films and white films have a deterrent effect. For maximum efficiency about 50 per cent of the ground should be covered with film.

Grafting Plants which are susceptible to a disease or soil pest are sometimes grafted on to the rootstock of a related species which is resistant. This is an established practice with tomatoes, when greenhouse soil has become 'tomato sick' through the build up of diseases. The Chinese graft cucumbers on to black seeded pumpkin (*Cucurbita ficifolia*) to overcome soil-borne fusarium wilt.

BIOLOGICAL CONTROL Biological control uses a natural predator, parasite or infection, normally multiplied under laboratory conditions, to control a pest. Not all forms are easy to apply, several requiring steady warm temperatures for the predator to operate successfully. This is one reason why biological control techniques are more widely used in warm climates. In cool climates use tends to be restricted to glasshouse crops. There is little risk of the introduced predator becoming invasive as once its 'host' has been cleared, it dies out itself. It is quite likely that new forms of biological control will be developed in the future.

The following examples of biological control are currently in common use.

Caterpillar controls A culture made from the bacterium *Bacillus thuringiensis* is effective against many types of caterpillar. It is sprayed on to plants where caterpillars are feeding; the caterpillars become infected and die within 24 hours. There are several strains, *B. thuringiensis* var. *kurstaki* being the one in common use against caterpillars, currently marketed under various brand names e.g. 'Dipel', 'BT', 'Thuricide', 'Bactospeine', 'Javelin'.

For maximum effectiveness spray when caterpillars are young. Spray in the evening on the underside of the leaves. The spray will stick better if 1 teaspoon of liquid detergent is added to each gallon (4.5 litres) of spray. It may be necessary to spray at weekly intervals. Never spray more than is necessary, to minimize the likelihood of insects developing resistance. Sachets can be stored for two to three years under dry conditions.

Some strains of *Bacillus thuringiensis* have proved effective against beetles, such as Colorado beetle. In the foreseeable future *Bacillus thuringiensis* may be 'genetically engineered' into plants, giving them natural immunity to caterpillar attacks.

As mentioned earlier, in China virus infections are used to control caterpillars.

In Taiwan I saw an experiment which attempted to control the diamond back moth—among the most serious brassica pests in the world—by the introduction of a small wasp which parasitized the caterpillars. The wasps were being accommodated in neat, white 'house-like' hives on stilts, dotted about the fields. A nice domestic touch were clumps of *Tagetes* marigolds planted outside the houses, to supply nectar to the wasps. As a control method it only proved successful at high altitudes in Taiwan.

Whitefly control The parasitic wasp *Encarsia formosa* is widely used in greenhouses to control greenhouse whitefly. The adult wasp lays eggs inside the whitefly larvae, which hatch and destroy them. The parasite must be introduced when the first whitefly are seen. Infected larvae are supplied on leaves, which are attached to pieces of card and hung in a greenhouse. Daytime temperatures must be at least 60°F (15.6°C), and night temperatures preferably above 54°F (12°C) for it to work effectively. It is unlikely to succeed in winter even in heated greenhouses.

Red spider mite control Another mite, *Phytoselius persimilis*, is used to control the greenhouse red spider mite. The adult mites capture and destroy the red spider. They are obtained by mail order, the predators delivered in packets which are cut open to liberate them. They immediately crawl onto the plants and get to work. The higher the temperature, the more effectively they work. They can work at temperatures as low as 55–60°F (12.5–15.5°C), but it will then take 6–7 weeks to clear the pest.

Aphid control Lacewings are sometimes introduced to control aphids. In China ladybirds are sometimes netted in a wheat field and liberated over a crop under attack from aphids. In the British Isles—unless spraying has taken place—there is a natural build up of parasitic wasps which help control aphids.

Plants that kill nematodes Certain plants appear to exude substances from their roots which can kill some of the serious soil pests—nematodes or eelworm. Among them are species of marigold, such as *Tagetes minuta* and *T. erecta*, which can be worked into a rotation plan to control bulb eelworm. Future research may reveal other nematicidal plants: flax and some types of mustard are among promising lines currently being investigated.

The safer sprays

The following are among the safer sprays (see Organic methods of control, page 172) which are currently approved by the organic bodies in the United Kingdom. Consult these bodies for up to date information on new approved products. (See Appendix, page 217.) Spraying may have to be carried out fairly frequently as the safer sprays lose their effectiveness rapidly. Although relatively harmless, they *are* poisons and should be treated with care.

POPULAR 'ORGANIC' SPRAYS

Derris/rotenone
- Extracted from roots of tropical legumes.
- Applied as powder or liquid.
- Very poisonous to fish, and theoretically toxic to some beneficial insects and wild life. In practice the toxic rotenoids break down very rapidly on exposure to light and air.
- Used to control aphids (greenfly and blackfly), some beetles (e.g. flea beetle), caterpillars, turnip fly, some weevils, thrips, suckers, red spider mite. Has some effect on Colorado beetle at double strength.
- 2–3 year shelf life *if kept in the dark*.

Pyrethrum/pyrethrins
- Derived from flowers of pyrethrum (*Chrysanthemum coccineum*).
- Harms bees and fish, but very low toxicity to mammals and birds.
- Breaks down very rapidly, so effectiveness short-lived, and can

be used close to harvest.
- Spray in the evening for maximum effectiveness.
- A broad-range insecticide used to control greenfly, whitefly, many beetles, caterpillars, leaf hoppers. NB Derris and pyrethrum are sometimes combined to make a more effective spray.

Insecticidal soap
- Based on blends of fatty acids of plant origin.
- Very safe for mammals, but damages some beneficial insects.
- Used to control all types of aphid, whitefly, red spider mite, leafhoppers. Sometimes used in greenhouses before the introduction of biological control.

Main groups of pests attacking oriental vegetables

The following are the main types of pests which attack oriental vegetables. (For further reading see Appendix, pages 215 and 217.)

ANIMALS AND BIRDS

Deer A problem in some rural areas where very high fencing, and in extreme cases electric fencing, is the only way of keeping deer out. The same applies to racoons, a common pest in parts of the United States. Both are extremely destructive.

Rabbits In rabbit-infested areas the entire vegetable garden has to be fenced with 2 ft 6 in (75 cm) high, 1 in (2.5 cm) mesh wire netting. Bury it at least 6 in (15 cm) below ground, turned outward to deter burrowing. Rabbits eat almost anything green.

Mice Mice are most active in winter and spring, attacking pea and bean seeds and young plants, and sometimes seedlings of anything tasty. Catch them in mousetraps.

Moles Their burrowing can be very damaging. Use humane mole traps to catch them: easier said than done in the loose soil of a vegetable garden. In my experience none of the claimed remedies—from moth balls to caper spurge—is any use.

Large birds Pigeons, jays, crows, partridges and pheasants are some

---

---

of the problem birds. Where they make cultivation impossible, the only answer is either to net the entire garden, or to net especially vulnerable crops like brassicas and peas during their most vulnerable periods in winter and spring. For short-term cages drive stakes in the ground, cover them with upturned jam jars, and lay netting over them. Humming wires and tapes are effective in some situations. Scarecrows such as plastic flappers, plastic cups on strings and other devices can be used in the short term, but birds quickly become accustomed to them unless they are moved around.

Small birds Sparrows are serious offenders, mainly going for young seedlings. When sowing seed outdoors, put sticks at either end of the row and run a single strand of strong black cotton between them. This normally deters small birds.

Upturned bottles stuck in the ground seem to have a deterrent effect for limited periods, as do most forms of scarecrow.

Slugs Without doubt slugs are the most serious pests on oriental vegetables, the soft leaves of the oriental brassicas being highly susceptible to their attentions. Slugs destroy young plants completely, and can render mature plants anything from unsightly to almost inedible. They are at their most active and damaging in mild, damp weather.

Most of the effective slug pellets on the market are damaging to the environment (even organically

'approved' products contain aluminium, which may be damaging to human health). So the principle remedies are hand picking and the use of barriers. Some people trap slugs in sunken 'slug pubs' filled with beer, but I have found these trap as many beneficial beetles as slugs. Barriers, ranging from upturned plastic pots to 'bottomless' bottles or jars, can be placed over young plants. (See Barriers, page 174).

Various agents sprinkled around plants are claimed to keep off slugs: lime, soot, rough bark, human hair and crushed egg shells are among those used.

In my experience the only really effective method of keeping numbers down is to hunt for them with a torch when they are feeding at night. They can also be found lurking under planks, under black plastic film, and beneath any firm mulching material. We immediately put them into steep-sided beer cans: they have difficulty escaping through the narrow hole in the lid. I'll come clean and admit I pour boiling water on them to kill them: it seems to be an instant death. They can also be fed to chickens.

Slugs have a lot of natural enemies: birds, hedgehogs, frogs and toads, and many species of beetles including the violet ground beetle and the Devil's coach horse beetle. One way of encouraging slug-eating beetles is to make slightly sunken beds, edged with a non-grip material, such as metallic lawn edging strips, a couple of inches high. The beetles drop over the edge into the bed, but are unable to crawl out. They eventually eliminate the slugs in the area.

All the above applies equally to snails.

SOIL PESTS

Several grub-like soil pests cause a lot of damage to young plants, eating the roots and stems at ground level or just below, often causing the plants to wilt suddenly and die. They are the immature larval stage of various flying insects. The following are the four chief offenders—their adult forms are given in brackets.

Chafer bugs (Chafer beetles) Solid grubs with a large brown head, 3 distinct pairs of legs, whitish body often swollen at the end, up to 1½ in (4 cm) long.

Cutworms (Various kinds of moths) Fat, hairless, caterpillar-like bodies usually soil coloured, up to 2 in (5 cm) long. In 'bad years' they devour foliage as well as nipping off stems.

Leatherjacket (Crane fly, daddy-long-legs) Fat, soft, earth-coloured grubs up to 1½ in (4 cm) long.

Wireworm (Click beetles) Tough wiry grubs about 1 in (2.5 cm) long. There are no organically approved controls for any of these pests, but in the course of digging over the soil many are exposed to birds and natural enemies. Chafer bugs and wireworm are worst in the first couple of years after digging up grassland. The cutworms are night feeders like slugs, and can often be caught at night with a torch. (See also Integrated control, page 172.) Young plants can sometimes be protected from cutworm by covering them with open-ended tins pressed into the soil.

Most soil pests can be attracted to 'traps' of scooped out potatoes on the end of a skewer, set a couple of inches deep in the soil during periods of peak activity. Large 'chips' of potato seem to trap wireworm. Examine traps daily to see what you have caught. If a plant wilts suspiciously suddenly, scratch carefully in the soil around it. It is often possible to catch a wireworm or leatherjacket in the act and so prevent it from moving on to the neighbouring plant.

Nematodes (eelworm) These are microscopic creatures, different species attacking a wide range of crops. Their numbers build up gradually in the soil, but most form cysts enabling them to survive many years in a dormant state in the absence of the crops they feed on. Once they have built up a sizeable population it is extremely hard to get rid of them. Rotating crops over a minimum 3-year cycle (in some cases a longer cycle is necessary) helps to prevent this stage being reached. (See also The bed system, Rotation, page 149.) Growing antagonistic plants may prove a method of control. (See Plants that kill nematodes, page 175.)

OTHER INSECT PESTS

For practical purposes the most serious of the remaining insect pests can be divided into two groups: the sucking insects and the biting insects.

The sucking insects pierce plant tissues and feed on the sap, weakening them and often transmitting virus diseases in the process. Affected plants develop twisted, distorted leaves and tend to wilt. Sucking insects often produce sticky honeydew, which becomes colonized by black, sooty moulds.

Aphids There are many species of aphids, most only attacking one type of plant. Greenfly and blackfly are the commonest aphids affecting vegetables. They tend to be most serious and multiply fastest in hot weather, 'soft' and underwatered plants being the most vulnerable.

They can be controlled by sticky yellow traps, very fine nets, fibrous film row covers and derris, pyrethrum and insecticidal soap sprays. They can sometimes be washed off plants with soapy water. Their natural predators include hoverfly, ladybirds and parasitic wasps, the work of the latter identified by the pale empty husks of aphid skins they leave behind.

Cabbage whitefly Clouds of these little white-winged insects rise from brassica plants in spring and summer. They may overwinter in old brassica stalks, so these should be lifted and burned or buried in spring. They can be controlled with insecticidal soap, and pyrethrum products.

Thrips (Thunderflies) These tiny sucking insects are most serious in hot climates. They generally cause silvery discolouration in leaves. Control with sticky yellow traps, derris and pyrethrum.

Greenhouse whitefly These little white flies are a much more serious pest, and much harder to control, than cabbage whitefly. They attack cucumbers and a very wide range of plants in greenhouses. The higher the temperature, the faster they develop.

In hot weather 'damp down' greenhouses by spraying with water several times a day if necessary, to slow down development. Interplanting with French marigolds (*Tagetes patula* and *T. tenuifolia* (*signata*)), the use of sticky yellow traps (starting early in the season), and spraying with pyrethrum at 5–7 day intervals help keep down numbers. Biological control is very effective (see page 175).

Red spider mite Most serious as a greenhouse pest, these minute mites initially produce speckling on the upper sides of leaves, which eventually become bronzed and die. They are best seen with a hand lens on the underside of leaves. They attack a wide range of plants, including cucurbits and beans, building up rapidly in warm dry conditions.

Damp down greenhouses as for greenhouse whitefly, spray with insecticidal soap, and use biological control. (See above.)

The biting insects damage plants by nibbling holes in various parts of the plant, mainly the leaves and stems. They include the caterpillars of moths and butterflies, the larvae of flies, and beetles.

Cabbage caterpillars Several different types of caterpillar, including the large and small cabbage whites and, in hot climates, the diamond back moth, commonly attack brassicas, causing serious damage if not spotted young. They can be controlled by hand picking, by fine nets and fibrous film covers to prevent the adult moths and butterflies landing to lay eggs, by spraying with derris, pyrethrum and soft soap, and with *Bacillus thuringiensis* biological control.

Cabbage root fly This pest can take a heavy toll on freshly planted young brassicas. The adult flies, which look like small houseflies, lay eggs at the base of the stem which hatch into small white larvae. These tunnel into the stems, causing the plants to keel over and die.

Protect plants from the adult flies with fine netting or fibrous film covers, or with discs or plastic pot barriers when planting.

Flea beetle These are several species of very small, jumping beetles which thrive in warm weather, nibbling the seedling leaves of brassicas and closely related vegetables like radishes. Freshly germinated plants seem to be the most vulnerable.

Crops can be protected with very fine netting and fibrous film covers, and beetles can be caught on greased boards. They are easily controlled by spraying with derris, pyrethrum or insecticidal soap. Californian growers with a very serious flea beetle problem were sowing pak choi under black shading net, which was removed once the seedlings were about ½ in (1 cm) high. This seemed to give a degree of protection. They also minimized the area sprayed chemically by 'herding' the flea beetles into one small patch with a water hose, then spraying them.

Pollen or blossom beetle These tiny, shiny, blue-black or green-black beetles are about ⅛ in (2 mm) long. They invade a wide range of crops in late spring, laying eggs in the buds and flowers. The larvae feed on the pollen and nectar before pupating in the soil. Pollen beetle can be a severe problem on the flowering brassicas and Chinese broccoli and on radishes grown for seed. Control as for flea beetle, though the use of nets is more difficult with tall plants.

Principal diseases of oriental vegetables

Diseases are mainly caused by fungi, bacteria and viruses. They can spread very rapidly in favourable conditions and, once established, it is very difficult to eradicate them. There are at present no practicable, environmentally safe sprays to control disease. So in most cases when disease strikes infected plants have to be pulled up and burnt, or infected parts cut out. Preventive medicine really is the key to avoiding disease. In almost every case, diseases arise where something is wrong with the growing conditions. (See Preventive medicine, page 173.)

The following are the main types of disease likely to be encountered in growing oriental vegetables.

Bacterial soft rot These unpleasant rots affect brassicas. The outer leaves wilt, rotting may then start at the base of the stem, and finally the internal leaves go slimy. This is often not noticed until the plants are harvested. Soft rot spreads rapidly at high temperatures.

Poor watering is often at the root of an attack. Good rotation, and keeping plants mulched help prevent attacks. The Chinese also believe planting on ridges keeps plants healthy.

Clubroot The most serious of all brassica diseases, clubroot is caused by an organism which makes the roots swell and develop gross lumps. The plants become stunted, and as the lumps decay (releasing spores into the soil), the roots rot and the plants die. Soil can remain infected for 20 years, even when no brassicas are grown in it. The long-term hope lies in the development of resistant varieties.

Good drainage, good rotation systems, preventing acidity (by liming soils to a pH of 7), and, probably, maintaining high levels of organic matter in the soil, are all measures which help prevent clubroot from becoming established, or its worse effects appearing. Take care not to introduce it on bought-in plants. Examine roots for suspicious lumps. Infected plants should be dug up (never pulled up) and burnt to avoid spreading infection. Never compost them.

Once soil is infected the only way to grow brassicas successfully is to raise them in modules and pot them up in 4 in (10 cm) pots before planting out. This usually gives them a sufficient start to produce a crop before the clubs decay, though plants *can* become infected within five weeks of sowing or planting. (See also Plant raising, Use of modules, page 153.)

Damping off diseases These are the diseases which cause seedlings to wither and flop over, often with blackening on the stems. It is most common on seedlings raised indoors. Hygiene, the use of sterilized compost, and good ventilation are the key preventive measures.

Leaf spots A range of diseases cause spots to appear on leaves. Infected leaves can often be removed without seriously damaging the plant.

Moulds and mildews There are very many types, causing a wide range of plants to rot and/or develop white moulds, mainly on the leaves. Some are worse in wet conditions, others in dry conditions. Keeping greenhouse plants well ventilated, and outdoor plants well grown and well watered, are the main methods of prevention.

Root rots A number of diseases which originate from soil infections result in the ultimate collapse of the plant, often rotting off at soil level. Cucurbits and beans are among the most susceptible. Careful watering and strict rotation are the best preventive measures.

Virus diseases Virus diseases are very infectious, incurable, and generally introduced and spread by insects such as aphids. Infected plants are characterized by stunted and distorted growth in the plant as a whole, with leaves becoming mottled, yellowing, rolled, or developing strange patterns.

Uproot and burn virused plants as soon as they are spotted. Take steps to control the 'vector' which carries it. Good soil fertility and adequate water can help plants overcome virus attacks. Use resistant varieties if available.

Part 3

Recipes

Introduction

I am most grateful to Ken Toyé, the Singing Chef of Ipswich, for helping me compile this short collection of recipes to supplement the general guidance on cooking given under 'Use' in each chapter.

In trying out the oriental vegetables in my garden, Ken has developed his own ideas on how to cook them, and what dishes to serve them with. He has become intrigued by the possibilities they present of marrying traditional European cookery with oriental. So in some of these recipes the Oriental influence is paramount, in others the Western. And we urge you to be experimental, adapting your own vegetable recipes to the oriental vegetables you have grown or bought. There is also plenty of scope to vary these recipes in your own way. In addition, many exciting 'ethnic' recipes can be found in the excellent books now available on Chinese, Japanese, Indian, Thai and Indochinese cookery. (See Appendix page 216.)

It is my belief that good quality, fresh, home-grown vegetables only need simple cooking. Most oriental vegetables lend themselves to cooking by one of the simple basic methods outlined below.

Cup measures Throughout this section, the cup used to measure volume is the British standard 10 fluid ounce cup, whose metric equivalent is 300 millilitres.

See also the conversion charts for weights and measures on page 197.

Basic methods of cooking oriental vegetables

Stir-frying

Stir-frying is the quintessential Chinese method of cooking vegetables. It is quick, economical and versatile. It preserves the flavour and nutrients of vegetables, while giving them a lovely crisp texture. Almost all oriental vegetables can be stir-fried, either alone or in combination with other vegetables, and/or meat, fish, poultry or egg. Westerners tend to be nervous of stir-frying, but there is no need: it is an easily mastered art. Stir-frying is traditionally done in a wok but can be done in a frying pan or heavy pot. However, I would urge anyone who grows oriental vegetables to 'adopt a wok'! It will be the best culinary investment you ever made.

METHOD
- Cut vegetables into small, equally sized pieces, generally an inch or so (3 cm) in length for stalks, root vegetables and pods, and somewhat larger for leafy vegetables.
- Heat the wok or pan until it starts to smoke.
- Put in 2–3 tablespoons of oil. For leafy greens, use approximately a tablespoon of oil per

Woks

handful of greens. As a general rule, use an oil *without* a strong flavour of its own, such as a good blended vegetable oil, groundnut oil or sunflower oil. Avoid strong-flavoured oils such as walnut or olive oil. A possible exception is *good quality* sesame oil; its distinctive flavour marries well with oriental vegetables.
- Swirl the oil in the base of the wok or pan, and up the sides.
- Where sliced garlic and sliced ginger are used as seasoning they are often added at this stage. Add garlic first, cooking it until it sizzles; then ginger, cooking until it sizzles.
- Add the prepared vegetables, tossing them around for 30–60 seconds, depending on the vegetables, until they are well coated in oil and partially cooked.
- Add other seasoning being used, such as sea salt, ground pepper, sauces, herbs, chopped onions. Add garlic and ginger at this stage if you prefer.
- If the mixture is dry add a little moisture. This could be water, white wine, stock, or soy sauce diluted in a little water.
- Cook until the vegetables are tender but crisp. This normally takes no more than a few minutes, depending on the vegetables and the quantities involved. If the vegetables are thick and bulky, cover the pan for this stage. It is unnecessary for small quantities.

NB Succulent vegetables such as cucumber help in the cookery as they add their own moisture to the vegetables.

Steaming

Steaming is a fast, efficient method of cooking vegetables. It preserves their delicate flavour, conserving more nutrients than when boiled. It is suitable for all leafy vegetables, and for root vegetables and beans, which should be sliced finely if they are large. Vegetables with a high moisture content, such as cucumber, are not generally very suited to steaming.

If available, use a metal steamer or a Chinese bamboo steamer, which can be set into a wok. Or improvise with a wire sieve on top of a saucepan, covered with some sort of lid or cooking foil.

METHOD
- Boil the water. Put the vegetables into the upper part of the steamer, making sure they don't touch the water but are permeated by the steam.
- Cover and steam for a few minutes.
- Test for readiness by breaking off a little piece of the vegetable and tasting.
- Season after steaming with salt, pepper, lemon, fresh herbs etc. (Lemon and salt help to bring out other flavours.) Fresh herbs tossed through freshly steamed vegetables are very good. Try it with chervil, Chinese chives, basil, mint, or any fresh herbs to hand. Serve with sliced raw radishes on top, allowing them just to absorb the warmth of the vegetables.

Boiling

Boiling is suitable for vegetables such as roots, dried and fresh beans, and vegetables with thick bulky stems or coarse leaves, all of which require a reasonable amount of cooking. It is not generally appropriate for fine-leaved, delicate vegetables. Boiling in water tends to degrade the nutrients and flavour, so vegetables should always be boiled in some kind of stock, such as good chicken stock or the basic stock below. Cooked this way vegetables retain their flavour.

A word about woks

A WORD ABOUT WOKS The basic wok is a thin-metalled, round-bottomed, high-sided pan. It is the ideal utensil for stir-frying, but can be adapted to steaming, braising and deep-frying. It heats up fast, distributes heat rapidly, uses a minimum of cooking oil, and has good capacity. It is best suited for cooking on gas, but we find it performs well on electricity. If you have problems, try a model with a slightly flattened base. Woks are made with either one long handle or two short handles. The former is steadier and better for steaming or deep-frying; the latter is more easily manoeuvred when stir-frying. A wok stand is used to steady the wok when steaming or deep-frying. (For gas cooking, it must have ventilation holes.) A wok should have a well-fitting domed lid for use when steaming or finishing off stir-fried vegetables. The best woks are made of iron or carbon steel; avoid cheap aluminium or light stainless steel woks. They should be about 14 in (35 cm) in diameter, and have high sides.

If you can learn to use chopsticks, you will find them very handy for turning and stirring vegetables in a wok. Extra-long chopsticks are often used for the purpose.

Frying pans and saucepans

FRYING PANS AND SAUCEPANS Don't be deterred by the lack of a wok. Stir-frying can be done *almost* as successfully in any large frying pan, such as a deep-sided sautéing pan, or even in a reasonably heavy saucepan. All require well-fitting lids.

Whatever utensil is used, try to reserve it for vegetables. It should be cleaned and seasoned before use as below. *Note:* Never use detergent to wash a wok or frying pan. It destroys the surface so food burns rather than slipping over the surface.

Cleaning the wok or pan

CLEANING THE WOK OR PAN
- Heat the wok or pan until it is searing hot.
- Add a little vinegar or water, allowing it to bubble furiously.
- Wipe it thoroughly with kitchen paper, a cloth, or a Chinese wok brush, a whisk-like brush usually made of bamboo splints.
- Warm it to dry. The surface should feel smooth.

Season the wok or pan

SEASONING THE WOK OR PAN
- Heat it until it is sizzling hot.
- Pour in a little cooking oil, then wipe it dry with paper.
- Repeat this two to three times if the pan has not previously been seasoned; once is sufficient if the pan is regularly used for vegetables.

METHOD
- Bring the stock (see below) to the boil, and add the vegetables.
- Boil them fast until they are cooked but still crisp.
- Drain and serve immediately.
- If they cannot be served at once, plunge them into ice-cold water to cool rapidly, drain and pat dry. Re-heat just before serving by fast stir-frying.

Basic Stock
- Chop carrots and onions, and simmer them for about 20 minutes with a sprig of celery, a bunch of herbs, sea salt, ground pepper and garlic.
- Drain. The stock can be kept in a fridge for a couple of days if it is not wanted immediately. Or it can be frozen in cubes for future use.

Parboiling

Parboiling implies boiling vegetables until they are *half* cooked, with the cooking process usually completed in a stir-fry. Parboiling is mainly for vegetables which require reasonably long cooking, to reduce the final cooking time to that required by other vegetables or ingredients in a mixture. The Chinese sometimes parboil bulky leafy greens before stir-frying. Parboil in a stock, as suggested above for boiling.

Blanching

Here vegetables are dipped or plunged into boiling water, for no more than a few seconds, to soften them and shorten the cooking time. Blanching is a useful method of softening leaves which will be stuffed.

Braising/stewing

In this gentle method of cooking, vegetables are stewed in a small amount of liquid. It is particularly suited to root vegetables and tubers, but can also be used for very firm cabbage (chopping the heart and stems), for fresh beans, and for the stems of mustards, pak choi and other oriental greens. The faster cooking leaves can be added halfway through the cooking. A mixture of braised roots and green vegetables creates a delicious vegetable *pot au feu*.

METHOD
- Prepare the vegetables in small cubes or thin slices.
- Toss them lightly in oil in a frying pan, wok or cooking pot.
- When piping hot add a little liquid, for example white wine or a well-flavoured stock. (See Boiling, above.) The liquid should be about a quarter of the volume of the vegetables.
- Cover and stew over a gentle heat, or cook slowly in an oven.
- Serve with large, crisp garlic-and-lemon croûtons (see below.)

How to hold chopsticks

To make croûtons
- Dry small cubes of crustless white bread in the oven with a splashing of oil on top and a little salt. Melt butter, garlic and lemon juice in a pan. Spoon over the croûtons. They can be heated in a low oven if wanted.

Deep-frying

From the nutritional point of view we should frown on deep-fried vegetables, but vegetables can be very tasty coated in batter and deep-fried—the classic example of this being the Japanese *tempura*. It is suitable for root vegetables, aubergines, peppers, many cucurbits, and flowers, and for certain leaves including chrysanthemum greens and perilla. Most vegetables will need to be sliced or cut into smallish pieces before cooking. Handle the vegetables with chopsticks or kitchen tongs.

Light tempura batter
1 large egg
½ pint (300 ml) water
pinch of salt
6½ oz (200 g) sifted plain flour
First, mix the batter. Whisk the egg in the water with the salt, then lightly whisk in the flour a little at a time.
  If the vegetable pieces are at all moist, sprinkle them lightly with flour, dusting off the excess, to help the batter to stick. Then dip them in the batter to coat them.
  Heat vegetable oil in a wok, deep frying pan, or deep-frier until it is very hot. (A cube of white bread dropped into it should turn golden-brown within about 40 seconds.)
  Drop in the vegetables, frying them briefly until they sizzle.
NB The vegetables can be marinated first, say in a mixture of lemon juice with a hint of soy sauce, then dried before coating with batter.

Salads and salad dressings

Oriental vegetables can be used in salads in the following ways:

Raw
The mild flavoured leafy brassicas, stem lettuce, and many forms of radish are among those often eaten raw with a salad dressing.

Cooked and cooled
This treatment is most suited to root vegetables, bean sprouts, and the strong-flavoured leafy mustards. Cook the vegetables lightly, cool and serve with a dressing.

Chinese hot salad
In a Chinese hot salad vegetables are stir-fried *very* briefly, just enough to take the edge off their rawness, then, while still in the pan, are tossed thoroughly with a dressing. The result is a superb flavour and an appetizing appearance. It can be adapted to many vegetables, alone or in a mixture, using different dressings.

BASIC METHOD
- Prepare vegetables as for stir-frying (see page 180).
- Mix up one of the Chinese dressings suggested below in a bowl.
- Stir-fry the vegetables for no more than 30 seconds in a mixture of cooking oil and a little sesame oil.
- Pour the dressing over the vegetables and toss them around thoroughly for another 30 seconds. Serve immediately.

Salad dressings

There is a wide choice of salad dressings for oriental vegetables, ranging from those with a distinct 'oriental' flavour, to more conventional Western dressings. A few suggestions are given below.

NOTE ON OILS, VINEGAR AND SAUCES
Oil Use a well-flavoured oil, e.g. olive oil, walnut oil, or sesame oil. Cold pressed sesame is excellent.
Vinegar Use wine, cider or sherry vinegar. The latter is particularly good with oriental greens.
Soy sauce Use light, not dark, soy sauce in salad dressings.

Vinaigrette
This is made in the proportion of 4 parts oil to one part of vinegar or lemon juice, blended with a little mustard, sea salt, ground pepper and crushed garlic. To finish, sprinkle fresh herbs over the salad.

Chinese dressing
Blend together 2½ tablespoons oil and 1 tablespoon vinegar. Gradually stir in the following: 1 tablespoon soy sauce, sea salt, ground pepper, 2 tablespoons finely chopped shallots or green onions, 2 tablespoons thinly sliced sweet peppers, 1 tablespoon ground sesame seeds, 1 chopped garlic clove.

Sweet and sour Chinese dressing
Make a syrup by warming a tablespoon of sugar in a little warm water. Add lemon juice and salt (or more sugar if necessary), until the required sweet-sour balance is obtained. Mix with a tablespoon each of sesame oil (or tahini) and wine vinegar, a little soy sauce, grated or sliced fresh root ginger and a pinch of sugar just before serving.

Ken's sesame seed dressing
Crush 2 tablespoons white or brown sesame seeds. Add to them 1 tablespoon sugar, 1 tablespoon soy sauce, 2 tablespoons vinegar and ½ teaspoon salt.

Lemon dressing
Blend together equal quantities of olive oil and lemon juice. Flavour with crushed garlic, and season with sea salt and ground pepper.

Lemon and green onion dressing
Blend together 2 tablespoons chopped green onion, the juice of half a lemon, a thin trickle of oil, sea salt and ground pepper.

Lemon and ginger dressing
For this clean, refreshing dressing, blend together 1 teaspoon freshly grated or sliced ginger, ½ teaspoon lemon juice, sea salt and ground pepper to taste.

Sauce gribiche
To ½ pint (300 ml) basic vinaigrette dressing add 1 chopped hard-boiled egg and 1 tablespoon chopped sweet/sour pickled gherkins. This sauce is excellent with cooked vegetables and Chinese greens.

French warm dressing
Chop 2 rashers streaky bacon, and cook in a pan until the fat runs. Take out the crispy bits and put in the salad. Add a tablespoon of wine vinegar (or wine), and a tablespoon of unhulled pumpkin seeds if you wish, to the fat and cook for about 2 minutes. Then pour over the salad, topped with garlic croûtons (see page 182). Eat immediately.

Raisin salad garnish
Mix raisins (soaked to soften), split seedless grapes and a pinch of sea salt through the salad so that the juice from the grapes and the raisins permeates the vegetables. Aim for a balance of sweetness from the raisins and sharpness from the grapes.

Soup

Many of the oriental vegetables are used in soups, especially the leafy greens. The following recipes are for 4 people.

Basic Western Recipe for Greens Soup
2 handfuls chopped greens
1 large onion, chopped
2 sticks celery, chopped
2 tablespoons chopped carrots
2 tablespoons radish or white turnip
oil for cooking
salt and freshly ground pepper
2 garlic cloves, chopped
ordinary or Chinese chives
1 tablespoon fresh tomato purée
grated hard mature cheese
spring onion, mitsuba or chervil
Soften the vegetables by cooking gently in a little oil in a large pan. Add salt, pepper, garlic, chopped chives, tomato purée. Mix together well.

Add 2 pints (1.2 litres) water. Simmer until the vegetables are just cooked. Check seasoning. Serve with crisp croûtons (see page 182), grated cheese, and chopped spring onion or fresh herbs.

Chinese-style Basic Soup for Leafy Greens
2 pints (1.2 litres) clear stock (see below)
a few mushrooms
1 clove garlic
handful of greens
sesame oil or soy sauce (optional)
Bring the stock to the boil, and simmer briefly.

Stir-fry the mushrooms and garlic together; add the greens and stir-fry for another minute.

Add the vegetables to the soup, and simmer for about 5 minutes. Season with a little sesame oil or soy sauce if liked.

Clear stock
To make a clear stock from chicken, cover about 1 lb (450 g) chicken pieces with 4 pints (2.2 litres) cold water. Bring it very slowly to just below boiling point, skimming off any fatty scum on the surface. Then add crushed garlic, sliced ginger, chopped green onion and seasoning, and simmer gently for at least 2 hours, skimming regularly. Strain well. The stock can be cooled and stored in the refrigerator for a few days, or frozen.

Ohitashi

This very popular Japanese method of cooking vegetables is used for leafy greens, all types of brassicas, and beans.

Boil the prepared vegetables until just cooked, then drain, gently squeezing out the moisture. (For leafy vegetables, it is sufficient just to drop them into boiling water, bring it back to the boil, then remove them.) Cut the cooked vegetables into 1½-in (4-cm) lengths if necessary. When cool sprinkle with soy sauce, and after a minute or so squeeze again to remove any more moisture. This increases the flavour.

The vegetables can be served in various ways. Typical Japanese methods are:
—Wrapped in dried seaweed, *nori*
—Dressed with a mixture of *dashi**, or as an alternative flaked tuna fish, and soy sauce

We recommend them as salad with sweet and sour Chinese dressing (page 183) or Ken's sesame seed dressing (page 183)

* **Dashi** is a Japanese clear stock made from seaweed and flaked dried bonito (a type of tuna fish). Make it from 'dashi-na-moto', a prepared concentrated form, if available. Otherwise use fish stock.

Oriental pickles

In Asia there is a long and rich tradition of preserving vegetables by salting, pickling, drying and fermentation. Many of the methods originated in areas with harsh climates, as a means of supplementing scarce supplies of vegetables during the winter months. But there is such a liking for the strong, unusual flavours produced by the preservation processes, that many 'short-term' pickles are made for immediate, daily use.

As in the West, pickles and preserves are used as snacks, appetizers and garnishes, chopped up and scattered over dishes. Small quantities (the flavour is very strong) are also used in cooking, generally to flavour simmering vegetable dishes or soups. Before being added to a dish they are soaked, drained, and parboiled for a minute or two.

Vegetables are preserved in a range of substances—from salt, vinegar, wine, and soy sauce to shrimp paste and fermented bean paste. There are innumerable permutations. Salt can be flavoured with garlic, soy sauce mixed with rice wine, and chillies, garlic, spices, sugar, dried seaweed, and numerous other ingredients added to give a distinct flavour, which can be spicy, sweet, sour or salty. While salting leads to a loss of vitamins, some of the fermentation processes actually increase the vitamin content of the vegetables.

Almost any oriental vegetable can be preserved: leafy greens and stems, turnips and radishes (turnip leaves and roots are pickled together), cucurbits . . . even delicate leaves such as perilla are pickled. They can be done alone, or in mixtures. A few guidelines are given below, but for further information consult specialist books on the subject. Western pickling recipes can be used for oriental vegetables.

Long-term pickles

Basic pickling method
This is suitable for a wide range of vegetables. There are normally two stages:
1 Dehydration.
2 Pickling in liquid such as vinegar.

DEHYDRATION
In hot climates vegetables may simply be dried in the sun; otherwise they are salted.
Dry salting Watery and fleshy vegetables, and some leafy vegetables are sliced or chopped where appropriate, then placed in a bowl in layers, with salt sprinkled over each layer. They can be left up to 24 hours, then drained and rinsed. They are often weighted to accelerate the process.
Salting in brine Solid vegetables such as onions and radishes can be soaked in brine, which is gentler in action than dry salt. For a basic brine dissolve 2 oz (50 g) salt in 1 pint (600 ml) water, bring it to the boil and cool it before dropping in the vegetables. Make sure they are well covered. They can be left from 12–48 hours, then drained.

PICKLING VINEGAR
Vinegar should be of good quality, with an acetic acid content of at least 5 per cent. Distilled vinegar, which is colourless, looks best, but malt, cider and rice vinegar tend to be better flavoured. The flavour can be improved by spicing the vinegar with *whole* spices (see below). You can often re-use the vinegar in jars of bought pickles. Vegetables can be put into hot or cold vinegar; hot vinegar is considered better for soft pickles, and cold for vegetables you wish to remain crisp. Make sure vegetables are well covered as the liquid evaporates with time. Store the pickles in screw top jars.
To make basic spiced vinegar
a) Slow method
For every quart (1.2 litres) of vinegar allow ½ oz (15 g) cinnamon bark, ¼ oz (7 g) cloves, ¼ oz (7 g) mace, ¼ oz (7 g) allspice. (Peppercorns, chilli peppers, etc can be added if liked. Chinese variants include ginger, garlic cloves, and sesame seeds.) Fill the jars with cold vinegar, add the spices and leave for up to 2 months, shaking the jars occasionally.
b) Fast method
Put spices and vinegar in a *covered* basin (to preserve the flavours) set in a pan of water. Bring the water to the boil, remove from the stove, and allow the spices to steep in the vinegar for 2 hours.
Plum vinegar The famous Japanese sour plums, *umeboshi*, are made by

sprinkling plums with salt and weighting them. The resultant juice makes an excellent pickling vinegar.

Oriental quick pickles

Here are some examples of popular, quickly made pickles.

Mizuna-greens Quick Salted Pickle

- Wash mizuna leaves. Sprinkle a bowl with salt, and cover it with a layer of leaves. Sprinkle salt over them, add another layer of leaves, sprinkle with salt and so on until the leaves are used up. Sprinkle salt over the top, and weigh the leaves down. They will be ready within 12 hours. Don't leave them longer or the flavour is destroyed. (The recommended ratio of leaves to salt is 25:1.)

Ruey Hua's Mustard Leaf Pickle

I must admit I was horrified to watch this apparently brutal treatment of common (leaf) mustard, but it resulted in an excellent flavour. We cooked the salted greens with minced beef and pork, adding red chillies for the contrasting colour.

Cover the leaves with salt and leave for a couple of hours. Take the leaves, scrunch them up, and wring them out as if they were wet clothes. (They are sometimes sold at this stage.) Wash in cold water, chop finely, and use in cooking.

Turnip Pickle

Cut turnips and leaves in half, sprinkle with salt. If sprinkled liberally, leave for ½ hour; if sparsely for 2 hours. Test the flavour by periodically removing a little, rinsing it, and tasting. When ready remove, rinse, and pickle in vinegar flavoured with soy sauce, sugar and salt to taste.

Cucumber Pickle

Make slits in ripe, yellow cucumbers, salt them and leave overnight. Pickle them in vinegar and sugar, adding chillies if you like a hot pickle.

Kelly Kindscher's Fermented Cambodian Pickle

Use any, or a mixture, of the following vegetables: Chinese cabbage, turnips, carrots, green onions, mung bean sprouts, cucumbers.

For the basic recipe fill a quart (1-litre) jar with chopped vegetables. Add 1 tablespoon each of vinegar, salt and sugar. Fill the jar three-quarters full with boiling water, place a lid lightly over the top, and put in the sun or somewhere warm. Check daily to see if fermentation is underway. If not, put it somewhere warmer. It should take 3 days. At that stage put it in a fridge, tightly covered, so that fermentation slows down. The flavour somewhat resembles sauerkraut. Variations to the basic recipe include adding more salt (for tougher vegetables and to make the pickle less sour), less vinegar, less sugar, hot peppers, garlic, etc.
—From *Gardening with Southeast Asian Refugees.*

Bruce Cost's Pickled Mustard Stems

3 bunches mustard with long straight stems
1⅓ tablespoons salt
2 cups mild white rice vinegar
1½ cups sugar
6 dried red chilli peppers
Trim mustard leaves off their stems and cut the stems into 3-in (7.5-cm) lengths. Sprinkle with 1 tablespoon salt. Leave 1 hour. Drain. Transfer to a quart (1-litre) jar. Bring the vinegar, sugar, chillies and 1 teaspoon salt to the boil, and pour over the stems. Cool. Cover and refrigerate. They will be ready within 24–48 hours.
—From *Asian Ingredients*, by Bruce Cost.

Sichuan Mixed Pickle

broccoli
cauliflower
carrots
red and white radishes
string beans
snow peas
cucumber
Chinese cabbage

Pickling mixture
2 tablespoons rice wine
2 tablespoons sea salt
2 teaspoons Sichuan peppercorns
1 pint (600 ml) water
3 fresh sliced chillies
6 slices ginger
1 sliced garlic clove
Use a selection of the vegetables listed above.

Wash and trim the vegetables, and cut into bite-sized pieces. Soak in cold, boiled water for 2 hours.

Meanwhile make up the pickling mixture.

Put the wine, salt and peppercorns with the water in a glass or china bowl. Add the chillies, ginger, garlic and drained vegetables. (They should be packed tightly into the bowl.) Cover with a small plate to keep them under the water, and cover the whole dish with clingfilm. Keep at room temperature for 2 days, then put into a refrigerator for 2 days. Eat within 10 days, draining before use. The longer they are left, the stronger the flavour will be.
—From *Highlight Chinese Cuisine*, by Madame Chin Hau.

Pickled Cabbage Peking Style

Served cold as an hors d'oeuvre, salad or side dish, this dish keeps well in the refrigerator for at least 2 weeks. Avoid eating the Sichuan peppercorns.

Serves 6–8
2 lb (1 kg) Chinese cabbage, quartered and cored
2 tablespoons salt
½–¾ in (1–2 cm) fresh ginger root, peeled and cut into silken threads
5 tablespoons sugar
2½ tablespoons groundnut or corn oil
2½ tablespoons sesame oil
3 dried red chillies, seeded and chopped
1 teaspoon Sichuan peppercorns
5 tablespoons rice vinegar
Shred the cabbage as finely as possible either in a food processor or with a knife. Put into a very large mixing bowl.

Sprinkle with salt and mix. Leave to stand at room temperature for 2–3 hours; the cabbage will decrease in bulk having released most of its water content. Taking a handful at a time, and using both hands, squeeze out the excess water but leave damp. Transfer to a clean bowl.

Place the ginger in a bunch on top of the cabbage in the centre of the bowl. Sprinkle on the sugar, taking care not to put it over the ginger.

Heat the groundnut or corn oil and the sesame oil in a small saucepan over a high heat until smoke rises. Remove from the heat and add the chillies and peppercorns.

Pour the mixture over the ginger first, and then the surrounding cabbage in the bowl. The sizzling oil partly cooks the ginger, enhancing the flavour.

Add the vinegar and mix well. Leave to stand at room temperature for 2–3 hours before serving.
—From *Yan Kit's Classic Chinese Cookbook*, by Yan-kit So.

Montrose Pumpkin Pickle

This delicious pickle is based on a Norwegian recipe. We make it every year as a substitute for mango chutney.

2 lb (1 kg) pumpkin
¾ pint (450 ml) malt vinegar
2 tablespoons sugar
⅔ oz (20 g) whole dry ginger.
Cut the pumpkin first into 4–8 'boats'. Peel, remove seeds and pith, and then cut into 2-in (5-cm) cubes. Boil in water for 5 minutes then strain.

Boil the vinegar, sugar and ginger together for 5 minutes. Add the pumpkin and boil until most of the liquid has evaporated (about 1 hour). Pack into screw-top jars, and store until needed.

Recipes for specific oriental vegetables

All recipes are for 4 people unless otherwise stated.

Adzuki beans
Japanese Anko Sweet

Cover dried adzuki beans with boiling water, leave for 30 minutes, drain and rinse. This procedure shortens the cooking time.

Cover the beans with fresh water, bring to the boil, and simmer until tender. (Cooking time varies with the age of the beans and other factors but is normally at least 1½–2 hours.) The beans should eventually be the consistency of yoghurt. Add a little sugar and salt, and eat with *mochi* (Japanese glutinous rice cakes) or vanilla ice cream.

Adzuki Bean Risotto

This is based on the Japanese dish *sekihan*, in which glutinous rice is boiled with the nearly cooked adzuki beans.
4 oz (100 g) dried adzuki beans
1 medium-sized onion, chopped
1 stick celery, chopped
cooking oil
handful of cooked green soya beans and/or cooked, sliced French beans
salt and freshly ground pepper
8 oz (225 g) cooked rice (preferably unpolished or brown rice)
1 chilli pepper, chopped
sesame seeds

Cook the adzuki beans as for the recipe above, with a little of the chopped onion and the celery, in water. Simmer until cooked but still just firm.

Toss rest of the chopped onion in a little oil in a large frying pan over a moderate heat to soften. Add the soya and/or green beans and seasoning. Mix well, add the rice and adzuki beans. Stir vigorously and when warmed through add the chopped chilli, and sprinkle with roasted sesame seeds (see below).

Use as an accompaniment to meat, poultry or fish dishes. To make a vegetarian meal serve with hard-boiled eggs and nuts.

TO ROAST SESAME SEEDS
Put the seeds in a dry skillet over low heat, stir constantly to prevent burning. As soon as you can smell the sesame, add a little salt, and cook for just a few seconds more. Keep dry in an airtight jar until required.

Alfalfa and Chinese clover
Vegetarian Light Lunch

Stir-fry a handful of young alfalfa or Chinese clover with a couple of chopped shallots, a few chopped nuts and seasoning. Add a sprin-

kling of wine to finish cooking. Serve with grilled tomatoes sprinkled with fresh herbs, and little mounds of lightly scrambled egg. Or add bean curd and use as a shortcrust pie filling.

Amaranthus
Spicy Amaranthus

1 lb (450 g) amaranthus, cut into 2 in (5 cm) pieces
butter or margarine
cooking oil
1 tablespoon chopped onion
Spice mixture
½ teaspoon cumin seeds or ground cumin
½ teaspoon grated fresh ginger
1 fresh green or red chilli, deseeded
1 garlic clove
Grind the spices together and stir the mixture into the amaranthus. Heat a knob of butter or margarine with a tablespoon of oil in a wok or frying pan and stir-fry the onion until just cooked. Add the spices and amaranthus—the thicker stalks first, then the leafier parts. Stir-fry until cooked, adding a little water if necessary. Cover for the last few minutes to retain the flavour.
Note: You can increase the quan-

tities of the spices, or vary them, to make a hotter dish.

Amaranthus, Lentils and Chick Peas

1 lb (450 g) amaranthus
butter or margarine
salt and freshly ground pepper
1 cup cooked red lentils
1 cup cooked chick peas

Braise the amaranthus in a minimum of water, a knob of butter or margarine and seasoning until just cooked. Drain.

Purée the cooked lentils in a food processor or mouli. Prepare the chick peas similarly.

Arrange the cooked amaranthus, red lentils and chick peas in strips on a hot plate. The deep green, red and beige colours contrast beautifully. Serve with grilled or roast pork, or firm-fleshed fish such as sea bass or tuna baked in the oven.
See also: Basella Quiche.

Artichokes see Chinese artichokes

Basella
Basella Quiche

8 oz (225 g) shortcrust pastry
8 oz (225 g) basella
salt and freshly ground black
    pepper
3 eggs
½ pint (300 ml) milk
freshly ground nutmeg
butter

Line a 9-inch (23-cm) flan tin or dish with the shortcrust pastry, and bake blind until golden brown.

Cook the basella until soft, e.g. stir-fry, with a little moisture if necessary, or steam, or parboil. Drain. Season, and put into the pie crust.

Mix together the eggs and milk. Season with salt, pepper and grated nutmeg. Pour over the basella. Dot the top with small pieces of butter and bake in a moderate oven (350°F, 180°C, Gas 4) until set.

Beans see Adzuki beans; Lablab beans; Yam beans; Yard long beans

Bean sprouts see Sprouting seeds

Bitter gourd see Cucurbits and gourds

Bottle gourd see Cucurbits and gourds

Broccoli see Chinese broccoli

Burdock
Japanese Kimpira Burdock (Sautéed burdock with carrots)

5 oz (150 g) burdock root
2 oz (50 g) carrot
1 dried red chilli pepper
1½ tablespoons sesame oil
1 tablespoon sugar
½ tablespoon sweet rice wine or
    sherry
1 tablespoon soy sauce
4 tablespoons fish stock or *dashi*
    (see page 184)
1 tablespoon roasted sesame seeds
    (see page 186)

Wash the burdock, gently scrape off the skin with the back of a knife, and cut into 2-in (5-cm), matchsticks. Soak in water immediately. Peel the carrot, and cut similarly into matchsticks. Soak the dried red chilli pepper in water to soften, cut in half and squeeze out the seeds under water. Chop finely and set aside.

Drain the burdock and pat dry with paper towel. Heat the sesame oil in a saucepan, and sauté the burdock and carrots over a high heat. Add sugar, rice wine or sherry, soy sauce and stock or *dashi*. Reduce to medium heat and simmer until the liquid is absorbed. Add pepper and sesame seeds and mix together well. Serve in a mound in a bowl.

—From *Japanese Home Style Cooking.*

Cabbage see Chinese cabbage

Chinese artichokes
Creamy Artichoke Soup

1 lb (450 g) Chinese artichokes
1 oz (25 g) butter or margarine
1 tablespoon cornflour

1 pint (600 ml) milk or milk and
    water mixed
freshly grated nutmeg
croûtons (see page 182)
chopped spring onions

Rub or scrub the artichokes gently to remove any soil. Put into a pan. Add enough salted water just to cover, bring to the boil and simmer for about 5 minutes. Drain, reserving the liquid to incorporate into the soup later. Return to the pan; add a knob of butter or margarine and stir over a gentle heat for about 10 minutes to soften further. Sprinkle over the cornflour, cover with the milk or milk and water mixture and the reserved artichoke stock. Simmer very gently for 10 minutes. Season with grated nutmeg and serve with bowls of small crisp croûtons and chopped spring onions.
Note: The soup could be passed through a blender to make a fine cream, but we prefer the artichokes whole.

Chinese Artichokes and Nuts

Lightly stir-fry Chinese artichokes. Season, and add a squeeze of lemon. Add strips of lightly grilled bacon and rough-chopped walnuts or almonds. Serve with lightly cooked amaranthus or a dressed salad.

Chinese broccoli
Chinese Broccoli with Pasta, Avocado and Radish

1 lb (450 g) Chinese broccoli
juice of ¼ lemon
salt and freshly ground pepper
8 oz (225 g) tagliatelle (preferably
    mixed green and white)
1 tablespoon butter
2 tablespoons hard cheese, grated
1 garlic clove, crushed (optional)
1 large avocado
3 tablespoons finely sliced or
    grated radish

Stir-fry the broccoli, adding a little water, lemon juice and seasoning. Cover and simmer until tender.

Boil the tagliatelle in plenty of salted water. Drain, but retain a few spoonfuls of the cooking water in the pan. Return the pasta to it, and stir in the butter, cheese and garlic over a gentle heat.

Serve the pasta in a mound, surrounded by the cooked broccoli. Top with scoops of avocado flesh and the radish.

Sunrise Seeds' Chinese Broccoli and Beef Stir-Fry

8 oz (225 g) good-quality lean
   beef (sirloin or rump)
1 lb (450 g) Chinese broccoli
cooking oil
freshly grated or ground ginger
salt
Marinade
1 tablespoon oyster sauce
2 teaspoons dry sherry
½ teaspoon sugar
2 teaspoons cornflour
Sauce
2 teaspoons dry sherry
½ teaspoon sugar
1 teaspoon cornflour
Cut the beef into ½-in (1-cm) thick slices, then into pieces 1 × 2 in (2.5 × 5 cm). Thoroughly mix the marinade ingredients in a bowl. Put in the pieces of beef, turn to coat in the marinade, then cover and leave for 30 minutes. In another bowl mix well the sauce ingredients.

Cut the broccoli into pieces roughly 2 in (5 cm) long, peeling the very thick stalks. Put 2 tablespoons oil, a little ginger and salt in a very hot wok; lower the heat and let them sizzle for a few seconds. Add the broccoli and cook for a minute; it will turn bright green. Add a little water to moisten, turn up the heat, cover and steam/sizzle the broccoli for 2–3 minutes until tender. Uncover, raise heat again, and stir-fry until the liquid is evaporated. Remove broccoli and spread out on a dish.

Reheat the wok with 1 tablespoon oil. Add the beef, and stir-fry for a minute. Return broccoli to the wok and stir in the sauce. Cook until the sauce thickens.

Chinese cabbage
Chinese Cabbage and Cashews

Use midribs, stems and crisp-hearted leaves, and the soft leaf tops as an accompanying salad.
1 lb (450 g) Chinese cabbage
a little oil for frying
sea salt and freshly ground pepper
2 garlic cloves, chopped
2 rashers lightly grilled and chopped bacon
1 oz (25 g) cashew nuts
a few tablespoons dry white wine
   or water.
Chop the cabbage leaves, stems and midribs roughly and stir-fry for a few minutes in a little oil with freshly ground pepper, sea salt and the chopped garlic.

When well impregnated with oil add the lightly grilled bacon and the cashew nuts. Toss together, add a little liquid, such as white wine or water, and cook a few minutes longer. The total cooking time should be no more than 5–7 minutes. Season to taste if necessary and serve right away.

Note: Ground almonds can be used instead of the cashews, and slivers of chicken or roast sliced pork instead of bacon. This would go well with fish or fried aubergine slices.

Chinese Cabbage Creamed with Yoghurt

1 small onion, chopped
1 small green or sweet red pepper,
   chopped
1 oz (25 g) margarine or
   1 tablespoon cooking oil
1 lb (450 g) Chinese cabbage,
   shredded
½ teaspoon caraway seeds
sea salt
5 fl oz (150 ml) yoghurt or soured
   cream
1 garlic clove, crushed
¼ teaspoon dried mint or ½
   tablespoon chopped fresh mint
   (optional)
freshly ground black pepper
Lightly fry the onion and pepper in the margarine or cooking oil. Add the shredded Chinese cabbage, caraway seeds, and a pinch of sea salt, plus a little water if necessary to prevent sticking. Simmer until tender, stirring occasionally.

Pour the yoghurt or soured cream into a small bowl and stir in the crushed garlic, and mint if using. Pour this mixture over the cabbage. Stir to heat through but don't allow to boil. Season with ground black pepper and serve.

—Adapted from *The Yogurt Book*,
      by Arto der Haroutunian.
See also: Pickled Cabbage Peking Style, page 185.

Chinese Leaves Stuffed with Rice, Peppers and Black Olives

8 large Chinese cabbage leaves
   (allow 2 leaves per person)
1 small onion, chopped
cooking oil
1 medium-sized sweet red pepper,
   chopped
handful of stoned black olives
8 tablespoons cooked rice
1 teaspoon grated fresh ginger
sea salt and freshly ground black
   pepper
1 tablespoon lemon juice
Plunge the cabbage for a minute into boiling salted water. Take out, drain and pat dry.

To make the stuffing for 8 large leaves, first toss the chopped onion in 1 tablespoon cooking oil in a wok or frying pan. Then add the chopped pepper, olives, cooked rice, grated ginger, and sea salt and ground pepper to taste. Stir well until they are warmed through. Lay out the leaves. Divide the stuffing among the 8 leaves, leaving the margins clear; turn in the sides of each, fold over like a cigar and tie with fine twine.

Heat a tablespoon of cooking oil in a saucepan or wok. Gently turn the stuffed leaves, one at a time, in the oil, then lay them all in the saucepan. Add water to come halfway up the leaves, lemon juice and more seasoning, and simmer for about 10 minutes.

Carefully remove the stuffed leaves, cut the twine, and serve. These are very good with pork chops or pork slices, fried with onion and celery.

Chinese chives
Chinese Chive Tempura Snack

Chinese chive leaves
tempura batter (page 182)
oil for deep-frying

Chinese seasoning sauce
3 tablespoons soy sauce
½ tablespoon chilli sauce
½ teaspoon sugar
pinch of salt
1 teaspoon grated garlic
Cut the chive leaves into about 9-in (23-cm) lengths and blanch for 30 seconds in boiling water to soften. Take three leaves at a time, knot them at the top, then make two more knots beneath so they are about 3 in (8 cm) long overall. Or fold them over two or three times and tie them with another leaf. Dip in tempura batter, and deep-fry until crisp.

Mix the Chinese seasoning sauce ingredients together and put into a little sauce dish. Slice the fried knots obliquely, and dip them in the seasoning sauce before eating.

For an attractive tempura mixed platter, deep-fry Chinese leeks, sliced aubergine, basil, amaranthus and ipomea, and serve together.

Chinese Chive and Mung Bean Sprouts Stir-fry

Chinese chive flowers or leaves
    cut into 1-in (2.5-cm) lengths
mung bean sprouts, topped and
    tailed (see note below)
cooking oil
salt
soy sauce or sesame oil
chicken stock (optional)
cornflour (optional)
Briefly stir-fry the Chinese chives and bean sprouts in a little oil. Add salt and a little light soy sauce or sesame oil, and stir well. If you wish add 2 tablespoons chicken stock mixed with 1 tablespoon cornflour, and stir until thickened.
Note: The ratio of Chinese chives to bean sprouts is unimportant: it is the combination of emerald green and white which is very appealing. A total quantity of 2 cups should give 4 servings.

Chinese clover see Alfalfa and Chinese clover

Chinese leaves see Chinese cabbage

Choy sum and co.
(Flowering brassica shoots)

Braised Choy Sum with Mushrooms

1 lb (450 g) choy sum shoots
a knob of butter
4 oz (100 g) mushrooms, sliced
1 onion, finely sliced
salt and freshly ground pepper
Wash the choy sum shoots carefully, pat dry, and make into small bundles tied with twine. Select a large pan, so the bundles can be laid across the bottom. Put them into the pan with just enough water to cover the base, a knob of butter, the mushrooms, onion and seasoning. Cover and simmer for 5 minutes, or until the thickest choy sum stems are tender.

This is delicious with new potatoes and braised chicken breasts; or with large prawns, crayfish tails or lobster.

Steamed Choy Sum with Nuts

1 lb (450 g) choy sum shoots
sesame oil
a handful of nuts (e.g. walnuts,
    cashews)
Make the choy sum into bunches as for the recipe above. Steam until tender, and drain.

Heat a little sesame oil in a wok or pan. Add the nuts, tossing them around until just toasted. Pour over the choy sum.
Note: Carnivores can add tiny pieces of crisp bacon. Mushrooms or other edible fungi can also be added with the nuts.

Chrysanthemum greens
Simple Chrysanthemum Soup

1 lb (450 g) chrysanthemum
    greens, cut in 2-in (5-cm)
    pieces
2 tablespoons vegetable oil
2 cups chicken stock
1 cup water
1 teaspoon salt
½ cup fresh tofu cut in 2-in
    (5-cm) squares (optional)
Stir-fry the chrysanthemum leaves in the cooking oil for not more than a couple of seconds. Add the stock, water, salt, and tofu if using. Bring to the boil. Serve.

Cucumber see Cucurbits and gourds

Cucurbits and gourds
Indonesian Gourd Stuffing (Petola Daging)

This stuffing, from Sri Owen's excellent book on Indonesian food and cookery was originally for stuffing luffa. However, it can be used to stuff all sorts of gourds or cucurbits, which are then either baked or steamed. If baked, they should first be parboiled, blanched or steamed to shorten the cooking time. Ordinary marrow, for example, would need to be parboiled for about 2 minutes. The texture of the gourds must be firm enough to withstand stuffing and cooking.
2 lb (1 kg) luffa or other gourd,
    thinly peeled
4 oz (100 g) shelled prawns
8 oz (225 g) minced lean beef or
    chicken breast
4 eggs
salt and freshly ground pepper
vegetable oil
1 medium-sized onion or
    2 shallots, thinly sliced
2 green chillies, deseeded, or ½
    teaspoon chilli powder
Halve the luffa or other gourd lengthwise and remove the seeds. Leave in cold salted water while preparing the stuffing. Chop the prawns and mix with the minced meat. Separate one egg, keeping the white to one side. Mix the yolk with the other whole eggs, season, and cook to make several thin omelettes. When cool, roll up and cut crosswise into thin slices.

Heat a little oil in a wok or pan, cook the onion or shallots and the chilli until just soft. Add the prawn and meat mixture and stir-fry for 3 minutes. Season, cool slightly and stir in the reserved egg white. Mix in the omelette pieces.

Drain and dry the luffa or gourd halves. Stuff the bottom half, and use the top half as a lid. Steam for 30 minutes or bake for 40 minutes in a moderate oven (350°F, 180°C, Gas 4). Cut into thick slices. Eat hot or cold.

—From *Indonesian Food and Cookery*, by Sri Owen.

Cucumber Soup

This is a good way to use up over-ripe cucumbers.

Peel cucumbers, remove seeds and cut into small pieces. Liquidize in a blender or food processor with seasoning, finely chopped onion to taste and just enough water to give the consistency you prefer.

Chill and serve in glass bowls, pouring over a trickle of single cream or a spoonful of creamy yoghurt. Add chopped parsley to garnish.

See also: Luffa and Tomato Ratatouille and Indonesian Gourd Stuffing, and the instructions for making a cucumber pickle on page 185.

Luffa and Tomato Ratatouille

1 medium onion, sliced
1 garlic clove, crushed
cooking oil
1 lb (450 g) sliced luffa
2 large tomatoes, skinned and sliced
salt and freshly ground pepper
6 large leaves fresh basil, shredded
béchamel sauce (optional)
grated cheese (optional)

Soften the onion and garlic in a saucepan in 2 tablespoons cooking oil. When transparent add the sliced luffa and simmer until soft. Add the tomatoes, seasoning and basil and simmer until all the ingredients are soft. Add a little water if necessary so that the mixture cooks evenly. Check seasoning.

Either serve as a vegetable, or spoon the ratatouille into small ovenproof dishes, cover with béchamel sauce, sprinkle with grated cheese and brown in the oven or under the grill.

Note: You can convert this dish into a typical Mediterranean ratatouille with the addition of sliced peppers and aubergines.

Sliced hot luffa garnish

Slice luffa very finely, and cook in a pan with a knob of butter, pepper, salt, garlic and very little water for not more than 3 minutes. Use as a garnish for chicken breast, pork chops, veal or firm-fleshed fish such as salmon, monkfish, sea bass or shark steaks.

See also: Indonesian Gourd Stuffing, page 000.

Sunrise Seeds' Simple Wax Gourd Soup

1½ pints (900 ml) chicken stock
1 lb (450 g) wax gourd
1 in (2.5 cm) wide strip dried, pre-soaked and scraped tangerine peel (optional)
3 dried mushrooms, pre-soaked and thinly sliced
4 water chestnuts, halved and sliced
2–4 teaspoons soy sauce
salt and freshly ground pepper
1 egg, lightly beaten (optional)

Bring the chicken stock to the boil. Add the wax gourd, tangerine peel, mushrooms, water chestnuts and 2 teaspoons soy sauce. Simmer until the wax gourd is soft (approximately 15 minutes). Season, adding more soy sauce if wished.

Add the egg, if using, and stir until it forms long, cooked threads. Serve at once.

Hairy Melon with Basil and Pasta Salad

2 hairy melons, coarsely grated
1 teaspoon salt
2 handfuls fresh basil leaves
6 tablespoons olive oil
3 garlic cloves
1 teaspoon fresh marjoram (or ½ teaspoon dried)
2¼ pints (1.25 litres) chicken stock
12 oz (350 g) small pasta shapes
fresh lemon juice
4 oz (100 g) grated Parmesan or other well-flavoured cheese
3 tablespoons chopped parsley

Put the grated hairy melon into a colander, sprinkle with the salt and leave for 20 minutes, stirring occasionally. Drain, pat dry and put in a large bowl.

Blend the basil, olive oil, garlic and marjoram thoroughly in a food processor or blender. Add to the hairy melon.

Bring the chicken stock to the boil in a large saucepan, add the pasta, reduce heat and cook for 10 minutes or until the pasta is just tender. Drain well and put into a warmed serving dish. Stir in the hairy melon. Add lemon juice to taste, grated cheese, parsley and seasoning and stir through.

Serve hot or cold. Excellent for picnics or barbecues or to accompany smoked fish.

See also: Luffa and Tomato Ratatouille.

Taiwanese Shredded Bottle Gourd and Red Pepper

1 lb (450 g) firm young bottle gourd
2 sweet red peppers or 2 tablespoons shredded red chilli
1 garlic clove, crushed
vegetable oil
1 teaspoon salt
1 teaspoon sugar
1 tablespoon cornflour

Peel the bottle gourd, cut in half, remove any seeds, and shred or grate the flesh coarsely.

Gently stir-fry the peppers or chilli and the garlic in a little oil. Add the shredded bottle gourd, salt and sugar, and simmer gently until soft, adding more oil if necessary during cooking. Mix the cornflour with 2 tablespoons water, stir through and heat gently until thickened.

—From *Chinese Vegetarian Dishes*, Hilit Publishing Co. Ltd.

Indonesian Stuffed Bitter Melon (Kembu Paria)

4 medium-sized bitter melons
salt
8 tablespoons freshly grated coconut

Stuffing
2 tablespoons vegetable oil
4 shallots, thinly sliced
1 garlic clove, thinly sliced
2 oz (50 g) minced beef, chicken or pork (optional)
½ teaspoon chilli powder or ground white pepper
pinch ground nutmeg
pinch ground turmeric
1 egg, beaten
2 medium-sized potatoes, mashed
seasoning
2 cups (600 ml) thick coconut milk (see below)

Cut the bitter melons in half lengthwise and remove seeds. Sprinkle with 2 tablespoons salt, leave upside down in a colander for an hour, then rinse well with cold water. Boil for 4 minutes; drain.

Stir-fry the grated coconut in a wok or frying pan *without* oil, until golden brown. Then grind it finely.

For the stuffing, first heat the oil in a wok or pan and fry the shallots and garlic for a minute, stirring constantly. Add the minced meat and stir. Add the ground ingredients, and stir again. Then add the mashed potato and beaten egg. Mix thoroughly, season and, when cool, stuff the bitter melons with this mixture.

Put the stuffed melons in a large saucepan and cover with the coconut milk. Sprinkle the ground roasted coconut over the top, and simmer for 10–15 minutes until the sauce is thick. Either serve as a snack, or to accompany a rice dish.

—From *Indonesian and Thai Cookery*, by Sri Owen.

TO MAKE THICK COCONUT MILK

Put 12 oz (350 g) desiccated coconut in a saucepan with 1 pint (600 ml) water. Bring to the boil and simmer for about 5 minutes. Allow to cool and, when tepid, strain, squeezing the coconut to extract as much milk as possible. (This can be done in a piece of cheesecloth or muslin.)

Daikon see Radish

Flat cabbage see Pak choi

Garlic

'Dry' Potatoes with Garlic and Ginger

Serves 4–5

It is best to make this dish in a large, non-stick frying pan or a well-used cast-iron one.

1 lb 6 oz (625 g) potatoes
a piece of fresh ginger about 2 × 1 × 1 in (5 × 2.5 × 2.5 cm), peeled and coarsely chopped
3 garlic cloves, peeled
3 tablespoons water
½ teaspoon ground turmeric
1 teaspoon salt

½ teaspoon cayenne pepper
5 tablespoons vegetable oil
1 teaspoon whole fennel seeds (optional)

Boil the potatoes in their jackets. Drain them and let them cool completely. Peel the potatoes and cut them into ¾–1 in (2–2.5-cm) dice.

Put the ginger, garlic, 3 tablespoons water, turmeric, salt and cayenne pepper into the container of a food processor or blender. Blend until you have a paste.

Heat the oil in a large, preferably non-stick, frying pan over a medium flame. When hot, put in the fennel seeds. Let them sizzle for a few seconds. Now put in the ginger-garlic paste. Stir and fry for 2 minutes. Put in the potatoes. Stir and fry for 5–7 minutes over a medium-high flame or until the potatoes have a nice, golden-brown crust on them.

You could serve these potatoes with an Indian bread and a yoghurt relish, or with grilled or roast meats.

—From *Madhur Jaffrey's Indian Cookery*.

Gourds see Cucurbits and gourds

Hairy melon see Cucurbits and gourds

Komatsuna (Spinach mustard)

Komatsuna Omelette

Ken Toyé loves to make a spinach omelette, but has often wished spinach had a bit more 'body'. Komatsuna seems to fit the bill. Use small leaves whole; cut larger leaves and stalks into pieces.

12 oz (350 g) komatsuna
lemon juice
8 eggs, plus 2 yolks
salt and freshly ground pepper
cooking oil
mushrooms and black olives to garnish
nuts (optional)

Wash and dry the komatsuna leaves and tender stalks, then chop them. Cook in just a little moisture, either lemon juice or water, until very tender. Keep warm.

Beat the eggs and egg yolks together lightly and season. Heat oil in a large, 12-in (30-cm) omelette pan until you get a colourless smoke. Pour the beaten eggs into the pan, and drive a spoon repeatedly through the eggs to build up the omelette. (If you only have a small, 7-in (18-cm) pan, make two small omelettes with half quantities.) When the eggs are still runny but the omelette has formed at the bottom of the pan add the cooked komatsuna, just mixing it into the egg. If you have a lot of vegetable filling don't fold the omelette. If not, fold it over.

Garnish with black olives and mushrooms tossed in oil. Add nuts for vegetarian protein. This makes a lovely starter.

Komatsuna Lobster Risotto

1 lobster, weighing about 2 lb (1 kg)
1 lb (450 g) komatsuna
12 oz (350 g) rice (unpolished brown rice, preferably)
2 sweet peppers, deseeded and chopped
1 large onion, finely chopped
2 sticks celery, finely chopped

Prepare the lobster by boiling or grilling. When cooked, split the claws and extract the meat; split the body in two and take the meat from the tail. Reserve the tail shells.

Wash and dry, then chop, the komatsuna leaves and tender stems. Cook until tender, either as in the recipe above or boiled in vegetable stock.

Make a risotto with the rice, sweet peppers, onion and celery, and mix the lobster meat into the risotto. Fill the tail shells with komatsuna and place on the risotto.

The dark green komatsuna in the pink shells, the white lobster meat and the brown rice make a colourful dish.

See also: Chinese Cabbage Creamed with Yoghurt, page 188.

'Glorious Garnish' dressing for 'heavy' brassicas

Mix vegetable oil and light soy

sauce in the ratio of 5:1. Add plenty of squeezed or crushed garlic. This can be kept in a fridge for a long time, shaking up before using on steamed or stir-fried greens. This dressing is particularly recommended for stronger greens such as komatsuna, mizuna, mustards and kales.

Lablab beans
Italian Green Bean Salad

Note: Any recipe for French beans can be used for lablab beans.

12 oz (350 g) lablab beans
salt and freshly ground pepper
vinaigrette dressing (see page 183)
lettuce leaves finely chopped onion
1 or 2 hard-boiled eggs, chopped
shavings of fresh Parmesan cheese
black olives
chopped fresh herbs

Boil or steam the lablab beans until just tender. Drain, season and dress with a vinaigrette dressing. Mix in some chopped onion to taste.

Serve piled on lettuce leaves, sprinkled generously with chopped hard-boiled egg, shavings of Parmesan cheese, black olives and chopped fresh herbs—basil and marjoram, or coriander, are especially good with this dish.

Lotus
Lotus Root Custard

3 eggs
4 tablespoons sugar
1 cup (300 ml) water
1 lb (450 g) shredded fresh lotus roots
2 oz (50 g) dates, shredded
1 oz (25 g) dried figs, shredded
2 oz (50 g) crystallized fruit
1 tablespoon cornflour

Beat the eggs in a bowl for 10 seconds. Add 1 tablespoon sugar and ¼ cup (75 ml) of water; beat together for 5 seconds. Pour the mixture into a dish 2 in (5 cm) deep. Place in a steamer and steam for 7–8 minutes until the egg has hardened.

Spread the shredded lotus roots on top, and arrange the shredded dates, figs and crystallized fruit in separate piles in the middle.

Blend the cornflour in the remaining ¾ cup (225 ml) of water together with the remaining sugar. Heat the mixture, stirring until it thickens into a syrup. Pour this syrup over the dish and serve either hot or chilled.

—From *Chinese Food* by Kenneth Lo.

See also: Thai Crispy Dessert, page 196.

Luffa see Cucurbits and gourds

Mallow
Mallow Soup

2 large handfuls mallow leaves
2 tablespoons olive oil
2 medium-sized onions, chopped
4 garlic cloves, crushed
6 coriander seeds, crushed
a little flour
¾ pint (450 ml) chicken stock
salt and freshly ground pepper
a pinch of sugar (optional)
a little cream

Wash and chop the mallow leaves.

Heat the oil gently in a saucepan, add the onions, cover and cook gently over a low heat. After a few minutes add the garlic and coriander. Sprinkle with a little flour, and stir until it is absorbed. Add the stock, stirring until the soup thickens. Bring to the boil, add the mallow leaves, and simmer for 10–15 minutes. Liquidize.

Season to taste, adding a pinch of sugar if required. Add cream, reheat before serving.

—From *Hedgerow Cookery*, by Rosamond Richardson.

Mibuna see Mizuna and mibuna

Mizuna and Mibuna

As the texture and flavour of these two vegetables is very similar, they can be cooked in the same way.

Mizuna Saffron Fish

4 oz (100 g) whole shelled almonds
1 garlic clove, finely sliced
cooking oil

8 oz (225 g) mizuna, chopped
At least two different kinds of fish, weighing in total 1½ lb (675 kg), e.g. cod and saith (rock eel) or, somewhat pricier, sea bass and monkfish
salt and freshly ground pepper
saffron or turmeric
fish or vegetable stock
a few prawns and mussels (both optional)

Stir-fry the almonds and sliced garlic in a wok in a little oil. Add the chopped mizuna and stir-fry lightly.

Cut the fish into 2-in (5-cm) pieces and press into the mizuna. Season with salt, pepper, and saffron or turmeric. Add just enough stock to cover the fish and mizuna, and simmer for about 10 minutes, until the fish is cooked. Add a few cleaned mussels when cooking is underway to impart a lovely clean seafood flavour, and a few prawns when nearly cooked.

After the initial cooking stage this dish could be finished in the oven.

Mizuna and Finely Sliced Beef

10 oz (275 g) lean frying beef
8 oz (225 g) mizuna
cooking oil
1 garlic clove, finely chopped
1 teaspoon cornflour
Marinade
⅓ teaspoon salt
1 tablespoon light soy sauce
1 tablespoon mixed cooking oil and dry white wine
2 teaspoons cornflour
Sauce
2 tablespoons light sauce soy sauce
1 tablespoon white wine
2 teaspoons vegetable oil
dash of tabasco sauce

Cut the beef into thin slices, then small pieces about 1½ in (3.5 cm) long. Mix the marinade ingredients well in a bowl. Put in the beef, turn to coat in the marinade, then leave for at least 10 minutes.

Cut the mizuna into 2-in (5-cm) pieces, separating leaves and stems. Stir-fry the stalks first, in a wok with a little oil, then add the leaves and cook until they become a paler colour. Remove and drain.

Clean the wok, heat in it about 3 tablespoons oil, stir-fry the garlic lightly, then add the marinated beef. Just before the beef is completely cooked add the mizuna and the sauce ingredients. Stir well. Then add 1 teaspoon cornflour moistened in 2 teaspoons water, and stir in to thicken.

See also: Mizuna-greens Quick Salted Pickle, page 185.

Mustard greens

The hot flavour of the mustards varies from plant to plant, and during the season. It is moderated with cooking, or by soaking the leaves for about 30 minutes before cooking.

Mustard Soup

1 oz (25 g) butter or margarine
1 tablespoon flour
1 pint (600 ml) milk and water, mixed half and half
salt and freshly ground pepper
8 oz (225 g) mustard greens
a knob of butter
1 garlic clove, crushed

Make a *roux* with the butter and flour. Heat the milk and water mixture to just below boiling point. Off the heat, stir a few spoonfuls into the *roux* and beat until smooth. On the heat, gradually add the rest of the milk mixture and simmer until you have a light, smooth sauce, still stirring. Season to taste.

Cut the mustard greens into thin strips, and cook lightly in a little butter, then add them to the light white sauce and simmer for 15 minutes. Add the crushed garlic and check the seasoning.

Note: Herbs can be added, but suspended in a muslin bag to prevent them 'speckling' the soup.

Duck with Mustard Leaves

The heat of mustard leaves goes well with the succulence of duck.

12 oz–1 lb (350–450 g) mustard greens, chopped
1 onion, grated
1 whole roast duckling or 3–4 grilled duck breasts
1 lb (450 g) cooked spiral or shell-shaped pasta

lemon juice
butter
freshly grated Parmesan cheese

Steam or stir-fry the chopped mustard leaves with the grated onion, adding a little water or wine if more moisture is needed.

Serve the duck on a bed of cooked mustard leaves, surrounded by a ring of pasta tossed in butter, lemon juice and grated cheese.

Young Mustard Leaves as a Warm Salad

Bring a large saucepan of water to the boil, seasoned with salt, pepper, grated onion and grated ginger. Plunge mustard leaves in the boiling water for 30 seconds to tenderize (mustards tend to become bitter if boiled too long). Drain and pat dry carefully. Cut the larger leaves into bite-sized pieces.

Serve while still warm with any of the salad dressings suggested earlier. Add chopped spring onions, almonds, apple to your taste.

See also: Ruey Hua's Mustard Leaf Pickle, page 185.

Mustard Greens and Potato Pie

12 oz (350 g) sliced boiled potatoes
12 oz (350 g) cooked mustard greens (steamed or blanched in boiling water)
1 hard-boiled egg, sliced
2 tablespoons béchamel sauce or thick cream
a little beaten egg or milk to glaze
Shortcrust pastry
12 oz (350 g) plain flour
pinch of salt
6 oz (175 g) very cold margarine
a few tablespoons cold water

First make the shortcrust pastry. Sift the flour and salt into a large mixing bowl. Cut the margarine into small pieces and rub into the flour with the tips of your fingers until the mixture has the texture of breadcrumbs. Use just enough cold water to enable you to form this into a dough. Turn the dough out onto a lightly floured surface and knead for 10 seconds with the heel of your hand. Wrap in cling film

and refrigerate for at least 30 minutes before using.

Roll out the pastry thinly and use half of it to line a pie dish large enough comfortably to hold the filling. Place in it the cooked sliced potatoes, cooked mustard, and hard-boiled egg. Mix in 2 tablespoons of well seasoned béchamel sauce or thick cream. Moisten the edges. Lay the rest of the pastry over the top, trim to fit and press down gently to seal all round. Brush a little beaten egg or milk over the top and bake in a preheated moderately hot oven (400°F, 200°C, Gas 6), for 10 minutes, then reduce the heat to 350°F, 180°C, Gas 4 and cook for a further 30 minutes or until the pastry is golden brown.

Mustard Greens and Chick Pea Pâté

Put equal quantities of cooked chick peas and cooked mustard greens through a food processor. Season well, adding crushed garlic and salt and pepper to taste. Serve in small pots with garlic bread.

Onion   see Oriental bunching onion

Oriental bunching onion

Ken's Green Onion Pancakes

several green onions (both the green leafy part and thickened lower stem)
cooking oil
little béchamel sauce or thick cream
Pancake batter for about fifteen 7 in (18 cm) pancakes
2 large eggs
5 oz (150 g) plain flour
pinch of salt
¾ pint (450 ml) milk
1 oz (25 g) butter, melted
1 tablespoon cooking oil

First make the pancake batter. Crack the eggs into the flour in a bowl, add salt, and work the eggs in well. Gradually add the milk and work into a paste, first with a wooden spoon then with an egg whisk until the mixture coats the back of the spoon. Add the melted butter and cooking oil and whisk in. If possible chill for an hour before making the pancakes. (The batter will keep 2–3 days in a fridge.) Make the pancakes. Put aside, covered, until ready to use.

Chop or finely slice the leafy onions and the thicker stems, which add a little bulk. Stir-fry in a little oil. Add a few spoonfuls of béchamel sauce or cream to moisten, and stuff the pancakes with the mixture. Pop them into a low oven (300°F, 150°C, Gas 2) to heat through and serve right away.

Stuffed Green Onion Hors d'Oeuvre

green onions (for this you will need fairly mature, substantial onions, with leaves ½–1 in (1–2.5 cm) diameter
cream cheese } (see below)
softened butter
finely chopped fresh herbs (e.g. thyme, marjoram, basil, parsley)
crushed or finely chopped garlic
salt and freshly ground pepper
Dip the green onions into boiling salted water for 30 seconds to soften. Make a paste with the cream cheese and softened butter (4 parts cheese to 1 part butter). Work in finely chopped fresh herbs, garlic, and seasoning to taste. Stuff the hollow onion stems with this mixture.

Pak choi

Pak Choi Sauce for Steak

12 oz (350 g) medium-sized pak choi
cooking oil
about 1 teaspoon grated fresh ginger
1 large onion, chopped
1 medium-sized carrot, chopped
dry white wine
1 large pepper, deseeded and sliced in strips
several large mushrooms, sliced
1 small garlic clove, crushed (optional)
salt and freshly ground pepper
4 thick, grilling beefsteaks
Stir-fry the *leaves* and leafy pak choi stems with grated ginger, half the chopped onion and the carrot. Add

a little white wine and cook, covered, for a few minutes. Set aside for use later as a vegetable. It would be good with sautéed potatoes mixed with sliced, cooked onion.

Braise the thick pak choi *stalks* in a saucepan with the rest of the chopped onion, the sliced pepper and mushrooms, a little crushed garlic if liked, and seasoning. Add just a little liquid (e.g. wine mixed with water), and cook until soft. Put through a food processor. Reheat, coat the grilled steaks with this sauce and serve.
See also: recipes for Chinese cabbage, page 188.

Rosette Pak Choi with Mussels

1 lb (450 g) medium-sized rosette pak choi
1 medium-sized onion, finely chopped
1 stick celery, finely chopped
cooking oil
herbs, e.g. marjoram, fresh sliced fennel, crushed fennel seed
2 pints (1 litre) mussels
½ glass dry white wine
1 bay leaf
1 garlic clove, chopped
freshly ground pepper
Chop the large pak choi leaves; use the small leaves whole. Stir-fry with the onion, celery and herbs in a little oil in a wok or frying pan.

Put the scrubbed, dry mussels into a large pan with the white wine, bay leaf, chopped garlic, and a few grindings of pepper. (*Don't* add salt.) Cover and cook until the shells open, occasionally shaking the pan. Drain, reserving the mussel stock.

Tip the mussels, still in their shells, onto the rosette pak choi in the wok or pan, and stir them well together. Add a little of the mussel stock to make the dish 'glister'. Ideally serve with rice.

Spiced Rosette Pak Choi

1 whole rosette pak choi weighing about 1 lb (450 g)
3 tablespoons cooking oil
2 tablespoons soy sauce
½ teaspoon sugar
⅓ teaspoon freshly ground nutmeg

a little salt
cornflour (optional)
Cut the rosette pak choi into quarters, wash and drain. Stir-fry briefly in the oil, seasoned with soy sauce, sugar, nutmeg and salt, then cover and simmer for about a minute (it turns a soft green when ready).

Uncover and stir-fry for a few moments more before serving. If you wish the liquid can be thickened by stirring in a little cornflour, dissolved in water, into the juice in the wok or pan.

Pumpkin

Italian Spiced Pumpkin Soup

2 lb (1 kg) slices of pumpkin
2 oz (50 g) butter
1 onion, chopped
12 coriander seeds
large pinch cumin
salt and freshly ground pepper
medium potato, peeled and chopped
3 pints (1.75 litres) stock (or stock cubes and water)
cream
chopped parsley or chervil to garnish
Peel and roughly dice the pumpkin. Put in a saucepan with the butter, onion, spices and seasonings, and the potato, and simmer, covered, for 20 minutes, stirring occasionally.

Remove the lid, add the stock, bring to the boil, and simmer for 30 minutes uncovered. Put through the coarse disc of a mouli, return to the pan and bring to the boil again. Check seasoning, add freshly milled pepper, and serve in bowls with a spoonful of cream in each bowl and chopped parsley or chervil as a garnish.

—From *Leaves from Our Tuscan Kitchen* by Janet Ross and Michael Waterfield.
See also: Montrose Pumpkin Pickle, page 186.

Radish

Ning's Recipes for Radish Soup

Ning, our guide in China, gave me her radish soup recipes. These would be made with any of the large radishes.

Version 1 (with meat stock)

Simmer meat and bones with a little rice wine (or sherry), small pieces of ginger, onions and salt until the meat comes off the bones easily. Add small pieces of radish, and simmer until they become soft and translucent.

Remove from the heat and add fresh coriander leaves.

Version 2 (with fish)

Stir-fry fish briefly in a wok with ginger, onion, wine and salt. Put in a pot, add water, bring to the boil then reduce to a simmer. Almost immediately, add small pieces of radish and continue simmering until cooked. (The radishes must be added early to avoid overcooking the fish.)

Version 3 (with meat balls)

Make meat balls with minced meat, a little rice wine or sherry, finely chopped onions and ginger, and salt. Add a little cornflour, egg white or water to bind the meat mixture together. Shape into meat balls with the hands. Boil small pieces of radish in water and, when nearly ready, add the meat balls and simmer until cooked.

Version 4 (a simple soup)

Heat a little cooking oil in a wok, and when very hot add shredded or sliced radish and stir-fry briefly. Add water and simmer over a low heat.

When the radish is nearly cooked, add salt and finely chopped onion and, a few minutes later, finely chopped coriander. Add pepper just before serving.

Jane Grigson's Recipe for Radish Foam

4 in (10 cm) piece of large radish
salt
5 fl oz (150 ml) double cream
½ teaspoon caraway seed or 1 oz (25 g) chopped walnuts

Process or grate the radish into julienne strips. Sprinkle with salt, leave 30 minutes, drain and squeeze out moisture.

Whip the double cream until stiff and fold in the radish shreds. Season to taste. Add the caraway seeds or walnuts.

This is used as a substitute for horseradish sauce, and is served with cold meats, fish, smoked poultry and game.

—From *Exotic Fruits and Vegetables*, by Jane Grigson and Charlotte Knox.

Bruce Cost's Daikon (Mooli Radish) in Orange Peel Sauce

1 piece dried orange peel
2 tablespoons sherry or sweet wine
¾ tablespoon dark soy sauce
¾ tablespoon sugar
pinch of salt
2 tablespoons water
1 lb (450g) mooli radish
1 garlic clove, chopped
1 teaspoon chopped fresh ginger
1½ tablespoons vegetable oil
1½ spring onions, cut in 1½ in (4 cm) lengths

Soak the peel in the sherry or wine for 30 minutes then chop and put back in the wine until required.

Combine the soy sauce, sugar, salt and water, and set aside.

Cut the radish into 1¼ in (3 cm) cubes and put aside also.

Combine the garlic and ginger and set aside.

Heat the oil in a wok or pan, add the radish and stir-fry briefly, stirring continuously. Add the garlic and ginger, and cook for 15 seconds, stirring constantly. Add the orange peel and wine, and cook until the liquid has evaporated. Stir in the soy sauce mixture.

Lower the heat to medium, cover and cook for 20 minutes, adding a little water if necessary.

When cooked, reduce the sauce by stirring over high heat until most of the liquid has been absorbed. Stir in the spring onions and serve.

—From *Asian Ingredients*, by Bruce Cost.

Namasu

Japanese Grated Radish and Carrots

12 oz (350 g) mooli radish
1 oz (25 g) carrots
salt
3 tablespoons rice vinegar
3 tablespoons wine vinegar
1 tablespoon *dashi* (see page 184)
1 tablespoon sherry
pinch of salt
2 teaspoons sugar

Peel the radish and cut into thin slices, then julienne strips. Prepare the carrots in the same way. Sprinkle the carrots and radish with salt, and leave for 10–15 minutes until limp. Squeeze to remove water.

Mix together the vinegars, *dashi*, sherry, sugar and a pinch of salt. Pour over the radish and carrots and either serve immediately or leave for 24 hours, which intensifies the flavour.

Note: In a simple but excellent Chinese version carrots and radish are cut into small pieces and stir-fried in oil. The sauce is thickened with cornflour for the last few minutes of cooking. A little sugar is added too. This looks very pretty if both white- and green-fleshed radishes are used.

—From *Japanese Home Style Cooking*.

Rosette pak choi   see Pak choi

Soya beans

Green Soya Beans and Sweetcorn

8 oz (225 g) shelled fresh soya beans
a knob of butter
3–4 spring onions, chopped
1 carrot, grated
salt and freshly ground pepper
squeeze of lemon juice
2 oz (50 g) freshly cooked sweetcorn

Cook the shelled, fresh soya beans until just tender by steaming, or boiling in a little water.

Melt a knob of butter in a pan, and lightly cook the spring onions and grated carrot. Add the beans, seasoning, and a squeeze of lemon juice. Mix with the freshly cooked sweetcorn for a colourful emerald-green and yellow dish.

Lamb Ragoût with Fresh Soya Beans

1 lb (450 g) cubed lamb (shoulder or leg)
cooking oil
1 large onion, chopped
1 carrot, chopped
1 tablespoon chopped celery
salt and freshly ground pepper
white wine
1 tablespoon tomato purée
8 oz (225 g) steamed fresh soya beans
the leaves from a sprig of fresh thyme or a few large leaves fresh basil, chopped

Toss the lamb in a little oil in a frying pan to brown. Add the onion, carrot and celery and mix well. Season. Cover with a mixture of half white wine and half water. Stir in the tomato purée. Either simmer on the stove in a saucepan, or transfer to an ovenproof dish and put in a moderate oven (325–350°F, 160–180°C, Gas 3–4). In either case, cover and cook until the lamb is tender (about 1½ hours).

Just before serving mix in the steamed soya beans. Warm through for about 5 minutes to blend the ingredients. Garnish with basil or thyme and serve with pasta, rice or potatoes, and whole small turnips.

Spinach mustard   see Komatsuna

Sprouting seeds

Stir-fried Bean Sprouts with Beef

cooking oil
1 small onion, chopped
8 oz (225 g) bean sprouts
12 oz (350 g) tender, finely sliced, beef
½ tablespoon wine
3 tablespoons soy sauce
1 tablespoon sugar
1½ teaspoons cornflour

Heat 2–3 tablespoons cooking oil in a wok or frying pan; stir-fry the onions lightly, add the bean sprouts and also stir-fry lightly. Add the beef and stir-fry until the colour changes. Add the wine, soy sauce and sugar and stir lightly.

Mix the cornflour with a little water, and add to the mixture. Stir until thickened, and serve.

Taro

Sunrise Taro Chips

8 oz (225 g) taro root
peanut oil
sesame oil (optional)
roasted sesame seeds (see page 186), grated Parmesan cheese or chilli powder, for coating

Scrub the taro root well and boil whole in water until tender (35–40 minutes). Peel, cool, and slice diagonally into ¼-in (5-mm) thick slices.

Pour enough peanut oil (mixed with sesame oil if wished) into a deep pan to give a depth of 2 in (5 cm). Fry the taro slices until golden brown, turning once. Drain on paper towelling.

Coat the chips by dipping them into toasted sesame seeds, finely grated Parmesan, or chilli powder.

Steamed Marinated Turnips

12 oz (350 g) turnips
Marinade
3 tablespoons wine or cider vinegar
1 tablespoon sugar
1½ tablespoons salt

Slice the turnips into thin slivers. Mix the marinade ingredients together in a bowl. Put the turnip in, turn to coat with the marinade and leave for 2 hours. Chill and use as a salad garnish.

Alternatively, steam the marinated turnips and serve with hot pork, goose or duck.

Creamed White Turnips

8 medium-sized turnips
2½ tablespoons butter
½ pint (300 ml) vegetable stock
salt and freshly ground pepper
½ pint (300 ml) cream or yoghurt
1 teaspoon grated fresh ginger
finely chopped parsley or chervil

Peel the turnips, cut each into small wedge-shaped pieces and fry in butter until they become transparent. Add the stock, season and cook until all the moisture is absorbed. Stir the ginger into the cream or yoghurt, add to the

turnips and cook a little longer over a low heat. Check seasoning and garnish with herbs.
See also: Turnip Pickle, page 185.

Watercress

Ken's Watercress Soup

4 handfuls watercress
1 large onion, chopped
a knob of butter
large garlic clove, squeezed or minced
salt and freshly ground pepper
1 cup (300 ml) creamy béchamel sauce
grated nutmeg, crushed red chilli pepper or paprika

Chop the watercress finely. Soften the onion in a pan in the butter, toss in the watercress and cook for a few minutes, turning it over, until it is wilted. Add 1 pint (600 ml) water, the garlic and seasoning. Simmer for 10 minutes.

Either add a cup of béchamel sauce, about the consistency of double cream, *or* first put the soup through the fine disc of a mouli to make it very smooth, and then add the béchamel to the mixture. Return to a clean pan and reheat.

Sprinkle with grated nutmeg, and crushed red chilli, pepper or paprika to garnish. Serve hot.
Note: The soup can also be served cold. Thin it with a little potato or vegetable stock, then chill. Check the seasoning, adding a little lemon juice if necessary.

Wax gourd   see Cucurbits and gourds

Yam bean

Thai Crispy Dessert

1½ cups sugar
few drops red food colouring
1 cup yam bean, cut into ¼-in (5-mm) cubes
1 cup cornflour
1 cup coconut milk (see page 191)
1 tablespoon roasted sesame seeds (see page 186)
1–2 cups crushed or shaved ice

Make a syrup by heating the sugar with ½ cup water until it dissolves. Bring to a boil, then simmer for 4–5 minutes. Cool and chill.

Mix the food colouring with a tablespoon of water. Add the yam bean cubes, mix well and set aside for 30 minutes. Then add the corn-flour and mix well to coat the yam bean cubes. Then separate each cube.

Bring 5 cups water to the boil in a saucepan. Add the coated vegetable cubes, and cook until they float. Drain and chill in iced water.

Mix together the cooked yam bean, coconut milk, sesame seeds and syrup, and put into serving glasses or dishes. Serve topped with crushed or shaved ice.

Note: This recipe can also be made with water chestnuts or lotus root.
—From *Tropical Cookery*, by Yoshiko Yoshida.

Yard long bean
Chinese Green Bean Salad

Stimulated by an excellent fresh yard long bean salad in a Chengdu restaurant, the Chinese present pooled their own bean salad recipes for my benefit. Here is one of the simplest and best:

Boil sliced beans for a few minutes in a little water until cooked but still crisp. Allow to cool, add salt, a little hot pepper, a little Sichuan (mild) pepper, and a little vinegar.

Optional additions Chopped raw onion; finely chopped garlic; fine slices of ginger; a little 'burned' vegetable oil made by heating oil quite high; sweet and sour sauce; sugar. Take your pick!

See also: Italian Green Bean Salad, page 192.

Yard Long Beans and Chopped Pork

1 sweet red pepper, sliced
cooking oil
1 lb (450 g) pork (from loin or leg) cut in ½-in (1-cm) cubes
1 medium-sized onion, chopped
1 teaspoon grated fresh ginger
1 chilli pepper, deseeded and crushed
6 oz (175 g) boiled or stir-fried yard long beans
1 tablespoon mango chutney
2 tablespoons dry sherry or sherry vinegar

Stir-fry the red pepper in a little oil for a few minutes, then add the cubed pork and stir-fry for about 2 minutes more.

Add the onion, ginger, chilli, cooked beans and mango chutney. Mix well. Sprinkle with the dry sherry or sherry vinegar and cook for 2 minutes more, stirring. Serve with a tossed salad.

Conversion charts

LIQUID MEASURES

US measures	Fluid ounces	Imperial measures	Millilitres
1 teaspoon	⅙	1 teaspoon	5
2 teaspoons	¼	1 dessertspoon	10
1 tablespoon	½	1 tablespoon	15
¼ cup	2	4 tablespoons	56
⅓ cup	2⅔		80
½ cup	4		110
⅔ cup	5	¼ pint/1 gill	140
¾ cup	6		170
1 cup/½ pint	8		225
2 cups/1 pint	16	generous ¾ pint	450
3 cups/1½ pints	24		675
4 cups/2 pints	32		900
5 cups	40	2 pints/1 quart	1120
6 cups/3 pints	48	scant 2½ pints	1350
7 cups	56	2¾ pints	1600
8 cups	64	3¼ pints	1800
9 cups	72	3½ pints	2000/2 litres
10 cups/5 pints	80	4 pints	2250

SOLID MEASURES

US and Imperial	Metric equivalent
1 oz	25 grams
2 oz	50
3 oz	60
4 oz/¼ lb	110
5 oz	150
6 oz	175
7 oz	200
8 oz/½ lb	225
12 oz/¾ lb	350
16 oz/1 lb	450
2 lb	900
3 lb	1 kg 350 g
4 lb	1 kg 800 g
5 lb	2 kg 250 g

Appendices

Starting points

Many of the Chinese and Japanese vegetables described in this book are unfamiliar to Western gardeners, so the question of where to start, what to try first, can be daunting. The answer to some extent depends on *why* you want to grow them. The short lists given below are examples of the more easily grown oriental vegetables, which will make good, rewarding 'starting points'.

FOR FLAVOUR
- Broad-leaved mustards
- Chinese broccoli
- Chinese chives
- Chrysanthemum greens
- Oriental bunching onion
- Pea shoots

FOR BULK
- Chinese cabbage – headed, and fluffy top loose-headed
- Komatsuna greens
- Loose-headed Chinese cabbage
- Oriental saladini

FOR QUICK RETURNS
- Oriental saladini
- Seedling pak choi
- Sprouting seeds

FOR SALADS
- Chinese cabbage – headed, and fluffy top loose-headed
- Oriental saladini
- Seedling pak choi
- Stem lettuce
- Radish – summer varieties of Japanese radish
- Radish – green fleshed varieties

FOR SOMETHING PRETTY
- Mizuna greens
- Chinese chives

IN HOT CLIMATES
- Amaranthus
- Basella
- Lablab beans
- Yard long beans
- Winter melon

IN COOL CLIMATES
- Komatsuna greens
- Green-in-the-snow mustard
- Mizuna greens

'Oriental saladini' Growing this mixture, for harvesting when a few inches high, is the ideal way of getting to know a few of the oriental brassicas. Either buy a prepared mixture, or make up your own. (See page 47.)

Tip for beginners Remember, with the brassicas and radishes in particular there is a risk of premature bolting if sown too early in northern latitudes. If in doubt, play safe by delaying sowing until late summer.

Glossary of gardening terms

Note 'See text' indicates further information in the text can be found via the index.

Annual Plant grown from seed that flowers, seeds and dies in less than 12 months.

Axil Angle between a leaf stalk and the stem, at which point new buds and stems arise.

Bare root transplant A young plant lifted from a seedbed for transplanting (a process liable to damage the root hairs), as opposed to a module-raised plant (see Module) which suffers no damage in transplanting.

Base dressing Fertilizer worked into the soil before sowing or planting.

Biennial A plant grown from seed whose life cycle normally spans two years. It develops a leafy tuft or rosette the first year and flowers, seeds and dies in the second year.

Blanch To exclude light from plants or parts of plants to render them white and tender. Often done as part of the forcing process. (See below.)

Block See Soil Block.

Bolting (running to seed) Flowering prematurely, usually due to unsuitable climatic conditions at certain stages of growth.

Bract Small modified leaves at the base of the flower stalk or beneath the flower head, sometimes resembling petals.

Brassica (USA: Crucifer) Strictly speaking, any plant in the genus *Brassica*, belonging to the plant family *Cruciferae*. The name embraces the many types of 'cabbagy' plants, mustards and turnips. (See text.)

Broadcasting Sowing seed by scattering it at random over the surface, rather than sowing in rows. (See text.)

Bulbil Small bulb-like organ which sometimes forms in place of flowers.

Catch crop A quick-maturing crop which is grown on a piece of ground primarily intended for other, slower-maturing crops. It may be grown alongside crops in the early stages, or be sown after one main crop is harvested, before the next main crop is sown.

Cell A single unit in a modular seed or sowing tray. (See Module.)

Clamp Method of storing root crops to protect them from frost, either outdoors or in a shed. Roots are piled on a base of straw, then covered with straw and soil.

Cloche Small glass or plastic unit, which can be put over plants to protect them. (See text.)

Cotyledon See Seed leaf.

Crucifer See Brassica.

Cultivar A variety raised in cultivation. Strictly speaking, vegetable 'varieties' should be known as cultivars, but few gardeners or seedsmen observe this convention.

Cutting Piece of leaf, stem or root used for propagation. Softwood cuttings are usually taken from young growths in spring; half ripe or semi-hardwood cuttings from slightly firmer growths in summer; hardwood cuttings from mature current year's growth towards the end of the growing season. Heel cuttings are side shoots pulled away from the main stem with a tiny piece of the stem attached.

Daylength The length of day and night varies with latitude and season. At the equator (0 latitude) daylength varies little from 12 hours; but in northern latitudes daylight hours increase progressively with latitude until mid summer (21 June), and decrease until the shortest day. The extreme case is 24 hours daylight at the north pole in mid summer. The reverse happens in the southern latitudes. At the equinoxes, 21 March and 21 September, daylength is 12 hours all over the world. **Photoperiodism** is the response of plants to different daylengths. As a generalization, short days are less than 12 hours daylight, long days more than 12 hours daylight. **Short day plants** develop and seed only when daylength is less than a critical maximum (i.e. mid summer to autumn in the United Kingdom); **long day plants** only when it is above a critical minimum (in spring to mid summer in the United Kingdom).

Direct sowing See 'In situ'.

Dormancy A quiescent period in which the whole plant, or parts such as buds or seeds, cease to grow. It can be part of a natural cycle or induced by unfavourable conditions.

Drawn Seedlings or plant which have become pale, etiolated and weak, because of being over-crowded, or grown with insufficient light.

Earthing up (USA: Mounding and hilling) Drawing soil up around the base and stems of a plant, in some cases over the top of the plant. It is done for several reasons: to cover tubers, to give additional support to stems, to blanch stems by excluding light (see Blanch), or to force fresh young growths in darkness.

Establish plants A plant is said to be 'established' when its roots have taken hold and started to function again after planting.

F1 hybrids Seeds bred by crossing two purebred inbred lines, to produce plants of exceptional vigour and uniformity. (See text.)

Film gauge A measurement of the thickness of plastic films; the higher the number the thicker the film. Various measurements are used: roughly speaking 100 microns = 400 gauge = 4 mls (USA).

Floating films (floating mulches, crop covers, floating row mulches, floating cloches) Lightweight films, made of perforated plastic, fleecy fibrous materials, or very fine netting, laid directly over a crop to accelerate growth and give protection.

Forcing Bringing a plant into earlier growth, generally by raising the temperature, or by transplanting into a warmer situation.

Frame Traditionally a simple, low, glass-roofed structure, made of wood or brick, free-standing or lean-to, used to shelter and grow plants. Modern frames are often made of steel or aluminium and glassed to the ground. Frames can be heated by electricity or a hotbed. 'Cold frames' are unheated. (See text.)

Genus See Species.

Grafting A union between two plants, whereby a shoot or scion (see below) of one, is joined to a rootstock (see below) of another so they eventually fuse and grow together. With vegetables it is usually done to obtain disease resistance.

Green manure The practice of growing a crop which is later dug into the ground to increase fertility. (See text.)

Growing days The number of days in a year between the point when average daytime temperatures reach about 43°F (6°C) in spring, and fall back to that point in winter. Most plants cease to grow below that temperature.

Growing point The tip of the plant's stem. It is often nipped out to encourage the development of side shoots.

Hardening off The process of gradually acclimatizing a plant that has been raised indoors to lower temperatures or more severe conditions, so that it is not severely checked when planted out. (See text.)

Hardy Term used in the temperate zone for plants which survive outside every year without protection. **Half hardy** plants survive only limited cold or very light frost unless in a sheltered site.

Hilum Scar on the surface of a seed, marking the point of its attachment to the seed stalk.

Hotbed A glass-covered bed of soil, usually heated by fermenting material such as animal manure, used for raising plants and forcing vegetables early in the year.

Hybrid A plant resulting from a cross between two distinct parents.

Hydroponics A method of growing plants without soil, plant foods being supplied in dilute solutions. Plants may be in an inert medium such as gravel, or suspended in water.

Indoors See Under Cover.

Inflorescence (truss) The flowering part of a plant, which may be composed of one or more flowers.

'In situ' (direct sowing) Sowing in the ground where the plant will grow, so there is no need for transplanting.

Larva The caterpillar or grub stage of an insect such as a moth, butterfly or fly, which will eventually metamorphose into the adult form. **Worm** (USA) is often used for grubs or caterpillars.

Lateral (side shoot) A side shoot or branch, coming off a main shoot. Laterals often develop when the growing point (see above) is removed. Sub-laterals are shoots which develop on the laterals.

Layering A method of propagation, in which the shoot or stem is usually pinned down or buried in the soil so that it will root. Once rooted it is severed from the mother plant.

Leaching The process whereby soluble plant foods are washed through or deeper into the soil out of reach of plant roots, by rain or excessive watering.

Legumes Plants in the *Leguminosae* family, such as peas and beans, whose fruits take the form of pods.

Loam An imprecise term, usually denoting a rich soil composed of clay, sand and humus.

Long day plants See Daylength.

Microclimate Very localized climatic conditions, for example in a part of a garden, or within the immediate surroundings of a plant.

Module Any kind of small pot, container, soil block, compacted pot, moulded plastic tray of cells or plugs, made of or filled with sowing or potting compost, in which individual seeds can be sown, or young plants or cuttings transplanted. Module-raised plants have no competition, pricking out (see below) is unnecessary and there is no setback on transplanting. (See text.)

Mulch A protective layer of material laid over the surface of the soil. (See text.)

Node The slightly swollen joint on a stem where leaves and buds arise. 'Internodal' cuttings are taken at a mid-point between nodes; nodal cuttings just below a node.

Offset Plant produced at the base of the parent plant, and easily detached from it.

Open pollinated Seed produced from natural, random pollination so that the resulting plants are very varied, as opposed to the uniformity of F1 hybrids. (See above.)

Perennial Plant that lives for several or many years, and does not die after flowering once.

pH scale A measure of the acidity or alkalinity of the soil. The pH scale runs from 1–14, the neutral point being 7. Soils with a pH below 7 become progressively more acid; and above 7 progressively more alkaline. The majority of vegetables grow best in slightly acid soils around pH 6.5. (See text.)

Photoperiodism See Daylength.

Pinching out See Stopping.

Pollination The transfer of pollen from the 'male' anther to the 'female' stigma, so enabling fruits to set and develop. Hand pollination may be necessary with cucurbits, where male and female flowers are separate. (See text.)

Polytunnels (USA: Polythene tunnels, hoop houses and grow tunnels) Structures covered with plastic films used for plant protection. 'Walk-in' polytunnels are approximately 6 ft (2 m) high at the ridge; low polytunnels are rarely more than 18 in (45 cm) high. (See text.)

Potting Placing a plant in a pot or container in a suitable soil or compost mix. **Potting on** is moving an established pot grown plant into a larger pot or container.

Potting compost (USA: Potting mix) A freely draining growing medium, traditionally soil or peat based, containing the minerals essential for plant growth, in which plants are grown in containers. (See text.)

Pricking out Transferring thickly sown seedlings from the pot, pan or seedtray in which they were sown into a larger container, giving them more space to develop. (See text.)

Propagation Increasing the stock of a plant, by sowing seeds, taking cuttings, or dividing the plant.

Protection See Under Cover.

Rhizome A thick, horizontal, underground stem, from which buds and shoots can develop.

Rootstock A rooted plant, onto which a compatible 'scion' (see below) can be grafted (see above). The rootstock bestows a beneficial character, for example disease resistance, to the grafted plant.

Running to seed See Bolting.

Scarify To scratch or chip the outer surface of a hard seed to aid germination. It can be done by rubbing the seed between two pieces of coarse sandpaper, or by chipping the seed coat with a sharp knife on the side opposite the hilum (see above).

Scion A piece from the upper part of a plant (such as a bud or shoot), which is grafted onto a rootstock (see above).

Seed leaf (cotyledon) The first tiny leaf or leaves (developed from the seed coat), produced by the seedling after germination. The 'true leaf/leaves' is/are the larger leaf/leaves which emerge next.

Self fertile Plants that will set seed without cross-pollination.

Short day plants See Daylength.

Soil block A cube of compressed soil (or growing medium), made with a blocking tool. A single seed, or sometimes a group of seeds is sown in the block. They develop without competition and are planted out in the block when roots have penetrated the block. (See text.)

Species Groups of plants which differ only slightly and will freely cross with each other. Fairly closely related species are grouped together in a **genus**. The Latin name of a plant denotes its genus and species. In *Medicago sativus* (Alfalfa), *Medicago* is the genus, *sativus* the species.

Station sowing Sowing small groups of seed at regular intervals along the drill. (See text.)

Stopping (pinching out) Removing the growing point (see above) of a plant or shoot, generally to en-courage the development of side shoots or to stimulate flower buds.

Stratification Exposing hard-coated seeds to frost to improve germination, or because they need a cold period to break dormancy (see above). Sow in shallow trays covered with sand and a pane of glass, and leave outdoors during winter. (Seeds can sometimes be stratified in a refrigerator.)

Successional sowing Making continuous sowings with a view to having a continuous supply of the vegetable (e.g. radish, lettuce). As a rule of thumb, make the next sowing as soon as the previous sowing is through the soil.

Temperate Climatic zone roughly halfway between the arctic or antarctic and the tropics. (See text.)

Tender Plants that can be injured by cold weather or frost.

Top dressing Generally the application of fertilizer to growing plants, but also the replenishment of the top layer of soil in a container with fresh soil.

True leaf See Seed Leaf.

Truss See Inflorescence.

Tuber Enlarged root or stem which functions as a storage organ and is usually underground.

Under cover (indoors, protection) Any form of protection for plants, from an indoor window sill to cloches, frames, low and walk-in polytunnels, and greenhouses.

Variegated Used mainly of leaves that are variously patterned, spotted or blotched with another colour.

Variety Distinct form of species that occurs in the wild. In popular use used for 'cultivar' (see above).

Vector An organism, usually an insect, which carries a disease within its body which it transmits to another plant.

Viability The ability of a seed to germinate, which diminishes with age. (See text.)

Growing information chart*

* For explanatory notes see pp. 208–209

● = Suitable
○ = Suitable dependent on variety

Brassicas

	Climate		Frost tolerance			Site				Plant characteristics				
	Temperate	Warm	None	Some	Good	Dry	Wet	Shade	Fertility index	Average spread (ins/cm)	Climber	Decorative	Cut/Come	VSR
Headed Chinese cabbage	●	○		●				●	3	9–12 (23–30)			●	★★★
Loose-headed Chinese cabbage	●	○		●	○			●	2–3	12–20 (30–50)		●	●	★★★
Pak choi	●	○		○				●	2–3	4–18 (10–45)		●	●	★★★
Rosette pak choi	●	○			●				2	12–18 (30–45)		●	●	★★
Choy sum	●	○	●						3	6–18 (15–45)				★★
Chinese broccoli	●	●		●					2	10–15 (25–37)				★★
Komatsuna	●	○			○				2–3	12–18 (30–45)			●	★★★
Mizuna greens	●	●			○	●	●		2	12–18 (30–45)		●	●	★★★
Mibuna greens	●			●					2	12–22 (30–56)		●	●	★★
Mustards Giant leaved	●	●			○		○		2	15–22 (37–56)		●	○	★★
Green-in-the-snow	●	●			●				2	12–15 (30–37)			●	★★
Leaf	●			●			○		2	12 (30)			●	★★
Japanese turnip Hinona-kabu	●			●					2	6 (15)				★★
Oriental saladini	●	○		○					2	1–2 (2–5)		●	●	★★★★
Ornamental cabbages & kales	●			○					1–2	12–18 (30–45)		●		★★

Sowing times						Main season of use											
Spring	Summer	Autumn	Growing season	Day length	Average days to maturity	January	February	March	April	May	June	July	August	September	October	November	December
●	○	●		●	65							▓	▓	▓	▓	▓	
●	○	●	●		55	▓						▓	▓	▓	▓	▓	▓
●	○	●	●		45						▓	▓	▓	▓	▓	▓	▓
	○	●			56	▓	▓	▓					▓	▓	▓	▓	▓
	●	●			50								▓	▓	▓	▓	▓
●	○	●	●		65						▓	▓	▓	▓	▓	▓	▓
●	○	●	●		55	▓	▓	▓	▓	▓	▓	▓	▓	▓	▓	▓	▓
●	●	●	●		70	▓	▓	▓	▓	▓	▓	▓	▓	▓	▓	▓	▓
	○	●			70	▓	▓	▓					▓	▓			
	○				100		▓	▓							▓	▓	▓
	○	●			70	▓	▓	▓							▓	▓	▓
	○	●			40	▓	▓	▓					▓	▓	▓		
	○	●		●	42								▓	▓	▓	▓	▓
●	○	●	●		25	▓	▓	▓	▓	▓	▓	▓	▓	▓	▓	▓	▓
●	●				92	▓								▓	▓	▓	

	Climate		Frost tolerance			Site			Fertility index	Plant characteristics				
	Temperate	Warm	None	Some	Good	Dry	Wet	Shade		Average spread (ins/cm)	Climber	Decorative	Cut/Come	VSR
Alfalfa	●	●		●		●			1	3 (8)		●	●	★★★
Amaranthus		●	●			●		●	2	4–12 (10–30)		●	●	★★★
Basella		●	●				●	●	1–2	12 (30)	●	●	●	★★
Beans Adzuki (dry)	●	●	●			●			2	12 (30)				★★
Lablab	●	●	●			●			1–2	12 (30)	●	●		★★★
Soya (fresh)	●	●	●						2	8 (20)				★★★
Yard Long		●	●						1–2	12 (30)	●			★★
Burdock	●			●					2	2–3 ft (60–90)				★
Chinese artichoke	●			●			●		1–2	10–12 (25–30)		●		★
Chinese boxthorn	●	●			●				1–2	12–24 (30–60)				★
Chinese celery	●			●			●		2–3	8–10 (20–25)		●		★★
Chinese chives	●				●			●	2–3	8–12 (20–30)		●	●	★★
Chrysanthemum greens	●			●				●	1–2	3–6 (8–15)		●	●	★★★
Cucurbits Luffa ridged		●	●						3	24 (60)	●	●		★★
Hairy melon		●	●						3	24 (60)	●	●		★★
Bitter gourd		●	●						2–3	24 (60)	●	●		★

Sowing times						Main season of use											
Spring	Summer	Autumn	Growing season	Day length	Average days to maturity	January	February	March	April	May	June	July	August	September	October	November	December
●	●	●	●		24				■	■					■	■	■
	●				50								■	■	■		
●	●			●	84							■	■	■	■		
	●			●	120								■	■	■		
	●			●	120								■	■	■		
	●			●	80								■	■	■		
	●			●	90								■	■	■		
●		●			155								■	■			
●					168	■	■									■	■
●		●			360				■	■					■	■	
●	●	●	●		60					■	■	■					
●	●	●			360		■	■	■								
●	●	●	●		32					■	■	■	■	■	■		
○	●			●	70								■	■	■		
●	●				90								■	■	■		
●	●				97								■	■			

	Climate			Frost tolerance		Site		Plant characteristics		
Japanese pumpkin	●	●	●				3	6 ft (180)	●	★ ★
Garlic bulb	●	●			●		1–2	5 (13)		★
Ipomea (Water spinach)		●	●			●	3	12 (30)		★ ★
Lettuce (Stem)	●	●		●		●	2–3	12 (30)		★ ★
Mitsuba (young)	●			●		●	1–2	9 (23)	●	★ ★
Oriental bunching onion	●	●			○		3	V		★ ★ ★
Pea shoots	●			●		●	2	4 (10)		★
Perilla	●	●	●				1–2	12–15 (30–38)	●	★ ★
Radish White mooli	●	○		●			1–2	14 (35)		★
Leaf radish	●	●		●			1–2	2–4 (5–10)	●	★ ★ ★
Radish seedling sprouts	●	●		●			0	1 (2.5)	●	★ ★ ★ ★
Seed sprouting	●	●	●				0	½ (1)		★ ★ ★ ★

Explanatory notes

The chart above summarizes data about the principal vegetables covered in the book. Its purpose is to help you decide if a vegetable is suitable for your area, and to give a rough indication of its growing requirements. All figures are approximations and conceal the wide variations which occur in practice. Sowing times and maturity are based on average conditions in temperate climates in northern latitudes.

Explanation of categories

CLIMATE
Temperate Based on average temperatures in the UK. (See Introduction, page 4.) *Warm* Ranging from above average UK temperatures to sub-tropical. (Warm season vegetables can often be grown in temperate zones with protection, and temperate vegetables can be grown in cool seasons in warm climates.)

FROST TOLERANCE
Some Will generally withstand about 4 degrees of frost. *Good* Will generally stand up to about 10 degrees of frost. Roots may survive frost when green parts are killed.

SITE
Dry Tolerates or thrives in fairly dry conditions. *Wet* Tolerates or requires wet conditions and/or high rainfall. *Shade* Tolerates some

Sowing times						Main season of use																			
●	●	●			120												░░								
●		●		●	280	░░	░░	░░	░░				░░												
●	●			●	60									░░	░░										
●	●				100								░░				░░								
●	●	●	●		60					░░	░░	░░	░░	░░	░░										
●	●	●	●		V	░░	░░		░░	░░								░░	░░						
●		●			30				░░	░░									░░	░░					
●	●				70								░░	░░											
●	●	●	●	●	70					░░	░░										░░				
●	●	●	●		28		░░	░░	░░	░░															
●	●	●	●		10	░░	░░	░░	░░																
●	●	●	●		5	░░	░░	░░	░░	░░	░░	░░													

shade, usually in mid summer. *Fertility index:* 1 = tolerates low to moderate levels of soil fertility (but may respond to higher fertility); 2 = needs fertile soil; 3 = needs very fertile soil.

PLANT CHARACTERISTICS

Average spread In most cases of a mature plant, but size depends enormously on growing methods, variety and conditions. The spread is a rough guide to spacing. *Climber* Natural habit is climbing, but plants can sometimes be trained in dwarf forms. *Decorative plant* has decorative qualities. *Cut/come* Plants regrow after first cut. *VSR* Value for space rating. Index of productivity, compiled on the basis of yield and length of time in the ground * = low returns, unless intercropped; ** reasonable returns; *** very good value; **** highly productive.

SOWING TIME

The correct variety must be sown in each season. Earlier and later sow-ings can often be made under cover. *Growing season* Can be sown throughout the growing season. *Day length* Daylength factors may be involved. (See main text.) In many cases early sowings may bolt. *Average days to maturity* From sowing to harvesting.

Main season of use Primarily for the fresh product grown outdoors. Usage can be extended by growing under cover and storage.

Key V = variable

Plant names

Note The name list gives the principal names for principal types of each
vegetable. See text for alternative names.
   Where no Japanese names or Chinese names are given, the original
Japanese or Chinese names are generally used in both countries

English	Latin	Mandarin	Japanese
BRASSICAS (B = Brassica throughout)			
Chinese broccoli	*B. rapa* var. *alboglabra*	Gai lan 芥蓝	Kairan かいらん
Chinese cabbage (headed)	*B. rapa* var. *pekinensis*	Da bai cai 大白菜	Hakusai はくさい
Choy sum	*B. chinensis* var. *parachinensis*	Cai xin 菜心	Saishin さいしん
Choy sum, purple flowered	*B. rapa* var. *purpurea*	Hong cai tai 红菜薹	Kosaitai こうさいたい
Komatsuna	*B. rapa* var. *perviridis*		Komatsuna こまつな
Mizuna greens	*B. rapa* var. *nipposinica*	Shui cai 水菜	Mizuna みずな
Mibuna greens	*B. rapa* var. *nipposinica*	Ren sheng cai 壬生菜	Mibuna みぶな
Mustard	*B. juncea*	Jie cai 芥菜	Takana たかな
Oil seed rape, edible	*B. rapa* var. *oleifera*	You cai 油菜	Aburana あぶらな
Ornamental cabbage & kale	*B. oleracea* var. *capitata* & var. *acephala*	Hua cai 花菜	Habotan はぼたん
Pak choi	*B. rapa* var. *chinensis*	Bai cai 白菜	Shakushina しゃくしな
Rosette pak choi	*B. chinensis* var. *rosularis*	Wu ta cai 乌塌菜	Tasai たあさい
Turnip	*B. rapa* var. *rapifera*	Wu jing 芜菁	Kabu かぶ

English	Latin	Mandarin	Japanese
OTHER VEGETABLES			
Adzuki bean	*Phaseolus angularis*	Hong xiao dou 红小豆	Azuki あずき
Alfalfa	*Medicago sativus*	Mu xu 苜 蓿	Arufarufa アルファルファ
Amaranthus	*Amaranthus gangeticus*	Xian cai 苋 菜	Hiyuna ひゆな
Arrowhead	*Sagittaria sagittifolia*	Ci gu 慈 姑	Kuwai くわい
Basella	*Basella rubra*	Luo kui 落 葵	Tsuru-murasaki つるむらさき
Bitter gourd	*Momordica charantia*	Ku gua 苦 瓜	Reishi れいし
Bottle gourd	*Lagenaria siceraria*	Hu lu gua 葫芦瓜	Hyotan ひょうたん
Burdock	*Arctium lappa*	Niu pang 牛 蒡	Gobo ごぼう
Chinese artichoke	*Stachys affinis*	Gan lu zi 甘露子	Chorogi ちょろぎ
Chinese boxthorn	*Lycium barbarum*	Gou qi 枸 杞	Kuko くこ
Chinese celery	*Apium graveolens*	Qin cai 芹 菜	Serina せりな
Chinese chives	*Allium tuberosum*	Jiu cai 韭 菜	Nira にら
Chinese clover	*Medicago hispida*	Cai mu xu 菜苜蓿	Chinizu kurohbah チャイニーズ クローバー
Chrysanthemum greens	*Chrysanthemum coronarium*	Tung hao 茼 蒿	Shungiku しゅんぎく
Garlic	*Allium sativum*	Suan 蒜	Nin niku にんにく

English	Latin	Mandarin	Japanese
OTHER VEGETABLES *cont.*			
Hairy melon	*Benincasa hispida* var. *chieh-gua*	Mao gua 毛 瓜	Heari meron ヘアリーメロン
Lablab bean	*Lablab niger*	Bian dou 扁 豆	Fujimame ふじまめ
Lettuce, stem	*Lactuca sativa* var. *augustana*	Wo sun 莴 苣	Stemuretasu ステムレタス
Lotus root	*Nelumbo nucifera*	Lian ou 莲 藕	Renkon れんこん
Luffa, angled	*Luffa acutangula*	Si gua 丝 瓜	Hechima へちま
Luffa, smooth	*Luffa cylindrica*	Si gua 丝 瓜	Hechima へちま
Mitsuba	*Cryptotaenia japonica*	San ye qin 三叶芹	Mitsuba みつば
Mung bean	*Phaseolus aureus*	Lu dou 绿 豆	Yaenari やえなり
Onion, oriental bunching	*Allium fistulosum*	Da cong 大 葱	Negi ねぎ
Pea shoots	*Pisum sativum*	Dou miao 豆 苗	Tohbyo とうびょう
Perilla	*Perilla frustescens*	Zi su 紫 苏	Shiso しそ
Pickling melon, oriental	*Cucumis melo* var. *conomon*	Yue gua 越 瓜	Uri うり
Pumpkin, Japanese	*Cucurbita moschata*	Nan gua 南 瓜	Kabocha カボチャ
Radish	*Raphanus sativus*	Luo bo 萝 卜	Daikon だいこん
Rakkyo	*Allium chinense*	Jiao tou 薤 头	Rakkyo らっきょう

English	Latin	Mandarin	Japanese

OTHER VEGETABLES *cont.*

English	Latin	Mandarin	Japanese
Soya bean	*Glycine max*	Da dou 大 豆	Daizu だいず
Taro	*Colocasia esculenta*	Yu 芋	Satoimo さといも
Water bamboo	*Zizania latifolia*	Jiao bai 茭 白	Uotabanbu ウォーター バンブー
Water caltrop	*Trapa bicornis*	Ling jiao 菱 角	Hishi ひし
Water chestnut	*Eleocharis dulcis*	Ma ti 马 蹄	Okuroguwai おおぐろくわい
Watercress	*Nasturtium officinale*	Xi yang cai 西洋菜	Uotakuresu ウォーター クレス
Watershield	*Brasenia schreberi*	Chun cai 莼 菜	Junsai じゅんさい
Water spinach	*Ipomea aquatica*	Kong xin cai 空心菜	Asagaona あさがおな
Wax gourd	*Benincasa hispida*	Dong gwa 冬 瓜	Tohgan とうがん
Yam bean	*Pachyrrhizus erosus*	Sha ge 沙 葛	Kuzuimo くずいも
Yam, Chinese	*Dioscorea batatas*	Shu yu 薯 蓣	Yamaimo やまいも
Yard long bean	*Vigna sesquipedalis*	Chang dou 长 豆	Sasage ささげ

HERBS AND WILD PLANTS

English	Latin	Mandarin	Japanese
Aralia cordata	*Aralia cordata*	Cong mu 楤 木	Udo うど
Black nightshade	*Solanum nigrum*	Long kui 龙 葵	Inuhoozuki いぬほおずき

English	Latin	Mandarin	Japanese
HERBS AND WILD PLANTS *cont.*			
Ginger	*Zingiber officinale*	Jiang 姜	Shooga しょうが
Ginger, myoga	*Zingiber mioga*	Xiang he 襄荷	Myohga みょうが
Lemon grass	*Cymbopogon citratus*	Xiang mao cao 香茅草	Remon gurasu レモングラス
Mallow	*Malva verticillata*	Dong han cai 冬寒菜	Zeniaoi ぜにあおい
Mugwort	*Artemisia princeps*	Ai 艾	Yomogi よもぎ
Polygonum	*Polygonum hydropiper* var. 'fastigiatum'	Liao 蓼	Azabutade あざぶたで
Salsola	*Salsola sp.*		Okahijiki おかひじき
Sesame	*Sesame indicum*	Zhi ma 芝麻	Goma ごま
Shepherd's purse	*Capsella bursa-pastoris*	Ji cai 荠菜	Nazuna なずな
Sichuan and 'sansho' pepper	*Zanthoxylum* sp.	Hua jiao 花椒	Sansho さんしょう
Sweet coltsfoot	*Petasites japonicus*	Bian fu cao 蝙蝠草	Fuki ふき
Sweet coltsfoot, giant	*Petasites japonicus* var. *giganteus*	Bian fu cao 蝙蝠草	Akita-buki あきたぶき
Velvet plant	*Gynura bicolor*	Zi bei tian kui 紫背天葵	Suizenjina すいぜんじな
Wasabi	*Wasabia japonica*	Shan yu cai 山崳菜	Wasabi わさび
Water dropwort	*Oenanthe stolonifera*	Shui qin 水芹	Seri せり

Bibliography and further reading

Bittenbender, H. C., *Handbook of Tropical Vegetables*, Michigan State University, USA, 1983

Buczaki, Stefan and Harris, M. Keith, *Collins Guide to the Pests, Diseases and Disorders of Garden Plants*, Collins, UK, 1981

Buishand, Tjerk, and Houwing, Harm P., and Jansen, Kees, *The Complete Book of Vegetables*, Uitgeverij Het Spectrum, Netherlands, 1986, Multimedia Publications, UK, 1986

Chan, Peter, *Better Vegetable Gardens the Chinese Way*, Storey Communications, USA, 1985

Chang, K. C. (ed), *Food in Chinese Culture*, Yale University Press, USA, 1977

Fukuoka, Masanobu, *The One Straw Revolution*, Rodale Press, 1978

Goldsmith, H. T. J. and Backhurst, A. E., *Market Gardening in China*, H. T. J. Goldsmith Market Research, Isle of Wight, UK, 1986

Grubben, G. H. J., *Tropical Vegetables and their Genetic Resources*, Royal Tropical Institute, Netherlands, 1977

Handbook of Japanese Herbs and their Uses, Brooklyn Botanic Garden, USA, 1976

Harrington, Geri, *Grow Your Own Chinese Vegetables*, Macmillan Publishing Co., USA, 1978

Herklots, G. A. C., *Vegetables in South-East Asia*, George Allen & Unwin, UK, 1972

Jones, Henry A. and Mann, Louis K., *Onions and their Allies*, Interscience Publishers, USA, 1963

Kelly, Kindscher, *Gardening with Southeast Asian Refugees*, SE Asian Gardening, USA, 1986

Keys, John D., *Chinese Herbs*, Charles E. Tuttle, USA, 1976

King, F. H., *Farmers of Forty Centuries*, Rodale Press, 1911

Lee, Gary, *The Chinese Vegetarian Cookbook*, Nitty Gritty Productions, USA, 1972

Ochse, J. J. and R. C. Bakhuizen van den Brink, *Vegetables of the Dutch East Indies* (English edition of *Indische Groenten*), Archipel Drukkerij Buitenzorg, Java, 1931. (1980 reprint: Asher & Co., Netherlands)

Oomen, H. A. P. C., and Grubben, G. J. H., *Tropical Leaf Vegetables in Human Nutrition*, Royal Tropical Institute, Netherlands, 1978

Organ, John, *Gourds*, Faber and Faber, UK, 1963
Rare Vegetables, Faber and Faber, UK, 1960

Oriental Herbs and Vegetables, Brooklyn Botanic Garden, USA, 1986

Plucknett, Donald L., and Beemer, Halsey L., Jr., (Eds), *Vegetable Farming Systems in China*, Westview Press, USA, 1981; Frances Pinter, UK, 1981

Richards, Betty and Kaneko, Anne, *Japanese Plants*, Shufunotomo Co., Japan, 1988

Rodale Research Center research papers. See below

Rogers, Brant and Powers-Rogers, Bev, *A New World of Fruit & Vegetables*, PRP-Powers, Rogers & Plants, Box 5403, Kent, WA, USA, 1986

Rogers, Brant and Powers-Rogers, Bev, *Culinary Botany*, PRP-Powers, Rogers & Plants, Box 5403, Kent, WA, USA, 1988

Shinohara, Suteki, *Vegetable Seed Production Technology of Japan*, Shinohara's Authorized Agricultural Consulting Engineer Office, Tokyo, Japan, 1984

The Unicef Home Gardens Handbook for People Promoting Mixed Gardening in the Humid Tropics, Unicef, New York, USA, 1982

Tindall, H. D., *Vegetables in the Tropics*, Macmillan Education Ltd., UK, 1983

Usher, George, *A Dictionary of Plants Used by Man*, Constable, UK, 1974

van Beek, Wim, *Exotische Gewassen zelf Geteeld*, DNA, Netherlands, 1988

Vilmorin-Andrieux, M. M., *The Vegetable Garden*, John Murray, 1885; Ten Speed Press, USA, 1986

Watercress: production of the cultivated crop, ADAS/MAFF Ref. Book 136, Grower Books, UK, 1983

Wenkam, Nao S., *Foods of Hawaii and the Pacific Basin*, College of Tropical Agriculture, University of Hawaii, Hawaii, 1983

Woodward, Lawrence and Burge, Pat (Eds), *Green Manuring*, Elm Farm Research Centre, UK, 1982

Yamaguchi, Mas, *World Vegetables*, Van Nostrand Reinhold Co., USA, 1983

Zee, S. Y. and Hui, L. H., *Hong Kong Food Plants*, Urban Council Hong Kong, 1981

CHINESE BOOKS ON VEGETABLE CULTURE (in Chinese)

Li Fang-ting, *Chinese Chives*, Liao Ning Sciences and Techniques Press, China, 1985

Beijing Vegetable Production Handbook, Agricultural Bureau, Beijing, China, 1981

Wang Hua, *Questions and Answers on Vegetable Production*, Shanghai Academy of Agricultural Sciences, Shanghai, China, 1985

Zhang Je Zhan, *The Family Vegetable Garden*, Nong Ye Chu Ban She, Beijing, China, 1983

RODALE RESEARCH CENTER, RODALE PRESS, USA RESEARCH PAPERS

Matthews, Diana and Flower, Robert and others, *Design Elements in Solar Grow Frames and Horticultural Adaptations for their Winter Use*, 1980

Matthews, Diana and Ganser, Stephen and others, *1981 Growing Frame Performance: design aspects and crop evaluation*, 1981

Palada, M., *Observations on the Use of Unheated Plastic Row Covers*, 1983

Palada, M. C., and Ganser, S., *Cultivar evaluation for Early and Extended Production of Oriental Greens in Northeastern States*, 1983

Palada, M. C., and Ganser, S., *Seasonal Planting of Cold Winter Vegetables in Northeast Pennsylvania*, 1981

Palada, M. C., and Ganser, S., *Winter Greenhouse Vegetable Production*, 1982

Palada, M. C., and Ganser, S. and others, *Varietal Observations of Field Grown Vegetables 1981*, 1981

Weinsteiger, Eileen, *Summary of Cool Weather Crops tested 1979–80 for Solar Structures*, 1981

Weinsteiger, Eileen and Wolfgang, Sarah and Harrington, Marie, *Summary of 1981–82 Winter Crops Variety Trial Observations*, 1983

Recommended cookery books

The following books are among those I have found very helpful.

Brennan, Georgeanne, Cronin, Isaac and Glenn, Charlotte, *The New American Vegetable Cookbook*, Aris Books, USA, 1986

Brennan, Georgeanne and Glenn, Charlotte, *Peppers Hot & Chile*, Aris Books, USA, 1988

Chin Hau, *Highlight Chinese Cuisine*, Hilit Publishing Co., Taipei, 1984

Cost, Bruce, *Asian Ingredients*, William Morrow, USA, 1988
Ginger East to West, Aris Books, USA, 1984

Cotterell, Yong Yap, *The Chinese Kitchen*, Weidenfeld & Nicolson, UK, 1986

der Haroutunian, Arto, *The Yoghurt Book*, Penguin Books, UK, 1983

Grigson, Jane and Knox, Charlotte, *Exotic Fruits and Vegetables*, Jonathan Cape, UK, 1986

Hmong Recipe Book, First Presbyterian Church, So. St. Paul, USA, 1985

Hom, Ken, *Chinese Cookery*, British Broadcasting Corporation, UK, 1984

Home Preservation of Fruits and Vegetables, HMSO Bull. 21, UK, 1984

Jaffray, Madhur, *Indian Cookery*, British Broadcasting Corporation, UK, 1982

Japanese Home Style Cooking, Better Home Publishing House, Japan, 1986

Kindscher, Kelly, *Gardening with Southeast Asian Refugees*, SE Asian Gardening, Rt. 2, Box 394A, Lawrence, KS, 66044, USA, 1986

Lin, Hsian Ju and Lin, Tsuifeng, *Chinese Gastronomy*, Thomas Nelson & Son, USA, 1969; Jill Norman & Hobhouse Ltd., UK, 1982

Lo, Kenneth, *Chinese Food*, Penguin Books, UK, 1972
Chinese Vegetable & Vegetarian Cookery, Faber & Faber, UK, 1974
New Chinese Cookery Course, Macdonald, UK, 1985

Owen, Sri, *Indonesian and Thai Cookery*, Judy Piatkus (Publishers) Ltd., UK, 1988
Indonesian Food and Cookery, Prospect Books, UK, 1986

Phillipps, Karen and Dahlen, Martha, *A Popular Guide to Chinese Vegetables*, South China Morning Post Hong Kong, 1982; Wokman Press Hong Kong, 1987

Richardson, Rosamund, *Hedgerow Cookery*, Penguin Books, UK, 1980

Shepherd, Renee, *Recipes from a Kitchen Garden*, Shepherd's Garden Publishing, USA, 1987

Shou, Tuan-Hsi, *Chinese Vegetarian Dishes*, Hilit Publishing Company, Taiwan, 1986

So, Yan Kit, *Yan Kit's Classic Chinese Cookbook*, Dorling Kindersley, UK, 1984

Sunrise Enterprises information sheets (See Seed suppliers)

Toyé, Kenneth, *Regional French Cookery*, David & Charles, UK, 1973

Traditional Recipes of Laos, Prospect Books, UK, 1981

Von Welanetz, *The Von Welanetz Guide to Ethnic Ingredients*, Warner Books, USA, 1982

Waterfield, Michael and Ross, Janet, *Leaves from our Tuscan Kitchen*, Penguin Books, UK, 1973

Xotus, *Exotische Groenten*, De Balie/Xotus/Novib, Netherlands, 1987

Yoshida, Yoshiko, *Tropical Cookery*, National Book Store, Philippines, 1981

Further reading

Container gardening
Beckett, Kenneth A. and Carr, David and Stevens, David, *The Contained Garden*, Frances Lincoln, UK, 1982. See also, in Bibliography, Harrington, Geri

Fluid sowing
Salter, P. J., and Bleasdale, J. K. A., and others, *The Complete Know & Grow Vegetables*, Oxford University Press, UK, 1991

Green manuring
Seed company catalogues, e.g. Suffolk Herbs, HDRA, Jonny's Seeds (USA). See also in Bibliography, Woodward, Lawrence

Herbs
Larkcom, Joy, *The Salad Garden*, Frances Lincoln, UK, 1984; Stickland, Sue, *Planning the Organic Herb Garden*, Thorsons Publishing, UK, 1986

Intercropping, Chinese
See Bibliography, Plucknett, Donald L.

Pests and diseases
See 'Organizations' for information leaflets and publications; see Jonny's Seeds catalogue (USA); *Common Sense Pest Control Quarterly*, Bio-Integral Resource Center, PO Box 7414, Berkeley, CA 94707, USA. See also Bibliography, Buczacki, Tindall

Raised beds and deep beds
See Jeavons, John, *How to Grow More Vegetables than You Ever Thought Possible On Less Land than you can Imagine*, Ecology Action, USA, 3rd ed 1982; Pears, Pauline, *Raised Bed Gardening the Organic Way*, Henry Doubleday Research Association, UK, 1963. See also entry in Bibliography for *Oriental Herbs and Vegetables*

Solar frames and low tunnels
Rodale Research Center, see organic research organizations

Solar greenhouses
Centre for Alternative Technology, Machynlleth, Wales; McCullough, James C. (Ed), *The Solar Greenhouse Book*, Rodale Press, Emmaus, USA 1978; Yander, Bill and Fisher, Rick, *The Solar Greenhouse*, John Muir Publications, Sante Fe, NM, USA, 1980. See also Bibliography, the section on Rodale publications

Worm compost
Appelhof, Mary, *Worms Eat My Garbage*, Flower Press, Kalamazoo, USA, 1982

Watercress cultivation
See entry in Bibliography for *Watercress: production of the cultivated crop*

Seed suppliers and organic research organizations

Note Companies marked with an asterisk are those with speciality lists of oriental vegetables; the other companies listed normally stock some oriental seed. Many also supply gardening equipment.

RETAIL MAIL ORDER SEED COMPANIES: UK

Boyce Seeds, Bush Pasture, Lower Carter St., Fordham, Ely, Cambs CB7 5JU

* Chiltern Seeds, Bortree Stile, Ulverston, Cumbria LA12 7PB

Dobies Seeds, Broomhill Way, Torquay, Devon TQ2 7QW

Fothergill Seeds, Gazeley Rd., Kentford, Newmarket, Suffolk CB8 7QB

* Henry Doubleday Research Association, National Centre for Organic Gardening, Ryton-on-Dunsmore, Coventry CV8 3LG

Johnson Seeds, Boston, Lincs PE21 8AD

* E. W. King and Co., Monks Farm, Coggeshall Road, Kelvedon, Essex CO5 9PG

S. E. Marshall, Wisbech, Cambs PE13 2RF

* Suffolk Herbs, Sawyers Farm, Little Cornard, Sudbury, Suffolk CO10 0NY

Suttons Seeds, Hele Rd., Torquay, Devon TQ2 7QJ

Thompson & Morgan, London Road, Ipswich IP2 0BA

Unwins Seeds, Histon, Cambridge CB4 4LE

* Xotus Seeds, Spoorlaan 15, 2267 AN Leidschendam, Netherlands

RETAIL MAIL ORDER SEED COMPANIES: USA, AUSTRALIA, NEW ZEALAND

W. Atlee Burpee, Warminster, PA 18974, USA

Bountiful Gardens, Ecology Action, 5798 Ridgewood Road, Willits, CA 95490, USA

Johnny's Selected Seeds, Foss Hill Rd., Albion, Maine 04910, USA

Kings Herb Seeds, PO Box 14, Glenbrook, NSW 2773, Australia

Kings Herb Seeds, PO Box 19–084, Avondale, Auckland, New Zealand

* Kitazawa Seed Co., 1748 Laine Avenue, Santa Clara, CA 95051–3012, USA

Le Marche Seeds, PO Box 190, Dixon, CA 95820, USA

Nichols Herb and Rare Seeds, 1190 North Pacific Highway, Albany, OR 97321, USA

Seeds Blum, Idaho City Stage, Boise, Idaho 83706, USA

* Sunrise Enterprises, PO Box 10058, Elmwood, CT 06110–0058, USA

Shepherd's Garden Seeds, 6116 Highway 9, Felton, CA 95018, USA

The Cook's Garden, PO Box 65, Londonderry, VT 05148, USA

Vermont Bean Seed Co., Garden Lane, Fair Haven, VT 07543, USA

ORIENTAL SEED COMPANIES

* Kaneko Seeds, 50–12 Furuichimachi 1-chome, Maebashi City, Gunma, Pref. 371, Japan.

* Known You Seed, 26 Chung Cheng 2nd Road, Kaohsiung, Taiwan

* Kyowa Seed, 15–13 Nanpeidei, Shibuya-ku, Tokyo, Japan

Mikado Seed Growers, 1203 Hoshikuki, Shiba City 280, Japan

* Sakata Seed, 1–7 Nagata Higashi 3 chome, Minami-ku, Yokohama, Japan 232

* Takii Seed, PO Box 7, Kyoto Central 600–91, Japan

* Tokita Seed, Nakagawa, Omiya-shi, Sataima-ken, Japan 330

Organic research organizations

Elm Farm Research Centre, Hamstead Marshall, Nr. Newbury, Berks, RG15 OHR, UK

Henry Doubleday Research Association, National Centre for Organic Gardening, Ryton-on-Dunsmore, Coventry, CV8 3LG, UK

Rodale Research Center, Box 323, RD1, Kutztown, PA 19530, USA

Acknowledgements

Where, oh where, do I begin to thank the many people who have helped me with this book. I'll start with the linguists. Big thankyous to Charles Aylmer for his endless patience in compiling and writing Chinese names, translating and teaching me; to Lee Ruey Hua, for her energetic help in translating and with recipes; and to Jin Li Xian, Zhang Zhong Chen, Sheng Yu Min, Bob and Jaqui Sloss for their various roles. Another very very big thank you to Ruriko Pilgrim, for the many hours she spent wrestling with Japanese translations for me.

Now to China, and thanks to the Royal Society and especially Catherine Donovan and Ling Thompson, for their hard work in arranging the vegetable study tour of China. In China, thanks to the China Association for Science and Technology for organizing our visit, especially to Chen Yan Hua in Beijing. Thanks too to our understanding guides, and to Yuan Ning and Xiong Jia Wei for their recipes. Our thanks to the staff at the institutes we visited whose kindness and helpfulness were boundless: Beijing Vegetable Research Centre, Beijing Agricultural University, the Vegetable Research Institute of the Chinese Academy of Agricultural Science in Beijing; the Jiangsu Academy of Agricultural Sciences in Nanjing; Shanghai Academy of Agricultural Sciences; Chengdu Vegetable Institute; South China Agricultural College and the South China Agricultural University in Guangzhou, and to the numerous people we met in communes, markets, workshops, factories and the fields. Very special thanks to Professor Jia Cui Ying, Jia Wen Wei and Shen Zheng Yan for their patience in answering my endless subsequent questions. Thanks also to Wang Zhu-Hao of the South China Institute of Botany, Guangzhou, and to Wang Hua and Zhang Je Zhan for their valued books. And thanks to my very long suffering companions on the trip, Alan Backhurst, 'Huff' Goldsmith

and Pam Toler, both for her enthusiasm for the project and perseverance with photography in often difficult conditions.

For my brief but highly productive visit to Japan I have Takii Seeds, Kyowa Seed Company and T. Sakata & Company to thank. My thanks also to Mr K. Nakasato of Horio Corporation for the many queries he subsequently answered, to Dr Tetsuo Nakajima, to Sei Sakamoto and a warm thank you to George Beaven for blazing the trail.

In Taiwan a big thank you to Dr Jack Gershon of the Asian Vegetable Research and Development Center for organizing a fascinating programme, and to my companions and guides Ma Shiu-Luan, Chen Li-Zhu, and Huang Yu-Hsiung. Also thanks to Dr Yu Chung Hsiung of Known You Seeds, and Dr N. S. Talekar of the AVRDC for their help.

I have another host of people to thank for helping to organize my research trip to Canada and the USA. Thank you all for hospitality, transport, use of phones, photocopying facilities, for arranging the talks which paid for it, but above all, for ferreting out people and places where oriental vegetables were being grown and sold. Thank you also to all those who gave up time to show me round your enterprises.

In Canada . . . Jill and Bill Lapper; Mike Barbolet, Susan Davidson and friends of Glorious Garnish Salads; Mike Levenston of City Farms; Veena and Mike Banga of Five B Produce Inc and G. Seguin-Swartz.

In the USA special thanks to my tireless 'organizers': Jane Pepper of the Pennsylvania Horticultural Society; Beverly Geist; Georgeanne Brennan and Charlotte Glenn of Le Marche Seeds; Mark Musick and his colleagues at the Seattle Tilth Association; Professor Paul Williams of University of Wisconsin – Madison; Eleanor and Bob Grant; Rene Shepherd of Shepherd

Seeds; Alice Waters of Cheq Panisse; Bill and Piyachart Hussey; Bruce Cost. And for setting the oriental ball rolling in 1984 thanks to Jane and Lee Taylor of Michigan State University, Skip Bittenbender and Sandy Hicks.

Warm thanks also to the following who supplied me with snippets of information, accompanied me, showed me round etc: Mark Becker, Harry Berg of Fuji Natural Foods, Dr Robert Bond, Linn Brown and Pete Forno, David Campbell of Alpha Beta, Karen Caplan of Frieda's Finest Produce Specialities, Tom Chino (please forgive the lack of footnotes), Insu Chon, Mark Dierkhising of Silverado Restaurant, David Lee, Steve Frowine of W. Atlee Burpee Seeds, Dr Stephen Garrison, Pam and Jo Helms, Cheu Mei and Henry Hsiao of Taiwan Farm, Niloufer Ichaporia, Kali Israel of Pragtree Farm, Caroline Kiang, Dr Tali Kuan and colleagues of Alf Christianson Seed Co., Robert W. Langlois, Moreno Brothers, Bruce Naftaly of the Gourmand Restaurant Seattle, Manuel Palada and Anne Schauer of the Rodale Research Center, Jim Quinn of Willow Run Farms, Brant Rogers, Gil and Carolyn Schieber, Esther Schmidt, Wendy Sekovich, Pat Simpson, Keming Song, Biff Soper and Zia of the Student Experimental Farm at the University of California, Davis, Tammi Tsuhuda, Noel Vietmeyer, Dr Bernie Zandstra . . . and the members of the American branch of our family who got involved: Mary Pollard, Paddy Pollard, Don and Anne Peters, Chrissie and Tom Pollard.

Back in England my thanks to the following for help of all kinds: AFRC Institute of Food Research Laboratory, Norwich; David Anthill; Lesley Bremness; Chris Brickell of the Royal Horticultural Society; R. A. B. Cook; Richard Dadd; Julian Davies of Arthur Rickwood; Mike Day of the National Institute of Agricultural Botany; Grahame Dixie; Jean-Claude Garnaud; Paul Graham-

Hyatt; Roy Grigson of A. L. Tozer; Peter and Jenny Groeneveld; Geoff Hamilton for growing so many Chinese brassicas for *Gardener's World*; Dr Nazumi Haq; the late Dr G. A. C. Herklots; Impact Photos; Shiro and Mina Mishima of Mikasa Engei Company; Pauline Pears, Margi Lennartsson and Sue Stickland of the Henry Doubleday Research Association; Graham Rice; Yan-Kit So, Peter Stanford; Jerry Tsang; John Twibell; Dr J. Waage; Wellesbourne Institute of Horticultural Research staff past and present; David Woodroffe; Jo Wicks, Dr Tony Wills . . . and the garden slaves, Ella Burley, Poppy Burke, Chris Stafford, John Walker, Colette Ingram without whom the trials here would have been impossible.

And a few final special thankyous . . . to Matt Nieburg of Rokewood Nurseries for technical help and allowing us to photograph; to John and Caroline Stevens of Suffolk Seeds, for collaboration over many years in introducing new seeds; to John Matthissen for advising on and nurturing the word processor; to Ken Toyé of the Singing Chef, Ipswich for his expert help with the recipes; to Jacqui Hurst for her photography in England; to Gert-

Jan Jansen of Xotus for endless encouragement, technical help and reading through much of the manuscript; to Dr Peter Crisp for reading the entire manuscript, correcting, advising, acting as courier to China . . . all with infinite patience; to Elizabeth Douglass, who tussled with all manner of reference material and impossible deadlines to produce the excellent line drawings; to June Pattinson for willing help with emergency typing; to my husband Don, who has given me such whole-hearted support throughout . . . growing the vegetables, cooking them, and looking after everything while I gallivanted in foreign fields; to Emma Manderson, for her skilful editing; to Caro Hobhouse, for her enthusiasm in the initial stages of this project, and to all those involved at the publishers John Murray, particularly Caroline Knox, who have put in so much effort and borne with me, as I have with them, in the long gestation of this book! If I have forgotten anyone, forgive me.

The author would like to thank the following publishers for permission to use recipes from the following books:

BBC Books – *Madhur Jaffray's Indian Cookery*
Better Home Publishing Company – *Japanese Home Style Cooking*
Dorling Kindersley – *Yan Kit's Classic Chinese Cookbook*
Hilit Publishing Company – *Highlight Chinese Cuisine* and *Chinese Vegetarian Dishes*
John Murray – *Leaves from our Tuscan Kitchen.*
Jonathan Cape – *Exotic Fruits and Vegetables*
Judy Piatkus (Publishers) – *Indonesian and Thai Cookery*
Kelly Kindscher – *Gardening with Southeast Asian Refugees*
Penguin Books Ltd. – *The Yoghurt Book*; *Hedgerow Cookery*; *Chinese Food*
Prospect Books – *Indonesian Food and Cookery*
Sunrise Seeds – information leaflets
William Morrow – *Asian Ingredients*
Yoshiko Yoshida – *Tropical Cookery*
The author would like to thank the following for permission to use their published material:
Rodale Research Center – various research papers
Suteki Shinohara – illustration of evolution of different types of radish as a basis for the illustration on page 112, from *Vegetable Seed Production of Japan* 1984.

Index